To Joe –

Whose internet skills are so advanced that he discovered this book even before it was published!

Happy Birthday!

[signature]

THE AMERICAN SKYSCRAPER

More than any other phenomenon, the skyscraper has determined the character of the American city, altering its physicality and land use patterns; prompting design, technological, and infrastructure developments; creating internal work environments; and redefining boundaries and expectations of individuals and groups defined by gender, class, and ethnicity. This volume examines the various dimensions of the skyscraper in its American urban context. Focusing on the major skyscraper cities of New York and Chicago between 1870 and 1960, the studies in this volume address many of the major aspects of the skyscraper through a diversity of disciplines, including planning and public policy, art and architectural history, labor and business history, and American studies. The result is a kaleidoscopic view of the skyscraper, a building type whose existence as object and icon is inextricably linked to the city itself.

Roberta Moudry is a historian of American architecture and urbanism. A recipient of support from the National Endowment for the Humanities, the Getty Grant Program, and the Graham Foundation for Advanced Studies in the Fine Arts, she has taught in the College of Architecture, Art, and Planning at Cornell University and is the author of the forthcoming *Met Life's Metropolis*.

"New York Sky Line." Reprinted with permission of the Keystone–Mast Collection, UCR/California Museum of Photography, University of California, Riverside.

THE AMERICAN SKYSCRAPER

Cultural Histories

Edited by

Roberta Moudry

CAMBRIDGE
UNIVERSITY PRESS

CAMBRIDGE UNIVERSITY PRESS
Cambridge, New York, Melbourne, Madrid, Cape Town, Singapore, São Paulo

Cambridge University Press
40 West 20th Street, New York, NY 10011-4211, USA

www.cambridge.org
Information on this title: www.cambridge.org/9780521624213

First published 2005

Printed in the United States of America

A catalog record for this publication is available from the British Library.

Library of Congress Cataloging in Publication Data

The American skyscraper : cultural histories / edited by Roberta Moudry.
p. cm.
Includes bibliographical references and index.
ISBN 0-521-62421-5 (hard cover)
1. Skyscrapers – United States. 2. Skyscrapers – New York (State) – New York. 3. Skyscrapers – Illinois – Chicago. I. Moudry, Roberta. II. Title.
NA6232.A44 2005
720′.483′0973 – dc22 2004024031

ISBN-13 978-0-521-62421-3 hardback
ISBN-10 0-521-62421-5 hardback

Contents

List of Illustrations

List of Contributors

Gail Fenske is an architect, historian, and Professor of Architecture in the School of Architecture, Art, and Historic Preservation at Roger Williams University. She has held visiting appointments at Cornell University and MIT. She has written numerous essays on the skyscraper, including "Corporate Identity and the New York Office Building, 1895–1915," co-authored with Deryck Holdsworth in *The Landscape of Modernity*, edited by David Ward and Olivier Zunz (Baltimore: Johns Hopkins University Press, 1997); "Cass Gilbert's Skyscrapers in New York: The Twentieth-Century City and the Urban Picturesque," in *Inventing the Skyline*, edited by Margaret Heilbrun (New York: Columbia University Press, 2000); and "The Image of the City: Cass Gilbert's Woolworth Building and the Creation of the New York Skyline," in *Cass Gilbert, Life and Work*, edited by Barbara S. Christen and Steve Flanders (New York: W. W. Norton & Company, 2001).

Lisa M. Fine is Associate Professor of History and Graduate Chair at Michigan State University. She is the author of *The Souls of the Skyscraper: Female Clerical Workers in Chicago 1870–1930* (Philadelphia: Temple University Press, 1990) and co-editor with Mary Anderson, Kathleen Geissler, and Joyce R. Ladenson of *Doing Feminism: Teaching and Research in the Academy* (Michigan State University Press, 1997) and *The Story of Reo Joe: Work, Kin, and Community in Autotown, U.S.A.* (Philadelphia: Temple University Press, 2004).

Antonello Frongia teaches history of photography and urbanism at the University of Trieste and the University of Venice in Italy. He is the author of *L'occhio del fotografo e l'agenda del planner. Studio su Jacob A. Riis* (*The Photographer's Eye and the Planner's Agenda. A Study of*

Jacob A. Riis) (Venice: Iuav/Toletta, 2000), and he is completing a book entitled *The Shadow of the Skyscraper: Photography and Urban Culture in America, 1890–1938.*

Lee E. Gray is Associate Dean of the College of Architecture at the University of North Carolina, Charlotte. He received his Ph.D. in architectural history from Cornell University and his Master's degree in architectural history from the University of Virginia. He is the author of *From Ascending Rooms to Express Elevators: A History of the Passenger Elevator in the 19th Century* (Elevator World, Inc., 2002) and he is currently working on a history of vertical transportation in the twentieth century.

Carol Herselle Krinsky is Professor of Fine Arts at New York University. She is the author of five books, including *Rockefeller Center* (New York: Oxford University Press, 1978). She has written many articles and book chapters on architecture of various periods as well as on studies of medieval and Renaissance art. A past president of the Society of Architectural Historians and of COPAR (Cooperative Preservation of Architectural Records), she has lectured widely around the United States, in Europe, and in China.

Roberta Moudry is an architectural and urban historian. She has taught architectural and urban history at Cornell University, and she has received research grants from the National Endowment for the Humanities, the Getty Grant Program, the Architectural History Foundation, and the Graham Foundation for Advanced Studies in the Fine Arts.

David E. Nye is Professor of History at Warwick University, Coventry, England. He has lectured throughout Europe on American history and culture and has been a visiting scholar at Harvard, MIT, the Netherlands Institute for Advance Study, Leeds, Cambridge, and most recently the University of Notre Dame. The sixteen books he has edited or written include *Electrifying America: Social Meanings of a New Technology, 1880–1940* (Cambridge, MA: MIT Press, 1990), which won the Dexter Prize and the Abel Wolman Award; *American Technological Sublime* (Cambridge, MA: MIT Press, 1994); and his most recent book, *America as Second Creation: Technology and Narratives of New Beginnings* (Cambridge, MA: MIT Press, 2003).

Max Page is Associate Professor of Architecture and History at the University of Massachusetts, Amherst. He wrote *The Creative Destruction of Manhattan, 1900–1940* (Chicago: University of Chicago Press, 1999), which won the Spiro Kostof Award of the Society of Architectural Historians. He is also the co-editor (with Steven Conn) of *Building the Nation: Americans Write Their Architecture, Their Cities, and Their Environment* (Philadelphia: University of Pennsylvania Press, 2003) and the co-editor (with Randall Mason) of *Giving Preservation a History* (London: Routledge, 2003). In 2003, he received a Guggenheim Fellowship.

Keith D. Revell is Associate Professor of Public Administration at Florida International University in Miami. He received his Ph.D. in American History from the University of Virginia. He is the author of *Building Gotham: Civic Culture and Public Policy in New York City, 1898–1938* (Baltimore: Johns Hopkins University Press, 2003), which received the Urban History Association's 2003 Award for the best book on North American urban history and the Public Works Historical Society's 2003 Abel Wolman Award for the best new book on public works history. His work has also appeared in *Studies in American Political Development*, the *Journal of Policy History*, and the *Journal of Urban Affairs*. His current research focuses on the redevelopment of South Beach and on efforts to regulate the market economy in the twentieth century.

Merrill Schleier is Professor of Art History at the University of the Pacific. She is the author of *The Skyscraper in American Art, 1890–1931* (New York: Da Capo Press, 1990); "Lewis Mumford's Classed and Gendered Modernism," *Architectural Theory Review* 3 (Nov. 1998):1–16; "Ayn Rand and King Vidor's The Fountainhead: Architectural Modernism, the Gendered Body and Political Ideology," *Journal of the Society of Architectural Historians* 61 (Sept. 2002):310–322. Her book *Skyscrapers/Gender/Film*, which was awarded a grant from the Graham Foundation for Advanced Studies in the Fine Arts, is forthcoming from University of Minnesota Press in 2005.

Katherine Solomonson is Associate Professor in the Department of Architecture at the University of Minnesota, where she also holds positions in the departments of American Studies, Art History, Cultural Studies, and Comparative Literature. She has worked with the Design Center for American Urban Landscape on public housing and on postwar suburbia, including the national conference, "Reframing the 1945–65 Suburb." Her publications include *The Chicago Tribune Tower Competition: Skyscraper Design and Cultural Change in the 1920s* (Cambridge: Cambridge University Press, 2001), which received the 2003 Alice Davis Hitchcock Award from the Society of Architectural Historians.

Sarah Watts is Professor of History at Wake Forest University. She is the author of *Order Against Chaos: Business Culture and Labor Ideology, 1880–1920* (New York: Greenwood, 1990) and *Rough Rider in the White House: Theodore Roosevelt and the Politics of Desire* (Chicago: University of Chicago Press, 2003).

Edward W. Wolner is Associate Professor of Architectural History and the Humanities, Ball State University. He has received research grants from the National Endowment for the Humanities, the Graham Foundation for Advanced Studies in the Fine Arts, the Wolfsonian/FIU, and the John Nicholas Brown Center for the Study of American Civilization at Brown University.

Acknowledgments

I extend a public and profound thanks to the authors of this anthology for their patience and the intellectual work that they have shared in conversations, text, and images. Beyond the texts you read here, the authors have contributed to discussions within various disciplinary and cross-disciplinary constituencies that began prior to the writing and compiling of this anthology. Groups of authors presented versions of the work contained here in a panel discussion, "The Skyscraper, the City and Urban Culture: Architecture and the Negotiation of Public/Private Urban Space," at the 1997 American Studies Association/Canadian Association for American Studies Annual Meeting; at a roundtable entitled "The Skyscraper and Its Cultural Context" at the 1997 Society of Architectural Historians Annual Meeting; and at the Gotham History Festival in October 2001. These interactions and the public commentaries that emerged were valuable to the development of these essays and their relationship to each other. Over an extended period, authors have shared ideas, sources, and images with each other: together they have shaped a virtual conversation marked by respectful debate, collegiality, and exciting discoveries. In this manner, the work herein has lived two lives, one as the process and one as the final product, which as a whole, is greater than the sum of its parts.

In addition, I would like to thank other individuals who lent support and criticism in the development and completion of this project: Edward K. Muller, Lauren O'Connell, Christian Otto, Dell Upton, and Carol Willis. I thank Stuart Blumin and John W. Reps for broadening my perspectives on the built environment. I would also like to acknowledge the influence of the late Theodore M. Brown. Our conversations about the skyscraper and modernism remain with me.

I thank the Graham Foundation for Advanced Studies in the Fine Arts for its generous support of the visual materials. Beatrice Rehl, Fine Arts Editor at Cambridge University Press, has been a steady supporter, and most essentially, a perceptive and critical guide.

Introduction

Roberta Moudry

A long tradition in this country grants the ceremonies of human life to architecture. Buildings enter their productive lives with fanfare: a flag raised at the top of a steel frame; a cornerstone bearing pedigree; a dedication with all the trappings of a christening. The skyscrapers of the twentieth-century American city were dramatic in their arrival and equally dramatic in their visual and spatial presence, changing the physical and social spaces of everyday life and giving to the city its visual signature – the skyline (Figure 1).[1]

As everpresent as the skyscraper on the skyline was its engagement with nearly every sector of the urban population. Architects, engineers, and workers in the building trades were directly involved in skyscraper design and construction, and corporate officers and executives and the army of clerks they employed determined the meaning and usage of the tall office building. Municipal officers, planners, and civic-minded laypersons worked to develop land use patterns, set building height and safety standards, and create or expand urban infrastructures that serviced the skyscraper's mechanical and human components. Inventors and sociologists developed machines and practices demanded by the consolidated workplace of the tall office building. Children, mothers, domestic help, and an assimilating immigrant workforce experienced the skyscraper as urban theater – free for the watching – and as the backdrop for nursery rhymes, socialist and consumer pitches alike. Urban muses – photographers, artists, poets, musicians, and journalists – took the skyscraper as the main character of their stories, the means for exploring the nature of modern urban life. Each of these urbanites walked daily among a growing number of tall buildings and viewed these structures, which were only partially visible from adjacent sidewalks, as constituent parts

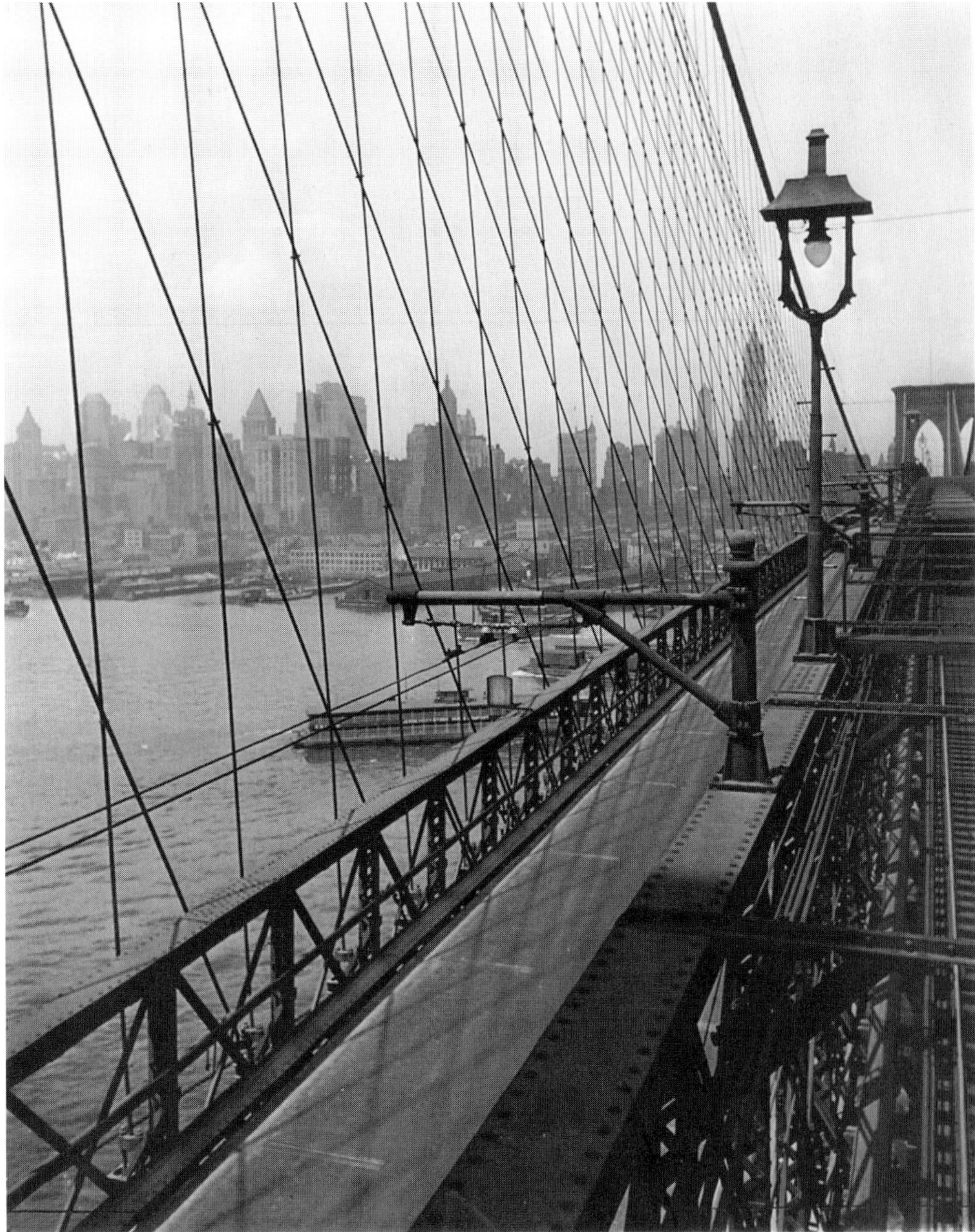

1. "New York City from Brooklyn Bridge." Reprinted with permission of the Keystone–Mast Collection, UCR/California Museum of Photography, University of California, Riverside.

of the skyline. Beyond the city limits, a flood of novels, magazines, three-dimensional stereoviews, and postcards, delivered cross-country for a penny stamp, brought the image of the skyscraper to the most remote household (Figure 2). This aggregation of meanings and experiences surrounding the skyscraper – its cultural identity – is the focus of this anthology.

The American skyscraper has spawned over a half-century of rigorous scholarship, largely

2. New York skyscrapers souvenir folder. Collection of the editor.

in the area of art and architectural history. Substantial book-length studies such as Carl W. Condit's *The Rise of the Skyscraper*, Sarah Bradford Landau and Carl W. Condit's *Rise of the New York Skyscraper, 1865–1913*, Merrill Schleier's *The Skyscraper in American Art*, and Carol Willis's *Form Follows Finance* focus on specifics of design and structure, representation, and economics.[2] Monographs of major buildings and architectural firms offer a cross-sectional study of building culture in a specific instance – of the specific and at times interlocking roles of client and urban context, architect, engineer and contractor, and building occupants.[3] Geographers, business historians, gender studies scholars, labor and urban historians, and historians of technology have contributed information and their distinctive disciplinary perspectives to skyscraper studies. However, most of these studies remain isolated in their intellectual arenas. To make aspects of this rich body of historical work available to a broad audience and to permit cross-disciplinary analysis and discussion, this volume collects work from scholars in diverse disciplines that addresses the engagement of the skyscraper with the experience and meaning of city life.

Purpose and Scope

Using the skyscraper, the signal architectural and spatial event of the modern American city, this volume's essays bring primary focus to the complex relationship between culture and the buildings and spaces it inhabits and inflects. They probe, among other things, how this building type shaped professional practices of developers, designers, and policymakers; the workplaces and streetscapes of workers and management; the image of corporations and organizations seeking cultural hegemony and financial success; and the vision of the city created by writers, artists, and photographers and handed back to its occupants. Collectively, the essays render a kaleidoscopic view of the skyscraper city and its cultural life – a multiplicity of overlapping histories, of public events and spaces, and of various professionally or politically homogeneous cultures.

The essays focus on a particular span of time in the history of the skyscraper: between the 1880s and the 1950s in the two major American skyscraper capitals, New York and Chicago. Thus, this collection does not grapple with the "first" or early skyscrapers, and it does not consider the tall building in its postwar, post-modern, or post-September 11 conditions. Nor does it offer a broad geographic survey of the building type beyond the two major centers of skyscraper production, although trends and practices that evolved in other urban centers may be observed in these two locations. Within these narrow parameters of time and place, depth and variety are provided by disciplinary diversity: the essays employ materials and methods from art and architectural history, urban planning, business and labor history, literary criticism, the history of photography, and the rich multidisciplinary field of American studies.

It is by design, then, that these stories overlap and intersect, for each investigation pivots upon the architectural/spatial reality of the skyscraper and its relationship with individuals, social and professional groups, and the ambient public culture. Therefore, certain events such as the World's Columbian Exposition of 1893 and New York's 1916 zoning ordinance, places such as Fifth Avenue, and buildings such as the Metropolitan Life and Woolworth towers appear in multiple essays. These points of intersection provide consistent referents for the reader moving from one interpretation to another, integrating a substantial body of information about a single urban building type. However, the intentions, concerns, uses, and interpretations related to these common places and recorded by the authors are wide-ranging and sometimes oppositional: the work of city-building and skyscraper design and the process of popular culture's absorption of the skyscraper as a norm in visual, spatial, and experiential realms look different through the lens of different stakeholders and through the medium of different materials. Thus, the result is not a generalized, but a relational history. Roland Barthes, in search of a semiology of the city, declared that it was "not so important to multiply the surveys or the functional studies of the city, but to multiply the readings of the city."[4] These essays articulate multiple cultural readings of the city, through study of its built environment and the singular urban monument of the skyscraper.

Organizational Themes

The essays are organized in four thematic sections. While every essay in this volume in some way considers skyscraper makers (clients, designers, engineers, and contractors) and/or users (workers, tenants, shoppers, passersby, or distant observers of visual material), the first part, "Makers and Users," gathers three essays that probe the complex culture of architects, planners, and clerical workers. Each of these professional groups was profoundly influenced by the quickening pace of skyscraper construction in the American city, and these essays indicate that there were both incredible opportunities and challenges posed by this urban phenomenon. Architects, engineers, and planners were compelled to develop new systems and strategies for collaborative work, as they encountered a design problem that demanded the coordinated contributions of an increasingly large number of professionals and tradesmen. Likewise, the internal work world of the skyscraper created an important niche for the female clerical worker that had to be defined, described, and codified by manuals as well as the popular press. The skyscraper shaped each of these professional groups beyond their specific contact with the building type, affecting how these groups would occupy and interact with the surrounding city.

In "The Beaux-Arts Architect and the Skyscraper: Cass Gilbert, the Professional Engineer, and the Rationalization of Construction in Chicago and New York," architectural historian Gail Fenske provides an in-depth look at prominent architect Cass Gilbert's efforts to maintain aesthetic control of the skyscraper, even as he realized that the contributions of skilled engineers and contractors were essential for a successful design. Her examination of the intricacies of Gilbert's practice and architectural theories suggest that Beaux-Arts aesthetic and urban design principles were neither irrelevant to nor irreconcilable with the realities of skyscraper design, but were a means of making the skyscraper a landmark, a beautiful and monumental "ornament" to the city.

Furthering the discussion of City Beautiful ideology in relation to skyscraper design, historian Keith D. Revell looks at the intersection of architecture and law and probes the interests and goals of planning professionals, including Edward Bassett, George Ford, and Nelson Lewis, who crafted New York's 1916 zoning ordinance. "Law Makes Order: The Search for Ensemble in the Skyscraper City, 1890–1930" details the means by which these men incorporated City Beautiful ideals about urban ensemble into zoning legislation. By regulating the skyscraper's vertical lines with a setback formula, they preserved individualistic design initiatives while protecting the collective goals of health and visual order. Legally defensible on the grounds of public health rather than civic beauty, skyscraper regulation ultimately enlarged the regulatory powers of municipal government and helped shape a skyscraper urbanism practiced by the most skilled of designers; the City Beautiful extended vertically onto the skyline.

Into this emerging skyscraper city, shaped by architects, planners, and corporate executives, arrived a flood of white-collar female clerical workers, altering the spatial reality and practices of the once-male realm of the business office and the nature of the urban downtown business district. The presence of women in the skyscraper office posed challenges to behavioral norms based on traditional gender roles that segregated work and spaces, and spawned entire genres of advice literature and secretarial pulp fiction. Labor historian and women's studies scholar Lisa M. Fine brings focus to "The Female 'Souls of the Skyscraper' " and describes the ways that the skyscraper and its workspaces transformed not only women's occupational opportunities but also their social and home lives, their image in the popular culture, and their public roles as individual citizens and as a collective presence in the urban business world.

Part Two, "In the Image of the Client," comprises four essays that examine the use of skyscraper design and publicity by specific corporate and institutional clients. Written by architectural historians, these essays draw on urban, advertising, and business history to explore the role of the skyscraper in a corporate or institutional agenda. Uncovering an array of goals and values that shaped clients' mandates concerning exterior design and internal spatial programs, these essays suggest that skyscraper design was far more complex than the confluence of economic requirements and engineering and aesthetic formulas. Using images, corporate records, and public statements, the authors show that attitudes about nationalism, citizenship, art, morality, and the role of men and women in an urban consumer society all contributed to clients' ideas concerning skyscraper form and function, and to the resulting interplay between public and private, inside and outside, culture and commerce.

The creation of a specific building type for the urban newspaper office is chronicled by Lee E. Gray in "Type and Building Type: Newspaper/Office Buildings in Nineteenth-Century New York." From the 1850s to the 1870s, New York City newspapers developed a commercial architecture that integrated mechanical systems and office workspaces in an efficient vertical arrangement, while employing siting and architectural design to declare the newspaper as a prominent institution in the modern city. Newspaper editors believed it was the role of commercial enterprise to furnish an appropriate civic architecture for the city, and they used their print resources to make clear their self-appointed roles as purveyors of architectural taste and the makers of new civic centers, such as Newspaper or Publishers' Row, and the subsequent Herald and Times squares.

In "Chicago's Fraternity Temples: The Origins of Skyscraper Rhetoric and the First of the World's Tallest Office Buildings," Edward W. Wolner brings into focus a critical but little-noted aspect of the Masonic Temple of 1890 and the 1891 unexecuted plan for the Odd Fellows Temple – the motivations of their clients, fraternal organizations steeped in archaic social hierarchies and rituals. Turning to the skyscraper as the means of achieving both social and financial prominence in an increasingly commercial urban culture, the Masons constructed the world's tallest building, which housed under one roof elaborate lodge rooms, first-class business suites, ten floors of luxury shops, and a glazed roof garden for 2,000 people. By closely examining the nature of Masonic and other fraternal cultures, this study documents the commodification of American fraternalism through the act of skyscraper building and the impact of this shift on both the societies and their urban environments. Also central to this study is a consideration of gender in relation to the skyscraper that focuses not on women clerical workers, but on men and their efforts to redefine masculine work and social identities in the changing environments of an increasingly mechanized, white-collar and mixed-gender skyscraper city.

Also eager to employ the skyscraper as advertisement were industries that had no tangible products such as banks and insurance companies. In "The Corporate and the Civic: Metropolitan Life's Home Office Building," I document the Metropolitan Life Insurance Company's embrace of the skyscraper office building as an efficient work center and as a vehicle for the dissemination of a corporate ideology that sought to influence all aspects of the built environment. The company's full-block complex and tower altered its immediate urban context and skyline, and its internal work systems were well publicized and influential. However, it was the form and symbol of the tower – wielded by architects, photographers, the popular press, and most extensively by the company itself – that loomed largest in the public eye. It carried to diverse viewers a multiplicity of messages and values, from American cultural superiority and technological prowess to corporate success and civic responsibility, blurring categories of public and private.

Katherine Solomonson's essay "The Chicago Tribune Tower Competition: Publicity Imagines Community" brings our attention once again to the newspaper industry, this time to the 1922 competition for the *Chicago Tribune*'s new office building in Chicago. This competition has been well documented as a landmark event in the architectural world, and Solomonson acknowledges the Tribune's architectural position while interpreting a broader range of evidence concerning the company's intentions and the political context of the immediate post–World War I era. Examination of the company's extensive publicity campaign surrounding the competition and subsequent building program reveals an "elaborate web of words and images" that shaped not only the skyscraper but also the set of values it represented and the community it would bind together.

Part Three, "Urban Contexts," collects three different perspectives of a city shaped by skyscraper form and meaning. Viewing New York City as both built and cultural landscape, these essays trace the conditions that shaped skyscraper development and the ways that this dense, tall urban landscape was interpreted by diverse constituencies. In these studies, the focus is not on specific buildings and their internal workings, but on the effect of the urban space and culture on the skyscraper, and the building type's reciprocal effect on the experience, meaning, and economics of the city.

In "The Heights and Depths of Urbanism: Fifth Avenue and the Creative Destruction of Manhattan," historian Max Page points to the skyscraper as the principal urban form representing the massive physical, economic, and social transformation of American cities. Looking at the urban landscape in the decades around the turn of the century, he describes the phenomenon of "creative destruction." This tumultuous cycle of tearing down and rebuilding reshaped the city, while presenting city dwellers with a chaotic physical landscape that mirrored the multiple social and economic changes wrought by waves of immigration, urban expansion, and the rise of corporations. At the center of this process, the skyscraper urged replacement of the nineteenth-century urban fabric with taller structures designed for spatial economy and symbolic power, structures that fundamentally changed the visual and experiential nature of the city.

Historian Sarah Watts views skyscrapers as the backdrop for labor protests and rallies, with focus on the 1913 Paterson Strike Pageant staged at Madison Square Garden. In "Built Languages of Class: Skyscrapers and Labor Protest in Victorian Public Space," Watts uses union records and published accounts of the strike and other labor actions to specify the meanings and values attached to the skyscraper by factory workers, civic leaders, and businessmen. Labor viewed skyscrapers as representations of their corporate owners, whose work processes, social behaviors, and economies increasingly controlled urban life beyond the walls of the office building. Businessmen and civic officials likewise acknowledged their influence on the city, but cast skyscrapers in a positive light, as symbols of civic order and capitalist progress. In contrast, they likened labor's irrational outbursts to the overcrowded and disordered tenement landscape, presenting the city in text and images as a built metaphor for the cultural clashes of labor with capitalist giants. Used by labor for mass marches and demonstrations and by corporations as venues for dramatic skyscraper construction, dedications, and operations, the city operated as a theatrical set upon which workers and management presented opposing views of labor's role in society. In this "urban dialogue," the skyscraper occupied center stage.

The creation of a skyscraper ensemble within the city is the subject of architectural historian Carol Herselle Krinsky's chronicle of Rockefeller Center, "The Skyscraper Ensemble in Its Urban Context." Built primarily between 1929 and 1940, the coordinated complex of skyscrapers, lower buildings, public art, and pedestrian plaza was the product of a collective of designers and a client's substantial financial resources and aesthetic insights. Krinsky shows how the project was further shaped by legal constraints, which orchestrated heights of periphery buildings and the length of the promenade and plaza to allow for the height and bulk of the central monolithic form of the RCA Building. Economic considerations determined the need for shops below grade, which in turn generated the slope of the promenade and the innovative use of the sunken plaza as an ice skating rink. Finally, Krinsky looks beyond the borders of this exceptional skyscraper ensemble to track and analyze its effect on the city around it.

The fourth and final section, "Popular Culture," follows the skyscraper as it was represented and interpreted through the media of photography, theater, and literature. Released of its specific architectural and functional obligations, the skyscraper in these realms existed as an image shaped by experience and meaning, by the perceptions of a diverse and cacophonous metropolitan culture, and by the experiences and aspirations of artists and writers. For millions who did not regularly engage with the skyscraper or the modern city, images and texts describing and analyzing this phenomenon were persuasive points of contact. For those who gazed upon and navigated the city on a daily basis – a diverse group that included white-collar workers, artists, children, rag pickers, and corporate captains – these "texts" referenced the familiar, both in recording fragments of popular culture and in creating new meanings, thus adding yet another layer to the metropolitan experience.

Three essays present the skyscraper as an article of cultural currency, underscoring what preceding essays suggest: the simultaneous operation of the skyscraper as an urban architecture and as an image. This image carried with it multiple conflicting meanings, signifying the exhilaration of corporate and technological accomplishment and/or the disorientation of a modern urbanity characterized by speed and a lack of physical and social coherence.

In "The Shadow of the Skyscraper: Urban Photography and Metropolitan Irrationalism in the Stieglitz Circle," Antonello Frongia, a historian of urban photography, focuses on the skyscraper as a subject of urban photography in the 1900s and 1910s. He locates in the skyscraper photography and criticism of Alfred Stieglitz and his colleagues Alvin Langdon Coburn and Sadakichi Hartmann, a "negative shadow-city" that expressed a pervasive cultural ambivalence about metropolitan modernism. Such classic images as Stieglitz's "Flatiron" and Coburn's "The Octopus" may be understood not only as products of technical experimentation and artistic interest, but also as efforts to subsume in a single image the "sunshine and shadow" of nineteenth-century urban commentaries. Thus, through the act of seeing and photographing, oppositional aspects of a fragmented and irrational urban environment could be revealed, organized, and resolved. Frongia's close reading of critical texts by Hartmann, the major spokesman for Pictorialism, and his consideration of urban photography from Jacob Riis to Lewis Hine uncover dialectical relationships between slums and skyscrapers, fact and fiction, rationality and fear.

Bringing a consideration of gender, class, mental health, and urbanism to skyscraper studies, architectural historian and women's studies scholar Merrill Schleier examines Sophie Treadwell's play *Machinal*, in which the main character is consumed both physically and emotionally by a mechanized and masochistic skyscraper culture. Considering the script and sets from the 1928 New York and 1933 Russian productions, Schleier documents the means by which Treadwell dramatizes the effects of the skyscraper and mechanized work environments on women. Based on a real-life murder trial, Treadwell's own experiences as an office worker, and her knowledge of contemporary psychiatric studies of gendered nervous disorders, *Machinal* recounts the "skyscraperization" of Young Woman. In the course of the play, the impersonal, mechanized, and male-controlled culture of the skyscraper office invades every physical and social aspect of her life, ultimately leading to her death. With exaggerated dialogue, characters, and sets, Treadwell theatricalized many concerns of feminists and the mental health profession about the modern city, skyscraper offices, and women's wellbeing.

The anthology's final essay, "The Sublime and the Skyline," shows how technology, nature, and history were woven into an urban and corporate mythology that defined the skyscraper in cultural terms. Using novels and the writings of architectural and cultural critics, as well as the work of commercial photographers, American studies senior scholar David Nye examines two paradigmatic experiences that forged the skyscraper's symbolic identity and shaped the public's experience and acceptance of "a landscape of skyscrapers": the view of the skyscraper as a constituent part of the skyline, and the view of the city from the top of the building.

These two ways of understanding the skyscraper, as skyline and vantage point, place the skyscraper at the center of the urban ensemble and the experience of urban modernity. Nye describes how the skyscraper, from a distance and from within, evoked a sense of the sublime, the sense of awe typically ascribed to experiences of natural power and beauty. The skyline, the collective of tall buildings, was overwhelming and cliff-like, at once naturalistic and a visual shout declaring victories of engineering and economics. As emphatically, the view from the top of a skyscraper denoted power and a command of both the built and natural visible landscape. Once positioned upon a public observation deck atop a corporate skyscraper, actually or virtually through the media of postcards or stereoviews, one could experience the magisterial gaze, the "solar eye" of the great corporations. These experiences are themselves not without complexity, however, and Nye points to the skyscraper's evocation of past and future and to the elevator's insistent inward focus on the individual, even as it moved upward to a platform of god-like height.

Collective Threads and Suggestions

The case studies presented here contribute to a growing body of research that builds upon and complements the foundational work of past skyscraper historians and critics. Although the essays cover a range of subjects, this collection is selective, both topically and methodologically, and many pieces of the skyscraper's kaleidoscopic story are not represented. The critical technologies of illumination, steel, and fireproof construction that made the skyscraper both structurally viable and then rentable and habitable; and communities of workers, like European immigrant custodians and Akwesasne Mohawk ironworkers whose very urban presence revolved around skyscraper employment, are just two avenues of study not pursued in this collection that yield additional insights into the skyscraper's urban cultural and spatial contexts.[5]

Within this collection, individual studies present methods, materials, and interpretations that generate further questions and observations. Read comparatively, these essays offer additional insights into the skyscraper, the city, and the discipline of history. For example, readers may find that topical or theoretical links between essays serve to highlight differences in sources and analytical strategies. Sarah Watts, Antonello Frongia, and I each consider in our studies Madison Square and its skyscrapers, the Met Life Tower and the Flatiron. However, to striking factory workers and labor advocates, corporate officers, and the Stieglitz circle, all of whom viewed and used Madison Square, this built landscape looked quite different. Our documentation of these differences of experience and perspective lends a "thickness," a historical articulation, to the much-used phrase "contested terrain," and suggests further productive study for historians. Likewise, the entangled processes of citybuilding and skyscraper design, and considerations of public versus individual rights are probed by Keith Revell and Max Page, yet they examine these issues in the context of different social and professional groups. The gendered qualities of skyscraper spaces and symbolism, and popular culture's absorption of the skyscraper as a spatial and experiential norm are at the center of Lisa Fine's and Merrill Schleier's essays, and the very nature of urban masculinity plays a significant role in Edward Wolner's study of fraternal orders and their skyscraper lodges.

This considerable topical and analytical overlap serves as a hinge between studies that are rooted in varied historical subdisciplines. This cross-disciplinary conversation, however, is enabled by a consistent *cultural approach* to the architectural history of the city.[6] The authors bring to this history observations concerning the spaces and structures in which personal and cultural forces operated, and they place aesthetic knowledge in a historical context that will explain motivations and perceptions. They identify the skyscraper as a focal point in the urban landscape – a physical place – where relationships and negotiations within and among groups defined by race, class, profession, and gender were concentrated and enacted.

The cultural history of architecture effectively engages Architecture with a capital A (signature or iconic buildings), as well as generic tall buildings that constitute the skyline, city streets, and office interiors. In these pages, a constellation of great American skyscrapers, urban ensembles, and planning milestones – the Chicago Loop and Rockefeller Center, the Woolworth Building, the Metropolitan Life and Tribune towers, the Flatiron Building, the World's Columbian Exposition of 1893, and the New York 1916 zoning ordinance – loom large. Authors make no attempt to sidestep these major monuments; in fact, they serve as the primary subject of a number of the essays. These studies, however, are not focused on authorship and architectural style, but on meaning, experience, and the relationship of these architectures and events with public spaces and social life. With a collective voice, the authors assert that the skyscraper, the major monument of the modern American city, is an excellent candidate for the cultural approach that frequently bypasses monuments to interpret "the spaces between," or the "nooks and crannies of the urban environment."[7]

Visual materials play a critical role in this collection, which suggests their significance as interpretive tools in urban architectural study. They document specific buildings, sites, and events, and they record cultural attitudes about the skyscraper and the modern city. Many images reproduced here are the work of commercial photographic companies, stock photographs intended for mass production as postcards and stereoviews. Others represent elaborate constructions by corporations and other groups or the creative experiments of art photographers, architects, and planners. Among their subjects are distant views and busy streets seen from atop skyscraper towers, panoramic skylines, the daily life of a skyscraper office, an imagined city of the future, and a city whose present is in constant dialogue with its past.[8]

Visual materials offer us a window, a nontextual commentary, on the urban experience. Commercial photographs of skyscraper offices, for example, not only provide valuable information about workspaces and behavioral norms, but also document corporate and municipal strategies to construct self-portraits legitimizing and boosting their political, economic, and social influence. "It is noticeable," stated one turn-of-the-century journalist, "that every American city and town that aspires to metropolitan importance wants to have at least one skyscraper – one that can be illustrated on a picture postcard and sent far and wide as evidence of modernity and a go-ahead spirit."[9]

Likewise, art photography of skyscrapers, frequently the subject of visual analysis or a survey of a photographer's technical and artistic accomplishments, is situated here in a literary and historical context. Photographers turned repeatedly to the skyscraper as *the* object of the modern city, a site for their experiments with technics and technique.[10] At the same time, they imprinted on film the disparate forces of urban culture – of history and invention, of creation and destruction, of fear and excitement – and sought there to reconcile them.[11]

Stereoviews, a valuable tool for documenting specific urban landscapes, are also rich in cultural content. These three-dimensional virtual glimpses of city architecture and life were originally offered to the parlor set, and a number of them appear in these pages. A view from a high

11162-Building one of New York's greatest skyscrapers, showing steel framework. Copyright Underwood & Underwood. U-107002

3. "Building one of New York's greatest skyscrapers." Singer Building under construction. Stereoview. Collection of the editor.

building looking past a dome of the Park Row Building at the Singer Building's unclad steel frame offers a dramatic perspective while juxtaposing the forms and values of history with that of engineering and corporate accomplishment (Figure 3). The view of the skyline through the cables of the Brooklyn Bridge is another carefully composed view (Figure 1). A street-level perspective of the Manhattan skyline appears at once so spectacular that it captured the attention of the photographer and yet so commonplace that it does not hold the attention of children who face the camera, backs to the city view (Frontispiece). Like the images captured in textual descriptions, these views capture on film glimpses of the skyscraper city. And from the choices that commercial photographers made in vantage point, subject, and composition, we may read attitudes, aspirations, concerns, about the nature and direction of American urban life, and the spectacle of the skyscraper.[12]

Finally, the essays collected here suggest a new theoretical path for skyscraper historians. Their cultural approach and their juxtaposition of diverse subjects and approaches forge a complex, discontinuous story of the modern city, in which the skyscraper functioned as both monument and locus of urban daily life. It was container of things sublime and banal – breathtaking and inspiring to witness under construction and as a finished structure, and yet utterly commonplace in a city where the cycle of creative destruction consumed and built ever higher. Thus, the skyscraper's histories contained here offer a window onto the urban everyday. This vantage point has been little explored by historians who traditionally locate the everyday in city streets and alleys, storefronts and public squares, and who view the skyscraper as a private realm, its form and spaces designed and controlled by a powerful professional elite.[13]

This anthology suggests quite the opposite – that the skyscraper, its makers and users, its form and spaces, its function, and its image were at the very center of the urban everyday, and that its history is complicated, with overlapping and at times contradictory meanings. The skyscraper occasioned great celebrations, it served as a symbol for causes corporate, civic, municipal, and national. It embodied history and the future. And yet it was everywhere, in mass-produced images, the subject of architectural and civics debates, of poetry and pulp fiction, theater and film. It was as prominent in the actual city, rising above sidewalk-covered scaffolding, casting steel-frame shadows, and adding to "the symphony of the city's noise" the sounds of pneumatic riveters high on steel beams.[14] Even the Flatiron Building, a favorite subject of art photographs (Figures 72 and 73) and an icon of the modern city (Figure 70), approaches the banal as captured in a construction photograph (Figure 4). Its steel frame rises half-clad, signs hawk for tenants, and scaffolding hides the adjacent sidewalks, at once sequestering passersby and the building. On the street beyond are people and vehicles: the monument rises and the city marches by what is on the one hand a major urban event, a slice of construction to view in awe; and on the other hand, another steel frame, another inconvenience of noise and detours.[15]

This position as urban icon and as a shaper of everyday spatial experience presents a challenge to the categories of high and low architecture, of the designed world and the spaces in between. As these essays detail, the skyscraper in the decades bracketing the turn of the century served as a dramatic spectacle. At the same time, the skyscraper in its many manifestations – as art and in photographs, as the subject of postcards, essays, plays, and novels, as a workplace and shopping venue, and as the ultimate shaper of urban space, both at the street level and on the skyline – was at the center of an urban experience widely shared. If the specific experiences or perceptions were not shared by all city dwellers – and the authors of the following essays indicate precisely this – the physicality of the skyscraper was a collector of these experiences, a focus for these fragments of experience and belief.

Further historical study of the skyscraper's form, use, and meaning may be enriched by a consideration of everyday life theory, an area of inquiry informed in part by the writings of Georg Simmel, Walter Benjamin, Henri Lefebvre, Michel de Certeau, and Jürgen Habermas.[16] Exploring the nature of modernity, these writers situated their critiques of daily life in the physical spaces of the city – the home, workplace, street, café, and shop. Benjamin's all-encompassing work in progress, his *Arcades Project*, has at its ostensible focus, a study of life practices among the city's capitalist institutions, where disparate fragments of everyday experience could be observed and analyzed. His materials and methods are inextricably caught up with the tactile and visual; the experiences and spaces he observes are fragments of a city both exhilarating and frightening, a condition Simmel had equated with the experience of modernity in his classic essay "The Metropolis and Mental Life."[17]

In recent decades, the fields of architecture, that is, its theory and practice and to a lesser extent its history, have used everyday life theory both to validate vernacular architecture studies and to shape a new trend in Architecture with a capital A (high-style architecture, characterized

4. Flatiron Building under construction. Courtesy of the Library of Congress, Prints and Photographs Div., Detroit Publishing Co. Collection [LC-D401-14278 DLC].

by signature buildings and celebrity architects). Both of these explorations attempt to study and then create spaces that are "in-between," "unmonumental and antiheroic," and "rooted in the commonplace and the routines of daily life."[18] Studies of everyday architecture and urbanism, then, find themselves in the domestic realm, in the yard, on the fence, or in the city streets, its shantytowns, and its alleys.[19]

These productive studies broaden the definition of architecture by considering environments and groups occupying positions of lesser power and visibility not typically celebrated by architects and their historians. They also contribute to a rich body of work by historians and geographers, prominent among them are Thomas Bender, David Harvey, and Richard Sennett, who have made the built environment an integral part of their urban studies.[20] However, studies of everyday architecture and urbanism have worked hard to detour around that very building that embodied so much of the physical and cultural work of the city. The skyscraper is to the American city what the arcades and cafés were to Benjamin's Paris, and the essays that follow begin the work of observing the urban culture located there.

This collection is not the first to assert the significance of the skyscraper city as both the physical frame for, and the production of, modern everyday experiences. Art critic Sadakichi Hartmann saw in the skyscraper city the essence of modern life, and he implored photographers to look to the city of the everyday, to its monumental skyscrapers and its streetscapes, for essential and aesthetic subjects. If Eugène Atget and Benjamin looked to shop windows and ragpickers as the physical objects and occupations of a commodified modern culture, Hartmann pointed the art photographer toward the skyscraper, to the commonplace of steel skeletons rising block after block, to the dramatic view of the city from a rooftop at dusk, where the natural light of day was overtaken by the pinpoints of window lights and illuminated skyscraper pinnacles. Through such images, he asserted, the photographer could "teach New Yorkers to love their own city as I have learned to love it, and to be proud of its beauties as the Parisians are of their city."[21]

E. B. White also advocated for the significance of the skyscraper as the icon of urban modernity at the center of everyday life. Undergirding his 1949 essay "Here Is New York" is an assertion that the city, its great buildings, and its ordinary spaces have imprinted upon them discontinuous, overwritten histories, fragments of past events and personalities that comprise the city's identity.[22] He also saw a city moving so fast as to find these traces at times imperceptible or incomprehensible. As a contemporary critic, he pointed to the skyscraper as the preeminent architecture of the city, which in his time represented both the potential for great human accomplishment in the rising form of the United Nations Secretariat and the possibility of death and devastation at a previously unmatched scale resulting from an atomic attack on the densely inhabited skyscraper landscape of Manhattan.

It is this interplay of the skyscraper's form and meaning and its relationship with the city that serve as the focus of the following essays. Like the barely perceptible shadow of the Met Life Tower in Alvin Langdon Coburn's famous photograph "The Octopus" (Figure 68), the skyscraper's impact on the city was sometimes subtle, and its cultural histories less obvious and dramatic than its physical presence on the skyline. It is to the practice of history that we turn to study the multiple meanings and experiences of this singular American building, which stood and continues to stand at the center of metropolitan culture.

NOTES

1. For a detailed discussion of life rituals as applied to architecture see Neil Harris, *Building Lives: Constructing Rites and Passages* (New Haven, CT: Yale Univ. Press, 1999); the elaborate dedication ceremonies of the Woolworth Building are recounted in *The Cathedral of Commerce* (New York: Broadway Park Place, 1916). For a recent and specific application of this trope, see M. Christine Boyer, "Meditations on a Wounded Skyline and Its Stratigraphies of Pain," Chap. 10 in *After the World Trade Center: Rethinking New York City*, eds.

Michael Sorkin and Sharon Zukin (London: Routledge, 2002), 109–20.

2. Carl W. Condit, *The Rise of the Skyscraper* (Chicago: Univ. of Chicago Press, 1952); Sarah Bradford Landau and Carl W. Condit, *Rise of the New York Skyscraper, 1865–1913* (New Haven, CT: Yale Univ. Press, 1996); Merrill Schleier, *The Skyscraper in American Art, 1890–1931* (New York: DaCapo, 1986); Carol Willis, *Form Follows Finance: Skyscrapers and Skylines in New York and Chicago* (New York: Princeton Architectural Press, 1995).

3. See, for example, Daniel M. Abramson, *Skyscraper Rivals: The AIG Building and the Architecture of Wall Street* (New York: Princeton Architectural Press, 2001); Robert Bruegmann, *The Architects and the City: Holabird and Roche of Chicago, 1880–1918* (Chicago: Univ. of Chicago Press, 1997); Sharon Irish, *Cass Gilbert, Architect: Modern Traditionalist* (New York: Monacelli, 1999); Sarah Bradford Landau, *George B. Post: Picturesque Designer and Determined Realist* (New York: Monacelli, 1998); Joseph Siry, *Carson Pirie Scott: Louis Sullivan and the Chicago Department Store* (Chicago: Univ. of Chicago Press, 1998); Katherine Solomonson, *The Chicago Tribune Tower Competition: Skyscraper Design and Cultural Change in the 1920s* (New York: Cambridge Univ. Press, 2001).

4. Roland Barthes, "Semiology and the Urban," in *Rethinking Architecture: A Reader in Cultural Theory*, ed. Neil Leach (London: Routledge, 1997), 171.

5. Issues of skyscraper technology are covered by Thomas J. Misa, *A Nation of Steel: The Making of Modern America, 1865–1925* (Baltimore: Johns Hopkins Univ. Press, 1995); Sara E. Wermiel, *The Fireproof Building* (Baltimore: Johns Hopkins Univ. Press, 2000); Lee E. Gray, *A History of the Passenger Elevator in the 19th Century* (Mobile, AL: Elevator World, 2002); and Dietrich Neumann, *Architecture of the Night: The Illuminated Building* (Munich: Prestel Verlag, 2002). A popular history of structural ironworkers and their bridge and skyscraper work is Jim Rasenberger, *High Steel: The Daring Men Who Built the World's Greatest Skyline* (New York: HarperCollins, 2004).

6. For examples of a cultural approach to architecture and the city, see Daniel Bluestone, *Constructing Chicago* (New Haven, CT: Yale Univ. Press, 1991); Dolores Hayden, *The Power of Place: Urban Landscapes as Public History* (Cambridge, MA: MIT Press, 1995); Lauren M. O'Connell, "Afterlives of the Tour Saint-Jacques: Plotting the Perceptual History of an Urban Fragment," *Journal of the Society of Architectural Historians* 60, no. 4 (Dec. 2001):450–73. For a general framing of the question of architectural history's purview, see Dell Upton, "Architectural History or Landscape History?" *Journal of Architectural Education* 44, no. 4 (Aug. 1991):195–9. Two historians who have devoted much of their writing to locating American urban culture in physical space are William R. Taylor and Thomas Bender. For William R. Taylor, see esp. *In Search of Gotham: Culture and Commerce in New York* (New York: Oxford Univ. Press, 1992) and Taylor, ed., *Inventing Times Square: Commerce and Culture at the Crossroads of the World* (New York: Russell Sage, 1991). For Thomas Bender, see esp. "Metropolitan Life and the Making of Public Culture," Chap.10 in *Power, Culture, and Place: Essays on New York City*, ed. John Hull Mollenkopf (New York: Russell Sage, 1988), 261–71; Bender, "The Modern City as Text and Context: The Public Culture of New York," *Rivista di studi Anglo-Americani (RSA)* 6 (1990):15–34; and Bender, *The Unfinished City: New York and the Metropolitan Idea* (New York: New Press, 2002).

7. Margaret Crawford, "Introduction," *Everyday Urbanism*, ed. Margaret Crawford (New York: Monacelli, 1999), 9, 10.

8. Simmons, Peter, and the Museum of the City of New York, *Gotham Comes of Age: New York through the Lens of the Byron Company, 1892–1942* (San Francisco: Pomegranate, 1999). In addition to the Byron Collection at the Museum of the City of New York, see the Detroit Publishing Co. Collection and the Gottscho–Schleisner Collection at the Library of Congress.

9. Frederic A. Delano, "Skyscrapers," *American City Magazine* 34, no. 1 (Jan. 1926):1.

10. In 1911, Sadakichi Hartmann commended "men who have preferred the city streets, the impressionism of life" for their contributions of motifs and compositional strategies to photographic art, citing in particular "Stieglitz's skyscrapers and dock scenes, and some of Coburn's interpretations of city views." See Sadakichi Hartmann, "What Remains" [1911], reprinted in *The Valiant Knights of Daguerre: Selected Critical Essays on Photography and Profiles of Photographic Pioneers by Sadakichi Hartmann*, ed. Harry W. Lawton and George Knox (Berkeley, CA: Univ. of California Press, 1978) 149–53.

11. For a discussion of urban photography, see Peter Bacon Hales, *Silver Cities: The Photography of American Urbanization, 1839–1915* (Philadelphia: Temple Univ. Press, 1984); Alan Trachtenberg, "Camera Work/Social Work," Chap. 4 in *Reading American Photographs: Images as History, Mathew Brady to Walker Evans* (New York: Hill and Wang, 1989), 164–230; and Trachtenberg, "Image and Ideology: New York in the Photographer's Eye," *Journal of Urban History* 10 (Aug. 1984):453–64.

12. The Keystone–Mast Collection at the California Museum of Photography, Univ. of California, Riverside,

holds the archive of the Keystone View Co., a maker of stereoviews. The Library of Congress, Prints and Photographs Div., also has an extensive collection of stereoviews.

13. Steven Harris, "Everyday Architecture," in *Architecture of the Everyday*, eds. Steven Harris and Deborah Berke (New York: Princeton Architectural Press, 1997), 3. This collection, as many contemporary architecture books and projects inspired by everyday life theory, expresses "a distrust of the heroic and the formally fashionable, a deep suspicion of the architectural object as a marketable commodity," and asserts that the everyday "is that which remains after one has eliminated all specialized activities" (p. 3). In this volume, the authors acknowledge the skyscraper as the ultimate object building, the symbol and container of a commodity-based culture, and a place of highly regulated, spatially ordered, specialized activities, but they assert that it is precisely the skyscraper and its landscape that created the context for the activities, ideas, and negotiations of everyday urban life.

14. A. D. F. Hamlin, "Architectural Art," *Forum*, 34 (July 1902):94.

15. For a survey of nearly a century of photographic images of the Flatiron Building, see Philip William Kreitler, *Flatiron: A Photographic History of the World' s First Steel Frame Skyscraper, 1901–1990* (Washington, DC: American Institute of Architects, 1990).

16. For an overview of everyday life theory, see Ben Highmore, *Everyday Life and Cultural Theory: An Introduction* (London: Routledge, 2002); Ben Highmore, ed., *The Everyday Life Reader*, (London: Routledge, 2002). See also the works of the individuals mentioned here, such as Georg Simmel, "The Metropolis and Mental Life," in *On Individuality and Social Forms*, ed. Donald Levine (Chicago: Univ. of Chicago Press, 1971), 324–39; Walter Benjamin, *Illuminations*, ed. Hannah Arendt (New York: Schoken Books, 1985), and Benjamin, *The Arcades Project*, trans. Howard Eiland and Kevin McLaughlin (Cambridge, MA: Harvard Univ. Press, 1999); Henri Lefebvre, *The Production of Space*, trans. David Nicholson-Smith (1974; London: Blackwell, 1991) and Lefebvre, *Writing on Cities*, trans. and ed. Eleonore Kofman and Elizabeth Lebas (London: Blackwell, 1995); Michel de Certeau, *The Practice of Everyday Life*, trans. Steven Rendall (1980; Berkeley, CA: Univ. of California Press, 1984); Jürgen Habermas, "Modern and Post-Modern Architecture," trans. Helen Tsoskounglou, *9H*, no. 4 (1982):9–14, reprinted in Leach, ed., *Rethinking Architecture*, 227–35.

17. Walter Benjamin, *The Arcades Project*, trans. Howard Eiland and Kevin McLaughlin (Cambridge, MA: Harvard Univ. Press, 1999); Vanessa R. Schwartz, "Walter Benjamin for Historians," *American Historical Review* 106, no. 5 (Dec. 2001):1721–43.

18. Harris and Berke, eds., *Architecture of the Everyday*, jacket copy.

19. See, for example, Harris and Berke, eds., *Architecture of the Everyday;* Crawford, ed., *Everyday Urbanism*; Chris Wilson and Paul Groth, eds., *Everyday America: Cultural Landscape Studies after J. B. Jackson* (Berkeley, CA: Univ. of California Press, 2003); Georges Teyssot, ed., *The American Lawn* (New York: Princeton Architectural Press, 1999); Gregory K. Dreicer, Diana Balmori, and the National Building Museum, *Building Fences* (New York: Princeton Architectural Press, 1996); and Annmarie Adams and Sally McMurry, eds., *Exploring Everyday Landscapes. Perspectives in Vernacular Architecture, No. 7* (Knoxville: Univ. of Tennessee Press, 1997) or the other volumes in this series created by the Vernacular Architecture Forum.

20. See note 6 for references to Thomas Bender's work; Richard Sennett, *The Conscience of the Eye: Design and Social Life of Cities* (New York: Knopf, 1990) and Sennett, *Flesh and Stone: The Body and the City in Western Civilization* (New York: Norton, 1994); David Harvey, *The Urban Experience* (Baltimore: Johns Hopkins Univ. Press, 1989) and Harvey, *The Condition of Postmodernity: An Enquiry into the Origins of Cultural Change* (Oxford: Blackwell, 1989).

21. Sadakichi Hartmann, "A Plea for the Picturesqueness of New York" and "Recent Conquests in Night Photography," in Hartmann, *The Valiant Knights of Daguerre*, 56–63 and 127–31, respectively.

22. E. B. White, *Here Is New York* (New York: Harper & Brothers, 1949).

PART ONE

MAKERS AND USERS

1

The Beaux-Arts Architect and the Skyscraper

Cass Gilbert, the Professional Engineer, and the Rationalization of Construction in Chicago and New York

Gail Fenske

Critics hailed Cass Gilbert's designs for skyscrapers, notably the West Street and Woolworth buildings, as the most architecturally distinctive of their day.[1] Technical authorities also regarded the designs as remarkably advanced from the standpoint of engineering and construction.[2] The Woolworth Building, the highest in the world upon its completion in 1913, was the culmination of several earlier developments in the engineering design of the skyscraper – chief among them were the caisson method for carrying concrete pier foundations to bedrock and the construction to increasingly greater heights with the fully wind-braced steel frame.[3] Gilbert's professional identity, however, was that of a Beaux-Arts architect. His office had the character of a small atelier (Figures 5, 6). He viewed the historical buildings of Europe as touchstones for his designs and the American city as a potential "city beautiful," which might rival Paris, London, or Rome in its order, dignity, and monumentality.

The skyscraper presented a special set of problems for Gilbert and his American Beaux-Arts contemporaries. The forces of modernization that it represented – among them new methods of financing, efficiency of office planning and engineering, and rapid construction – seemed totally at odds with the Beaux-Arts architect's perception that buildings should be timeless and ennobling works of art. As compositions, such works of art were to have a monumental and dignified presence in the public spaces of American cities. To that end, Beaux-Arts architects emphasized formal principles such as organizing a plan around clearly defined axes of circulation and the expression in elevation of a clear hierarchy of volumes.[4]

I thank Roberta Moudry for her perceptive comments on an early draft of this essay.

5. East Twenty-fourth Street #1, Entrance Lobby, Cass Gilbert's Office, ca. 1912. Reprinted with permission of the Museum of the City of New York, Wurts Collection, 114603.

The skyscraper, typified by a thinness of metal construction, a standardization of building components, and hence a visual uniformity, seemed to most Beaux-Arts architects tenaciously irreconcilable with such time-honored formal principles. Gilbert optimistically believed, nonetheless, that in masterminding an artistically designed as well as professionally engineered skyscraper, he might overcome the disparity. Indeed, it was possible to have it both ways – an architecture that evoked the character of a European capital as well as an architecture that served the functional needs of the twentieth-century city. To that end, Gilbert employed his prodigious skills as an architectural administrator to synthesize his own artistic contribution with those of the skyscraper's new team of experts, chief among them being the structural engineer and the large-scale general contractor. Together they would harness the forces inciting the modernization of cities and press them into the service of Beaux-Arts aesthetic and cultural ideals.

At the turn of the twentieth century, the modern criteria governing the financing and planning of the office building were widely known and accepted. Independent speculative developers, development companies, and business corporations functioning as speculative investors conceived ingenious financial mechanisms for expediting the construction of well-lit and well-serviced office structures in the hearts of major American cities. These buildings generated respectable profits while also fulfilling an established architectural need.[5] By the mid-1880s, a special branch of professional structural engineering developed that was dedicated to the design of the foundations and skeletal framing systems for the new office buildings. Concurrently, the general contractor rose

6. East Twenty-fourth Street #1, Drafting Room, Cass Gilbert's Office, ca.1912. Reprinted with permission of the Museum of the City of New York, Wurts Collection, 114603.

to importance with the deployment of increasingly sophisticated organizational methods for rapidly constructing large-scale projects. The architectural community's response to the new building type involved its dissection and analysis in detail, as illustrated by the technical investigations of Barr Ferree, the theoretical writings and standardized plan diagrams of George Hill, and the architectural criticism of Louis Sullivan.[6] These new types of urban professionals' defined their roles in the contemporary world of architecture through their contributions to the rapidly developing body of technical expertise associated with the skyscraper.

The growth of professional knowledge associated with skyscrapers took place for the most part in Chicago and New York. Gilbert benefited significantly from his experience with various professional communities in both cities. The engineers, contractors, and architects of Chicago were known for their shared devotion to the skyscraper as a new building type and, in particular, to the modern technologies that made its construction possible. Architectural discourse in journals and papers presented at professional meetings showed an intensity of enthusiasm for the new type's iron and steel framing, elevators, and electrical illumination.[7] The architectural community of New York, by contrast, did not as a group collaborate with the city's engineers and builders in their devotedness to the skyscraper's modern technologies. The most prominent among New York's architects were trained at the Ecole des Beaux-Arts or in American offices modeled on the ateliers of the Ecole. Many viewed their professional identity as that of artists. As such, they believed they were charged with the representation of an individual's or an institution's nobler cultural sentiments. In the hierarchy of building types that the Beaux-Arts architect aspired to design, institutions occupied the highest tier, and commercial types, by contrast, the lowest.[8]

Some New York architects were known for their markedly critical stance toward the skyscraper. The Beaux-Arts-trained Charles McKim and Stanford White, for instance, both spoke out against skyscrapers and refused to accept commissions to design them.[9] Even George Post, called the "father of the tall building in New York" and respected for his early experimentation with new technologies such as the elevator in the Equitable Building and "cage construction" in the Produce Exchange, spearheaded the city's professional discussions over height restrictions. These originated at the Architectural League in 1894 and culminated with New York's 1916 zoning ordinance.[10]

Among these New York architects, few were so vociferously critical of the skyscraper as the Beaux-Arts-trained Ernest Flagg. Flagg had studied at the Ecole during 1888–91 and upon his return from Paris, rapidly built up a reputation as the city's doctrinaire proponent of Ecole methods of design. Flagg's criticism, particularly scathing in its attack of the skyscraper's absence of propriety, compositional aesthetics, and the proper protection to withstand fire, could be read as a summation of the day's antagonistic views toward the new building type.[11] Flagg designed the Singer Tower in 1906, widely known as the tallest skyscraper in the world, but justified his design as a demonstration of his proposal for skyscraper reform (Figure 3). Afterward, he wrote that "we have a lurking inward consciousness that [tall buildings] do not belong to the highest type of art" and he never designed another such major skyscraper again.[12] In general, the Beaux-Arts architect's perception of the skyscraper ranged from an outright avoidance of the building type to a deep desire to reform a kind of construction that many of them considered the aesthetically and ethically depraved product of brutal market forces.

One consequence of the New York architectural community's adverse view of the skyscraper was the extremely slow process by which the professional engineer and the large-scale general contractor eventually came to establish themselves independently in the city. Corydon T. Purdy, of the Chicago engineering firm Purdy & Henderson, recalled that in 1894, the year he set up practice in New York, the city's architects relied on three or four great iron manufacturers for their structural iron and steel designs.[13] Prior to the arrival of the Chicago-based George A. Fuller Company in New York in 1896, which enlisted Purdy to establish a branch office in the city, architects continued to coordinate the individual building trades responsible for constructing skyscrapers. Among these trades were the iron and steel contractors, masonry and terra-cotta contractors, and carpenters. As late as 1895–98, George Post served as the structural engineer and organizer of the individual trades responsible for constructing the tallest skyscraper of the day, the twenty-six-story St. Paul Building.[14]

Gilbert was uniquely positioned in relation to the professional communities of architects, engineers, and general contractors working in both New York and Chicago. On the one hand, his attitude toward designing skyscrapers was influenced by his Beaux-Arts training at MIT during 1878–79 and his apprenticeship in the Beaux-Arts atelier of McKim, Mead & White in New York during 1880–82. On the other hand, his attitude was also conditioned by his early years of practice in the midwestern city of St. Paul, which had strong links to Chicago. There, he drew upon the expertise of Chicago engineers for the design of office buildings. Chief among them was Louis E. Ritter, whom Gilbert retained to design the foundation and the internal iron framing of the Endicott Building, a large six-story office building in St. Paul of 1890–91.[15] For the design of the eleven-story Brazer Building in Boston, his first fully steel-framed skyscraper of 1894–97,

7. The Brazer Building, State Street, Boston, 1894–97. Photograph by Halliday Historic Photograph Co. Courtesy of the Society for the Preservation of New England Antiquities.

Gilbert chose Ritter again (Figure 7). Ritter, in turn, consulted with Henry S. Pritchard of the New Jersey Iron & Steel Company. Together, they devised an inventive system of portal arch wind bracing, which supported the building without obstructing the daring open corners of Gilbert's elevations. In the end, however, Gilbert relied on the engineer Corydon T. Purdy of Purdy & Henderson to check and oversee the construction of the Brazer Building's structural design; Purdy was the choice of the George A. Fuller Company, the project's builder.[16] By the mid-1890s, then, Gilbert was working very closely with Chicago's most experienced engineering professionals. This collaboration, combined with his Beaux-Arts training, would be essential to his formation as an architect who would go on to design some of the most technologically sophisticated and visually stunning skyscrapers in New York during the early years of the twentieth century.

While in St. Paul, Gilbert organized his practice as a Beaux-Arts atelier. His objective was to maintain full artistic command of his projects. Even after he moved to New York in April 1899, the size of his office remained relatively small; it never exceeded more than twenty-five assisting designers and draftsmen.[17] Beginning in the early 1890s, however, the commercial office building assumed an increasing level of importance in Gilbert's architectural practice. As a consequence, he faced the challenging question of how to uphold his Beaux-Arts architectural ideals while also properly serving his modern, investment-oriented clients. These clients, in turn, expected efficient engineering design and construction; the skyscraper as a potentially profitable speculative enterprise imposed severe time contingencies. Gilbert's solution was to infuse his small atelier with a newly rigorous level of hierarchical organization. Once in New York, he established clear lines of command between himself as the sole principal and mastermind of a project, his key assistants in office management, design, and construction, and in turn, their supporting staffs of apprentices and draftsmen. The new functional clarity of Gilbert's small but well-organized office was widely recognized by colleagues in the profession; visitors to the office frequently made note of Gilbert's efficient and systematic work methods.[18]

Another one of Gilbert's solutions to his clients' requirements for efficient design and construction was to strengthen his ties with the engineering professionals and construction contractors upon whom he had since the early 1890s already come to strongly rely. In doing so, he would become ever more facile in his methods for tapping related areas of professional and technical knowledge, these in turn having continued to develop significantly in their own right.[19] Ultimately, Gilbert would thoroughly depend upon the skills of those assisting professionals with whom he formed close working relationships, and furthermore, upon their own large and organized staffs of supporting professionals and draftsmen. He also would continue to streamline the process of work within his own office, while relying on his professional consultants to streamline their methods of work as well.

Gilbert's administrative methods were unique among those of his major Beaux-Arts contemporaries. At the twentieth century's turn, the prominent model of a Beaux-Arts architectural practice specializing in the commercial skyscraper was D.H. Burnham & Company of Chicago. Even while known as Burnham & Root during the 1880s, the firm had developed a reputation as one of the biggest and most elaborately organized architectural offices of the day. Contemporaries compared it to the corporate hierarchies of big business. According to a young visitor of 1889, the drafting room of Burnham & Root "impressed [him] like a large manufacturing plant."[20] By 1912, the Burnham office staff totaled 180. It was under the direction of a managing partner, who coordinated the efforts of middle-level managers in charge of design, production, and construction supervision. The middle-level managers in turn oversaw teams of designers, draftsmen, and construction supervisors.[21] Gilbert admired Burnham's abilities as an administrator. In 1891, while Burnham was serving as the chief of construction for the World's Columbian Exposition, Gilbert seriously considered forming a partnership with him. When Burnham died in 1912, Gilbert described his mentor in a eulogy as a "man of affairs ... [who] would have been successful in any walk of life." When called for, Burnham could be "direct and practical," but he was also "a great citizen and a great architect."[22] Gilbert, as it turned out, was as skilled as Burnham in administration and could have similarly organized his office for the purpose of producing a large volume of commercial work. Yet even during the fifty-five-story Woolworth Building project of 1910–13, the largest skyscraper that any architectural office had yet to see, Gilbert resisted augmenting the size of his relatively small office staff of twenty to twenty-five assistants. He was determined to preserve the character of a Beaux-Arts atelier.

The high significance that Gilbert placed on the Beaux-Arts model for professional practice was based in part on his encounter with Henry Hobson Richardson's office in Brookline, Mass., which he visited as a young architect in the early 1880s. There, Gilbert later recalled, Richardson "presided like a medieval potentate over a group of devoted adherents." The library in which they met he described as "a room of unusual dimensions, on one side was a huge fireplace and in the middle an enormous table covered with architectural books of large dimensions."[23] Gilbert's experience with Richardson was reinforced by his apprenticeship with McKim, Mead & White in New York during 1880–82, as one of among ten to twelve assistants. There he experienced an environment strongly influenced by the character of Richardson's atelier. Even as McKim, Mead & White's office increased in size, boasting a staff of over 100 from the mid-1890s, making it the largest architectural practice in New York, the ideal of the atelier remained paramount.[24] McKim, Mead & White refused to become a "syndicate" or "plan factory" like D.H. Burnham & Company, according to H. Van Buren Magonigle, who apprenticed there in the late 1880s. The main drafting room was decorated with plaster casts of ornament, pieces of Venetian wrought-iron work, and "all manner of interesting odds and ends." There existed little system and organization in the office; that is, it lacked the hierarchy of "division heads" and "'efficiency' was unknown." The freewheeling artistic atmosphere, Magonigle noted, was personified by Stanford White, whose assistants he called "an association of artists working in architecture as their principal medium," adding, "that fact colored everything that went on."[25] Regardless of Magonigle's perceptions, however, by the mid-1890s the realities of late-nineteenth-century American architectural practice forced compromises in the ideal of the Beaux-Arts atelier. Both White and McKim eventually delegated design tasks and Henry Hobson Richardson's successor firm, Shepley, Rutan & Coolidge, was known at the time for a hierarchical division of responsibility and labor.[26]

Gilbert, in aspiring to the model of the Beaux-Arts atelier, endeavored to create a smaller, more compact version of McKim, Mead & White's office, even while he developed multiple commissions for major commercial skyscrapers. His "highly cultivated artistic sensibility," as one of his apprentices, Guy Kirkham, later described it, made him especially resistant to the Burnham model for architectural practice.[27] Furthermore, Gilbert's reputation rested strongly on his nationally known Beaux-Arts works, that is, on his design for the Minnesota State Capitol in St. Paul (1895–1905) and the United States Custom House in New York (1899–1907). Like Richardson, Charles McKim, and Stanford White, Gilbert exerted a high level of artistic control over his office's designs; Kirkham noted that a "master spirit" pervaded Gilbert's work as a whole. In this, Gilbert followed the pattern of his Beaux-Arts mentors; he communicated his design objectives with "off-hand studies," or conceptual thumbnail sketches similar to a Beaux-Arts "parti," which "would check up closely with laborious mechanically-executed drawings."[28] Gilbert's work, however, reflected far more frequently than that of his mentors the contributions of various designers employed in his office at various times. The United States Custom House project, during which the Ecole-trained Ernest Hìbrard assumed an important designing role, for instance, significantly differed in character and detail from the Woolworth Building project, for which Thomas R. Johnson served as Gilbert's key assistant in design. Gilbert, evidently, was more willing than Richardson, McKim, or White to delegate design authority. His artistic process was in part a consequence of having to also secure, organize, manage, and oversee the design and construction of some of the largest commercial and institutional projects of his day.

Gilbert's concerted effort to integrate the commercial skyscraper into his Beaux-Arts practice was not entirely new; he was preceded at least a decade by the New York architect, George Post. Post apprenticed in the Beaux-Arts atelier of Richard Morris Hunt, the first such office established in America, during 1858–60. By 1881, however, Post had fully transformed the model of Hunt's earlier atelier into a modern commercial office, the "first of a new type."[29] Post's office was distinguished by its immense number of commercial projects, the "industrial" appearance of its main drafting room, the relatively large size of its staff for the time – a total of twenty-one in 1881 – and by the clear hierarchical organization that Post established between himself and his closest assistants. Post's early study of engineering at New York University, along with his habit of serving as a project's engineer, architect, and coordinator of separate contracts for construction – essentially functioning as a general contractor – allowed him to tailor his practice to the design of the modern commercial skyscraper more broadly and comprehensively than any other practice in the city at the time.[30] In Gilbert's office, however, commercial building types never really predominated as they did in Post's. Nor did Gilbert have Post's sophisticated level of knowledge in engineering and construction, choosing instead to utilize the expertise of outside professional consultants. Most significantly, Gilbert's office continued to be identified with monumental Beaux-Arts projects for major institutions of culture and government.[31] Through such monumental projects he developed and secured his reputation nationally.

When Gilbert designed skyscrapers during the 1890s in St. Paul, he recognized that employing Chicago's professional structural engineers significantly extended the reach of his Beaux-Arts practice. Furthermore, he clearly understood the difference between the engineer's work and his own. This sharply distinguished his office methods from those of Post's. As far as Gilbert was concerned, the engineer designed a skyscraper's inner supporting construction, that is, the foundation and the steel-framed superstructure, in accordance with the architect's preliminary sketches in plan. The architect, by contrast, designed ornamental Beaux-Arts exteriors. Working together as professionals, the engineer and the architect had the potential to introduce a wholly new kind of monumentality within the city. This they would achieve through a synthesis of the new steel-framed technology, and particularly its potential for height, with Beaux-Arts compositional and aesthetic ideals.

Historically in America, the architect and engineer were often identified with a single person, as illustrated by the careers of Benjamin Henry Latrobe, Ithiel Town, William Strickland, Robert Mills, and Thomas U. Walter.[32] Even as late as the 1880s, the architects who pioneered in the design of metal-framed skyscrapers were also frequently trained as engineers. George Post and William Le Baron Jenney of Chicago stand out as two prominent examples of such well-rounded professionals. As the influence of the Ecole des Beaux-Arts over American architectural practice began to increase and eventually dominate in the 1890s, however, architects came to view themselves instead primarily as creators of monumental and artistic compositions that embellished their urban surroundings. In giving prominence to the architect's role as an independent artistic creator, the Ecole directed the development of the profession away from the earlier and potentially fruitful American architectural tradition in which an artistic personality was combined with that of a technological innovator.

Gilbert, who was trained as a Beaux-Arts architect but was also determined to design skyscrapers, looked for instruction at the close professional alliances that architects formed with engineers in Chicago during the 1890s. As it turned out, even William Le Baron Jenney found it essential for his practice to employ additional consulting engineers. Jenney hired Louis E. Ritter as his office's chief structural engineer in 1892, for instance, one year after he formed a partnership with the architect William B. Mundie.[33] When Burnham's office grew in size, he too decided to hire talented in-house engineers, employing E. C. Shankland as his office's chief engineer in 1893. By the end of the century, however, Chicago's engineering profession had changed as well; many engineers had established themselves independently in practice as consulting professionals. Burnham, for instance, sought out the expertise of an independently practicing professional engineer, the Norwegian-American Joachim G. Giaver, shortly after Shankland resigned from his office in 1898.[34]

The architects of New York, by contrast, only gradually came to appreciate the value of such professional engineering collaborators. Corydon T. Purdy observed as late as 1905 that regardless of the "enormous expansion of problems involving technical knowledge," the foundations and structural frames of skyscrapers in the city, many of which were designed by steel fabricators or builders, continued to vary in strength, stability, and cost.[35] Structural engineers had yet to strongly and decisively establish their professional authority as independent consulting practitioners in New York, which suggested that the profession's potential contributions to the design of skyscrapers had yet to be fully understood.

Given Purdy's assessment of the engineer's predicament in New York, Gilbert's effort to forge a strong working relationship between the architect and the independently practicing professional engineer might have stood out as unusual among his colleagues in the profession when he arrived in the city in 1899. Construction began on his Broadway Chambers Building that year and Gilbert's association with the engineering firm Purdy & Henderson was well established (Figure 8). Significantly, the George A. Fuller Company had formed an exclusive working relationship with Purdy & Henderson, and its new vice president, Harry S. Black, prepared the project's detailed financial scenarios.[36] Purdy & Henderson provided Gilbert with the full range of engineering services. By 1899, Purdy had designed the Broadway Chambers's concrete-bedded steel grillage foundation and steel frame using detailed calculations, produced all of the required structural steel shop drawings, and wrote a complete set of specifications.[37] By contrast, the engineer Louis E. Ritter, with whom Gilbert had worked initially on the Brazer Building project in 1894, relied heavily on the detailed shop drawings supplied by the New Jersey Iron & Steel Company. During the Broadway Chambers project, then, Gilbert was in the position to observe the development of an increased precision and clarity in the definition of the engineer's professional role as well as a clearer division of professional responsibilities among the architect, engineer, and the steel fabricator. As a consequence, Gilbert considered the Broadway Chambers Building, which the Fuller Company built in less than four months, a marvel of efficient design, engineering, and construction, calling it a "triumph of organization."[38]

After Gilbert designed the Brazer and Broadway Chambers buildings, however, he also recognized that his role as the architect for such large-scale skyscraper projects had become somewhat limited. His principal contributions to the projects were office planning and the design of a terra-cotta and brick-masonry envelope. Indeed, Gilbert noted in 1900 that he was awed by the degree to which the Fuller Company, in conjunction with Purdy & Henderson, took nearly complete control of the Broadway Chambers project as a phenomenon of engineering and construction, reducing the architect's contribution to a mere "measure of

8. Broadway Chambers Building, New York, under construction, 1899–1900. *Architects' and Builders' Magazine* 11 (Nov. 1900):48. Courtesy of the Trustees of the Boston Public Library.

beauty."[39] In an effort to strengthen and decisively establish the architect's professional authority, Gilbert envisioned reconfiguring the professional relationships among the architect, structural engineer, and general contractor; in particular, he sought the formation of a stronger professional alliance between the architect and the engineer. When he retained the structural engineer, Gunvald Aus, for his Custom House project in 1899, Gilbert discovered a well-grounded professional expert with whom he could form such an alliance. This, he may well have foreseen, would facilitate the renewal of his artistic command over the problem of the skyscraper. Gilbert was introduced to Aus through his former partner James Knox Taylor, who was at the time the supervising architect of the United States Treasury Department. Aus had served as the department's chief construction engineer since 1895. Ultimately, Aus would enhance Gilbert's practice with more than just seasoned technical expertise. To Gilbert's designs for the West Street and the Woolworth buildings, he contributed a new level of brilliant as well as highly compatible engineering talent.

When Aus began working for Gilbert in 1899, he was already a prominent member of his profession, his training and career having followed the typical pattern of the structural engineering professionals who preceded him in Chicago.[40] He received a civil engineering degree from the Polytechnic Institute in Munich in 1879 and had experience as a bridge designer with the Long Island Railroad and the Phoenix Bridge Company in Pennsylvania. Aus, like Burnham's consulting structural engineer, Joachim G. Giaver, was among a distinguished group of professional engineers who emigrated in the 1880s from Norway via Munich to America.[41] As a consequence of his training, Aus immediately brought a new level of professional distinction to Gilbert's office. His proposal for laterally stabilizing the triple-shell dome of the Minnesota State Capitol, for instance, ultimately salvaged the dome's weak construction.

9. West Street Building, New York, 1905–07. Photograph by Irving Underhill, 1907, Neg. 32071. Collection of The New-York Historical Society.

The West Street Building project of 1905–07 was the first skyscraper in Gilbert's office to which Aus contributed as a structural engineering professional (Figure 9). Gilbert was seeking a monumental image for a skyscraper that was to house an array of interrelated railroad, steamship, iron, and coal enterprises. For this, he turned to medieval Flemish compositional prototypes – *hotel de villes*, cloth halls, and belfries – to produce a design that originally sported a seven-story tower. Gilbert was also seeking the proper character for the skyscraper as a modern building type. In consultation with Aus, he studied in depth the steel frame's relationship to the skyscraper's thin envelope of terra cotta, achieving for the first time a "rational" accentuation of verticality. Gilbert clarified his intentions in 1909, after the completion of the West Street Building; and Aus did so in 1913, after the completion of the Woolworth. Gilbert insisted that a skyscraper's height "should be recognized, insisted upon, and expressed by vertical lines," and Aus claimed that "from an engineering point of view, no structure is beautiful where the lines of strength [are] not apparent."[42] Gilbert later observed not only that his own decision to use "vertical lines" in the West Street Building was inspired by the Chicago architect, Louis Sullivan, but also that "my logic and my judgment told me that it was the right thing to do" and "out of it grew a certain type, a decision that was fundamental to my practice."[43] Gilbert's decision, supported by Aus's shared philosophical viewpoint and engineering expertise, ultimately accounted for the West Street Building's high level of refinement as a modern "skyscraper Gothic" design.

The Woolworth Building of 1910–13, Gilbert's second major "skyscraper Gothic" project, derived its monumental character as the F.W. Woolworth Company's headquarters from the same Flemish medieval compositional strategy that Gilbert employed in the West Street Building. Its tower, which projected significantly higher from the main office block, was the tallest in the world. As such, the Woolworth presented a major structural challenge that called for an especially close collaboration between Gilbert and Aus. Besides working together as architect and engineer to solve the usual problem of column placement, both argued that the exterior's veneer of terra cotta should be detailed to emphasize and so seemingly reveal the steel frame's supporting uprights (Figure 10). Gilbert and Aus shared not only the rational articulation of structure, but also the goal of enhancing the exterior's illusion of Gothic openness and attenuated verticality. Aus, in proposing the most extensive use of portal arch wind bracing that had ever appeared in a skyscraper before or since, provided the rigid yet open steel-framed armature necessary for creating elevations of an unparalleled screenlike delicacy. "Fortunately architects are gradually recognizing that steel and stone should act together," Aus asserted after completing the Woolworth Building's engineering design. Gilbert proudly observed in a similar vein that "the Woolworth Tower is a thing of steel and fireproofing terra-cotta and is an endeavor to acknowledge that fact."[44] Aus's wind bracing, coupled with Gilbert's minimum of terra-cotta protection, were ultimately responsible for the Woolworth Building's overall lightness of scale and experience of soaring uplift. In no other building type was the engineer's reasoned and thorough attention to the visual consequences of a structural design so crucial.

Gilbert's skill at joining his own artistic vision with that of an exceptionally talented structural engineer might have been enough to ensure the Woolworth Building's high level of distinction – aesthetically and structurally – as a Beaux-Arts skyscraper. Yet, as Gilbert realized during his earlier experience with the George A. Fuller Company on the Brazer and Broadway Chambers projects, the architectural success of the skyscraper also entailed the formation of an effective working partnership with the project's builder. By the turn of the century, the construction industry, now headquartered in Chicago and New York, was dominated by builders who had organized themselves into large corporate firms or "national builders." Such an advanced level of size and organization represented little more than the industry's managerial response to the speculative investor's imperative that the construction process be totally rationalized. The more rapidly that a skyscraper was completed, the sooner it would realize the projected financial returns.

However, the general contractor's effort to rationalize construction, along with assuming control of the entire construction process under a single contract, posed a serious threat to the artistic standards of the Beaux-Arts architect. Beaux-Arts architects, ideally, would command the processes of construction and craftsmanship entirely themselves, if only for the sake of ensuring designs of high artistic quality. Gilbert acutely recognized the dilemma and so endeavored as a consequence to bring to the Woolworth Building's construction site a heightened level of professional authority. Gilbert's professional jurisdiction over the Woolworth's construction devolved from the architect's contractual right to supervise the entire building process. The architect legally had the right to either approve or disapprove the quality of the general contractor's work.

Probably the earliest example of a general contractor was the Norcross Brothers of Worcester, Mass. In 1875, Norcross provided construction services described at the time as "uniquely complete." Orlando Whitney Norcross, a gifted builder, expert cost estimator, and innovative engineer, functioned as "a working branch" of Henry Hobson Richardson's office.[45] However, the large-scale general contractor who specialized in the erection of big commercial skyscrapers under a single contract was clearly a Chicago phenomenon. The George A. Fuller Company, founded in 1882, rapidly rose to dominance in the construction industry by assuming total financial control over the entire commercial building process. From the outset, Fuller's overarching goal was to erect structures rapidly and systematically within a contractually guaranteed period of time for a fixed and predetermined price.[46] In Chicago, Fuller earned a reputation for major skyscrapers such as Holabird & Roche's Tacoma (1887–89) and Marquette (1895) buildings and D.H. Burnham & Company's Reliance Building (1895).[47] Shortly after the company opened its New York branch office in 1896, it closed the contract for Gilbert's Broadway Chambers project. By 1900, Fuller was known as a "national builder," working in several other cities besides Chicago and New York.[48]

10. Woolworth Building, New York, with diagram of the tower wind bracing, 1911. *Engineering Record* 63 (May 27, 1911):592. Courtesy of the Trustees of the Boston Public Library.

Gilbert, having already established a close professional relationship with the Fuller Company during the Brazer Building project of 1894, stood in advance of his New York contemporaries in the coordination of his architectural expertise with that of the general contractor. However, after the century's turn, Gilbert and other architects based in Chicago and New York increasingly reported conflicts over territorial boundaries. While a few expressed fears that the construction industry would absorb the architect's function altogether, the more common battle for territorial control was fought over the architect's role during construction supervision.[49] Daniel Burnham, for instance, earned a reputation for abrasiveness on the job site during the construction of Washington, D.C.'s Union Station by Ralph and Theodore Starrett 1903–07.[50] Gilbert, keenly aware of such territorial issues, defended the architect's authority to approve or disapprove the work of the general contractor before the Minnesota Chapter of the American Institute of Architects in 1894, shortly after he began working on the Brazer Building with the Fuller Company. By 1909, however, Gilbert had developed a wholly new stance toward what he now considered the increasing monopolization and control of the construction industry by the excessively large general contracting corporations. In his address as president before the American Institute of Architects, Gilbert called the big construction corporations a "serious menace to the interests of the architect." As a solution to the problem, Gilbert proposed "returning to the old-fashioned system of letting the various sections of construction to minor contractors." In essence, Gilbert argued that architects should resume their earlier roles as general contractors.[51]

Gilbert's territorial battles with the large-scale contracting corporations such as Fuller may explain in part why he welcomed the opportunity in the West Street Building project of 1905 to allow single contracts with the John Peirce Company, the granite masonry contractor for the United States Custom House, and others. After the death of George A. Fuller in 1901, Harry S. Black assumed the helm at the Fuller Company. He subsequently set up the still larger United States Realty & Construction Corporation, which he capitalized at $66 million and in the process, turned Fuller into a mere subsidiary. Black's goal was to control as large a share of the building industry as possible, including the architect's function of "drawing up plans." It was probably Black's company that the *Brickbuilder* criticized in 1902 for seeking in-house architects.[52] Such an effort to monopolize the construction industry, indeed to squeeze the architectural profession out of the building process entirely, may have been what ultimately alienated Gilbert from Black, besides the latter's notoriously unscrupulous business practices.[53]

In 1910, Frank Woolworth insisted upon securing a large-scale general contractor to construct the Woolworth Building project rapidly and efficiently; the size of the project, moreover, was such that it would have tested even Gilbert's administrative capacities as a separate-contract project. Woolworth and Gilbert, as a consequence, then, had two choices. They would employ one of the two largest construction companies headquartered in New York, that is, either Fuller or the newer Thompson–Starrett Construction Company. Fortunately, Thompson–Starrett had recently become large enough to compete with Fuller. Like Fuller, Thompson–Starrett pioneered in the rationalization of large-scale construction projects. Founded by Theodore Starrett and Henry S. Thompson in 1900, it was organized according to methods that Starrett learned while in partnership with George A. Fuller during the 1890s.[54] Fuller and Thompson–Starrett competed vigorously for the Woolworth Building contract, and after months of indecision, Woolworth chose Thompson–Starrett.

Shortly after the Thompson–Starrett Construction Company arrived on the Woolworth Building project's site in April 1911, the company's new president, Louis Horowitz, lucidly described the large-scale general contractor's goals for rationalizing the construction industry in his essay, "The Modern Building Organization." Significantly, Horowitz called the Thompson–Starrett Company a "machine."[55] Indeed, such large-scale general contractors, now commonly known as "corporate contractors," functioned as well-tooled mechanisms for securing big construction projects at a single price under a single contract and then completing them with a systematic order and efficiency. Horowitz's efforts to rationalize the construction industry echoed the methods recently proposed by the mechanical engineer and contractor, Frank Bunker Gilbreth. On a smaller scale, Gilbreth had devised precise

11. Woolworth Building, New York, under construction, 1911–13. Photograph by Irving Underhill. Reprinted with permission of the Milstein Division of U.S. History, Local History & Genealogy, The New York Public Library, Astor, Lenox and Tilden Foundations.

time and motion techniques for streamlining the craft of bricklaying. Both were indebted to the still earlier time and efficiency methods proposed by Frederick Winslow Taylor for rationalizing the industrial work process.

Speed on the construction site, according to Horowitz, was governed by the "comprehensive time schedule," which was enforced through the records of timekeepers and the daily reports of each trade's foreman. It dictated the coordination of materials deliveries and compelled the close monitoring of all construction costs. Horowitz's schedule thoroughly controlled the process of construction at the Woolworth Building's worksite and, in fact, served as a benchmark that workers endeavored to rival or surpass. The project's steelworkers, notably, set a speed record for assembling the project's structural steel – 1,153 tons in six consecutive eight-hour days. In addition, they topped off the steel frame twenty days ahead of schedule (Figure 11).[56] In a popular commemorative publication, *Master Builders of the World's Greatest Structure*, both Gilbert and Woolworth elaborately praised Louis Horowitz and Thompson–Starrett's construction crew for rapid and systematic completion in "record time."[57]

Although the Woolworth Building's rationalized construction process had the advantage of saving money for Woolworth, it also imposed a new set of time-contingent demands upon Gilbert's relatively small Beaux-Arts architectural office. First of all, Gilbert's staff faced the prospect of producing thousands of detailed construction drawings at a pace that could not have contrasted more thoroughly with the freewheeling, creative atmosphere characteristic of an "atelier." Second, the staff had to effectively supervise a time-and-money-driven sequence of construction that by now had taken on a mechanical momentum of its own. For the sake of efficiency, Gilbert relied heavily on the skills of his key assistants, Thomas R. Johnson, John Rockart, and George Wells. Johnson oversaw the development of the exterior's craft details, Rockart managed the project within the office, and Wells assumed responsibility for the onsite supervision of the construction process.[58] Furthermore, Gilbert, determined to prevent his office from becoming a "plan factory," employed the temporary hands of draftsmen and designers working outside the confines of his office. Among these were the Gunvald Aus & Company's approximately thirty engineers and draftsmen and the Atlantic Terra Cotta Company's twenty-five "ornamental draftsmen."[59] The fabrication of the project's steel and terra cotta was, in turn, overseen and approved at the factory sites by Wells. Gilbert's superintendent for the project, William Sunter, coordinated the project with Wells and Thompson–Starrett's superintendent. Together, they monitored the sequential arrival of materials, along with their assembly and craftsmanship to Gilbert's standards on the building site.[60]

The Thompson–Starrett Company never functioned as a "working branch" of Gilbert's office, as Norcross did for Richardson. Still, its staff, in assuming the role of expediters during the Woolworth Building's construction, facilitated a seamless interface of responsibility between the contractor and the architect. Gilbert, meanwhile, exercised the architect's supervisory authority throughout the entire construction process. He instructed Wells to "hold [the foremen] strictly to the contract... no matter how much they protest."[61] As a consequence, the Woolworth Building, although built in "record time," still had a quality of craft detail that accorded with both Gilbert and Woolworth's vision of the Beaux-Arts skyscraper as an "ornament" in the city.

The architectural success of the Woolworth Building can be attributed ultimately to the ethos of mutual cooperation and respect promoted by Gilbert among the new set of professionals involved in the skyscraper's design and construction process. Significantly, both Aus and Horowitz frequently acknowledged Gilbert's autonomy as the overall coordinator of the project and showed respect for the centrality of his artistic role. Gilbert similarly expressed appreciation for the contributions of his collaborators, but also recognized the need to enlarge and redefine the Beaux-Arts architect's professional sphere. This he accomplished by combining his knowledge with that of the structural engineer, by renewing the architect's supervisory authority during the construction process, and by augmenting the scope of his practice through enlisting the help of countless assisting designers, draftsmen, and technical experts. Only then could the Beaux-Arts architect effectively secure his professional position within the rapidly changing world of construction. As a consequence, the Beaux-Arts vision of the skyscraper as a landmark – with monumentality, beauty, and ornamental decorum – might find an important place within the twentieth-century American city.

NOTES

1. See, for example, Claude Bragdon, "Architecture in the United States, III: The Skyscraper," *Architectural Record* 26 (Aug. 1909):96; and Montgomery Schuyler, "The Woolworth Building," in *American Architecture and Other Writings*, vol. 2, ed. William Jordy and Ralph Coe (Cambridge: Harvard Univ. Press, 1961), 610–21.

2. Models of the Broadway Chambers Building, one of which showed the foundation and the steel frame, were exhibited and received medals at the International Exhibition in Paris of 1900. *Broadway Chambers: A Modern Office Building* (New York: George A. Fuller Co., 1900), 5–7. Sarah Bradford Landau and Carl Condit, *Rise of the New York Skyscraper, 1865–1913* (New Haven: Yale Univ. Press, 1996), 272. The Woolworth Building was published on the cover of *Scientific American* 108 (March 8, 1913).

3. Mario Salvadori calls the Woolworth Building the "first skyscraper." See *Why Buildings Stand Up: The Strength of Architecture* (New York: Norton, 1980), 107.

4. On the Beaux-Arts principles of composition as they were understood among U.S. architects at the time, see John Beverly Robinson, *Principles of Architectural Composition* (New York: Architectural Record, 1899) and John Vrendenburgh Van Pelt, *A Discussion of Composition* (New York: Macmillan, 1902).

5. For a good recent assessment of the social forces that influenced early office buildings and the financial instruments that made them possible, see Robert Bruegmann, *The Architects and the City: Holabird & Roche of Chicago, 1880–1918* (Chicago: Univ. of Chicago Press, 1997), 65–9, 71–3, 112–15. See also Sharon Irish, *Cass Gilbert, Architect: Modern Traditionalist* (New York: Monacelli Press, 1999), 53.

6. See, for example, Barr Ferree, "The Modern Office Building," *Journal of the Franklin Institute* 141 (Jan.–Feb. 1896): 47–55, 124–40; George Hill, "Some Practical Limiting Conditions in the Design of the Modern Office Building," *Architectural Record* 2 (Apr.–June 1893):445–68; Louis Sullivan, "The Tall Office Building Artistically Considered," in *Kindergarten Chats and Other Writings* (1918; repr. New York: Dover, 1979), 202–13.

7. Sibel Bozdagon Dostoglu, "Towards Professional Legitimacy and Power: An Inquiry into the Struggle, Achievements, and Dilemmas of the Architectural Profession through an Analysis of Chicago, 1871–1909" (Ph.D. diss., Univ. of Pennsylvania, 1982), 42.

8. Mardges Bacon, *Ernest Flagg: Beaux-Arts Architect and Urban Reformer* (New York and Cambridge: Architectural History Foundation and MIT Press, 1986), 171.

9. Leland Roth, "The Urban Architecture of McKim, Mead & White, 1870–1910" (Ph.D. diss., Yale Univ., 1973), 739; Charles C. Baldwin, *Stanford White* (1931; repr. New York: Da Capo Press, 1971), 227–8.

10. Daniel Burnham of Chicago conceived the title for Post (Landau and Condit, *Rise of the New York Skyscraper*, 66–7, 120–1). On the meetings at the Architectural League in 1894, see Gail Fenske, "The 'Skyscraper Problem' and the City Beautiful" (Ph.D. diss., MIT, 1988), 29–30. Post was president of the League at the time.

11. Bacon, *Ernest Flagg*, 49–50. See especially Ernest Flagg, "The Dangers of High Buildings," *The Cosmopolitan* 21 (May 1896): 70–9.

12. Ernest Flagg, "Public Buildings," in *Proceedings of the Third National Conference on City Planning* (Boston, 1911), 43. Flagg did design a few other commercial buildings of moderate height, however. See Bacon, *Ernest Flagg*, 171–208.

13. Corydon T. Purdy, "The Relation of the Engineer to the Architect," *American Architect and Building News* 87 (February 11, 1905):43. Purdy was a leading structural engineer. He received bachelor's and master's degree's in civil engineering from the University of Wisconsin, worked for Keystone Bridge Co. during 1888–89, and founded a partnership with Lightner Henderson in Chicago in 1893. His structural design for the Old Colony Building in Chicago was among the first in which steel was used extensively and portal arches were employed for wind bracing. In 1900, Purdy was awarded a medal at the International Universal Exposition in Paris for his design of Cass Gilbert's Broadway Chambers Building and in 1909, the Telford Premium by the Institute of Engineers of Great Britain. In 1907–08, Purdy's firm designed the structural steel for the Metropolitan Life Insurance Tower. Carl Condit, "Corydon Tyler Purdy," in *Dictionary of American Biography*, suppl. 3 (New York: Charles Scribner's Sons, 1973), 611–12. Landau and Condit, *Rise of the New York Skyscraper*, 184, 272, 417 n.74.

14. Landau and Condit, *Rise of the New York Skyscraper*, 238, 426 n. 4 mentions the contractors for the steelwork (J.B. & J.M. Cornell) and the plumbing (Rossman & Bracken Co.), but not a general contractor.

15. Sharon Irish, "West Hails East: Cass Gilbert in Minnesota," *Minnesota History* 53 (Spring 1993):201–2; *St. Paul, History and Progress: Principal Men and Institutions* (St. Paul: Pioneer Press, 1897), 80–1.

16. Gilbert chose Ritter after consulting with Daniel Burnham and William Le Baron Jenney. By Nov. 1896, Fuller Co. had compared Ritter's and Purdy's designs for structural economy and cost and insisted upon using Purdy as the project's structural engineer. Gilbert later credited Ritter and New Jersey Iron & Steel's Henry S. Pritchard for the design. For correspondence related to the structural engineering of the Brazer Building project, see Cass Gilbert Papers, Minnesota Historical Society, Box 2.

17. The size of Gilbert's office in New York is documented in the office ledgers, Cass Gilbert Collection, New-York Historical Society.

18. On the organization of Gilbert's design team for the U.S. Custom House competition of 1899, see Sharon Irish, "Beaux-Arts Teamwork in an American Architectural Office: Cass Gilbert's Entry to the New York Custom House Competition," *New Mexico Studies in the Fine Arts* 7 (1982):10–13. Francis Swales, "Master Draftsmen, 18: Cass Gilbert," *Pencil Points* 7 (Oct. 1926):585; Guy Kirkham, "Cass Gilbert, Master of Style," *Pencil Points* 15V (Nov. 1934):541.

19. Purdy, "The Relation of the Engineer to the Architect," 43, noted that the body of technical knowledge constituting the discipline of structural engineering had expanded enormously within the last thirty years.

20. Andrew Saint, *The Image of the Architect* (New Haven, CT: Yale Univ. Press, 1983), 87.

21. After 1900, D. H. Burnham & Company had branch offices in San Francisco and New York. Thomas S. Hines, *Burnham of Chicago: Architect and Planner*, 2nd ed. (Chicago: Univ. of Chicago Press, 1979), 268–9. Bernard Michael Boyle, "Architectural Practice in America, 1865–1965 – Ideal and Reality," in *The Architect: Chapters in the History of the Profession*, ed. Spiro Kostof (New York: Oxford Univ. Press, 1977), 315.

22. Burnham was considering Gilbert as a partner who would replace John Wellborn Root, but the association never materialized. For the correspondence associated with the partnership, see Box 17, Cass Gilbert Papers, Minnesota Historical Society. Cass Gilbert, "Daniel Hudson Burnham: An Appreciation," *Architectural Record* 32 (August 1912): 175–6.

23. Cass Gilbert to DeLisle Stewart, Jan. 26, 1914, Cass Gilbert Papers, Library of Congress, Box 8. On Richardson's atelier, see Mary N. Woods, *From Craft to Profession: The Practice of Architecture in Nineteenth-Century America* (Berkeley: Univ. of California Press, 1999), 106–10, and James O'Gorman, *H. H. Richardson and His Office, A Centennial of His Move to Boston, 1874: Selected Drawings* (Cambridge, MA: Department of Printing and Graphic Arts, Harvard College Library, 1974).

24. Richard Guy Wilson, *McKim, Mead & White, Architects* (New York: Rizzoli, 1983), 14–15.

25. H. Van Buren Magonigle, "A Half Century of Architecture, 3: A Biographical Review," *Pencil Points* 15 (March 1934):115–16. The atelier ambiance was augmented by the teaching role of McKim, Mead & White; it reportedly trained about 800 apprentices over the years.

26. Boyle, "Architectural Practice in America," 316.

27. Kirkham, "Cass Gilbert," 543.

28. Kirkham, "Cass Gilbert," 541, 547.

29. Diana Balmori, "George B. Post: The Process of Design and the New American Architectural Office (1868–1913)," *Society of Architectural Historians Journal* 46 (December 1987):342.

30. Balmori, "George B. Post," 350–1. Landau and Condit, *Rise of the New York Skyscraper*, 62–75, 78–83, 116–25, 149–55, 205–8, 238–42 documents Post's role in the architectural and engineering design of New York's major skyscrapers, from the Equitable Building (1868–70, 1886–89) to the St. Paul Building (1895–98).

31. On Gilbert's desire to balance his Beaux-Arts projects for public institutions with his commissions for large commercial skyscrapers, see Sharon Irish, *Cass Gilbert*, 114.

32. Woods, *From Craft to Profession*, 158–60.

33. Misa, *Nation of Steel*, 45, 65. Ritter graduated from the Case School of Applied Science in 1886 and before joining Jenney's office, worked for the Erie Road.

34. Shankland worked with Burnham on the World's Columbian Exposition (Hines, *Burnham of Chicago*, 268). Giaver also worked on the exposition. In 1896, Giaver offered his engineering services to Gilbert for the Brazer Building project (Joachim G. Giaver to Cass Gilbert, July 11, 1896, Box 2, Cass Gilbert Papers, Minnesota Historical Society). Giaver went on to serve as the chief structural engineer for Burnham's Flatiron and Equitable buildings. Kenneth Bjork, *Saga in Steel and Concrete* (Northfield, MN: Norwegian-American Historical Association, 1947), 222–7.

35. Purdy, "The Relation of the Engineer to the Architect," 43–4.

36. Condit, "Corydon Tyler Purdy," in *Dictionary of American Biography*, 611. Harry S. Black to Cass Gilbert, Nov. 12, 1896, Cass Gilbert Papers, Minnesota Historical Society, Box 3.

37. *Broadway Chambers: A Modern Office Building*, 9, 52. Landau and Condit, *Rise of the New York Skyscraper*, 272.

38. Cass Gilbert, "Building Skyscrapers," *Real Estate Record and Builder's Guide* 45 (June 23, 1900):1089.

39. Cass Gilbert, "Building Skyscrapers," 1091. Gilbert also felt compelled to justify the "measure of beauty" as having "income-bearing value."

40. Aus became a member of the American Society of Civil Engineers in 1895 and participated actively in the intellectual development of his discipline. He published a number of articles, among them "Special Fireproof Construction in the U.S. Appraiser's Warehouse, New York City," *Engineering News* 40 (November 3, 1898): 278–9.

41. Bjork, *Saga in Steel and Concrete*, 24–39, 41–4.

42. Cass Gilbert, "Tenth Birthday of a Notable Structure," *Real Estate Magazine of New York* 11 (May 1923):344; Gunvald Aus, "Engineering Design of the Woolworth Building," *American Architect* 103 (March 26, 1913):158.

43. Cass Gilbert, "The Relation of the Architect to His Client, to the Builder, and to His Brother-Architect, and the Organization of an Architect's Work," lecture delivered at the School of Architecture, Harvard Univ., Feb. 20, 1912, Cass Gilbert Papers, Manuscript Div., Library of Congress, Box 16.

44. Aus, "Engineering Design of the Woolworth Building," 158; Gilbert, untitled essay on progress in the arts, Dec. 26, 1921, Cass Gilbert Papers, Manuscript Div., Library of Congress, Box 17.

45. The Washington, DC, architect Glenn Brown, who worked for Norcross during the mid-1870s, recorded his observations in *Memories, 1860–1930* (Washington, DC, 1931). The Boston architect Robert D. Andrews recollected that Norcross became "one of the earliest of our local builders to take general contracts." See James O'Gorman, "O. W. Norcross, Richardson's 'Master Builder': A Preliminary Report," *Society of Architectural Historians Journal* 32 (May 1973): 109–10.

46. David Van Zanten, "The Nineteenth Century: The Projecting of Chicago as a Commercial City and the Rationalization of Design and Construction," in *Chicago and New York: Architectural Interactions* (Chicago: Art Institute of Chicago, 1984), 38, 42.

47. George A. Fuller studied architecture at MIT and then apprenticed in construction supervision with Peabody & Stearns in Boston. "Mr. George A. Fuller," *American Architect and Building News* 70 (Dec. 22, 1900):90. Woods, *From Craft to Profession*, 157. Van Zanten, "The Nineteenth Century," 44.

48. "The National Builder," supplement to the *Real Estate Record and Builder's Guide* 64 (July 28, 1900):1–4.

49. See for instance, "Architect and Builder," *Brickbuilder* 11 (Dec. 1902):257. Woods, *From Craft to Profession*, 158.

50. Hines, *Burnham of Chicago*, 286–7.

51. Irish, "West Hails East," 200. Gilbert, "President's Address, American Institute of Architects," Cass Gilbert Papers, Manuscript Div., Library of Congress, Box 16.

52. Timothy John Houlihan, "The New York City Building Trades, 1890–1910" (Ph.D. diss., State Univ. of New York at Binghamton, 1994), 34–6. "Architect and Builder," 257.

53. On Harry S. Black, see Paul Starrett, *Changing the Skyline* (New York: McGraw-Hill, 1938), 69, 86–90.

54. In the late 1880s, Theodore Starrett was employed as an engineer by Burnham & Root in Chicago; he oversaw the construction of the Rand McNally, Rookery, and Monadnock buildings. "Theodore Starrett," in *The National Cyclopaedia of American Biography* 24 (1935; repr., Ann Arbor, Mich.: Univ. Microfilms, 1967), 41–2. Starrett supervised the construction of Gilbert's Broadway Chambers Building for Fuller Co. in 1899–1900 (Irish, *Cass Gilbert*, 57).

55. Horowitz joined Thompson–Starrett in 1903. Louis Jay Horowitz, *The Modern Building Organization* (New York: Alexander Hamilton Institute, 1911), 11.

56. "Steel Erection of the Woolworth Building," *Engineering Record* 65 (June 29, 1912):715.

57. Frank Woolworth, "Foreword," in *The Master Builders: A Record of the Construction of the World's Highest Commercial Structure* (New York: Hugh McAtemney, 1913), 5; Gilbert, "The Architect's Approbation," in *The Master Builders*, 9.

58. The responsibilities of Johnson, Rockart, and Wells during construction are documented in the office memoranda associated with the project, dated May 16, 1911, to May 1, 1915. Woolworth Building, Cass Gilbert Collection, New-York Historical Society.

59. Frank W. Skinner, *Woolworth Building, New York City* (New York: American Bridge, n.d.), 33; Hildegard J. Safford, "The Terra Cotta Industry and the Atlantic Terra Cotta Company," *Staten Island Historian* 31 (Apr.–June 1974):161.

60. "Construction of the Woolworth Building," *Engineering Record* 66 (July 27, 1912):100.

61. Cass Gilbert, as quoted in Sharon Irish, "Cass Gilbert's Career in New York, 1899–1905" (Ph.D. diss., Northwestern Univ., 1985), 300.

2

Law Makes Order

The Search for Ensemble in the Skyscraper City, 1890–1930

Keith D. Revell

"The architectural condition of our cities is the price we have paid for liberty!" exclaimed Cass Gilbert, architect of the Woolworth Building, at the National Conference on City Planning in 1915. For Gilbert, as for many architects and planning advocates, the American predilection for individual property rights doomed attempts to "create civic order and civic embellishment."[1] American cities would retain their patchwork appearance, they feared, because the law would simply not allow municipal authorities to regulate the height, use, shape, and location of private buildings to produce more aesthetically pleasing urban landscapes.

Nowhere was this battle between the aesthetic and legal dimensions of urban planning more evident than in skyscraper regulation, which involved two interrelated problems growing out of contemporary architectural and constitutional discourses. The aesthetic problem centered on the difficulty of incorporating vertical structures into a planning model, epitomized by the World's Columbian Exposition of 1893, which employed "horizontal visual unity" to give public significance to urban space.[2] This aesthetic debate was complicated by the strictures of constitutional law. Well into the first decade of the twentieth century, American municipalities had limited legal means to carry out city plans. Although states and cities did have extensive police powers to restrict the use of property to protect public health, safety, and morals, these powers did not extend to the regulation of private rights for civic beautification.

The attempt to beautify American cities by regulating the height of skyscrapers thus

My thanks to Olivier Zunz, Charles McCurdy, John Stuart, and Roberta Moudry for their insightful criticisms of earlier versions of this essay.

created a dialogue between law and architecture, not so much about specific architectural styles, but about buildings in the context of a planned city. The encounter between the police power and skyscraper architecture encouraged a wide-ranging discussion over the city as "ensemble" – a collection of complementary elements contributing to a unified urbanistic effect – with the tension between individualism and civic life at the center of both the aesthetic and legal aspects of this exchange. In the process of attempting to reconcile private liberties and public goals, a generation of progressive architects, lawyers, and planners transformed the architecture of skyscrapers, the regulatory power of municipal government, and the aesthetic ideal of the planned city. This essay combines insights from legal, architectural, and planning history to explore how these transformations occurred by focusing on the ways aspiring planners used (and changed) legal discourse to incorporate City Beautiful ideals into zoning regulations, thus ushering in a new generation of skyscrapers and a modern version of the city ensemble.

This debate over the aesthetics of the modern city took an important turn with the World's Columbian Exposition of 1893, for as Henry Adams observed, "Chicago was the first expression of American thought as unity; one must start there."[3] It was in Chicago that the ideal of the city as "ensemble" was first realized. As the renowned architectural critic Montgomery Schuyler observed of the Court of Honor, the centerpiece of the exposition, its "success is first of all a success of unity, a triumph of ensemble. The whole is better than any of its parts and greater than all its parts, and its effect is one and indivisible." That effect had been achieved by the use of the classical architectural style for all the buildings in the ensemble and, more significantly, by a uniform sixty-foot cornice line, which created a "virtually continuous skyline all around the Court of Honor" while "preventing that line from becoming an irregular serration" (Figure 12). By choosing individual architects to design each building in the court, Director of Works Daniel Burnham had ensured variety among individual buildings, but by restricting both style and cornice line, Burnham prohibited that variety from "degenerat[ing] into a miscellany."[4] In this way, Burnham endowed the exposition's architecture with the three crucial elements that Charles Mulford Robinson would later canonize as the City Beautiful aesthetic: unity, harmony, and variety.[5]

The City Beautiful emerged from the confluence of Beaux-Arts neoclassicism, Olmstedian landscape design, and American municipal reform; thus it had both aesthetic and civic significance. As an American adaptation of *la belle ville* of Beaux-Arts city planning, it idealized the low-rise city, crowned with a nearly uniform cornice line, accentuated here and there by church steeples and the domes of public buildings, and traversed by wide, uncluttered, tree-lined boulevards.[6] The compositional elements of the city – buildings, streets, parks, lampposts, fire hydrants – worked together to create a unified "picture" of the city. The uniform cornice line was especially important for realizing this effect, for it provided the disparate elements of the street and the skyline with horizontal visual unity, monumentalizing the public space of the city. For devotees of the City Beautiful aesthetic, that grand, unified public space embodied the "soul of the metropolis," suggesting that the disordered, competitive, polyglot city had a collective purpose and spirit.[7]

Skyscrapers violated the City Beautiful aesthetic at almost every turn.[8] "These things have turned the skyline of New York into a horribly jagged sierra," complained Schuyler.[9] Skyscrapers disrupted the horizontal lines of the low-rise city with their powerful vertical forms. As the embodiment of corporate

12. View of the Court of Honor, World's Columbian Exposition, Chicago, 1893. This classic view of the court illustrates the way the uniform cornice line provides a horizontal visual unity, creating an ensemble effect while permitting diversity among individual structures. Photograph by C. D. Arnold. Reprinted with permission of the Chicago Historical Society (ICHi-13883).

capitalism, skyscrapers imposed commercial rather than civic significance on the collective portrait of the city.[10] Skyscrapers robbed pedestrians of light and air, turning streets into canyons and casting a gloom over neighboring buildings. Some commentators also believed that tall buildings posed a threat to public health by blocking the salubrious rays of the sun;[11] and architect Ernest Flagg warned that streets flanked by skyscrapers could not accommodate all the inhabitants of surrounding buildings in the event of fire.[12] Skyscrapers thus rendered narrow downtown streets all the more dark, cramped, and unhealthy – the antithesis of the open, spacious City Beautiful ideal.

This criticism of tall buildings as inappropriate within a planned city was complicated by the growing number of aesthetically noteworthy skyscrapers. By the end of the first decade of the twentieth century, Ernest Flagg's Singer Tower (1908) and Napoleon LeBrun & Sons' Metropolitan Life Tower (1909) illustrated that skyscrapers could be symbols of corporate power *and* welcome additions to the skyline.[13] Even Schuyler, who in 1903 concluded that "there is no example of the modern and extreme skyscraper which commends itself as an architectural success," had to concede that there were a handful of tall buildings worthy of architectural acclaim, such as George B. Post's Union Trust Building in New York (1890) and Burnham and Root's Monadnock Building in Chicago (1891).[14] Furthermore, Schuyler was positively effusive in his praise of the Woolworth Building (1913).[15] The "Cathedral of Commerce" trumpeted private wealth and dominated the city around it, but it did so in ways that suggested that skyscrapers could contribute positively to the collective image of the city.[16] En masse, the new wave of skyscrapers nearly "redeemed" the city from "ugliness," endowing New York, one critic noted, with "the first suggestion of beauty that the city has ever laid claim to."[17]

13. Singer Building, City Investing Building, and Hudson Terminal Building with Trinity Church steeple, New York, between 1904 and 1910. The steeple of Trinity Church struggles for space amid skyscrapers in Lower Manhattan. The bulky Hudson Terminal Building, center right, was the largest office building in the world and housed the station of the Hudson and Manhattan Railroad, which moved commuters between New York and New Jersey via the first successful tunnels underneath the Hudson River. Ernest Flagg's Singer Tower rises in the upper left. Skyscrapers flanking Broadway can be seen receding into the left background. Courtesy of the Library of Congress, Prints and Photographs Div., Detroit Publishing Co. Collection [LC-D418-10238 DLC].

In spite of the growing number of notable individual skyscrapers, the problem of tall buildings in the context of the city remained a pivotal issue of civic aesthetics throughout the early twentieth century, and here the conflict between individualism and civic life took center stage. "The fundamental unit of design in architecture is not the separate building but the whole city," affirmed Werner Hegemann and Elbert Peets, co-authors of *The American Vitruvius: An Architects' Handbook of Civic Art* (1922); "the well-designed individual building in order to be fully enjoyed must be part of an aesthetically living city, not of a chaos."[18] And it was chaos that skyscraper critics saw surrounding the substantial individual achievements of American architects. Even attractive skyscrapers were so closely juxtaposed, so randomly packed together, so inappropriately placed, that they created "a mere formless jumble."[19] Skyscrapers thus represented "rampant individualism" and a blatant disregard for both urban context and collective effect (Figure 13).[20] "The development of the tall building has been secured at the expense of the rights of the public at large," remarked architectural critic Charles Rollinson Lamb in 1898.[21] "This is a case in which individualism cannot fight individualism, in which the power of the community must be invoked to protect the community against the individual," warned Schuyler.[22] "Nothing but a statute will stop them."[23]

When this debate over skyscraper regulation began in earnest in the mid-1890s, the only ruling on building heights from an American court – an 1888 case from New York City – was unfavorable, leaving planners with few legal tools at their disposal.[24] Attorney Walter Fisher, who prepared the legal appendix for the Chicago Plan of 1909, admitted that the city would have to rely principally on the power of eminent domain (and thus the expenditure of public monies), rather than the police power, to carry out architect Daniel Burnham's vision; the inability to restrict the height and character of buildings left the city with no regulatory means to protect the areas surrounding the monumental buildings and public spaces Burnham called for in the downtown area.[25] As late as 1915, *The American City* editorialized that, while many cities had developed plans, "adequate consideration has not ordinarily been given to the very important question of the legal power of the municipality to carry out the physical improvements advocated. As a result the plan has been left somewhat up in the air."[26] Underdeveloped public powers thus kept the best American city plans on the shelf.

To be sure, throughout the mid-nineteenth century many cities had developed a phalanx of building regulations, which, arguably, bespoke a robust sense of the public sphere. As New York Supreme Court Justice Rufus Peckham, later author of the infamous *Lochner* decision, noted in an 1895 case, "anyone in a crowded city who desires to erect a building is subject at every turn almost to the exactions of the law in regard to provisions for health, for safety from fire, and for other purposes."[27] In 1871, for example, New York building regulations covered everything from the thickness of walls and the placement of beams to the proper ratio of mortar ingredients and the appropriate methods of securing gutters and cornices to exterior walls. In one sense, therefore, cities did have a significant array of regulatory powers over private structures.[28]

For planning advocates, however, such regulations represented only a very narrow conceptualization of municipal authority.[29] Aesthetic considerations in particular never fell within the police power of even the most legally well-equipped city. "Aesthetic considerations are a matter of luxury and indulgence rather than of necessity," a New Jersey court affirmed in 1905, and therefore did not meet the most basic test of constitutionality – the substantial relation test – which courts used to ascertain whether new regulations fell within the scope of legitimate government authority. In the eyes of most judges, limiting the use of private property to enhance civic beauty bore no clear relationship to established police power goals, such as halting the spread of fire or reducing the likelihood of epidemics.[30]

Planning advocates attributed the narrowness of the police power to a judicial preference for individual property rights as embodied in the Fourteenth Amendment, which guarantees that no state "shall deprive any person of life, liberty, or property, without due process of law; nor deny to any person . . . the equal protection of the law." The due process and equal protection clauses seemed to provide private property with considerable fortification against regulation. Expanding the police power meant convincing the courts that the public interest required superseding those explicit guarantees and thus overcoming, as Cincinnati lawyer and zoning supporter Alfred Bettman noted in 1914, "the extreme individualistic interpretation of the Constitution of the United States."[31]

The legal debate over the limits of the police power found common ground with the aesthetic debate over skyscrapers in the conflict between individualism and the public interest. In both discourses, unrestrained individualism was seen as a barrier to a more deliberate assertion of the civic good. But City Beautiful discourse translated very poorly into legal strategy, for to speak of "public" in City Beautiful terms was to speak of beauty, and beauty, as a legal value, was not recognized as a legitimate reason for restricting private rights.

Disguising aesthetic regulations as health and safety measures was one response to this legal impasse, an approach tried first in Boston and later in Baltimore.[32] Boston succeeded in outlawing skyscrapers in 1891 (limiting their height to 125 feet) because members of the conservative real estate establishment saw the need to protect both their investments and the city's "sacred skyline." Residents of the Back Bay area, especially, prided themselves on their city's profile, with its low, even line of edifices, punctuated by church steeples. The construction of the 183-foot Fiske Building (1887) and the 190-foot Ames Building (1889) threatened the serenity of that skyline and promised to overwhelm key public monuments like Trinity Church and the State House.[33]

When Boston's ordinance was challenged in 1904, after a second, lower residential height district of 80 feet was added, its aesthetic origins made it legally vulnerable. Opponents of the ordinance claimed that the second height district was a thinly disguised attempt "to preserve architectural symmetry and regular skylines" and bore no substantial relation to legitimate police power goals, such as protecting health and safety.[34] To defend against this line of attack, attorneys for the city employed the health and safety strategy while scrupulously avoiding any mention of architectural beauty. Predictably, they emphasized the importance of height regulation for fire prevention.[35] The Massachusetts Supreme Court in 1907 and the U.S. Supreme Court in 1909 upheld Boston's height limit, with both tribunals affirming that the real purpose of the ordinance was to prevent fire. Although each decision acknowledged that aesthetics played some role in the height limits, they characterized it as merely an "auxiliary" consideration and therefore not a fatal feature of the measure.[36]

Baltimore went through a similar process of burying the aesthetic features of building height limits by using the health and safety strategy. Baltimore's "anti-skyscraper" ordinance of 1904 (limiting the height of buildings to seventy feet) emerged from the efforts of the Municipal Art Society to preserve the character of Mt. Vernon Square, a four-block area around the Washington Monument, dominated by the stately homes of the city's "silk stocking" elite. Like dozens of other planning groups around the country, Baltimore's Municipal Art Society had been inspired by Burnham's White City at the World's Columbian Exposition of 1893, with its emphasis on horizontal monumentality, architectural ornamentation, and open spaces. Two recent additions to Mt. Vernon Square, the 130-foot Stafford Hotel (1894) and the 115-foot Severn Flats (1895), had violated that aesthetic.[37]

The aesthetic goals of Baltimore's building height limit were carefully hidden during the legal process, however. Fortuitously for advocates of the ordinance, the business section of Baltimore had been severely damaged by fire in 1904. That fact facilitated the passage of the ordinance and played a crucial role in its defense, even though the fire never reached Mt. Vernon Square. When the height limit was challenged in court, counsel for the city successfully argued that the fire had been spread between "skyscrapers," such as they were. The fire left enduring images of building skeletons standing amid the smoldering rubble – images powerful enough to convince the courts that an aesthetic height ordinance was really a fire protection measure (Figure 14).[38]

The effort to regulate building heights in New York City differed legally and aesthetically from the efforts in Boston and Baltimore and represented a more constructive encounter between architecture and the law. New York's 1916 zoning ordinance emerged from the intersection of three key debates: the first addressed regulating building height; the second, planning the modern metropolis; and the third, the limits of the police power. Members of the New York zoning team wanted to create practical tools to carry out a comprehensive city plan and that meant, above all else, expanding their ability to regulate private property in all five boroughs, especially building heights in Manhattan. This turn toward the practical aspects of urban planning did not mean that the ideals of the City Beautiful movement were abandoned, however. Instead, the experts who wrote the New York ordinance debated ways to update, modify, and disguise the values of City Beautiful planning – unity, harmony, variety, and the city as ensemble – and make them applicable where the vertical monumentality of skyscrapers had already become the defining feature of the city. In the case of the New York ordinance, considering the city as ensemble meant engaging the legal matters that the City Beautiful left unresolved and crafting a new language to express changing aesthetic aspirations.

New York thus produced a considerably more complex ordinance regulating building height than either Boston or Baltimore. The New York ordinance had five height districts, with height limits ranging from one to two times the width of the street. Buildings beyond that height could rise higher only by stepping back from the street wall, thus creating a distinctive terraced, setback effect. These height districts worked in conjunction with three use districts (residential, business, and unrestricted) and five area districts (A through E), which mandated progressively more open space at the rear and sides of buildings.[39]

As is well known, the movement that produced this elaborate measure began as a call for skyscraper regulation. Fifth Avenue merchants zealously advocated a Baltimore- or Boston-style height limit to protect both the appearance of their neighborhood and the value of their property. By the second decade of the century, real estate owners in other sections of Lower Manhattan joined the campaign for skyscraper regulation. Although the 612-foot Singer Building, the 700-foot Metropolitan Life Tower, and the 792-foot Woolworth Building were embraced even by skyscraper critics, the completion of the massive Equitable Building on lower Broadway provided a dramatic reminder that not all new skyscrapers would be welcome additions to the city's skyline.[40] The Equitable was big and bulky, and it rose straight up from the street, casting a huge shadow across neighboring buildings and reviving all the familiar criticisms of skyscrapers as anti-civic structures.[41]

The Equitable was exceptional, however, for New York's skyline had become more intriguing with the addition of other new skyscrapers. Even J. Horace McFarland, one of the country's leading proponents of the City Beautiful, conceded in 1908 that New York was becoming "a city of wonderful beauty. This I say as one willing to stifle his prejudice against the predominance of 'skyscrapers,' when he sees those same towers of commerce creating not only a new skyline, but a general modeling of new city lines that grows into majestic beauty."[42] Those new lines were vertical, not horizontal.[43] Unlike the height limit campaigns in Boston and Baltimore, the regulation of skyscrapers in New York City reflected this important change in civic aesthetics, as architects and planning advocates considered the possibility of creating a planned city of skyscrapers, rather than

14. Downtown Baltimore after the fire of 1904. The skeletons of burned-out skyscrapers haunt the Baltimore skyline. Images like this one convinced the courts that building height restrictions for Mt. Vernon Square, which was not affected by the fire, were really for fire protection. Courtesy of Maryland Department, Enoch Pratt Free Library, Baltimore.

eliminating skyscrapers from the ideal of the planned city.[44]

The authors of the 1916 zoning ordinance were caught up in this transition from the horizontal to the vertical city. Most of them shared a civic aesthetic that was deeply influenced by the City Beautiful movement. Edward Bassett, who headed the commission that wrote the ordinance and is best known for his criticism of skyscrapers as inefficient, was a prominent member of the Brooklyn City Plan committee, which hired Beaux-Arts-trained architect Edward H. Bennett, Daniel Burnham's assistant, to design the borough's Municipal Building, Court House, and Park Plaza in 1912.[45] Nelson Lewis, chief engineer of the New York City Board of Estimate and Apportionment, was an advocate of City Efficient principles and a more scientific approach to planning, but his criticisms of the modern metropolis – "injudicious tree planting... hideous billboards and gaudy facades..., a riot of inharmonious color in electric advertising signs [which] may proclaim the bad taste and vulgar commercialism of the people" – came directly from the City Beautiful movement.[46] George Ford, who had been inspired to become an architect after seeing the World's Columbian Exposition, remained an advocate of City Beautiful principles throughout his life, arguing for more street trees, fewer billboards, and "interesting 'street pictures'" as late as 1929.[47] Otto Eidlitz, a prominent builder in the city and one of Bassett's closest allies, was also deeply interested in architecture and civic aesthetics. He shared this concern with his cousin, Cyrus Eidlitz, architect of the Times Building (1904), and with his famous uncle, Leopold Eidlitz, architect of Christ Church in St. Louis, St. George's Church in New York, and the Brooklyn Academy of Music, among other buildings, who urged that architecture become "a living and creative art" rather than "an archeological toy-shop."[48] Bassett and his colleagues were also advised by leaders in the City Beautiful movement, such as architect Arnold Brunner, who chaired the commission that proposed height limits along Fifth Avenue and co-authored (along with Daniel Burnham and John M. Carrère) the Cleveland Group Plan of 1903, with its grand civic center so reminiscent of the World's Columbian Exposition.[49] Even a few of the real estate developers who opposed flat height limits recognized the aesthetic value of the uniform cornice line along prominent boulevards.[50]

Though the City Beautiful aesthetic was a powerful influence on the zoning debate, key members of the zoning team recognized that New York was a distinctively vertical city and they were drawn to the aesthetic possibilities presented by the new lines the downtown was taking. George Ford "entirely relish[ed] skyscrapers" and considered New York "thrilling." Nelson Lewis, who criticized the bulky Equitable Building for overwhelming the streets around it, admitted that "some really beautiful effects" had been achieved in American skyscraper architecture. For Ford and Lewis, the problem in New York was not tall buildings per se, but the prospect of more bulky, unimaginative skyscrapers crammed into the already overcrowded skyline.[51]

Important though it was, this aesthetic debate over skyscrapers was subordinated to larger concerns about planning the city as a whole. Members of the zoning team were anxious to move beyond a narrow concern with beautification toward a more comprehensive approach to urban planning. Nelson Lewis reproached City Beautiful planning for neglecting the metropolis beyond downtown civic centers and public forums. Too often, around these "show places" lay crowded streets, poor quality housing, and inefficient public works. Political scientist Robert Whitten, the commission's legal expert, recognized the aesthetic shortcomings of American cities but was more concerned with the social and economic consequences of the lack of urban planning. "The distinguishing characteristic of an American city as compared with a European city is its ragged, unfinished, unevenly developed appearance," Whitten told his colleagues. "The ugliness of a sprawling building development is its most apparent evil, but is really comparatively unimportant beside the great social and economic loss due to this method of city building. We are interested primarily in this enormous social and economic loss and not in the concomitant violation of symmetry and beauty." Lawson Purdy, head of the city's Department of Taxation and Assessment, who was well known for his criticism of skyscrapers ("a skyscraper is either a monument, an advertisement, or a failure") and whose aesthetic tastes were drawn from Ruskin's *Seven Lamps of Architecture*, backed zoning as a way to stabilize property values and tax revenues.[52] Perhaps most important of all, the zoning team had to persuade politicians, real estate developers, and mortgage lenders that height and use regulations would benefit them in tangible ways.[53] Thus, while City Beautiful ideals were an important part of the New York zoning effort, Bassett's team of experts was moving beyond a traditional horizontal civic aesthetic and a narrow concern for municipal beautification.

This debate over skyscrapers, civic aesthetics, and the proper goals of planning was decisively shaped by omnipresent legal concerns that encouraged proponents of municipal beautification to adopt a new language to pursue their aesthetic goals. In 1914, Bassett wrote to Manhattan Borough President George McAneny (a major advocate of city planning) that laying the legal foundation for zoning "is not at all clear to any of us, largely on account of the vagueness of the police powers. I am afraid that if Messrs. Purdy, Whitten, Ford and I do not have our own ideas rather safely grounded, we may all be carried off on some false trail."[54] Whitten, who conducted a thorough analysis of the police power, knew that critics of skyscraper regulations had attacked height limits in Boston and Baltimore on the grounds that they were aesthetically motivated. From his research, Whitten also knew that in both cases judges characterized the ordinances as fire prevention measures, downplaying the role of civic beautification. Whitten's research confirmed Bassett's belief that the only safe trail for the New York team to follow was to frame every aspect of the ordinance using the health and safety strategy.[55]

Because of their legal concerns, Bassett's team used health and safety to hide the housing goals of the New York zoning effort. Ford, Whitten, Purdy, and Bassett were all anxious to offer legal protection to residential areas, but Bassett felt that the promotion of single-family housing districts (as distinct from multifamily apartment buildings) would not be recognized by the courts as a legitimate use of the police power. As a consequence, the zoning team created one broad residential category and left the distinction between single and multifamily dwellings to area districts (relating to the bulk of structures): "Fine distinctions of uses would not, we thought, appeal to the courts, but distinctions in the area regulations having to do directly with light, air, ventilation, etc., would always afford a handle on which the court could hang a favorable decision." Bassett thus buried single-family housing regulations in "D" and "E" area distinctions where they could be more readily connected to public health through light and air.[56]

Concerns about the police power also encouraged the suppression of the aesthetic debate over skyscrapers. Early in the deliberations of the Heights of Buildings Commission, builder Otto Eidlitz and architect Burt Fenner urged their colleagues to consider the "artistic value of different skylines and setbacks." Housing expert Lawrence Veiller, one of the authors of New York's Tenement Law of 1901 and thus someone familiar with the legal problems of regulation, counseled his colleagues that " 'aesthetic consideration' [should] be struck entirely out of the program, on the ground that even the mention of the term would cause the public and the law-making bodies to feel that the Commission was wasting time, as the courts of New York do not recognize aesthetic considerations" as a valid reason for exercising the police power. Purdy, Fenner, and architect C. Grant La Farge responded that "it would be fatal to a comprehensive consideration of the subject not to take into account the aesthetic side" of the problem. Rather than drop the discussion of beauty, however, the commission decided to disguise its interest in it, referring only to "aesthetic considerations in relation to rentability and the value of land."[57] The next step was avoiding entirely any mention of aesthetics.

But the New York zoning team did more than simply hide its aesthetic goals using the health and safety strategy. Instead, the team engaged the law, translating aesthetic concerns into terms that the courts recognized and reconstructing City Beautiful ideals to suit their practical planning mentality.

The reconstructed civic aesthetic of the 1916 zoning ordinance was largely the work of architect George Ford. Ford earned a degree in architecture from MIT in 1901 and attended the Ecole des Beaux-Arts in Paris from 1903 to 1907, where he studied in the atelier of Jean-Louis Pascal.[58] Ford's professional career can be viewed as an extended attempt to incorporate the ideals that had inspired him at the World's Columbian Exposition and Ecole des Beaux-Arts into the practical aspects of planning.[59] Although Ford criticized the narrow focus of the City Beautiful movement, he never repudiated its ideals of unity, harmony, and variety, striving instead to make them more realizable. In this effort, he was very much like Frederick

Law Olmsted, Jr., who argued in 1910 that "the demands of beauty are in large measure identical with those of efficiency and economy, and differ merely in demanding a closer approach to practical perfection in the adaptation of means to ends than is required to meet the merely economic standard." Ford, who quoted this passage in one of his most important essays on City Beautiful ideals, shared Olmsted's desire to translate civic beautification into the language of engineers, lawyers, and real estate developers, and thus increase the likelihood that modern planning would create beautiful as well as functional cities – a vision that necessarily included weaving skyscrapers into the urban fabric more successfully.[60] Form would follow function, but on a metropolitan scale and with the skyscraper as part of the planned city.

Ford brought three key aesthetic considerations to the debate over skyscraper regulation and city planning in New York. First, he believed that the search for solutions to the aesthetic and urbanistic problems of the skyscraper was ongoing. Ford had joined the celebrated architectural firm of George B. Post and Sons in 1907 (Post had designed the Manufactures and Liberal Arts Building at the World's Columbian Exposition) and knew well Post's own attempts to deal with ever taller buildings, including such noteworthy skyscrapers as the Mills Building (1883), the Havemeyer Building (1892), and the St. Paul Building (1899).[61] Although Ford admired Post's work, he believed that the basic approach to designing skyscrapers (at least as it had developed in New York City), that is, hang some variation of a historical style on a steel frame, had not yet produced fully satisfactory results.[62] Second, Ford felt that height limits in other cities had produced boring architecture. He recognized the tendency of builders to push structures to the edge of the height limit, resulting in a sameness to streets that he wanted to avoid.[63] Third, long before Ford started to think about disguising aesthetic concerns in the legal garb of health and safety, he had a passion for light and air. Along with Robert Whitten, Ford had been deeply involved in housing reform and believed that well-lit and properly ventilated surroundings were aesthetically and medically essential, especially in increasingly crowded American cities.[64]

Ford wrote these considerations – continued architectural experimentation, visual diversity, and the preservation of light and air on all sides of buildings – into the 1916 ordinance in an effort to redefine the parameters of the debate over skyscraper regulation, not in terms of height limits but in terms of public values that should be preserved in private construction projects.[65] Through his encounter with the law, Ford reformulated the traditional emphasis on horizontal visual unity, pursuing instead visual and urbanistic compatibility among the vertical elements of the city.[66] In this process, the law acted not merely as a disguise, but also as a new lexicon for expressing aesthetic values. Rather than restricting building height to attain visual unity and harmony, the ordinance encouraged "a certain measure of uniformity" of building heights so that each property owner "should contribute in substantial equality to the common stock of light and air." Rather than criticizing bulky skyscrapers as ugly and unimaginative, the ordinance mandated open spaces around buildings to prevent "the stagnation of the air between them."[67] Ford thus recast the key aesthetic concepts of unity, variety, and harmony as legally defensible planning tools, allowing architectural freedom to create new vertical forms (indeed, forcing tall buildings to take on new shapes) while offering streets and surrounding structures some protection from tall, bulky buildings. Although he thought the ordinance could have gone further than it did, Ford "prophesied that a great new era in architecture of a brilliance and daring hitherto undreamed of" would be inspired by the regulations, particularly as architects experimented

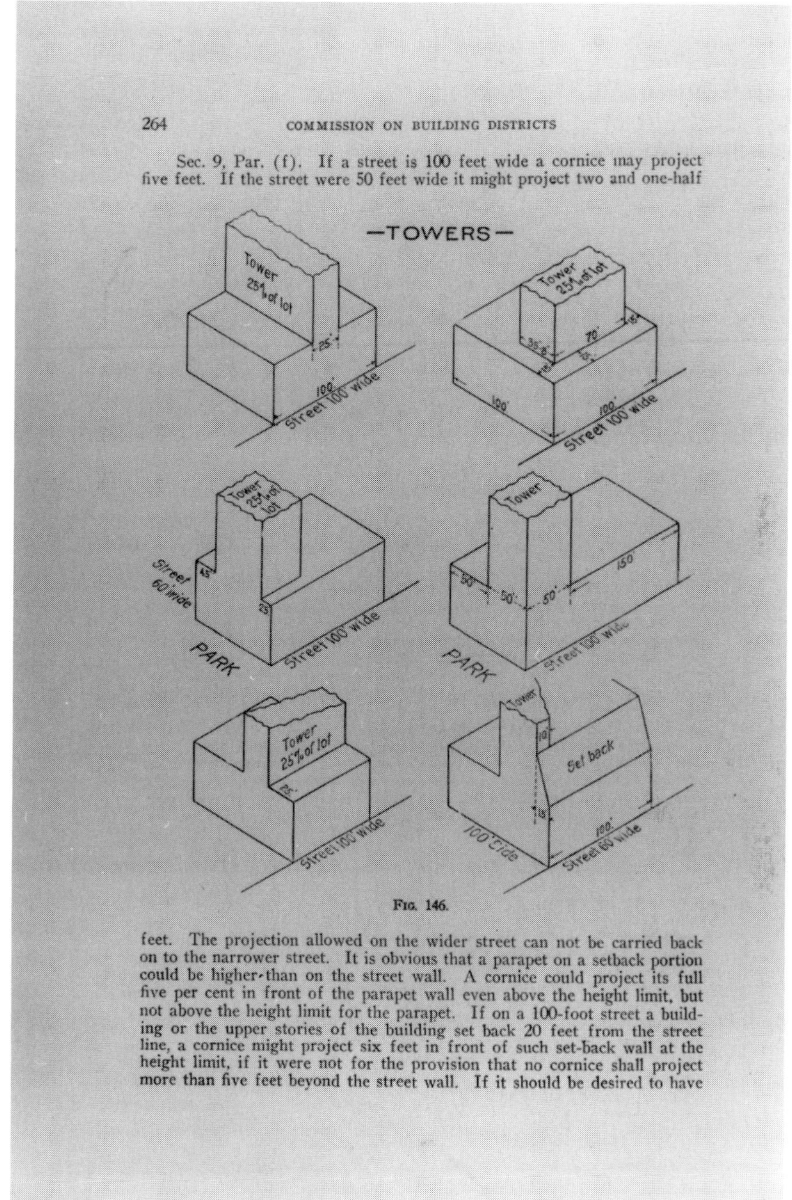
264 COMMISSION ON BUILDING DISTRICTS

Sec. 9, Par. (f). If a street is 100 feet wide a cornice may project five feet. If the street were 50 feet wide it might project two and one-half

Fig. 146.

feet. The projection allowed on the wider street can not be carried back on to the narrower street. It is obvious that a parapet on a setback portion could be higher than on the street wall. A cornice could project its full five per cent in front of the parapet wall even above the height limit, but not above the height limit for the parapet. If on a 100-foot street a building or the upper stories of the building set back 20 feet from the street line, a cornice might project six feet in front of such set-back wall at the height limit, if it were not for the provision that no cornice shall project more than five feet beyond the street wall. If it should be desired to have

15. "Towers" figure from New York City's 1916 zoning report. Architect George B. Ford intended the zoning ordinance to encourage architectural experimentation, especially in skyscraper design. Although clearly not as visionary as the work of Hugh Ferriss (see Figure 17), these line drawings give a sense of the diversity the ordinance promoted. Courtesy of the New York City Department of Records, Municipal Archives.

with the different tower configurations the ordinance permitted (Figure 15).[68]

Ford and his colleagues thus thought explicitly about the artistic value of different skylines and setbacks, but clothed these considerations in the language of rentable space, property values, and the medical role of sunlight. They did this to give judges as many familiar legal handles as possible on which to hang a favorable decision and to avoid giving their opponents any opening to brand zoning as civic beautification. What made this formula work was the legal role of light and air. Both light and air were easily connected to public health and such connections went a long way toward satisfying the substantial relation test. The preservation of light and air for reasons of public health became the leitmotif of the zoning ordinance, camouflaging several legally suspect motives – the most important being the protection of single-family homes and the sculpting of the skyline. Under the guise of preventing tuberculosis, the ordinance thus encouraged architectural experimentation in the downtown and expansion in the suburbs.[69] By this sleight of hand, the authors of the 1916 zoning ordinance reconstituted the language of civic beautification – which they inherited from the City Beautiful – through the language of public health – which the courts recognized as a legitimate reason for infringing on private property. At the same time, they accepted the skyscraper as part of a planned city, taking a crucial step toward reconciling the individualism represented by skyscrapers with the civic values comprised by planning. By regulating (rather than outlawing) the vertical city, they opened up new aesthetic possibilities both for planning and for architecture.

In 1921, architectural critic Aymar Embury observed that the 1916 zoning ordinance had quite unexpectedly produced distinctive architectural results. "One cannot help suspecting," he mused, "that the architects on the committee must have perceived at least their possibility, although as these were aesthetic rather than practical, one can imagine that they were not particularly urged as reasons for the passage of the law since any purely aesthetic reason is received with suspicion and doubtfully regarded as a detriment by our sound business men."[70] The "unanticipated" architectural consequences of the setback regulations further encouraged the transition from a horizontal to a vertical civic aesthetic, making it possible to think of skyscrapers as the primary elements of a planned city. The interaction of legal and aesthetic discourses thus produced an ordinance that updated the key values of City Beautiful planning, realizing diversity and harmony in the skyline and suggesting the possibility of a unified city of tall buildings.

During the postwar building boom, the hidden aesthetic elements of the ordinance helped produce a new skyscraper style of sculpted, massed forms and limited exterior ornament, and encouraged (paradoxically) variety and "uniformity" in the skyline.[71] Although the first skyscraper constructed under the zoning ordinance, the Heckscher Building (1918), seemed torn between the demands of the law and a dogged commitment to historicism, architects soon found a multiplicity of ways to make setbacks work aesthetically.[72] Raymond Hood combined Gothic detail and setback massing in his widely acclaimed American Radiator Building (1924), while Carrère and Hastings produced classicized setback skyscrapers such as the Fisk Building (1922) and Standard Oil Building (1922).[73] Increasingly, however, the ordinance inspired architects to abandon historicism in favor of a more sparing modernism. Arthur Loomis Harmon took an important step in that direction with the Shelton Hotel (1925). Harmon used Venetian Gothic detail to decorate the first three floors of the building, but covered the rest of the structure in simple brickwork, relying instead on fenestration and massing to create the building's powerful effect (although the Shelton seems ornate when compared to later skyscrapers, such as Schultze and Weaver's Waldorf-Astoria Hotel, completed in 1931 only a few blocks away).[74] In structures like the Two Park Avenue Building (1927), Ely Jacques Kahn further illustrated how architects were "slough[ing] off the cluttered detail of the past" in order to emphasize building "shapes that are more a series

16. View from the Empire State Building to Chrysler Building and Queensboro Bridge, 1932. A product of economics and architectural imagination, the mid-Manhattan skyline also bore the stamp of the 1916 zoning ordinance. On the far right, a slice of Raymond Hood's Daily News Building. The Chrysler Building (William Van Alen, 1930) emerges in back of the Chanin Building (Sloan and Robertson, 1929) on the center right. In the left foreground are the 10 East Fortieth Street Building (Ludlow and Peabody, 1928) and the 22 East Fortieth Street Building, also known as 277 Madison Avenue (Kenneth Franzheim, 1931). The Lefcourt Colonial Building, 295 Madison Avenue (Charles F. Moyer Co., 1929), and the Lincoln Building, 60 East Forty-second Street (J. E. R. Carpenter, 1930), are partially covered by the shadow of the Empire State Building. The twin towers of the Waldorf-Astoria Hotel (Schultz and Weaver, 1931) are visible as well. Note the contrast between high-rise Manhattan and low-rise Queens. Reprinted with permission of the Museum of the City of New York, Gottscho-Schleisner Collection.

of planes that become attractive through the play of light and shadow."[75] By the mid-1920s, the new style was so influential that architects were using setbacks even when the ordinance did not require it. The daring setbacks on Raymond Hood's Daily News Building (1929) – which has one of the most striking silhouettes of any of New York's skyscrapers – were purely aesthetic.[76] While these innovative structures were quite distinctive, they nonetheless appeared to comprise "a single architectural species." By producing "variety within quite definite limits," the ordinance thus encouraged diversity while maintaining a sense of harmony among the new generation of skyscrapers (Figure 16).[77]

The ordinance had its most unexpected effect on run-of-the-mill, utilitarian skyscrapers in Lower Manhattan.[78] Thanks to the efforts of entrepreneurs like cloak and suit manufacturer A. E. Lefcourt and real estate developer Max Aronson, by the early 1920s a new Garment District emerged between Sixth and Eighth avenues below Times Square, complete with a new generation of tall buildings earmarked by the zoning ordinance.[79] The Lefcourt Buildings on West Thirty-seventh and West Thirty-eighth streets, the Gilbert Building on West Thirty-ninth Street, and the Aronson Building on West Thirty-sixth Street, all demonstrated the effects of the setback envelope, with architects taking advantage of the dormer exceptions written into the ordinance.[80] Architect Ely Jacques Kahn was particularly impressed with the collective effect of these buildings: "Miraculously groups like the millinery buildings on Thirty-seventh, Thirty-eighth and Thirty-ninth Streets gather and poke their heads together into the air. The jewelry trade district on Forty-sixth and Forty-seventh Streets makes an amazing jumble of silhouettes. The garment trade buildings scattered through the thirties, between Seventh and Eighth Avenues, are fantastic in their grouping." The result even impressed so discerning an observer as architectural historian Fiske Kimball, who noted in 1928, "Some of these raw novel products of law and economics, . . . with their vast bulk stepped in receding stories, already show elements of style and achieve a new aspect."[81] Although the buildings in the Garment District are not generally recognized as treasures of New York architecture, the setback style they were compelled to adopt transformed these workaday skyscrapers into urbanistic architecture, in effect harmonizing elements of the skyline which, without the ordinance, might have had little aesthetic relationship to one another or to the city around them.

The resulting skyline portended the fulfillment of a vertical civic aesthetic. Architect Harvey Wiley Corbett argued that the zoning ordinance "pointed the way to a type of city such as the world had never known, a city of symmetrical towers" where "the more thoughtful designers eradicated all signs of the horizontal in their buildings" and "mass and line were made to serve the vertical."[82] In this sense, the growing acceptance of the vertical aesthetic signaled that the zoning ordinance had nearly civilized the skyscraper. "Zoning may be described as a demand that architecture conform to the needs of civilization," affirmed architectural visionary Hugh Ferriss in 1922. By forcing individual builders to consider the wider needs of the community – such as the desire for light and air, and the health and efficiency of the city – the ordinance encouraged structures that resulted in "a city ensemble." A generation earlier, skyscrapers had disrupted the ensemble of the low-rise city; with zoning, the ensemble effect was achieved anew, not by eliminating the skyscraper through height limits, but by encouraging an architectural style that made the skyscraper city an aesthetically appealing reality. A new era of "civic architecture" was dawning.[83]

In this way, the ordinance revived the notion that the whole city, rather than the individual building, was the proper focus of architecture. Zoning, Ferriss emphasized, "regards building operations not from the point of view of the individual plot, or owner, or designer, but from the argus-eyed view-point of the city itself."[84] Admittedly, the "closely juxtaposed verticals" of contemporary cities posed "a serious menace," for skyscrapers continued to cause congestion and aggravate traffic problems.[85] But the new architecture suggested a unity yet to be realized – an ideal that Ferriss developed in his *Metropolis of Tomorrow* (1929) and in his drawings for the Regional Plan of New York (1929–31). In Ferriss's metropolis, skyscrapers were set nearly a half-mile apart at the intersections of wide boulevards. There, skyscrapers retained their individuality while contributing to a harmonious collective result (Figure 17). This imagined city remained oddly reminiscent of the City Beautiful, however; so reminiscent, in fact, that Frederic Delano, Chairman of the Regional Plan Association, could compare the city of the future, with its "beautifully designed and well-placed skyscrapers," to "the almost uniform skyline and wide open spaces of Paris,"

17. Hugh Ferriss. "An Imaginary Metropolis." Ferriss's imagined skyscraper city preserved stupendous height and architectural individuality without the congestion and competition for space so evident in New York City. Here, skyscrapers are set a half-mile apart at the intersections of wide boulevards, thus accommodating very tall buildings while retaining the ensemble effect of the City Beautiful. *American City Magazine* 34, vol. 1 (Jan. 1926):9. Reprinted with permission of publisher.

the epitome of Beaux-Arts city planning.[86] Although it had more towers than Burnham's Plan of Chicago, as historians Thomas Bender and William Taylor observed of the Regional Plan, it was nonetheless "an attempt to express civic unity by producing a neoclassical urban form for the modern American city."[87] Within the old format, the regulated vertical lines of the setback skyscraper had become the new civic aesthetic.

The New York zoning formula thus accomplished what flat height limits could not: it protected the city against some of the worst features of tall buildings while permitting architectural experimentation with great height and yet encouraging a unified urbanistic effect. That balancing of public needs and private liberties proved to be a formula worth emulating, inspiring both Chicago and Boston to forego their flat height limits for setback formulas as a way to satisfy developers' demands for increased rentable space and to emulate the architectural experimentation that had been so successful in New York City.[88]

By the late 1920s, the legal progress of comprehensive zoning had created a veiled openness about the aesthetic aspects of building regulations. In the decade after 1916, hundreds of cities around the country followed New York's lead and drafted their own zoning ordinances. Of course the judicial record on zoning was mixed until the U.S. Supreme Court upheld an Ohio ordinance in the landmark case of *Euclid v. Ambler* in 1926. However, where state courts did uphold zoning, they appeared to endorse (or at least tolerate) what seemed to be civic beautification measures. Prohibiting businesses in residential areas, distinguishing between apartment buildings and single-family homes, and "bring[ing] order, coherence, and coordination into city life," appeared to many zoning enthusiasts to be aesthetic considerations, regardless of the pretense of basing such regulations on the preservation of public health, municipal efficiency, or property values.[89] In 1926, one legal observer frankly declared that "the primary purpose of municipal zoning is to make the city more attractive and to prevent the individual from using his property so as to injure the property of his neighbor." The legal charade was still necessary, however: "Of course, it would be difficult to prove that a comprehensive zoning plan has no relation at all to the public health, safety, or morals. And, hence, we find courts upholding regulations *primarily* aesthetic, which the public knows are aesthetic but, nevertheless, demands, but the terms 'aesthetics, beauty, or attractiveness' are notoriously absent from the opinions."[90]

Thus, only a decade after Cass Gilbert despaired of ever moving beyond the legal barriers to city planning, the pursuit of civic beautification through skyscraper regulation had transformed the scope of the police power. As with the regulation of billboards, automobiles, streetcars, and railroads, which also changed the physical environment of the city and precipitated the search for new policy tools, the regulation of skyscrapers was part of a larger debate over the need for legal change in a society that had outgrown its individualistic foundations.[91] In the case of skyscrapers, advocates of regulation struggled to create the legal means to integrate tall buildings into a vision of the planned metropolis while preserving the individualism of American architects like Gilbert – to create the policy tools, in other words, to forge a new relationship between individualism and collective life. The result was neither a repudiation of the skyscraper nor an abandonment of City Beautiful principles nor an acquiescence to outdated conceptions of property rights. Instead, the dialogue between law and architecture initiated by the City Beautiful movement significantly expanded municipal legal authority over private property while encouraging a new era in skyscraper design. The tension between individualism and the public good so evident in both discourses was resolved, strangely enough, by an emphasis on public health rather than on civic beauty. By claiming to pursue cleaner, safer, healthier streets, city planners fashioned legal restrictions, which, in the hands of innovative architects, produced a skyscraper urbanism that retained the City Beautiful's emphasis on ensemble by incorporating vertical monumentality into a modern conceptualization of the city as a whole. By forcing the law to recognize beauty in this roundabout way, advocates of skyscraper regulation were able to reconcile their civic goals, robust commercialism, and architectural freedom in ways that had previously seemed impossible.

NOTES

1. In Gilbert's estimation, the American devotion to private rights "produces a skyline that is . . . interesting and picturesque, but seldom well organized and rarely beautiful." Cass Gilbert, "Discussion," *Proceedings of the Seventh National Conference on City Planning* (1915):209–10.

2. I borrow the vertical versus horizontal, private versus civic dichotomy from Thomas Bender and William R. Taylor, "Culture and Architecture: Some Aesthetic Tensions in the Shaping of Modern New York City," in *Visions of the Modern City: Essays in History, Art, and Literature*, ed. William Sharpe and Leonard Wallock (Baltimore: Johns Hopkins Univ. Press, 1987), 189–219, 194. For an overview of the problem of skyscraper regulation, see Robert M. Fogelson, *Downtown: Its Rise and Fall, 1880–1950* (New Haven, CT: Yale Univ. Press, 2001), 112–82.

3. Henry Adams, *The Education of Henry Adams: An Autobiography* (1918; repr., Dunwoody, GA: Norman S. Berg, 1975), 343.

4. Montgomery Schuyler, "Last Words About the World's Fair," in *American Architecture and Other Writings*, vol. 2, ed. William H. Jordy and Ralph Coe (Cambridge, MA: Belknap Press, 1961), 559, 560. Originally published in *Architectural Record* 3 (Jan.–Mar. 1894):271–301.

5. Charles Mulford Robinson, *Modern Civic Art, or, The City Made Beautiful*, 4th rev. ed. (1918; repr., New York: Arno Press, 1970), 30–1; see also William H. Wilson, *The City Beautiful Movement* (Baltimore: Johns Hopkins Univ. Press, 1989), 62–3.

6. Wilson, *City Beautiful Movement*, 9–95; Donald Drew Egbert, *The Beaux-Arts Tradition in French Architecture: Illustrated by the Grand Prix De Rome*, ed. David Van Zanten (Princeton, NJ: Princeton Univ. Press, 1980), 156. On the Ecole des Beaux-Arts, see also *The Architecture of the Ecole Des Beaux-Arts*, ed. Arthur Drexler (New York: Museum of Modern Art, 1977) and James Philip Noffsinger, "The Influence of the Ecole des Beaux-Arts on the Architects of the United States" (Ph.D. diss., Catholic Univ. of America, 1955). Although I stress the aesthetic aspects of the City Beautiful movement in this essay, it is quite clear from Wilson, *City Beautiful Movement*, that it had many other dimensions.

7. Bender and Taylor, "Culture and Architecture," 195, 196, 200; Charles H. Caffin, "Municipal Art," *Harper's Monthly Magazine* 100 (Apr. 1900):658.

8. Gail G. Fenske, "The 'Skyscraper Problem' and the City Beautiful: The Woolworth Building" (Ph.D. diss., MIT, 1988), provides a thorough analysis of the topic; see 8–57 and esp. 1, 2, 16, 17, 19, 25, 36–7, 53, 55, 222, and 225. Skyscrapers were not the only modern form to violate the City Beautiful aesthetic; billboards were similarly problematic.

9. Montgomery Schuyler, "The Skyscraper Problem," in *American Architecture and Other Writings*, 2:446; originally published in *Scribner's Magazine* 34 (Aug. 1903):253–6.

10. Bender and Taylor, "Culture and Architecture," 190.

11. Charles Rollinson Lamb, "Civic Architecture from Its Constructive Side," *Municipal Affairs* 2 (March 1898):58.

12. Ernest Flagg, "The Dangers of High Buildings," *The Cosmopolitan* 21 (May 1896):70–9.

13. Mildred Stapley, "The City of Towers," *Harper's Monthly* 123 (Oct. 1911):698.

14. Along with Louis Sullivan's Guaranty Building in Buffalo (1895) and Bayard Building in New York (1898); Schuyler, "The Skyscraper Problem," 2:445. See also Rollin Lynde Hartt, "Economic Forces for Beauty," *World's Work* 15 (Mar. 1908):10025.

15. Montgomery Schuyler, "The Towers of Manhattan and Notes on the Woolworth Building," *Architectural Record* 33 (Feb. 1913):99–122.

16. The Woolworth Building furnished "irrefutable proof of the fact that the much maligned American skyscraper is not of necessity ugly." See "The High Building," *American Architect* 103 (Mar. 26, 1913): 171–2.

17. Giles Edgerton, "How New York Has Redeemed Herself from Ugliness – An Artist's Revelation of the Beauty of the Skyscraper," *Craftsman* 2 (Jan. 1907):458, 468. New York City's forty-story Municipal Office Building (1913), designed by William Kendall of McKim, Mead, & White, also violated the horizontal tradition for civic architecture, but in this case we have a public building taking on vertical rather than horizontal form. In so doing, the building managed to "bring the values of the City Beautiful movement – classical forms, noble civic spaces – to the skyscraper," architectural critic Paul Goldberger observed in *The Skyscraper* (New York: Knopf, 1981), 41–2; see also Nelson P. Lewis, *The Planning of the Modern City: A Review of the Principles Governing City Planning* (New York: Wiley, 1916), 160–1.

18. Werner Hegemann and Elbert Peets, *The American Vitruvius: An Architect's Handbook of Civic Art*, ed. Alan J. Plattus (1922; repr., New York: Princeton Architectural Press, 1988), 1, 2.

19. "The Skyscraper and Silhouette," *American Architect and Building News* 92 (Sept. 21, 1907):89.

20. Montgomery Schuyler, "To Curb the Skyscraper," *Architectural Record* 24 (Oct. 1908):300; Charles H. Caffin, "The Beautifying of Cities," *World's Work* 3 (Nov. 1901):1429. See also Caffin, "Municipal Art," 656. Thomas Hastings noted that "it is almost discouraging to spend one's energies upon fifty or one hundred feet of an avenue or street, when, however good the result in itself may be, we are only making a blot upon the *ensemble* of the general line of building. Legal limitations would give us that monotony so essential to the general appearance of a city"; Thomas Hastings, "High Buildings and Good Architecture," *American Architect and Building News* 56 (Nov. 17, 1894):67.

21. Lamb, "Civic Architecture," 57.

22. Schuyler, "The Skyscraper Problem," 2:446.

23. Montgomery Schuyler, "The Skyline of New York, 1881–1897," *Harper's Weekly* 41 (Mar. 20, 1897): 295.

24. *People ex rel. Kemp v. D'Oench*, 111 N.Y. 359. In this case, the New York State legislature had passed a law limiting the height of tenements and the city had tried to use that law to limit the height of hotels. The judge struck down such use of the legislation by arguing that, while the height of tenements could be regulated because of the well-known health and safety problems they posed, the same reasoning could not be applied to hotels – prompting Montgomery Schuyler to conclude: "So that it appears that not only is this monster [the skyscraper] *ferae naturae*, but that the courts will give

us no help toward reducing him to subjection" ("The Skyscraper Problem," 2:447).

25. See Walter L. Fisher, "Legal Aspects of the Plan of Chicago," in Daniel H. Burnham and Edward H. Bennett, *Plan of Chicago*, ed. Charles Moore (1909, repr. New York: Princeton Architectural Press, 1993), 127, 140–1. The Chicago Plan, a direct descendant of the World's Fair, was an attempt to create "the city as an organic whole, each part having well-defined relations with every other part." To achieve that cohesion, especially in the downtown area, Burnham called for strict controls on the heights of buildings: "Along the curved avenues and the diagonals the architectural design should avoid the building up of the thoroughfare structure by structure, each one following the whim of its owner or the struggle for novelty on the part of its architect. Without attempting to secure formality, or to insist on uniformity of design on a large scale, there should be a constant display of teamwork, so to speak, on the part of architects. The former days when each architect strove to build his cornice higher and more elaborate than the adjoining cornice are giving place, happily, to the saner idea of accepting existing conditions when a reasonable line has been established. There is as much reason why facades should live together in harmony as there is for peace among neighbors. In the case of open spaces, effectiveness of architectural design is to be obtained only by a large unity in the entire composition." It is worth remembering that the tallest structure in Burnham's downtown was the central dome of the Civic Center, which was surrounded by acres of buildings restrained by a uniform cornice line. Thomas Hines, however, has pointed out that the buildings in Burnham's downtown were nearly twenty stories high. Thomas S. Hines, *Burnham of Chicago: Architect and Planner* (New York: Oxford Univ. Press, 1974), 334–5. In Burnham's conception, downtown Chicago looks much more like Washington, DC, or Paris than the commercial city of skyscrapers that it was (*Plan of Chicago*, 4, 14, 29, 86–7).

26. "The Lawyer as a City Planning Advisor," *American City* 13 (Sept. 1915):172.

27. *Health Department v. Rector*, 145 N.Y. 32 at 44.

28. By 1871, the State of New York had consolidated and expanded statutes applying to buildings housing gunpowder and petroleum to cover all urban structures. See *Laws of New York, 1871*, Chap. 625, Sec. 11, 19, and 22; *Laws of New York, 1866*, Chap. 873, Sec. 4 and 5. By 1907, the building code in Massachusetts specified the unit stresses in pounds per square inch required of various types of pine and spruce and detailed the thickness, weights, and diameters of pipes used in waterclosets and sinks. See *Massachusetts, Acts and Resolves, 1907*, Chap. 550, Sec. 14 and 121.

Indeed, historian William Novak has gone so far as to argue that the expansion of the police power during the nineteenth century represented "a full-fledged science of government" in which "the public interest was superior to private interest." Novak has shown that cities had extensive power to regulate everything from wooden buildings, to weights and measures, to taverns, ports, and public highways. William J. Novak, *The People's Welfare: Law and Regulation in Nineteenth-Century America* (Chapel Hill: Univ. of North Carolina Press, 1996), 1, 9, 66–71, 97, 117–28, and 157–61.

29. While it is certainly true that nineteenth-century fire limits and building codes served as the legal precursors to twentieth-century zoning ordinances, it was still quite a leap (both legally and administratively) from protecting cities against catastrophic conflagrations and shoddy construction to creating more livable neighborhoods, efficient business districts, and beautiful skylines. Novak, *People's Welfare*, 67.

30. *Passaic v. Patterson Bill Posting*, 72 N.J.L. 285 (1905) at 287. Cities were not entirely powerless to pursue some forms of aesthetic enhancement, even when those efforts interfered with private property rights. Although not within the police power, civic beautification did fall within the power of eminent domain, the power of the state to take private property for public use. Here, however, courts were really authorizing the expenditure of public monies for the creation and preservation of parks, rather than the beautification of the skyline. The City of Boston, to cite the leading example, passed an ordinance in 1898 limiting building heights to 90 feet around Copley Square (site of Henry Hobson Richardson's masterpiece of American architecture, Trinity Church), a limit enforced by the city's compensating property owners for lopping off the tops of buildings above 90 feet (which occurred in only one case, where the roof of a 96-foot building was lowered by 6 feet). The State Supreme Court upheld the ordinance, but it did so by arguing that its real motive was to protect Copley Square as a public park – a recognized use of the power of eminent domain. *Attorney General v. Williams*, 174 Mass. 476 (1899). "In all respects the statute is in accordance with the laws regulating the taking of property by right of eminent domain, if the Legislature properly could determine that the preservation or improvement of the park in this particular was for a public use. . . . It is only within a few years that lands have been taken in this country for public parks. Now the right to take land for this purpose is generally recognized and frequently exercised. . . . Their aesthetic effect has never been thought unworthy of careful consideration

by those best qualified to appreciate it. It hardly would be contended that the same reasons which justify the taking of land for a public park do not also justify the expenditure of money to make the park attractive and educational to those whose tastes are being formed and whose love of beauty is being cultivated" (at 478, 479, and 480). See also Michael Holleran, "Boston's 'Sacred Skyline': From Prohibiting to Sculpting Skyscrapers, 1891–1928," *Journal of Urban History* 22 (July 1996): 563–5.

The Copley Square decision in 1899 hardly signaled a judicial embrace of regulatory measures limiting the use of private property for aesthetic reasons, however. Only six years later the same Massachusetts court struck down another ordinance prohibiting advertising signs along parkways – an undisguised effort to beautify a public road. In its opinion the court emphasized that while it was acceptable *to spend public monies* to promote civic beauty and pleasure (as in the Copley Square case), it was beyond the scope of the law *to regulate the use of private property* for something which, at most, was "an offense against good taste." *Commonwealth v. Boston Advertising Co.*, 188 Mass. 348 (1905) at 351. As one student of the legal aspects of civic beautification concluded in 1907, "although public aesthetic ends may be effectuated by statute or ordinance through the exercise of eminent domain, the same object may not be accomplished by legislation under the police power." Wilbur Larremore, "Public Aesthetics," *Harvard Law Review* 20 (1906–07):43. Noted legal scholar and police power authority Ernst Freund was more sanguine; he speculated that the police power might be extended from the suppression of offensive noises and odors to the suppression of unsightly advertising. See Larremore, "Public Aesthetics," 43.

31. Alfred Bettman, "Discussion," *Proceedings of the Sixth National Conference on City Planning* (1914):111.

32. Although several American cities, including Washington, DC, and Chicago, had adopted height limits by the 1890s, the task of making the legal case for skyscraper regulation fell first to Boston and later to Baltimore. As with height limits in other cities, those in Boston and Baltimore emerged from an array of practical, economic, and aesthetic motives. In each case, however, attorneys traded the language of beautification for the language of health and safety to justify limiting building heights.

33. Unlike their counterparts in New York City, few Boston developers thought of skyscrapers as a sound investment. In a city that favored decentralization, skyscrapers represented unwanted concentration and congestion (Holleran, "Boston's 'Sacred Skyline,' " 559–61, 558–9).

34. Holleran, "Boston's 'Sacred Skyline,' " 562, 566; *Brief for Plaintiff in Error* (Francis C. Welch v. George R. Swasey et al.), 18. The plaintiffs accepted the legitimacy of the 125-foot limit, however.

35. *Brief for Defendants in Error* (Welch v. Swasey), 10, 11. In perhaps the most innovative aspect of their defense, attorneys for the city insisted that the health and safety of women and children required the lower height limit. They cleverly connected the problem of building height to the U.S. Supreme Court's recent decision upholding a labor law for women, *Muller v. Oregon*, arguing that the safety of women and children required the state to intervene and restrict the use of private property. Historical sociologist Theda Skocpol has shown that the protection of women and children proved to be an especially important line of argument during the early battles leading to the creation of the welfare state; see *Protecting Soldiers and Mothers: The Political Origins of Social Policy in the United States* (Cambridge, MA: Belknap Press, 1992).

36. *Welch v. Swasey*, 193 Mass. 364 at 373, 377, and 375 ("if the primary and substantive purpose of the legislation is such as justifies the act, considerations of taste and beauty may enter in, as auxiliary"); and *Welch v. Swasey*, 214 U.S. 91. After discussing the dangers of fire (and the threat to women and children), Justice Peckham concluded "that in addition to these sufficient facts, considerations of an aesthetic nature also entered into the reasons for their passage, would not invalidate them" (at 108). It should be added, however, that Peckham made it clear that he was deferring to local authorities (especially to the state court decision) in this case (at 105–6).

37. As historian Garrett Power observed, both buildings "were not single family residences and they were not to scale. They cast a shadow over nearby residences and detracted from the neighborhood's centerpiece, the Washington Monument." See Garrett Power, "High Society: The Building Height Limitation on Baltimore's Mt. Vernon Place," *Maryland Historical Magazine* 79 (Fall 1984):202–6, 205.

38. Power, "High Society," 207; *Cochran v. Preston*, 70 Atl. Rep. 113 at 115. See also Joseph M. Rogers, "The Baltimore Fire," *Review of Reviews* 29 (Mar. 1904):298–303, and Sherry H. Olson, *Baltimore: The Building of an American City* (Baltimore: Johns Hopkins Univ. Press, 1980), 246–7.

39. Together, these designations created some 75 possible combinations of height, area, and use limits, although the original ordinance employed only 36 such combinations. See Herbert Swan, "Making the New York Zoning Ordinance Better," *Architectural Forum* 35 (Oct. 1921):126, and Keith D. Revell, "Regulating

the Landscape: Real Estate Values, City Planning, and the 1916 Zoning Ordinance," in *The Landscape of Modernity: Essays on New York City, 1900–1940*, ed. David Ward and Olivier Zunz (New York: Russell Sage, 1992), 20–1.

40. "Heights of Edifices," *American Architect and Building News* 108 (November 3, 1915): 301.

41. For a full discussion of the ordinance, see Keith D. Revell, *Building Gotham: Civic Culture and Public Policy in New York City, 1898–1938* (Baltimore: Johns Hopkins Univ. Press, 2003), 185–226; Carol Willis, "A 3D CBD: How the 1916 Zoning Law Shaped Manhattan's Central Business Districts," in *Planning and Zoning in New York City: Yesterday, Today, and Tomorrow*, ed. Todd W. Bressi (Rutgers: Center for Urban Policy Research, 1993), 3–26; Marc A. Weiss, "Density and Intervention: New York's Planning Traditions," in *The Landscape of Modernity*, 46–75; Revell, "Regulating the Landscape," 19–45; S. J. Makielski, Jr., *The Politics of Zoning: The New York Experience* (New York: Columbia Univ. Press, 1966); M. Christine Boyer, *Dreaming the Rational City: The Myth of American City Planning* (Cambridge, MA: MIT Press, 1983); M. Christine Boyer, *Manhattan Manners: Architecture and Style, 1850–1900* (New York: Rizzoli, 1985); Seymour I. Toll, *Zoned America* (New York: Grossman, 1969), 143–87; and Harvey Kantor, "Modern Urban Planning in New York City: Origins and Evolution, 1890–1933" (Ph.D. diss., New York Univ., 1971).

42. J. Horace McFarland, "The Growth of City Planning in America," *Charities and the Commons* 19 (Feb. 1, 1908):1525.

43. Stapley, "The City of Towers," 698. Stapley noted that architects were gradually awakening to the fact that classic horizontal lines did not suit the skyscraper. "A tall building demanded, for any sort of congruity, a strong expression of verticality." See also Bender and Taylor, "Culture and Architecture," 200, 204, 207, 209.

44. Since the 1890s, the practical difficulties of enacting flat height limits had inspired alternative schemes for regulating skyscrapers and thus coming to terms with the vertical city. In 1896, George Post, who had designed the Manufactures and Liberal Arts Building at the Chicago World's Fair, proposed limiting the height of buildings in New York to 15 times the square root of the width of the street they fronted. Ernest Flagg advocated a "tower and base" formula – as in his design for the Singer Building – limiting the percentage of the lot where towers would be permitted. And Philadelphia architect David Knickerbocker Boyd, who blamed the absence of height limits on "the spirit of rampant commercialism" that prevailed in American cities, proposed to step back the upper portions of skyscrapers. See "George B. Post's Building Bill," *New York Times*, Jan. 28, 1896, 9:2; "Tower Skyscrapers Planned for Future," *New York Times*, May 30, 1908, 16:3; Flagg, "The Dangers of High Buildings," 70–9; Mardges Bacon, *Ernest Flagg: Beaux-Arts Architect and Urban Reformer* (Cambridge, MA: MIT Press, 1986), 220–3; David Knickerbocker Boyd, "The Skyscraper and the Street," *American Architect and Building News* 44 (Nov. 18, 1908):162, 161–7.

45. "To the Members of the Brooklyn Committee on City Plan," June 1, 1912, Edward Murray Bassett Papers, Cornell Univ., Box 13, File 34, and "Supplemental Report Submitted to the Comptroller with the Three Perspective Drawings on Sites for Public Buildings and Re-Location of Tracks in Lower Fulton Street, Borough of Brooklyn," July 26, 1913, Bassett Papers, Box 11, File 10; on Bennett, see Hines, *Burnham of Chicago*, 180, 270, 348. On Bassett's use of "efficiency" in the skyscraper debate, see Olivier Zunz, *Making America Corporate, 1880–1920* (Chicago: Univ. of Chicago Press, 1990), 122–4.

46. As did his models for the grouping of public buildings and the arrangement of park space; see Lewis, *The Planning of the Modern City*, 220, 130–74.

47. George B. Ford, "What Makes 'The City Beautiful'?" *Planning Problems of Town, City and Region: Papers and Discussions at the Twenty-First National Conference on City Planning* (1929):170–8, 177; see also Wilson, *The City Beautiful Movement*, 299, describing Ford's article as "perhaps the most amazing restatement of the City Beautiful ideal."

48. Leopold Eidlitz, *The Nature and Function of Art: More Especially of Architecture* (1881; repr. New York: Da Capo, 1977), viii, vi; "Leopold Eidlitz Dead," *New York Times*, Mar. 23, 1908, 1:4.

49. Minutes of the Heights of Buildings Commission, June 19, 1913, New York City Municipal Archives, Box 2507; Hines, *Burnham of Chicago*, 170; Robert I. Aitken et al., *Arnold W. Brunner and His Work* (New York: American Institute of Architects, 1926), esp. 18–20, 25–6, and 30.

50. Alrick H. Man to Lawson Purdy, July 3, 1913, Heights of Buildings Commission, New York City Municipal Archives, Box 2507.

51. Biographical Notes, George B. Ford, Apr. 1931, Harriet Ford Papers, Sophia Smith Collection, Smith College, Northampton, MA, Box 1, 5, 9; Lewis, *Planning the Modern City*, 36, 12.

52. Lewis, *Planning the Modern City*, 23; Robert Whitten, "Preliminary Report to the Heights of Buildings Commission," Heights of Buildings Commission Papers, New York City Municipal Archives, Box 2507, 40–1; and Lawson Purdy et al., *Zoning: As an Element*

in City Planning, and for Protection of Property Values, Public Safety, and Public Health, American Civic Association pamphlet, ser. 2, no. 15 (June 30, 1920), 3; see also Revell, "Regulating the Landscape," 35–40, and Keith Revell, "Beyond Efficiency: Experts, Urban Planning, and Civic Culture in New York City, 1898–1933," (Ph.D. diss., Univ. of Virginia, 1994), 269–71.

53. In 1926, Lawson Purdy recalled that the two most important constraints the zoning team had struggled with a decade earlier were first whether the ordinance would be upheld in New York state courts and second whether the members of the city's Board of Estimate and Apportionment would ever approve the measure – a possibility he thought of as "very, very remote." As a result of these concerns, "with everything that we did, cautions of extreme prudence prevailed." See Remarks of Hon. Lawson Purdy at Meeting of Zoning Div., Oct. 28, 1926, Mayor William J. Gaynor Papers, New York City Municipal Archives, Box GWJ-231.

54. Bassett to McAneny, Sept. 28, 1914, Bassett Papers, Box 4, File 65.

55. Whitten, "Preliminary Report to the Heights of Buildings Commission," 5, 27, 31–3.

56. Commission on Building Districts and Restrictions, *Final Report* (New York: Board of Estimate and Apportionment, Committee on the City Plan, 1916), 19, 40–1 (hereafter, CBDR, *Final Report*); Bassett to Leon Hornstein, Jan. 3, 1922, Bassett Papers, Box 3, File 133.

57. Minutes of the Heights of Buildings Commission, May 26, 1913, New York City Municipal Archives, Box 2507, 4.

58. Biographical Notes, George B. Ford, 1–3, 6. Thomas Hastings and Paul Cret were also pupils of Pascal; see John J. Burnet, "Jean-Louis Pascal," *Journal of the Royal Institute of British Architects* 27 (June 26, 1920): 400–1.

59. Like Ernest Flagg, who attended the Ecole a decade before him, Ford struggled to reconcile beauty and rationality, although Ford sought to balance the two through city planning, while Flagg concentrated on architecture. See Bacon, *Ernest Flagg*, 42–3 on Flagg's ongoing efforts to reconcile the polarities of "intuition and reason, art and construction."

60. George B. Ford, "Phases of Architectural Education," *Technology Review* 12 (Jan. 1910):1–6; George B. Ford and E. P. Goodrich, *Preliminary Report to the City Plan Commission, Newark, New Jersey* (June 1, 1912), 4–7, and George B. Ford, "City Planning in New York City: How All Can Cooperate," paper presented at New York Political Academy, Apr. 18, 1912, George B. Ford Papers, Francis Loeb Library, Harvard University, Cambridge, MA. Or as Ford put it, "The 'City Beautiful' will come easily if the structure is right"; undated letter from George B. Ford on George B. Post and Sons letterhead, Ford Papers. Frederick Law Olmsted, "The Basic Principles of City Planning," *American City* 3 (Aug. 1910):72; quoted in Ford, "What Makes 'The City Beautiful'?" 171.

Ford is a key link between the American and French planning communities. The connections between urban design, health, housing, aesthetics, and political reform were central to contemporary debates among French planners and architects, just as they were in the U.S. Ford, who joined the American Red Cross relief effort in postwar France and oversaw the replanning of Rheims, contributed significantly to the debate. His approach, as historian Gwendolyn Wright observed, "sought to connect aesthetic and economic development . . . through 'scientific' principles." "Le plan Ford," as it came to be called, was an attempt to modernize French cities by improving sanitation, traffic flows, and land use patterns while retaining the charm associated with the narrow, crooked streets of European villages. See Gwendolyn Wright, *The Politics of Design in French Colonial Urbanism* (Chicago: Univ. of Chicago Press, 1991), 20, 25, 27, 32, 49–50, and George B. Ford, *Out of the Ruins* (New York: Century, 1919).

61. On Post, see Winston Weisman, "The Commercial Architecture of George B. Post," *Journal of the Society of Architectural Historians* 31 (Oct. 1972):176–203.

62. George B. Ford, "Another Architectural Renaissance," Feb. 2, 1908, Ford Papers, 7–16, esp. 9 and 12.

63. George B. Ford, "Prevention by 'Housing': The Relation of the 'Social' to the 'Architectural' in Housing and Town Planning," 1910, Ford Papers, 2; Ford, "City Planning in Europe," address given at City Hall, Philadelphia, May 24, 1911, Ford Papers, 4; and Ford, "City Planning and Housing Reform," address delivered at the N.J. State Housing Conference, Trenton, Jan. 22, 1914, Ford papers, 5. Robert Whitten expressed this concern as well; see Whitten, "Preliminary Report," 18.

64. George B. Ford, "Practical Planning of Residential Streets," paper read at the First National City Planning Congress, Washington, DC, May 22, 1909, Ford Papers.

65. Louis Sullivan was ahead of his time in suggesting the setback skyscraper as a way "to preserve in a building of high altitude the equities of both the individual and of the public." His sketch for a setback skyscraper city in 1891 prefigured the terracing plans offered by other architects in the coming decades. See Donald Hoffmann, "The Setback Skyscraper City of 1891: An Unknown Essay by Louis H. Sullivan," *Journal of the Society of Architectural Historians* 29 (May 1970):181–7.

66. It is not my contention here that Ford created the specific skyscraper style that emerged in the 1920s, for as fellow architect C. Grant La Farge argued, the

aesthetic consequences of the ordinance "could hardly have been foreseen, except dimly as conjectures." See C. Grant La Farge, "The New Skyline," *American Mercury* 1 (Jan. 1924):89. Toward the end of his life, Ford claimed to have envisioned the skyline more or less as it did emerge: "The new skyline of New York, with its stepback terraces, towers and gables, is not an accident. Far from it! When we were zoning New York and trying to see how we could get the greatest amount of light and air down into the street we tried at the same time to picture how terraced-back buildings were going to look. To keep them from being monotonous and standardized we made little models in harness soap of virtually all the new types of skyscrapers and many other types besides, and we drafted our stepback regulations so that they would permit all the variety and spontaneity of treatment we are reveling in today." See Ford, "What Makes 'The City Beautiful'?" 174. See also "Report of Committee on Methods of Improving the General Architecture, Mass and Appearance of Buildings," n.d., Ford Papers. Ford's colleagues also credited him with "a profound influence on modern 'skyscraper' architecture." Henry Vincent Hubbard, editor of *City Planning*, noted in an article eulogizing Ford: "The conception of the 'Zoning Envelope' within which the form of the restricted building must lie, the first visualization of the architectural forms so brought about which now create a new architectural style – these were primarily the work of George B. Ford during the drafting of the New York Zoning Ordinance passed in 1916." And in recognition of Ford's concern with the city ensemble, Hubbard added: "Perhaps more than any other architect, he faced squarely and studied completely the factors of the economics of construction, upkeep, use, and mutual amenity of city buildings, as an inseparable and underlying part of the whole problem the final solution of which is the efficient and beautiful neighborhood or district rather than the individual structure" (H. V. H., "Editorial," *City Planning* 6 [Oct. 1930]:282). Given what I have been able to discover in his prezoning writings, I am persuaded that Ford was concerned with light and air, architectural diversity, and civic beauty. If he carved his harness soap models in strict accordance with the ordinance – in effect, prefiguring Hugh Ferriss's now famous sketches of the evolution of the skyscraper under the zoning law – then it seems at least plausible that Ford might have envisioned the skyline of the 1920s. In the absence of more direct evidence, however, I am inclined to conclude only that he at least thought seriously about how the skyline would look under the new zoning law, holding out the possibility that he foresaw the setback skyscrapers of the future "dimly as conjectures."

67. CBDR, *Final Report*, 25, 28.

68. Biographical Notes, George B. Ford, 13. On the tower configurations, see CBDR, *Final Report*, 264. Ford probably thought that the new era would include more dormers, mansards, and parapets than it ultimately did, for the ordinance specifically allowed buildings to exceed the setback envelope when using such features; see CBDR, *Final Report*, 257–60. Ford's drawings were quite spare when compared to Hugh Ferriss's renderings of setback skyscrapers; see Carol Willis, "Drawing Toward Metropolis," in Hugh Ferriss, *The Metropolis of Tomorrow* (1929; repr. Princeton, NJ: Princeton Architectural Press, 1986), 157.

69. Keith D. Revell, "The Road to *Euclid v. Ambler*: City Planning, State-Building, and the Changing Scope of the Police Power," *Studies in American Political Development* 13 (Spring 1999):50–145.

70. Aymar Embury II, "New York's New Architecture: The Effect of the Zoning Law on High Buildings," *Architectural Forum* 35 (Oct. 1921):119.

71. La Farge, "New Skyline," 89. This observation was made by Fiske Kimball, *American Architecture* (1928, repr. New York: AMS Press, 1970), 212, and Carol Willis, "Zoning and *Zeitgeist*: The Skyscraper in the 1920s," *Journal of the Society of Architectural Historians* 45 (Mar. 1986):47–59, esp. 57. It did not take long for the emerging trends to appear, as zoning became one of several important elements in the design process. As a result of the setback regulations, increasingly architects had to work backward, from the zoning envelope inward, in addition to working from the floor plan upward. Because of the premium placed on space within the envelope, architects did away with interior light courts. The ordinance also encouraged building on larger lots, since towers of unlimited height were restricted to 25 percent of the lot area. See, for example, La Farge, "New Skyline," 91; John Taylor Boyd, "The New York Zoning Resolution and Its Influence Upon Design," *Architectural Record* 48 (Sept. 1920):192–217; James B. Newman, "Factors in Office Building Planning," *Architectural Forum* 52 (June 1930):881–90; Walter H. Kilham, *Raymond Hood, Architect: Form Through Function in the American Skyscraper* (New York: Architectural Book Publishing, 1973), 18, 89; Harvey Wiley Corbett, "The Planning of Office Buildings," *Architectural Forum* 41 (Sept. 1924):89–93; Ely Jacques Kahn, "The Office Building Problem in New York," *Architectural Forum* 41 (Sept. 1924):94–6; and Willis, "Zoning and *Zeitgeist*," 48.

72. Kilham, *Raymond Hood, Architect*, 86–7.

73. Hood is an interesting architect in this respect, for he exemplifies the shift from "the Beaux-Arts 'Gothic' toward a gothicized modern aesthetic" that architectural historian William Jordy described in *American Buildings*

and Their Architects: The Impact of European Modernism in the Mid-Twentieth Century (New York: Doubleday, 1972), 59; see also Goldberger, *The Skyscraper*, 61, 54.

74. Claude Bragdon, "The Shelton Hotel, New York," *Architectural Record* 58 (July 1925):1–18, esp. 3–8; and Kimball, *American Architecture*, 213; Goldberger, *The Skyscraper*, 61.

75. Ely Jacques Kahn, "Our Skyscrapers Take Simple Form," *New York Times*, 4 (Magazine), May 2, 1926, 11. According to Kahn, architects were discarding the moldings and reliefs of "dead leaves, swags, bull's heads and cartouches" and turning to surface modeling that emphasized the "play of light and shade, voids and solids," thus reinforcing the "unbroken lines, immense surfaces, planes, angles, sharp contrasts of light and shade [that] are essentially New York." On Kahn, see Kilham, *Raymond Hood, Architect*, 88, and Jewel Stern, "Ely Jacques Kahn: The Modernist Years, 1925–1931" (MA thesis, University of Miami, 1978). The same tendency can be seen in the work of Starrett and Van Vleck; see John Taylor Boyd, "A New Emphasis in Skyscraper Design," *Architectural Record* 52 (Dec. 1922):496–509, esp. 507.

76. The same was true of buildings Hood helped design for Rockefeller Center. (See Kilham, *Raymond Hood, Architect*, 23, and Jordy, *American Buildings and Their Architects: The Impact of European Modernism in the Mid-Twentieth Century*, 48.) According to critic R. W. Sexton, architects in cities without zoning ordinances began to design setback skyscrapers, such as the Pacific Telephone Building in San Francisco – a trend that led him to conclude: "This reborn skyscraper, though still in its infancy, represents a new style of architectural design. It is based throughout on architectural principles, and neither adapts nor reproduces old-world motifs in its design, nor breaks any of the basic and fundamental laws on which architecture has ever been founded. The American skyscraper has come into its own! It is American now throughout." See R. W. Sexton, "Unifying Architecture in America," *International Studio* 83 (Feb. 1926):45. In this sense, the setback skyscraper seemed to have answered Ernest Flagg's call for the creation of "a national style of our own." See Ernest Flagg, "American Architecture as Opposed to Architecture in America," *Architectural Record* 10 (Oct. 1900):180.

77. Ferriss, *The Metropolis of Tomorrow*, 46; Embury, "New York's New Architecture," 120.

78. The 1916 ordinance did not give merchants a flat height limit along Fifth Avenue, but it effectively restricted the heights of new buildings in the retail district by limiting their street wall to one and one-quarter times the width of the street. It also restricted the amount of space in new buildings that could be used for manufacturing purposes, thus limiting the conversion of lofts to sweatshops. Moreover, it designated most of Fifth Avenue and its side streets for either business or residential use, rather than for unrestricted (industrial) purposes. This allowed some proximity of factories, showrooms, warehouses, and retail stores, but prevented mixed-use districts from converting to industrial areas (CBDR, *Final Report*, 110–20, Fig. 128; CBDR, *Tentative Report*, 10). However, when it became clear that the ordinance would not be retroactive, Fifth Avenue merchants launched the "Save New York" campaign – a public relations blitz designed to force garment manufacturers out of the Fifth Avenue district. By July of 1916, just as the ordinance was enacted, 95 percent of the garment manufacturers threatened with the boycott had promised to relocate. See Seymour I. Toll, *Zoned America* (New York: Grossman, 1969), 175–9. This pushed them north toward the new garment district, which was created after the war.

79. By 1919, a consortium of cloak, suit, and fur manufacturers began to develop land west of Seventh Avenue between Thirty-fifth and Thirty-ninth streets. That area had been zoned as a "2 times" height district and an "unrestricted" use district. See Walter Stabler, "Some of the Effects of City Planning on Real Estate Values," an address before the City Plan Committee of the Cleveland Chamber of Commerce, Dec. 18, 1919, MetLife Archives, 5; CBDR, *Final Report*, Figs. 123 and 128; on the other forces encouraging the relocation of the garment district, see Nancy L. Green, "Sweatshop Migrations: The Garment Industry Between Work and Home," in *The Landscape of Modernity*, 213–32.

80. "Many New Buildings for Garment Trades Reveal Seventh Avenue's Business Growth," *New York Times*, Aug. 27, 1922, 1:3–6.

81. Kimball, *American Architecture*, 212; Kahn, "Our Skyscrapers Take Simple Form," 22.

82. Harvey Wiley Corbett, "New Heights in American Architecture," *Yale Review* 17 (July 1928):694. Corbett argued that, prior to the zoning ordinance, "the ordinary skyscraper was simply an elongation of the five or six story building," and "was in no sense a new form" but "a distortion of the old form." The zoning ordinance changed the way architects approached skyscrapers, "revolutionizing the exterior of tall buildings" and compelling designers "to treat every building as a free-standing structure." One of the great benefits of this approach, Corbett observed, was that it helped "to make the exterior [of buildings] big enough to cover the inside. In case you think there is a joke in that statement, look at the forest of roof tanks, elevator penthouses and bulkheads that jut up against the sky over any American city, or keep an eye for fire escapes and suchlike

excrescences, and you will come to the conclusion that the practice of putting undersized exteriors on our buildings is altogether too common." See "New Stones for Old," *Saturday Evening Post* 198 (May 8, 1926):186.

83. Hugh Ferriss, "Civic Architecture of the Immediate Future," *Arts and Decoration* 18 (Nov. 1922):12.

84. Ferriss, "Civic Architecture," 12.

85. The skyscraper's old antagonists were spurred on by the threat of congestion posed by the new breed of tall buildings. "Skyscrapers are the craziest buildings in New York," insisted Thomas Hastings in 1926; "they pour a flood of humanity into the streets that taxes them beyond all limits, and are the cause of nearly all our congestion ills" – a view seconded by Ernest Flagg, who continued to call for lower height limits following the example of European cities. See "Divergent Views by Architects on City Planning and Skyscrapers," *New York Times*, Oct. 31, 1926, 1:1; Ernest Flagg, "Limiting Building Heights," *New York Times*, Nov. 27, 1926, 16:7; Thomas Hastings, "Are Skyscrapers an Asset?" *Forum* 77 (Apr. 1927):570–7. The redoubtable Thomas Edison joined the debate briefly, predicting that increasing traffic congestion would lead to the prohibition of skyscrapers in some parts of the city. "Edison Predicts End of Skyscraper Era," *New York Times*, Nov. 15, 1926, 1:4. Even Edward Bassett had second thoughts about his own handiwork, regretting that the city ever permitted buildings over ten stories. "Finds Skyscrapers Blot on City Beauty," *New York Times*, Dec. 12, 1926, sec. 2, 21:5.

86. Frederic A. Delano, "Skyscrapers," *American City* 34 (Jan. 1926):6, 9. See also Bender and Taylor, "Culture and Architecture," 216, and Orrick Johns, "Architects Dream of a Pinnacle City," *New York Times Magazine*, Dec. 28, 1924, 10.

87. Ferriss, *Metropolis of Tomorrow*, 15, 16, 46, 62, 109, 110; Bender and Taylor, "Culture and Architecture," 216, 212–16.

88. Following New York's example, Chicago made the switch from flat height limits to the setback formula in 1923. The city's previous height ordinance, which put a 264-foot limit on buildings while permitting *unoccupied* towers up to 400 feet, proved to be unworkable. Architectural historian Katherine Solomonson has argued that pressure to raise the height limit increased during the Chicago Tribune competition in 1922 because the company considered the 400-foot limit to be "commercially irksome and artistically deadening," preventing them from creating the tallest *and* most beautiful skyscraper in the world. Shortly after the competition, the city adopted a new setback ordinance (Katherine Solomonson, email to author). See Katherine Solomonson, *The Chicago Tribune Tower Competition: Skyscraper Design and Cultural Change in the 1920s* (New York: Cambridge Univ. Press, 2001). In addition to permitting building projects with "the utmost in rentable space," the new ordinance promised to be an aesthetic boon. As architect Arnold Rebori observed in 1925, "Chicago's zoning law . . . opens up a new vein rich in architectural possibilities." See A. N. Rebori, "Zoning Skyscrapers in Chicago," *Architectural Record* 58 (July 1925):88–90.

The combination of aesthetics and economics also persuaded Bostonians to abandon their height limits in favor of the New York formula. Boston's consensus for the 125-foot height limit unraveled by the mid-1920s as builders demanded more rentable space and architects praised the architectural possibilities of the sculpted skyscraper. Encouraged by the results of the New York ordinance, the city finally adopted a setback zoning envelope in 1928. See Holleran, "Boston's 'Sacred Skyline,' " 571, 575–9.

89. Boyd, "New York Zoning Resolution," 217, and Revell, "The Road to *Euclid v. Ambler*."

90. Newman F. Baker, "Aesthetic Zoning Regulations," *Michigan Law Review* 25 (Dec. 1926):136, 139.

91. Morton Keller, *Regulating A New Economy: Public Policy and Economic Change in America, 1900–1933* (Cambridge, MA: Harvard University Press, 1990), esp. 43–85, 171–91; Revell, *Building Gotham*.

3

The Female "Souls of the Skyscraper"

Lisa M. Fine

Between the former site of old Fort Dearborn and the present site of our newest Board of Trade there lies a restricted yet tumultuous territory through which during the course of the last fifty years, the rushing streams of commerce have worn many a deep and rugged chasm. Each of these canons [sic] is closed in by a long frontage of towering cliffs, and these soaring walls of brick and limestone and granite rise higher and higher with each succeeding year, according as the work of erosion at their bases goes onward – the work of that seething flood of carts, carriages, omnibuses, cabs, cars, messengers, shoppers, clerks and capitalists, which surges with increasing violence for every passing day... along with the Tacoma, the Monadnock, and a great host of other modern monsters – towers the Clifton. From the beer-hall in its basement to the barber-shop just under its roof the Clifton stands full eighteen stories tall. Its hundreds of windows glitter with the multitudinous letterings in gold and silver, and on summer afternoons its awnings flutter score on score in the tepid breezes that sometimes come up from Indiana. Four ladder-like constructions which rise skyward stage by stage promote the agility of the clambering hordes that swarm within it, and ten elevators – devices unknown to the real, aboriginal inhabitants – ameliorate the daily cliff-climbing for the frail of physique and the pressed for time.

The tribe inhabiting the Clifton is large and rather heterogeneous. All told, it numbers about four thousand souls. It includes bankers, lawyers, "promoters"; brokers in bonds, stocks, pork, oil, mortgages; real-estate people and railroad people and insurance people – life, fire, marine, accident; a host of principals, agents, middlemen, clerks, cashiers, stenographers, and errand-boys; and

Adapted from *The Souls of the Skyscraper: Female Clerical Workers in Chicago, 1870–1930* by Lisa M. Fine. Reprinted with permission of Temple Univ. Press I would like to thank Maureen Flanagan and Peter Berg for helpful readings of this article but take full responsibility for its shortcomings.

the necessary force of engineers, janitors, scrub-women, and elevator-hands.

All these thousands gather daily around their own great camp-fire. This fire heats the four big boilers under the pavement of the court which lies just behind, and it sends aloft a vast plume of smoke to mingle with those of other like communities that are settled round about. These same thousands may also gather – in installments – at their tribal feast, for the Clifton has it own lunch-counter just off one corner of the grand court, as well as a restaurant several floors higher up. The members of the tribe many also smoke the pipe of peace among themselves whenever so minded, for the Clifton has its own cigar-stand just within the principal entrance. Newspaper and periodicals, too, are sold at the same place. The warriors may also communicate their messages, hostile or friendly, to chiefs more of less remote; for there is a telegraph office in the corridor and a squad of messenger boys in wait close by. In a word, the Clifton aims to be complete within itself... [1]

When it first appeared on the scene in Chicago in the 1880s, the skyscraper could have hardly been associated with anything feminine. Its presence, shape, and size conjured up images of the male form and related characteristics of strength, empiricism, and system. Tall buildings were then and are now edifices to capitalism, industrialization, and urbanization. They were designed and paid for by men and in the minds of the architects, engineers, planners, intellectuals, and captains of industry involved in creating these potential money makers and workspaces, they were to be inhabited by men.[2] Nevertheless, the changing economy and city conspired to create an unexpected development by the late nineteenth century: the ubiquitous "business girl." She might have been a file clerk, a stenographer, a typewriter (the machine and the operator of the machine had the same appellation), a bookkeeper, or any combination of these; more than likely, she worked in one of these new skyscrapers downtown and her lot, many noted, was taking over not only the buildings but also the streets and the downtown business district itself.

As the ubiquitous business girl dashed from the street car to the office building, up the elevators and to her seat in front of the typewriter, contemporaries watched, worried, and warned of the outcome of this new development. One hundred years later, contemporary scholars in the fields of labor, urban, and architectural history have often overlooked her. In a recent work on the history of the late nineteenth century "Chicago School" of commercial architecture, the author describes skyscrapers, their offices, and the business districts in which they were found as masculine domains and the residential suburbs with detached houses and green spaces as feminine domains.[3] And in another otherwise wonderful book on space and architecture in Chicago, the author claims that the middle classes saw the downtown department stores as "public imitators of private consumption that facilitated respectable female presence in downtown." Skyscrapers, however, were "workplaces for white-collars and professionals, arenas for sales, advertising, and marketing."[4] Even though it has been acknowledged that skyscrapers were devised as "new workplaces and new symbols of a refined form of work," helping to redefine the downtown, "as an acceptable arena for both respectable gentlemen and ladies," there has been little acknowledgment or consideration of whether or how the female workers in these urban workplaces contributed to or abetted this development.[5]

By the 1890s, the female office worker had become a regular feature of the downtown business office. In fact, the appearance of the skyscraper containing the business office, the growth of white-collar work, the widespread use of office technologies like the typewriter and telephone, and the presence of the female office worker were concurrent and interrelated features of the late-nineteenth-century city. These two new features of city life – urban commercial architecture (the skyscraper) and the female white-collar worker – needed to be accommodated and reconciled to each other, and even if contemporary scholars have been blind to this, many who lived through the period between 1870 and 1930 in cities like Chicago understood that a new female worker and mixed-gender workspaces were distinctive features of these new urban edifices.[6]

The mixing of the sexes on urban streets, in public accommodations, and in business establishments challenged the standards governing appropriate and respectable (read middle class) gendered behavior, particularly the doctrine of "separate spheres." As the primarily young, white, single daughters of immigrants took advantage of the new occupational opportunity of clerical work, business leaders, reformers, social activists, and artists took notice and often issued warnings.[7] Young women themselves contemplated the changes wrought by their conquest of office work and space. In both fictional representations (such as novels, short stories, and films) and nonfictional (scholarly and professional) writings, the role, behavior, character, and future of the new "souls" of the city's skyscrapers were negotiated.

In the late nineteenth century, the size, anonymity, and newness of the work and experience in the skyscrapers were daunting to young women and scandalous to many social commentators who believed that business offices were no better than brothels and the female office workers who worked there were at best, girls on the make and at worst, prostitutes. In trade journals, the business girls themselves, who were determined to make it in their new jobs, recognized this negative press and enjoined their sisters to set a good example and change the nature of the business environment themselves. Over time, the presence of women did alter the image and reality of the downtown business office in the tall building. Female spaces carved out by the extension of the sexual division of labor within the office occupations made the experience of working in the skyscraper more commonplace and less dangerous. In the real world of the office workers as well as in the depictions of office work in film and novels, working in the skyscraper in the big city became a new opportunity for young women to make a decent living under good conditions, to experience "life," and maybe even to catch a rich husband. As these new "souls" left their distinctive mark and affected the history of the skyscraper, they contributed to creating a new acceptable place for women to work.

Chicago and the Skyscraper

During the 22 years between the Great Chicago Fire of 1871 and the World's Columbian Exposition of 1893, Chicago mushroomed into the second largest city in the United States. Between 1870 and 1890, its population increased from 298,977 to 1,098,570, while its area increased from 35.2 square miles to 178.1 square miles.[8] Important economic changes during these years accounted for this growth. Because of its advantageous location, rich hinterland, and connections to Eastern U.S. capital, Chicago became the commercial center of the Midwest by the 1860s and by the 1890s, a national manufacturing center.[9] In 1884, the *Chicago Tribune* commented on Chicago's "metamorphosis from a city of commerce to a city of manufacturing."[10] Chicago's growth coincided with the major waves of European migration, and the city's burgeoning manufacturing base found its workforce in the ever-increasing pool of foreigners migrating to the city. Young men and women from small towns and rural areas in the region also gravitated to Chicago in search of job opportunities and a more exciting life in the city.[11]

During this period, Chicago also became a significant service-oriented, merchandising, retail, and distribution center within the national market.[12] The downtown business district, the Loop, became the city's center of economic activities. An observer in 1910 stated that "within an area of less than a square mile there are found the railroad terminal and business offices, the big retail stores, the wholesale and jobbing businesses, the financial center, the main offices of the chief firms of the city, a considerable portion of the medical and dental professions, the legal profession, the city and county government, the post office, the courts, the leading social and political clubs, the hotels, theaters, Art Institute, principal libraries, the labor headquarters, and great number of lesser factors of city life."[13]

The catharsis and fear resulting from the 1871 fire, late-nineteenth-century growth and prosperity, the local architects, technological advances in building techniques, and the desire to speculate on downtown land all contributed to the emergence of this innovative and distinctive development of the 1880s and 1890s – tall urban commercial buildings, the first skyscrapers. The downtown prospered as office buildings and transportation and communication services completed the look of this urban landscape. Office building construction in the city that witnessed the construction of what many consider our nation's first skyscraper, boomed during the late nineteenth and early twentieth centuries.[14] In 1910 alone, 1.5 million square feet of office space was opened for use.[15] In 1906, the electrically powered street railroad system replaced the cable cars that had been in use for over 20 years. By 1910, these elevated trains, the "els," circled or looped around the central business district. This rapid transit system brought large numbers of workers into the central business district each day.[16] In addition, facilities such as post office service, electric lights, and telephones grew in response and contributed to the enlargement of the business sector.[17]

The central business district created precisely the conditions necessary to support the kinds of firms that would employ a large number of clerical workers. Manufacturing firms established downtown business offices where managers and planners conducted their activities. By the middle of the 1890s, Chicago had become the headquarter city of thirty-six of the country's largest industrial combinations. By 1920, Chicago was home to the second largest number of headquarter offices in the United States.[18] In addition, those firms involved in the purchase and resale of commodities, banking, credit, brokerage, investment, and insurance relied heavily on large numbers of clerical workers.[19]

Cultivating "Foreign Soil"

When women entered the new tall buildings of the downtown business district in Chicago, they were taking jobs and spaces that were understood by members of late-nineteenth-century society to be for men (Figure 18). Women's entrance into clerical positions directly challenged the commonly held belief that not only was the office a male space and office jobs men's work, but also all sorts of urban settings – elevators, street cars, restaurants, boarding houses – were inappropriate for respectable women. Women's entrance into these places set in motion a redefinition of the woman's sphere within the world of work and the city that continued throughout the twentieth century. But during these years, the outcome was never certain. Once given the opportunity to enter this previously forbidden world, women had to isolate their own space, forge a code of behavior, and legitimize their presence in these heretofore male environments.

This was necessary because women's entrance into offices posed a direct threat to a number of Victorian prescriptions for respectable behavior, not just for women, but

18. Circuit Supply Co., Chicago, 1910. Reprinted with permission of the Chicago Historical Society (890-B).

between the sexes. The prevailing belief in nineteenth and at least early twentieth-century society that men and women should naturally occupy "separate spheres" has been well documented.[20] This concept of separate spheres was intimately related to the concept of the sexual division of labor, originally evident in the preindustrial domestic economy in both agricultural and artisan households, and then translated into an industrial economy with the delineation of men's public sphere outside the home and women's private sphere within the home. (Of course, it is important to remember that these were ideals and not often adhered to in reality.) Under ideal economic circumstances, men's work would provide all the money necessary to support the family. The ability of the male head of household to make a "family wage" was a persistent goal of organized labor specifically and of all working men in general.[21] Women's proper and natural role, therefore, was to perform duties within the home.

Of course, women did not stay home. And, throughout the period, women's participation in the paid labor force and specifically office work increased (Figure 19). Because women had entered the paid labor force well before they entered clerical work, explanations existed to justify this activity out of their sphere. Women who worked outside the home could usually rely on three explanations for their activity. First, women could perform functions outside the home that they had traditionally performed within the home, usually within a closely monitored "family" setting. Second, women could engage in work outside the home on a temporary basis to help their families. Third, women could work outside the home for a limited period of time, usually for a few years before marriage. These rationalizations functioned to support, not threaten, the concept of the "family wage," the sexual division of labor, and the ideology of separate spheres.

Within the world of wage work, a number of other implicit rules also seemed to operate based upon these assumption about women's work. "Respectable" middle-class members of Victorian society believed that it was morally dangerous for unrelated men and women to work together in the same physical space. It was also considered unnatural for a man to work in a position subordinate to a woman and this allowed for restricting women's promotion within firms. Many members of nineteenth- and twentieth-century society saw women as secondary workers, providing wages that merely supplemented but did not support their families. The family wage idea justified the lower salaries and wages for women. Society also assumed that women were physically weaker than men, which limited the type of work possible as well as the time and length of shifts. Finally, many employers believed that since a female worker's primary commitment was to her present or future family, she was less willing to move geographically or make a long-term commitment to employment.[22]

Women's presence in clerical occupations posed a threat to many of these assumptions. Simply going to work placed women in unsupervised and potentially dangerous "public" settings. In an office, a woman would work closely with men. If no changes were made within the office hierarchy, she could attempt to work her way up through the ranks, posing the possibility of a woman supervising one or more men. If a woman did become a manager, supervisor, or even boss, her earning power would pose a direct threat to the ideal of the family wage. Her success at work might damage her "natural instinct" to abandon work for marriage. Furthermore, if a woman attempted to succeed within this setting, she would necessarily adopt certain behaviors that might "unsex" her or render her more masculine than feminine in the eyes of her co-workers, associates, and family.

The concern over the female clerical worker taking office positions in the skyscraper came from a number of quarters and was expressed in both nonfictional and fictional representations of these new workers and their workspaces. Prominent authorities on the position of women such as the editor of the *Ladies Home Journal* and Chicago's famous reformer Jane Addams saw the entrance of women into the offices of the tall buildings for office positions as a dangerous, unfortunate development. In 1900, the *Journal*'s editor baldly stated that it "is a simple fact that women have shown themselves naturally incompetent to fill a great many of the business positions which they have sought to occupy.... The vast number of majority of women in business to-day have absolutely no taste for it. They are there simply because necessity drove them to it." These women, the editor believed, will leave the "foreign soil" of the business office and return to their "natural sphere," domestic service, either in homes of their own or others.[23]

Jane Addams was concerned that the skyscraper office environment and the meager wages of many female workers created situations in which women accepted money and gifts in exchange for sexual favors. Despite the relatively better wages and working conditions in offices, female clerical workers were not exempted from the temptation to "fall into a vicious life from the sheer lack of social restraint." In 1912, Addams wrote, "perhaps no young woman is more exposed to the temptation of this sort than the one who works in an office where she may be the sole woman employed and where the relation to her employer and to her fellow-clerks is almost on a social basis.... The girl is without the wholesome social restraint afforded by the companionship of other working women and her isolation in itself constitutes a danger."[24]

Clara E. Laughlin's 1913 study of Chicago working girls confirmed these fears as she reported that many girls who worked in offices and stores supplemented their wages by receiving the attentions of men. "Many girls who work in offices and stores spend one or two or three nights a week in some 'resort' and earn the difference between shabby insufficiency and the ability to compete with or even dazzle the girls who work beside them." She reported on Eugenia, a high school and private business school graduate, who came from a small town

YEAR	TOTAL[a]	NUMBER OF MALES	PERCENT MALE	NUMBER OF FEMALES	PERCENT FEMALE
1870[b]	154	145	94.2	9	5.8
1880[b]	1,120	996	88.9	124	11.1
1890[c]	41,015	32,391	79.0	8,624	21.0
1900[d]	74,866	52,476	70.1	22,390	29.9
1910[e]	105,257	62,539	59.4	42,718	40.6
1920[f]	190,615	93,652	49.1	96,963	50.9
1930[g]	238,124	111,232	46.7	126,892	53.3

Source: U.S. Bureau of the Census, *1870 Census on Population Statistics*, vol. 1, p. 782; U.S. Bureau of the Census, *1880 Census of the Population of the United States*, vol. 1, p. 870; U.S. Bureau of the Census, *1890 Census of Population*, vol. 1, part 2, pps. 650–652; U.S. Bureau of the Census, *Special Report on Occupations, 1900*, pps. 516–523, and 558–560; U.S. Bureau of the Census, *Statistics of Women at Work, Based on Unpublished Information Derived from the Schedules of the 12th Census* (Washington: D.C., U.S. Government Printing Office, 1907), pps. 29, and 228–233; U.S. Bureau of the Census, *Population—Occupational Statistics, 1910*, vol. 4, pps. 165, and 544–547; U.S. Bureau of the Census, *Population—Occupations, 1920*, vol. 4, pps. 149, and 1076–1080; U.S. Bureau of the Census, *Population—Occupations by States, 1930*, vol. 4, pps. 423–429, 447–450, 456–457, and 463–465.

[a]All workers 10 years of age and over.

[b]Only included clerks and bookkeepers in manufacturing establishments and clerks and copyists, not specified. This figure is low because no clerks and bookkeepers in trade, transportation, or professional service, or stenographer-typists, were included.

[c]The 1890 census classified clerical workers by function rather than by type of establishment. The classification is: bookkeepers and accountants, clerical and copyists, and stenographers and typists. The 1890 count of female clerical workers is probably high because census collectors included some saleswomen in the category of clerks and copyists. See U.S. Bureau of the Census, *Statistics of Women at Work*, p. 100.

[d]Same classifications as 1890 census.

[e]The classifications used for 1910 were: bookkeepers, cashiers, and accountants; clerks (not in stores); and stenographers and typists.

[f]The classifications used for 1920 were: accountants and auditors; bookkeepers and cashiers; clerks (except in stores); and stenographers and typists.

[g]The classifications used in 1930 were: bookkeepers, cashiers, and accountants; clerks (except in stores); and stenographers and typists.

19. Number and Percentage of Male and Female Clerical Workers in Chicago, 1870–1930. From Lisa M. Fine, *Souls of the Skyscraper*, 30. Reprinted with permission of Temple Univ. Press.

to earn her living as a stenographer in the city. She answered an advertisement from the Union Novelty Company. The office was overwhelmingly masculine, menacing, and messy. "Inside were two men. The office was scantily furnished. There was a cheap roll-top desk . . . a giant cuspidor, a swivel chair, and two others that look like stray members of an erstwhile dining-room set. Smoking and aiming at the cuspidor seemed to be the only business of the place; and while the smoke was voluminous, the other half of the enterprise evidenced some lack of expertness."[25]

Other writers in the technical journals concerned with office work practice believed that even if women were not helpless victims and men hopeless lechers, the proximity between the two sexes made the businesslike running of the office almost impossible. Janette Egmont, who considered "the Woman Stenographer as a Moral Factor" for the *Phonographic World*, claimed that women held a share of responsibility for the problem that arose when women entered the office as well as the solution to these problems. Women "in an office are disconcerting. They demand more privileges than men." She also cautioned that "whenever a girl happens to be in an office, there is always too much discussion, and when there are two or three girls, the male clerks will compare the blonde with the brunette, and the discussion is apt to last a little too long." She enjoined these female pioneers to steer "well between the Scylla of prudery and Charybdis of familiarity, to raise the standard (and in this generation, even establish the standard) by which men will judge her sex in this profession."[26]

What was needed to answer these critics was some explanation of how women's supposedly innate morality could be of positive benefit to the office. Kathryn Chatoid, who briefly wrote a column in the *Phonographic World* called "The Fem-Sten's Retreat," asserted that female stenographers must "never lose sight of the fact that women were not employed because of their superior mentality but because their innate qualities admirably advantage them to certain work and make their presence desirable in an office." After all, "if a man were needed, [an] employer could secure the genuine article without very much trouble, and not be compelled to accept a poor imitation of masculine gender." Women's "habits, principles, neatness, quiet manner, and carefulness" were considered superior and "possessed in the highest degree by the womanly woman."[27]

Others in the trade journals concurred. Not only were women workers free from addiction to the "same habits as men," but they also tended to alter the atmosphere of an office by their very presence.[28] Women "bring with them order and refinement, banish tobacco smoke and profanity, and set an example of regularity and decency."[29] The female office worker, one commentator suggested, "has been a missionary," rendering offices more like parlors. Men have "modified their habits and dress, and the office has taken on a moral aspect."[30] The female clerical worker, enjoined to moralize the business office, was depicted as a new type of woman, no less feminine, but equipped to deflect threats to her nature. Her behavior and demeanor cast no doubt upon her womanliness as she not only "solved her individual part of the woman question," but also disproved the statement that business unsexes the woman or makes her less worthy of respect." "Womanliness," female clerical workers were counseled, "is their ornament and protection."[31]

Not everyone agreed. The usually young, white, educated, and unmarried woman engaging in office work in the skyscraper was an interesting phenomenon to late-nineteenth-century society. Her presence was tantalizing, challenging, provocative, dangerous, exciting, and "modern" to any number of artists, writers, and urban commentators.[32] Perhaps the most sensational depictions of these urban pioneers was seen in the early films. The earliest movies about female clerical workers presented them as women who, because of misfortune or worse, desire, had placed themselves in an immoral environment. These early films were short comedies that were shown in local, small nickelodeons, primarily to audiences with large percentages of working-class wives, mothers, and daughters. They were actually filmed vaudeville skits with simple, formulaic plots and characterizations. Nevertheless, these motion pictures potentially reached enormous numbers of people, providing those newly arrived immigrants (and their daughters who were the largest group of potential office workers in Chicago) with a powerful image of American working womanhood and the world of the office.[33]

In these films, the possibilities of crossing sex, age, and class boundaries in the office provided the raw material for the comedy.[34] *The Typewriter* (1902) best exemplifies this sort of film in its simplest form. It involves a young, pretty typist who first received the attention and then the embraces of her grey-haired boss. They are interrupted by a severe old woman, undoubtedly the boss's wife, who, brandishing an umbrella, drags her husband out by his ear. In the 1905 *Broker's Athletic Typewriter* (the title refers to the operator of the machine, not the machine itself), the boss misinterprets an innocent interaction between a young male employee and his typist and reprimands the young man. After the young man goes, the boss, another gray-haired man, makes advances to the typist, but she resists. She begins, in fact, to throw her boss around the room. While the boss is on the floor, his wife, yet another severe old woman wearing black, comes in and begins hitting him with yet another umbrella. In *She Meets with His Wife's Approval* (1902), the boss and his secretary conspire to trick his wife. A matronly, tall woman enters the business office to find her husband and his secretary hard at work. She scrutinizes the young woman, but is apparently mollified by the woman's appearance, and she leaves after her husband gives her some money. As soon as she is well gone, the secretary takes off a mask that she had been wearing on her face, and the boss and his secretary begin to kiss.

20. "How would you like my job?" Color postcard, ca. 1909. Collection of the author.

These cultural representations seem intended to both shock and to elicit laughter. A woman engaging in clerical work was a titillating prospect to the general public. Whether a young female resisted or encouraged the advances of her boss, some interaction between the two seemed inevitable. Whether she was cast as a victim or the vamp in the office setting, she was not a respectable, good girl. Yet, alternative "readings" or viewings were possible here. As Kathy Peiss states, "visually and thematically, these films constructed a notion of modern American womanhood that reaffirmed the flamboyant cultural style popular among many young American-born working women and...created new aspirations among the foreign-born."[35] The young, pretty typist or stenographer stood in sharp contrast to the doughty, unfashionably dressed, bespectacled matron married to the boss. Clearly, the young female office worker represented a new type of woman, not altogether acceptable, but not completely unsympathetic either (Figure 20).

This transitional status and what it represented about fundamental changes in the American social and cultural cityscape was the subject of an important realistic novel of the period, Henry Blake Fuller's *The Cliff Dwellers* (1893), a novel that tells of the web of relations among the business men and women who worked in one of the first tall buildings in Chicago. Set in Chicago during the 1890s, the novel comments on the period of explosive growth and social dislocation, the penalties of greed, and the false values of the rich and those aspiring to social station. Cornelia McNabb, the building's public stenographer, is one character designed to illustrate these themes. In the novel, Cornelia leaves her modest rural home in Wisconsin for the pleasures and opportunities of Chicago. She learns quickly that the only way for a woman to make a decent living and mix with the right sort of people is to become a stenographer. While she works as a waitress, she studies stenography and typewriting at a private business college; she also studies the ways of the rich and powerful in the society pages of the newspaper. As she tells the main character of the novel, "Now then, why shouldn't I be wearing heliotrope satin to dinner sometime? – if not under the name of Cornelia McNabb, then under some other as good or better. Anyway, I'm going to keep my hands as nice as I can; a girl never knows what she may have a chance to become. I don't imagine it will disfigure me much to operate a typewriter."[36]

Cornelia McNabb soon becomes the general public stenographer for many of the businesses in the Clifton office building. She learns the ways of society people through her contact with both the businessmen and their wives, who frequently visit their husbands on their downtown shopping excursions. One wife in particular, Mrs. Floyd, quite inadvertently provides Cornelia with pointers on costume, speech, and behavior. From this interaction with Chicago's society, Cornelia learns "what to do and what to avoid." These lessons pay off. Before long, Cornelia becomes a particular favorite with Mr. Brainard, an important banker, and his son. And ultimately, Cornelia's manipulations, intelligence, spunk, perseverance, and even her refreshing coarseness are rewarded. With his father's approval, Mr. Brainard's son marries Cornelia McNabb just a few months later.

To Henry Blake Fuller, this democracy, brought about by the mixing of various sorts of people, with their vulgar and enlightened desires, was not a good development. The organization of the workspace in the Clifton office building did not simply reorient vertically what had previously been horizontal. As the quote at the start of the essay reveals, with its evocation of tribes and campfires, the society in these buildings could be brutally primitive in a new way. This realistic novel was a cautionary tale, one that used the tall building as a symbol of the larger forces of urbanization, commercialization, and immigration that prompted the disruption of old hierarchical relationships while devising new social relations. A building such as the Clifton gave new meaning to the social climbing of a character like Cornelia McNabb.[37]

By the beginning of the twentieth century, writers in the *Phonographic World*, the most important trade journal for office practice, noted how the appearance of female clerical workers had become more respectable over the years. Female clerical workers had been the "butt of jokes... receiving the fond caresses of her elderly employer;... a successful adventuress," who "used rouge, bleached her hair; she winked at strange drummers who came into the boss's office to sell dime bills of codfish or pig iron; she flirted outrageously with the bald-headed bookkeeper; she accepted caramels from the office-boy, the janitor, the letter-carrier, and the elevator man." According to one writer, however, this sensational depiction was thankfully changing to a proper image of the female clerical worker as "Americanism in skirts!"[38]

The short stories that appeared in the *Phonographic World* between 1887 and 1907, many written by women, were included for the enjoyment and profit of their readers, mostly female office workers.[39] Many of them served didactic functions, instructing the new arrival to foreign soil on how to act, survive, and even prosper under these circumstances. These stories carried important messages: if a woman conducted herself in a refined, dignified, feminine manner, if she worked diligently and seriously, and if she attempted to serve her boss and others less fortunate than she, then she would not only gain acceptance and respect in the world of the office but also earn more responsibility and money. The relationship between a female office worker and her boss did not have to pose a problem as long as she did not relinquish her "womanliness, ornament and protection." In the stories without romances, we see good girls doing good deeds and receiving their just reward in success at work. A minority of the short stories playfully explored, in a nonsensational, nonthreatening way, the new romantic possibilities opened to both men and women when women entered offices in tall buildings to work.

Martha Ellsbeth's "For the Sake of the Office" (May 1902) exemplifies this type of short fiction. Stylish and competent as chief clerk, Miss Middleton is reprimanded by the business manager, Mr. Grantly. For the second time, he has had to warn her away from having contact with Mr. McAllister, a married man. He admits that

> yesterday afternoon I was in an office directly opposite this, across the court. From where I was, Miss Middleton, I could see you distinctly as you sat at your window, and I also had a partial view of McAllister's window on the right of the court ... I was angry and shocked at what I saw ... You were in full view of all the offices on the other side, but seemed oblivious to the fact. I saw you first lean out of the window and smile. You then waved your handkerchief in response to one waved at you from McAllister's window, and beckoned. Then – I saw it with my own eyes – you began to throw kisses at him. I was astounded – I had always considered you so – [40]

The melodrama that follows further sets up the sight gag and the misunderstandings possible in the courts of the new office buildings.[41] As the discharged clerk leaves, the manager admits his love and his raging jealousy to which Miss Middleton, the clerk, blushingly admits that the man she had been consorting with is her brother-in-law and the kisses blown across the building were to his and her sister's baby, obviously not visible to Mr. Grantly from his vantage point. Meetings, melodrama, misunderstandings, and love – all made possible by the tall building and its new inhabitant, the business girl.

Women and Their Work in Tall Buildings

In the real world, not all women were comfortable in these new jobs in the tall buildings. In 1885, Isabel Wallace took a temporary position as a copyist in an office in Chicago, where her uncle worked. She apparently took the position to supply her mother with some needed cash. In letters to her mother, she described the atmosphere in this office as essentially pleasant, and yet she never enjoyed the experience. Even though "the desks are comfortable, the chairs, etc. light, good, and room well heated," and "there seemed a very pleasant set of ladies," Isabel claimed she "felt like somebody else all day. Out of my element and sphere somehow. It made me feel less womanly and somehow as if I was doing something I didn't approve of. I suppose," Isabel continued, "it's because it's in the Court House and in an office."[42]

Even though a small number of women during the 1870s and 1880s did copying work as Isabel Wallace had done, most female office workers from the 1880s onward took advantage of new jobs created by the invention and widespread adoption of the typewriter, the most important of which was the stenographer-typist, sometimes referred to as the business or commercial stenographer or simply the stenographer. Stenographers could have varied work experiences within the skyscraper. Stenographers and typists were distinguished from earlier female office workers such as copyists because of the requirement of some advanced training beyond basic literacy and writing skills. The stenographers and typists elected to train in these areas with the express intention of taking these new jobs.[43]

A small group of stenographers – usually older, more experienced, more frequently married, and/or with dependents – were often established as independent entrepreneurs in tall buildings. They, like our fictional Cornelia McNabb, were the buildings' public stenographers. In firms, in partnerships, or as individuals, they worked in their own rooms in an office building and took in work from the various establishments in the building. They billed their services by the hour and the volume of work done. One such stenographer, Astrid Rosing, recalled how her start as a stenographer helped her ultimately to run her own company. She reported that "it was the year after the panic [either 1893 or 1907] – I was in my early twenties then – that I rented an office in the Rookery Building, hired a stenographer and myself, went out after business from dealers, contractors, and large manufacturers." Astrid Rosing claimed that when she started, her greatest obstacle, "despite the small amount of initial capital and hard times, was that I was young and a woman." By 1921, when this article about her life appeared, much had changed. "Today, that [working as a stenographer] wouldn't seem so unusual, but then, girls were not doing such things."[44]

Most young women who entered offices in tall buildings during the end of the nineteenth century did so as stenographer-typists in a variety of business and professional offices (Figure 21). Effie Jones exemplifies the experience. In 1890, Effie left her Iowa home for Chicago. She lived in a boarding house west of the Loop, and upon arriving, she took a course in a business college to learn stenography and typewriting. Her first position was in an import agent's office in the Loop. Soon after, she wrote her father, and in contrast to Isabel Wallace, Effie described her work and setting quite favorably. She began as a substitute stenographer, as the usual male stenographer was on a two-week vacation. She wrote, "I write about twenty-five letters a day, and address the envelopes, and that is all. The office boy folds and seals the letters after they look them over and they do their own copying, so it is a very easy position. They only pay me $6.00 a week, but say they will pay me more next week if I suit them." Perhaps they were ambivalent about Effie because "they always had a man before, and they said they did not know whether a lady would do or not, but," Effie believed, "I think I will do just as well." Effie did not feel at all uncomfortable in the space; she reported that the "office is very nice and I have a nice desk right by the window. We are opposite the Post Office and I amuse myself looking at the people who are always around there, when I am not busy."[45]

Two years later we find Effie Jones working at a demanding yet satisfying job as a stenographer in a law office on LaSalle across the street from City Hall. Because of the adoption of office technology, the work has become even more intense, but Effie seems to enjoy the challenge. She describes one particularly busy period

> as positively amusing. Every desk in this office is connected with electric bells and speaking tubes with every other desk, and I would be in one room, writing away for dear life, and would hear my bell going. Then would come an ominous silence, then a head would be poked into the room where I was, "Going to keep Miss Jones long?" "Yes, been waiting all day for her, and how I am going to finish this." "Well, Miss Jones, you done in to my room as soon as you are through there" and before I would finish there, I would have a date or two made in some of the other rooms.[46]

The years of working had not made Effie Jones uncomfortable, bitter, or tired, but worldly and enthusiastic about the world around her. She rapturously and in great detail described her participation in the festivities for the World's Columbian Exposition and her adventures in the city with her friends: "All the high office buildings, with their hundreds of windows, had flags in every window, and the

21. Auditor's office, Bowman Dairy Co., 1912. Reprinted with permission of the Chicago Historical Society (86:49 B2F4).

effect was beautiful."[47] She acknowledged the flirtatiousness of the young lawyers in her office and took it upon herself to protect her young assistant from "the frivolity of mankind in general." She was not, however, above a little flirtation herself. Similiar to the short story "For the Sake of the Office" described earlier, Effie describes a flirtation made possible by the court in her office building. She ends a letter to her mother, "By the way, I must tell you of the fun I have been having. You remember the first letter I wrote you after I came here? You remember I said there was a fellow on the floor above – across the court – who smiled on me? Well, he met me on the street a few days afterward and spoke – but I hadn't been introduced, so gave him the cut direct. A few days afterward he came into the office and had McCartney introduce him. Since then he watches until I start out to lunch, or to go home, and then goes down in the elevator with me, and walks as far as he can with me. He imagines he is more than 'rushing a flirtation' but it will be sometime before I fall in love with him. I just happened to think of it, for he is sitting at the window watching me now."[48] Even though the correspondence does not allow us to determine whether anything developed with this gentleman, the final letter from the 1920s reveals that Effie was a happily married housewife and mother.

Women's invasion and capture of stenography-typing positions had a profound impact on women's work experiences as offices began to systematize their work processes and adopt business machines. As office workforces increased in size and began to drain more of the profits of firms, managers sought to increase the productivity and profitability of their office employees. The functions of the stenographer-typist were sometimes divided into smaller actions that were measured, separated from individual bosses in pools of workers, and paid for by piece rates rather than by straight salaries. Although it is unlikely that even a majority of those firms employing office workers systematically incorporated these

22. Male office space, Pullman Co., Chicago, 1916. Reprinted with permission of the Chicago Historical Society (P. 18774).

principles into their office practices, efficiency in office design and work flow was undoubtedly a popular goal among managers as early as the 1910s. Attention to efficiency and the rational flow of work created a consciousness among office managers about the interior space of offices. The rationalized office reflected not only the economic exigencies of the bureaucratized firm, but also the rank and status of the workers involved, as these characteristics were informed by assumptions about gender. Some office workers remained in spaces with both sexes, but many also found themselves in "pools" of machine tenders who most often were all women (Figures 22 and 23).[49]

"Ancient Barriers" Felled

Less than a decade after Jane Addams warned young women of the dangers and difficulties of clerical work, female clerical workers had become a commonplace feature of the business office, and institutional accommodations suited to the needs of the female clerical worker began to appear throughout the city. In 1923, the journal of Chicago's business community, *Chicago Commerce*, ran a story that highlighted the fifty-year history of the typewriter. The anonymous writer believed not only that the typewriter had improved business methods, but also that it had contributed greatly to the "economic emancipation" of women. "The typist blazed the path by which other women entered every department of business." The entrance of the girl stenographer and typist into the business world felled "ancient barriers."[50]

The rapid increase in the number of women engaging in a wide variety of clerical occupations after 1910 prompted many members of private and public civic and reform organizations concerned with the physical and moral health of working women to redefine the nature of their services. By the late teens and early 1920s, young women were no longer considered in need of charity (or the object of ridicule), but of guidance.[51] The services provided by these organizations not only helped to "conventionalize" the lives of Chicago's clerical workers, but also revealed how the leaders of these organizations defined the needs of this

23. Female office space, Pullman Co., Chicago, 1916. Reprinted with permission of the Chicago Historical Society (P. 19553).

new occupational group. Female office workers were now regarded as permanent fixtures of the downtown business district.

Safe, affordable, and respectable housing for women away from their families was the concern of many organizations. Between 1870 and 1930, the number of working women living on their own increased, particularly during the World's Columbian Exposition and World War I. Generally, three options were available to working women: boarding with a family, renting a room in a lodging house, or living in a residential club. Although most independent working women lived in lodging houses and rooming houses, residential clubs founded and sponsored by a myriad of groups became popular among working women during these decades.[52]

Another concern was the atmosphere of some sections of the downtown where saloons were found in abundance. "Virtually every street and most of the intersections had at least one bar, and some blocks seemed to be given over completely to drinking purposes." Bars often offered modest free lunches with their main fare, which may have been an incentive for office workers on limited budgets to frequent these establishments. According to Perry Duis, who wrote on public drinking in Chicago, "concern with the well-being of lunching women had fostered a rapid increase in the number of tearooms near the turn of the century."[53]

Many groups concerned with the life of the working woman began to provide a wide variety of other social services to the business woman who worked in the Loop. Reformers believed that these women needed safe, respectable, inexpensive eateries; restrooms where they could meet friends during and after the workday; organized recreational, cultural, and educational activities; and an outlet enabling business women to serve each other and the community in general.

The Eleanor Association, a privately funded social service organization founded by Ina Law

Robertson to ease the transition of working girls to the city, for example, offered various services to business women who did not live in the association's residences.[54] In addition to the six residences the organization ultimately offered working women, the association's leaders met the immediate needs of the business women away from home by providing refuge during the working day at the Central Eleanor Club located in the Loop. In 1918, after moving to larger quarters, the club's membership increased to 2,000 "self supporting business girls," who could eat lunch or dinner at the club, take courses in business English, commercial law, rhetoric, literature, gymnastic dancing, dramatics, chorus, or French, attend lectures on political or cultural topics, or participate in the Eleanor organization through the fellowship, vocational guidance, finance and membership, or civics committees. These committees functioned not only to provide services to business women in need but also to offer an opportunity for successful business women to help their less fortunate sisters.

The Chicago Woman's City Club, a club of upper- and middle-class women involved in a variety of civic activities, also supplied services for the business woman who worked in the Loop. Starting in 1917, the club opened its rooms, with a chaperone on hand, between 5:00 and 9:00 p.m. for any young people who wished to keep appointments or rest until time for their evening appointment. In addition, the board of directors for the club decided to hold a meeting one evening a week each month "for the benefit of business and professional women who... are unable to attend the noon meetings."[55] In 1922, the club oriented its services even more directly to the needs of business women. The rooms of the club were opened all day and business women were encouraged to take advantage of the magazines and books available in the "civic library." The club offered restrooms where business women could "wash-up" after leaving the office and an inexpensive cafeteria "to which she can feel proud to invite her friends." The club also offered talks and lectures on civic and political issues during the noon hour and after 5:00 p.m. so that the business women could take advantage of them.[56]

The Chicago Woman's City Club also encouraged business women to become involved in civic issues through its Young Woman's Auxiliary. Founded in 1921, these groups, located throughout the city and suburbs, consisted of 500 business girls whom the leaders of the club described as "potential citizens of the city," who "have not had the advantage of a complete education, nor have they ever been reached before by any organization of civic interest." The threefold objective of the organization was "service, education, and recreation." Recreation, the club leaders decided, was the easiest way to reach these girls. Not only would wholesome recreation relieve the stress and strain of their labor, but it would also "teach them how to find the right kind of recreation, instead of leaving them to the prey of commercialized amusements."[57]

Perhaps the organization that changed the most in response to the appearance of the female office worker in the business district was the Young Women's Christian Association. Starting in 1917, the National Board of the Young Women's Christian Association (YWCA) began acknowledging the need to direct attention and services to the business woman. A writer in the association's journal rhetorically asked her readers, "Have we given enough consideration to the part the women downtown have in creating the atmosphere of the town?" and answered that "the signs of the times indicate that the hosts of earnest, efficient business women are about to come into their own. Their entrance into civic life in other than its commercial phases is going to mean a very wholesome stimulus."[58] At the

National Convention of the YWCA in 1922, 100 business women of the association met for what they referred to as their "Continental Congress," designed to "put the business girls on the map." These women discussed the special needs and desires of the business women of the association, and more importantly, sparked the formation of business and professional women's organizations throughout the country.[59]

In 1923, the Chicago YWCA moved its employment bureau from the central YWCA residence just south of the Loop to the central branch in the middle of the Loop. Annie Trotter, the director of the employment bureau, apparently orchestrated this move as a way to better serve the needs of business women.[60] Trotter reported that at its former location, "the major work had been supplying families with governesses and children's nurses." When the bureau moved, however, "great numbers of applicants for business positions crowded the waiting room daily," and "it soon became apparent that a reorganization of the Bureau was imperative to meet the needs of the new clientele."[61] The employment bureau stopped its placement service for domestic positions and focused on office positions, institutional positions for middle-aged women, and dissemination of vocational information. By 1924, 92 percent of the placements from the YWCA employment bureau were in business firms,[62] and most of the women taking courses at the central branch were business women who worked in the Loop.[63] The central club's program was a mix of what the club leaders wished to teach its new constituency and what business women themselves desired. It included social and recreational activities such as courses in personality, dramatics, ukulele, citizenship, vocational education, and world fellowship and "talks on suitable dress, business etiquette, and other topics of practical appeal to business girls."[64]

"A Taste for a Daily Going Out into the World"

In 1919, a resident in a women's boarding house provided by the Eleanor Association in Chicago wrote that "no matter how independent the woman, a home is the thing to which she looks forward. But the office experience of many of these girls will create a taste for a daily going out into the world.... There is a satisfaction and contentment in the triumphs and trials of earning one's bread that is not to be gained in the dependency on human affection; and numberless women are now enjoying making the wheels turn noiselessly in some office who in other decades got their satisfaction from a kitchen or apartment."[65] Women worked in the offices in Chicago's tall buildings from the very beginning. Whether it was an economic necessity or a desire for independence, given the prevailing gender system, taking an office job was a contested development. It was also not a one-sided development. Whether feared or lauded, women's presence in the skyscraper changed the way late-nineteenth-century society thought about the downtown business district, the urban workspace, and the nature of women's work. As Carl Sandburg reminded his readers nearly 100 years ago,

> Ten-dollar-a-week stenographers take letters from corporation officers, lawyers, efficiency engineers, and tons of letters go bundled from the building to all ends of the earth.
>
> Smiles and tears of each office girl go into the soul of the building just the same as the master men who rule the building.[66]

The smiles and tears of those office girls changed the skyscraper forever.

NOTES

1. Henry Blake Fuller, *The Cliff Dwellers* (NJ: Gregg Press, 1893), 1, 4–5.

2. According to Daniel Bluestone, "Skyscrapers are best understood as part of a larger cultural reformulation of urban commerce . . . a downtown commercial space and a workplace." See Bluestone, *Constructing Chicago* (New Haven, NJ: Yale Univ. Press, 1991), 108.

3. Arnold Lewis, "The Domain of Women," Chap. 7 in *An Early Encounter with Tomorrow: Europeans, Chicago's Loop, and the World's Columbian Exposition* (Urbana, IL: Univ. of Illinois Press, 1997).

4. Bluestone, *Constructing Chicago*, 145.

5. Bluestone, *Constructing Chicago*, 115, 143. Other important works on women and office work include Cindy Sondik Aron, *Ladies and Gentlemen of the Civil Service: Middle Class Workers in Victorian America* (New York: Oxford, 1987); Margery Davies, *Woman's Place Is at the Typewriter: Office Work and Office Workers, 1870–1930* (Philadelphia: Temple Univ. Press, 1982); Ileen A. DeVault, *Sons and Daughters of Labor: Class and Clerical Work in Pittsburgh* (Ithaca, NY: Cornell Univ. Press, 1990); Angel Kwolek-Folland, *Engendering Business: Men and Women in the Corporate Office, 1870–1930* (Baltimore: Johns Hopkins Univ. Press, 1994.); Elyce J. Rotella, *From Home to Office: U.S. Women at Work, 1870–1930* (Ann Arbor, MI: UMI Research Press, 1981); and Sharon Hartman Strom, *Beyond the Typewriter: Gender, Class, and the Origins of Modern American Office Work, 1900–1930* (Urbana, IL: Univ. of Illinois Press, 1992).

6. On how clerk jobs in the federal bureaucracy underwent this transition from male-only to mixed-gender workspaces and the sexual politics this created see Aron, Chap. 7 in *Ladies and Gentlemen of the Civil Service*.

7. Lisa M. Fine, *Souls of the Skyscraper: Female Clerical Workers in Chicago, 1870–1930* (Philadelphia: Temple Univ. Press, 1990), 33, Table 4.

8. Wesley G. Skogan, *Chicago Since 1840: A Time Series Data Handbook* (Urbana, IL: Institute of Government and Public Affairs, Univ. of Illinois, 1976), Table 1. For a rich, wonderful environmental, economic, and cultural history of Chicago, see William Cronon, *Nature's Metropolis: Chicago and the Great West* (New York: Norton, 1991).

9. Bessie Louise Pierce, *A History of Chicago*, vol. 2 (New York: Knopf, 1937), 77. See also Elmer A. Riley, "The Development of Chicago and Vicinity as a Manufacturing Center Prior to 1880" (Ph.D. diss., Univ. of Chicago, 1911); Allan Pred, *The Spacial Dynamics of United States Industrial Growth, 1800–1914: Interpretive and Theoretical Essays* (Cambridge, MA: MIT Press, 1966), 54; Carl Abbott, *Boosters and Businessmen: Popular Economic Thought and Urban Growth in the Antebellum Middle West* (Westport, CT: Greenwood Press, 1981); David Ward, *Cities and Immigrants: A Geography of Change in Nineteenth Century America* (New York: Oxford, 1971), 36–7; Earl Shepard Johnson, "The Natural History of the Central Business District with Particular Reference to Chicago" (Ph.D. diss., Univ. of Chicago, 1941), 9.

10. Quoted in Pierce, *History of Chicago*, vol. 3, 145.

11. Pierce, *History of Chicago*, vol. 3, 21–2, and Ward, *Cities and Immigrants*, 78.

12. N. S. B. Gras, "Development of a Metropolitan Economy in Europe and America," *American Historical Review* 27 (1922):702–5; James Heilbrum, *Urban Economics and Public Policy* (New York: St. Martin's Press, 1974), 33; Ward, *Cities and Immigrants*, 94.

13. As quoted in Harold Mayer and Richard Wade, *Chicago: Growth of a Metropolis* (Chicago: Univ. of Chicago Press, 1969), 226.

14. Frank A. Randall, *History of the Development of Building Construction in Chicago* (Urbana, IL: University of Illinois Press, 1949), 11; S. Ferdinand Howe, *Chicago: Commerce, Manufacturing, Banking, and Transportation Facilities* (Chicago: S. Ferdinand Howe, 1884), 8; Heilbrun, *Urban Economics*, 32. See also Bluestone, *Constructing Chicago*, Chap. 4; Carl W. Condit, *The Chicago School of Architecture* (Chicago: Univ. of Chicago Press, 1964); George H. Douglas, *Skyscrapers: A Social History of the Very Tall Building in America* (Jefferson, NC: McFarland, 1996), Chap. 2; Kenneth Turney Gibbs, *Business Architectural Imagery in America, 1870–1930* (Ann Arbor, MI: UMI Research Press, 1984); Lewis, *An Early Encounter with Tomorrow*; and Donald L. Miller, *City of the Century: The Epic of Chicago and the Making of America* (New York: Simon and Schuster, 1996), Chap. 10.

15. Randall, *History of the Development*, 11; Carl W. Condit, *Chicago, 1910–1929: Building, Planning, and Urban Technology* (Chicago: Univ. of Chicago Press, 1973), 89.

16. Mayer and Wade, *Chicago*, 214.

17. A. T. Andreas, *History of Chicago* (Chicago: A.T. Andreas Publishers, 1884), 554; and, Pierce, *A History of Chicago*, vol. 3, 224–30.

18. Johnson, "The Natural History," 259, 376.

19. Harry Braverman, *Labor and Monopoly Capital: The Degradation of Work in the Twentieth Century* (New York: Monthly Review Press, 1974), 300.

20. For the standard works see Alice Kessler-Harris, *Out to Work: A History of Wage Earning Women in the United States* (New York: Oxford Univ. Press, 1982); Nancy Cott, *The Bonds of Womanhood: "Woman's Sphere" in New England, 1780–1835* (New Haven, CT: Yale Univ. Press, 1977); Kathryn Kish Sklar, *Catherine Beecher: A Study in American Domesticity* (New York: Norton, 1973); Carroll Smith-Rosenberg,

"The Female World of Love and Ritual: Relations Between Women in Nineteenth-Century America," *Signs* 1(Autumn 1975):19; and Jeanne Boydston, *Home and Work* (New York: Oxford Univ. Press, 1990).

21. The most recent work addressing the issues of the family wage and living wage ideals is Lawrence B. Glickman, *A Living Wage: American Workers and the Making of Consumer Society* (Ithaca, NY: Cornell Univ. Press, 1997).

22. These ideas were formed by my general reading in the literature on the sex-typing of occupations. See, for example, Valerie Kincade Oppenheimer, "The Sex-Labeling of Jobs," *Industrial Relations* (May 1969), 219; Sam Cohn, *The Process of Occupational Sex-Typing: The Feminization of Clerical Labor in Great Britain* (Philadelphia: Temple Univ. Press, 1985); Barbara Reskin, ed., *Sex Segregation in the Workplace: Trends, Explanations, Remedies* (Washington, DC: National Academy Press, 1984); Shirley Dex, *The Sexual Division of Work: Conceptual Revolutions in the Social Sciences* (New York: St. Martin's Press, 1985); Julie A. Matthaei, *An Economic History of Women in America* (New York: Schocken Books, 1982); Barbara Reskin and Heidi Hartmann, eds., *Women's Work and Men's Work: Sex Segregation on the Job* (Washington, DC: National Academy Press, 1986); Martha Blaxall and Barbara Reagan, eds., *Women and the Workplace: The Implications of Occupation Segregation* (Chicago: Univ. of Chicago Press, 1976); and Ava Baron, ed., *Work Engendered: Toward a New History of American Labor* (Ithaca, NY: Cornell Univ. Press, 1991).

23. "The Return of the Business Woman," *Ladies Home Journal* (Mar. 1900), 16.

24. Jane Addams, *A New Conscience and an Ancient Evil* (New York: MacMillan, 1912), 213–14.

25. Clara E. Laughlin, *The Work-A-Day Girl: A Study of Present Day Conditions* (Chicago: Fleming H. Revill, 1913), 52, 107–24.

26. Janette Egmont, "The Women Stenographer as a Moral Factor," *Phonographic World* (July 1890):341; "Uncle Sam Prefers Male Stenographers," *Phonographic World* (Nov. 1911):222; and "Women in Government Service," *Gregg Writer* (Nov. 15, 1911):157.

27. Kathryn Chatoid, "Does Business Contaminate Women?" *Phonographic World* (Nov. 1900):140–1.

28. "The Efficiency of Women Stenographers," *Phonographic World* (May 1900):529.

29. S. S. Packard, "The Girl Amanuensis," *Phonographic World* (Oct. 1888):40–1.

30. W. N. Ferris, "The Old Education and the New," *Phonographic World* (Nov. 1902):398–401; see also, "Girl Stenographers and Their Employers," *Phonographic World* (Feb. 1891):184. See also Angel Kwolek-Folland, "The Domestic Office: Space, Status, and the Gendered Workplace," Chap. 4 in *Engendering Business: Men and Women in the Corporate Office, 1870–1930* (Baltimore: Johns Hopkins Univ. Press, 1994).

31. Egmont, "The Woman Stenographer as a Moral Factor," 341.

32. My book has a full discussion of many cases and types of cultural representations of the female office worker. I am merely highlighting those that were particularly sensitive to setting.

33. Kathy Peiss, *Cheap Amusements: Working Women and Leisure in Turn-of-the-Century New York* (Philadelphia: Temple Univ. Press, 1986), 139–62. I found this section on the gender images in the early films extremely helpful. See also Larry May, *Screening Out the Past: The Birth of Mass Culture and the Motion Picture Industry* (New York: Oxford, 1980), 147–8; and Roy Rosenzweig, *Eight Hours for What We Will: Workers and Leisure in an Industrial City, 1870–1920* (Cambridge: Cambridge Univ. Press, 1983), 191–208.

34. Peiss, *Cheap Amusements*, 156. I screened these early films at the Motion Picture, Broadcasting, and Recorded Sound Division of the Library of Congress. For summaries of these motion pictures, see Kemp R. Niver, *Motion Pictures from the Library of Congress Paper Print Collection, 1894–1912* (Berkeley, CA: Univ. of California Press, 1962); and Rita Horwitz and Harriet Harrison, *The George Kleine Collection of Early Motion Pictures in the Library of Congress: A Catalogue* (Washington, DC: Library of Congress, 1980).

35. Peiss, *Cheap Amusements*, 158. Peiss cites Elizabeth Ewen, "City Lights: Immigrant Women and the Rise of the Movies," *Signs* 5 suppl. (Spring 1980):S45–S65.

36. Fuller, *The Cliff Dwellers*, 70.

37. Even though I have presented my own reading of this work, two helpful sources on Fuller are Da Zheng, *Moral Economy and American Realistic Novels* (New York: Peter Lang, 1997) and Kenneth Scambray, *A Varied Harvest: The Life and Works of Henry Blake Fuller* (Pittsburgh: Univ. of Pittsburgh Press, 1987).

38. "The Typewriter Girl," *Phonographic World* (Mar. 1906):203–4; "Young Women Who Do Eat with Their Employers," *Phonographic World* (Nov. 1901):252–3.

39. Citations for dozens of short stories examined in my book are listed in Fine, *The Souls of the Skyscraper*, 218–19, fns. 43, 44.

40. Martha Ellsbeth, "For the Sake of the Office," *Typewriter and Phonographic World* 19 (May 1902):249–53.

41. Interior courts were common features of some of the first tall buildings in Chicago. See Bluestone, *Constructing Chicago*, 132–5.

42. Letter from Isabel Wallace to her mother, Nov. 23, 1885. Wallace–Dickey Family Papers, Illinois State Historical Society.

43. During this early period, most women (and men) learned these skills in private business colleges. See Janice Weiss, "Educating for Clerical Work: The Nineteenth Century Private Commercial School," *Journal of Social History* (Spring 1981):407; John L. Rury, "Vocationalism for Home and Work: Women's Education in the United States, 1880–1930," *History of Education Quarterly* 24 (Spring 1984):33–4; and Albie Frances Mrazek, "Development of Commercial Education in Chicago's Public Schools" (Master's thesis, Univ. of Chicago, 1938).

44. M. E. Chase, "From Stenographer to the Ownership of a $100,000 Business," *Fort Dearborn Magazine* (Dec. 1921):8. See also *Chicago Central Business Directory, 1908* (Chicago: Winter's Publishing Co., 1908), where stenographers' offices are listed by office building.

45. Letter from Effie Jones to her father William Griffith Jones, Aug. 11, 1890. William Griffith Jones Papers, 1854–1925, Iowa State Historical Society. I thank my friend Mary Neth for bringing these wonderful letters to my attention.

46. Letter from Effie Jones to her mother, Oct. 27, 1892.

47. Letter from Effie Jones to her mother, Oct. 27, 1892.

48. Letter from Effie Jones to her mother, Sept. 21, 1892, p. 4.

49. Strom, *Beyond the Typewriter*, Chap. 1; Margaret Hedstrom, "Automating the Office: Technology and Skill in Women's Clerical Work, 1940–1970," (Ph.D. diss., Univ. of Wisconsin-Madison, 1988), esp. Chap. 1; Braverman, *Labor and Monopoly Capital*; Davies, *Woman's Place Is at the Typewriter*.

50. "Will Celebrate the Jubilee of Typewriter," *Chicago Commerce* (July 21, 1923):13–14.

51. Joanne J. Meyerowitz, *Women Adrift: Independent Wage Earners in Chicago, 1880–1930* (Chicago: Univ. of Chicago Press, 1988). Meyerowitz also describes this shift in the focus of reformers. On the general efforts of middle-class white women reformers to respond to the challenges of the city, see Maureen A. Flanagan, "The City Profitable, the City Livable: Environmental Policy, Gender, and Power in Chicago in the 1910s," *Journal of Urban History* 22 (Jan. 1996):163–90; and Maureen A. Flanagan, "Gender and Urban Political Reform: The City Club and the Woman's City Club of Chicago in the Progressive Era," *American Historical Review* (Oct. 1990):1032–50.

52. Meyerowitz, *Women Adrift*, 46, 47.

53. Perry Duis, *The Saloon: Public Drinking in Chicago and Boston, 1880–1920* (Urbana, IL: Univ. of Illinois Press, 1983), 184–6.

54. *Eleanor Record* (Mar. 1918):14. For more on this organization, see my book as well as "Between Two Worlds: Business Women in a Chicago Boarding House," *Journal of Social History* (Spring 1986):511.

55. *Bulletin* (Feb. 1917): 1, Women's City Club of Chicago Collection.

56. "Club Privileges for the Business Woman," *Bulletin* (June 1922):41, Women's City Club of Chicago Collection.

57. Esther J. Wanner, "News of the Young Woman's Auxillary," *Bulletin* (July/Aug. 1922):63, Women's City Club of Chicago Collection.

58. Margaret E. O'Connell, "Business Women and the YWCA," *Association Monthly* (Jan. 1917):529.

59. "Business and Professional Women's Conference," *Association Monthly* (July 1922):354; YWCA of Chicago, *47th Annual Report* (1924), 25; YWCA of Chicago, "Business and Professional Women," *Report of the National Board of the YWCA of USA, 9th Annual Convention at Milwaukee, Wisconsin* (Apr. 21–28, 1926), 59.

60. YWCA of Chicago, *Minutes of the Board of Director's Meeting* (Nov. 9, 1922), 2.

61. YWCA of Chicago, *46th Annual Report* (1923), 21.

62. YWCA of Chicago, "The Girl and the Job," *The Tiny Y* (Dec. 1922):3; *Board of Director's Meeting* (Dec. 13, 1923), 2; *47th Annual Report* (1924), 17.

63. YWCA of Chicago, "Education," *44th Annual Report* (1921), 10.

64. YWCA of Chicago, "Central Branch," *45th Annual Report* (1922), 8; *Board of Director's Meeting* (Apr. 12, 1923), 4; "Business Courses," *The Tiny Y* (Jan. 1925):2; "Young Business Women's Club," *47th Annual Report* (1924), 25.

65. *Eleanor Record* (Jan. 1919):13.

66. Excerpt from "Skyscraper" in Carl Sandburg, *Chicago Poems* (New York: Holt, Rinehart and Winston, 1916). Copyright renewed 1944 by Carl Sandburg, reprinted by permission of Harcourt Brace Jovanovich, Inc.

PART TWO

IN THE IMAGE OF THE CLIENT

4

Type and Building Type

Newspaper/Office Buildings in Nineteenth-Century New York

Lee E. Gray

The London *Times* is, up to the present, issued from a dull, besmeared, unpretending pile of old and decayed bricks, and in one of the dingiest parts of that metropolis, while here the *World*, *Times*, *Clipper*, *Ledger*, and others, have already led off with costly and aspiring structures, and we understand that the N.Y. *Tribune* and *New Yorker Staats Zeitung*, with the *Courrier des Etats Unis*, propose shortly to construct their majestic literary temples, which we expect will cap the climax by taking the lead in architectural splendor.[1]

In the early twenty-first century, with an often bewildering quantity of information communicated across an equally complex array of media, it is perhaps difficult to imagine the importance of newspapers in the nineteenth century. Beginning in 1850, newspapers served as the principal purveyors of general news, commercial and business information, political propaganda, entertainment, and culture. During the 1860s and 1870s, New York City's newspapers also actively responded to the public's growing interest in architectural and urban issues. The papers featured increased coverage of new buildings, plans for future urban growth, and architectural editorials that ranged in topic from aesthetics to fireproof construction. Furthermore, the press did not restrict itself to simply reporting the news. Between 1858 and 1875, almost every newspaper publisher in the city constructed a new building, works that were often promoted as architectural models in terms of their aesthetic quality and technological innovations.[2]

These new buildings also represented a new architectural type, the newspaper/office building. This new building type combined the newspaper building – an established use type dependent on the latest technology – with the commercial office building, an emerging use type with a lesser reliance on technology. This merging of use types produced a series of buildings that contained some of the technological origins of the modern skyscraper. However, their primary technical innovations did not concern the development of the steel skeletal frame, the typical focus for most discussions of skyscraper technology. Instead, their focus was on the internal building systems necessary to a successful business operation such as communication systems, material transportation, and heating and ventilating systems. The exterior received attention with regard to the role of newspaper/office building as an exemplar of architectural taste.

Beginning in 1840, the city's newspapers began to occupy buildings along Park Row opposite City Hall and City Hall Park. These buildings gradually defined a triangular space formed by the irregular street pattern of Lower Manhattan. Although the space was not a true urban square, it nonetheless constituted a strong enough break in the street pattern for it to be readily perceived as a distinct urban space, which became known as Printing House Square. Newspapers sought this location in part because of its proximity to the political heart of the city for, although City Hall was one attraction, Tammany Hall, the New York Democratic party headquarters, was also located on Park Row. The Democratic party moved their headquarters in the late 1860s, and the building was renovated as the home of the *New York Sun*; but the site was further enhanced in the early 1870s by the construction of the new Post Office at the southern tip of City Hall Park. In fact, the city's papers played a critical role in determining the site of the Post Office, having lobbied for the nearby location that would increase the area's value and prestige.

The future architectural importance of Printing House Square was not evident in its modest beginnings. By the mid-nineteenth century most New York businesses were housed in buildings known as rookeries: multistory, functional boxes typically three to four stories high. They lacked aesthetic pretensions, having unarticulated exterior walls with a simple grid of window openings. Within this simple shell, the newspaper's operation was distributed according to pragmatic functional needs. The basement contained the mechanical operations, printing presses, and other equipment, often located in extensive underground vaults that extended beneath the adjacent sidewalks. The basement also housed the steam engines required to run the presses (in some instances the engines were located in a cellar below this level) and the vaults permitted the easy delivery of large rolls of paper through hatches in the sidewalks.

The main business office, known as a counting room, was located on the first floor to provide convenient access for customers. The chief editor's office was typically found on a floor above the counting room, as were additional offices for subeditors and workspaces for reporters. Placed as high in the building as possible – the preferred location was the top floor – was the composing room. This was where the paper was "put together," the lead type was set by hand into forms that were then transported to the press room in the basement. Extensive windows and skylights were required to provide the best possible light for the typesetters. Linking all of these spaces together was a centrally located, exposed mechanical core that included a hoist to carry the type forms between the composing and press rooms, smaller copy boxes that carried print samples to the editors, speaking tubes, bell annunciators, and heating and ventilation shafts.

This logical distribution of a paper's operation resulted in a use type that remained unchanged during the nineteenth century even as its architectural articulation changed dramatically. The early home of the *New York Tribune* illustrates the rookery version of the newspaper building type. Founded in 1841 by Horace

Greeley, the paper moved in 1843 to quarters on Nassau Street, a site at the center of Printing House Square. The Tribune Building burned in early February 1845, and Greeley decided to rebuild on the existing site. By the end of May the new building was complete.[3] It occupied both the original site and an additional corner lot on Spruce and Nassau streets and consisted of a basement level and five upper stories.[4] The basement contained the press room, the furnace and boiler rooms (located in a vault under Spruce Street), and the folding room, mail room, and vault for stereo-type plates (located under Nassau Street).[5] The *Tribune* publication and business offices were located on the first floor with the counting room occupying the corner. The first floor also housed the bookstore of William H. Graham and the "Law Book, Blank, and Stationary" store of Messrs. Jansen & Bell. The central mechanical core, which pierced the heart of the counting room, was "a perpendicular viaduct... with speaking pipes, copy boxes, and bells, running from the low ceiling through the center of the room, like the succulent branch of a banyon tree."[6] Offices for Greeley, other editors, and reporters were located in the upper stories. The composing room occupied the entire fifth floor, receiving light from three sides and from "ample" skylights.

The building's pragmatic nature reflected, in part, the personality of its founder as well as the character of the city's most common commercial building type. However, a rival appeared in 1851 in the person of Henry Raymond, the editor of the newly created *New York Times*, who quickly offered both journalistic competition and a new architectural vision for newspaper buildings. In early 1857, Raymond decided to construct a building specifically designed for his increasingly popular paper. In fact, the *Times* first proposed a radical notion to their competitors. When property adjacent to City Hall Park, at the intersection of Nassau Street, Spruce Street, and Park Row became available, they proposed that the *Herald*, *Tribune*, and *Times* purchase the entire site and erect a unified block of newspaper buildings.[7] Following the rejection of this proposal, the *Times* purchased the entire site and the resulting building defined the southern boundary of Printing House Square and marked the first departure from the rookery building type.

Construction began on May 1, 1857, and the building, designed by Thomas R. Jackson, was completed one year later.[8] The building consisted of a basement and five upper stories and it contained roughly 50,000 square feet of space with 29,000 square feet occupied by the *Times* and 21,000 square feet intended for commercial use. The building's size and substantial rental space for retail stores and commercial offices clearly set it apart from its predecessors and the *Time's* leading competitors: the Herald Building had only 12,250 square feet (with 875 square feet of leasable space) and the Tribune Building had 13,500 square feet (with 1,100 square feet of leasable space).

The design also expressed Raymond's awareness of the value of architectural effects. Known as the Times Block, the building featured elaborate facades on Park Row and Spruce Street to serve the paper's business office and the prime rental spaces, and a relatively plain facade on Nassau Street due to the narrowness of the street and the more utilitarian nature of this side of the building. Although it has been described by architectural historians as both a Romanesque variation of the commercial palace type and as "floridly Italianate," it is important to note that the *Times* refused to apply any stylistic label to its new building, declaring instead that "the architectural appearance of the building is singularly bold and striking, and though designed with a total disregard of classical models and artistic rules, the two principal facades display great inventive genius, and a most harmonious combination of apparently incongruous elements."[9]

However, perhaps the most telling descriptive term is the least obvious. The paper chose to call its new home the Times Block. The notion of a "block," a term that typically denotes a series of contiguous buildings, is reflected in the building's Spruce Street and Park Row facades. The division of both facades into three distinct components, albeit united by a consistent (if slightly ambiguous) theme, may have been an effort to reduce the visual scale of the building or an attempt to provide a clear architectural identity for the building's tenants (Figure 24).

Within this intriguing exterior, the diverse worlds of the metropolitan newspaper and the commercial office were both interwoven and segregated. By the 1850s, commercial buildings in New York also featured well-established patterns of use and internal zoning. The most valuable rental spaces were those nearest to the street with the first and second floors perceived as prime locations. The first floor had immediate access from the street, and the second floor, up a single flight of stairs, had a similar accessibility and the added advantage of placing users above the noise and dust of the street. Above the second floor, the attractiveness of the spaces decreased as the length of the climb increased.

In the Times Block the counting room was the only newspaper space located on the first floor. The remaining space was designed for retail businesses and the entire second and third stories were designed as office space, described as intended "chiefly for lawyers."[10] The merging of commercial and newspaper use types required the integration of the paper's mechanical systems (plumbing, heat and ventilation, communication, and vertical transportation) into the building's fabric. The exposed mechanical shaft found in older buildings now required concealment as the functional needs of the paper were not permitted to intrude into the world of the commercial office. However, while some systems were hidden (the press-form elevator, speaking tubes, etc.), others required extension into the rental spaces. The offices were supplied with steam heat and may have been furnished with running water, as most first-class offices had a washbasin.

The building's tenants encountered the newspaper's operation in the same discrete manner in which they benefited from its mechanical systems. The building was carefully zoned so that commercial tenants and their clients had limited contact with the paper's staff. Tenants used an entrance located on Park Row, which provided access to a lobby and main staircase. This stair extended to the second and third floors and to the *Times'* editorial offices on the fourth floor. A separate stairway on Nassau Street, used solely by *Times'* employees, provided access to the fifth-floor composing room. Thus, tenants could mingle with the paper's leadership and editorial staff while avoiding the press and composing room workers.

While the Times Block was clearly not a skyscraper, it did serve as an important precedent for later works. It was one of the first attempts to integrate, on a large scale, clerical, commercial, and newspaper activities. The specific mechanical needs of newspapers and the need for their discrete concealment hinted at the future complexity of the skyscraper. It also addressed a key aesthetic issue. The Times Block required an architectural expression that clearly represented the building's owner, reflecting the success and stability of the *New York Times*. However, this expression was also required to serve the needs of the building's many commercial tenants who sought an identifiable address without sacrificing their own identities. The building's somewhat fragmented facade reflected this latter concern just as the building's size and strategic site – at the confluence of three streets at the head of City Hall Park and Printing House Square – gave the building a dynamic setting.

In spite of the building's commercial success, there were no immediate imitators. The

Times' rivals delayed any future building plans in large part because they soon found their attention and resources focused on coverage of the American Civil War. However, following the war, New York entered an unprecedented, albeit short-lived, building boom. The papers reported in January 1867 that in the previous year, new building construction had increased dramatically.[11] While there was unanimous agreement that this building boom would continue, concerns were expressed about its impact on the growth of the city. All the city's papers published numerous articles on architectural issues and future growth, but only one attempted to promote a specific urban aesthetic. The *New York Herald* suggested that contemporary Paris and the planning efforts of Baron Georges-Eugène Haussmann provided the best urban model. In an editorial published on November 17, 1867, the paper asked the following questions:

24. New York Times Building, 1857–58. Views looking South, at the Spruce Street & Park Row facades. © Collection of The New-York Historical Society, Neg. 4851.

> Why should our architects persist in encouraging the whims that lead to the disfigurement of our principle [sic] streets by such a wide irregularity in the heights of the splendid marble buildings which are, one after the other, towering, like so many Babels, to the sky? Could not something like what the French call alignement be introduced in our street architecture that would secure the combined advantages of a general uniformity and of the utmost variety in detail?[12]

The *Herald* also offered its new building, built in 1865–67 by John Kellum, as an architectural exemplar. They described their building as "bearing a closer resemblance to the new Louvre, at Paris than, perhaps, to any other edifice known to the traveling public."[13] Travelers familiar with the Louvre may have questioned this claim. While its mansard roof followed current French fashion, Kellum's restrained facade lacked the plasticity and sculptural quality of its alleged inspiration (Figure 25).

The Herald Building was the first to follow the precedent set by the *Times* and it offered a variation on the direction implied by the earlier building. Its scale, visual clarity, and attendant urban vision suggested an alternative to future unbridled upward growth and to the earlier 'block' aesthetic. Although the *Herald* failed to persuade New York to adopt building height restrictions and embrace Haussmann's urban vision, it was persuasive in its presentation of the newspaper/office building as a coherent, unified architectural work. This presentation was enhanced by the building's prominent site at

25. New York Herald Building, 1865–67. © Collection of The New-York Historical Society, Neg. 33605a.

the intersection of Ann Street, Park Row, and Broadway. However, this location, one block south of the Times Block, placed it outside of Printing House Square; thus, it was not able to exert any direct influence on the development of that area.

The *Herald* restated its urban vision in 1893 with a new building designed by McKim, Mead, & White. Like its predecessor, this building promoted a different commercial aesthetic from its rivals; its form was derived from a Renaissance palazzo and it was emphatically not a skyscraper. Unlike its predecessor, this building had a significant urban impact on New York. Its site, the intersection of Sixth Avenue, Thirty-fourth Street, and Broadway, became known as Herald Square, giving the paper an urban presence that, in some ways, surpassed Printing House Square and was only equaled by the new New York Times Building of 1904.

While the *Herald* was completing its new home, another building effort was underway in the heart of Printing House Square, in the same block as the Tribune Building. This effort involved the literal transformation of an existing rookery into a newspaper/office building. In 1867, Charles A. Dana purchased old Tammany Hall with the intention of refurbishing it as the headquarters for the *New York Sun* and, when the renovation was completed in January 1868, it garnered high praise from the New York press. Although not a commercial structure, the building, built in 1811, possessed a rookery-like architectural character in its simple facades. This plain exterior was altered by the addition of a new fifth floor housed in a mansard roof, the refacing of the upper floors, and a new iron front on the first floor facing City Hall Park. The mansard roof also allowed the *Sun*, at least temporarily, to literally overshadow its nearest rival, the *New York Tribune*. In this architectural aspect and desire to physically dominate its surroundings, the building was a subtle harbinger of things to come.

As was common during this period, the *Sun* maintained an active presence on its building's exterior through a corner bulletin board where breaking news items were posted. Among the many items featured in 1868 were notices concerning the new home for the Equitable Life Assurance Society. Designed by Arthur Gilman and Edward Kendall (assisted by George Post), the Equitable Building clearly offered a new architectural paradigm for the commercial office building in its unprecedented height and use of passenger elevators. Of course, while it was the first office building to take advantage of this technology, the Equitable Building did not introduce these devices to New Yorkers. The passenger elevator had been present in New York's department stores and hotels for over a decade. In a similar fashion, the mechanical systems employed for heating, ventilation, and internal communication owed much of their development to their use in newspaper buildings. However, unlike the newspaper/office building, the Equitable Building utilized these new technologies in a completely clerical environment devoid of any manufacturing or industrial activities. The Equitable Building also presented a unified architectural expression that allowed the entire building to serve as a corporate symbol, perhaps following the precedent set by the Herald Building.

26. New Yorker Staats-Zeitung Building, 1872–73, on the right. The old Hall of Records is to the left. © Collection of The New-York Historical Society, Neg. 50918.

One of the first buildings to follow the Equitable was built for the *New Yorker Staats-Zeitung*. Established in 1834, the *Staats-Zeitung* by the 1870s had become the city's most successful foreign language newspaper. The new building, designed by Henry Fernbach and completed in 1873, occupied a large site at the junction of Center Street, Tryon Row, and Chatham Street with a combined street frontage of over 200 feet (60 feet along Center, 99 feet along Tryon Row, and 50 feet along Chatham). Its height, 100 feet from sidewalk to the top of the mansard roof, allowed it to tower over neighboring buildings (Figure 26). The new building consisted of a cellar, basement, four upper floors, and a fifth floor contained in a mansard roof. As with the Equitable Building, its height was made economically feasible by the passenger elevator. Although earlier newspaper/office buildings had utilized freight hoists, the Staats-Zeitung Building was the first to employ passenger elevators.

The elevators were integrated into the use pattern established by earlier newspaper/office buildings. The western half of the first floor was intended for banks and insurance companies and the western portion of the basement was perceived to be the ideal location for a "first-class restaurant." The entire second and third floors and half of the fourth floor were designed as rental office space. The main entrance, located on Tryon Row in the center pavilion, provided entry to a hall that divided the building in half and led to the main stair and passenger elevators located at the rear of the building. The hall separated commercial from newspaper spaces on the first floor and provided an impressive entrance sequence for businesses located in the upper floors.

The Staats-Zeitung Building set a new standard for newspaper/office buildings. Labeled a "mammoth printing house" by the New York press, it clearly marked the northern boundary of Printing House Square. Its scale was also a direct counter to the *Herald*'s call for restraint, and its success seemed to prove that size was important. Reinforcing this notion was the building that immediately followed, one that not only learned from this example, but also surpassed it in every way. Located between the Staats-Zeitung Building and the Times Block, adjacent to the refurbished Sun Building, was Horace Greeley's Tribune Building. By the late 1860s the building was commonly referred to as the "old rookery," a phrase that reflected its humble origins and its rustic occupant. Unfortunately, Greeley was not destined to occupy the building that replaced his old rookery. Although he did establish a building fund in 1870, Greeley died in late November 1872 and the planning of the *Tribune*'s new home was left to his successor, Whitelaw Reid.

Reid had joined the *Tribune* staff in 1868 and served as managing editor from 1869 to 1872. Following Greeley's death and a brief power struggle for control of the paper, Reid emerged in January 1873 as the paper's chief editor and primary owner. The first item on his agenda was the construction of a home for *his* newspaper. The new building was intended to serve two distinct purposes. It was to be visible proof of the continued vitality of the newspaper (Greeley had so personified the paper that many people could not imagine its continued existence without him at its helm); and it was to represent the power and vision of the paper's new editor/owner. Indeed, in the same manner that the *Tribune* had been associated with Horace Greeley, the new building was inexorably linked to his successor for it was characterized by the New York press and known to the public, even before the completion of its first phase in 1875, as the "Tall Tower of Whitelaw Reid."

The building's design reflected the desires of its owner, the established use patterns of the newspaper/office building, and the architectural skills of Richard Morris Hunt. In March 1873, Reid composed a fifteen-point memorandum that constituted the building's architectural program. This program reflected the requirements of a typical newspaper building and the additional planning issues resulting from the introduction of extensive commercial rental space. These issues included the clear separation of the newspaper offices and tenant spaces, separate entrances and circulation systems, and the need for fireproof construction. Reid also established the basic architectural form, set the height at eight stories, and specified an attached tower with an illuminated clock.

Hunt carefully followed the points outlined in Reid's memorandum: the finished building was nine stories tall, with the eighth and ninth floors contained in a mansard roof, and it had a prominent clock tower facing City Hall Park (Figure 27). When the building opened in 1875, Reid described his new building as one in which "every ornament has its uses: the

27. New York Tribune Building, Phase One, 1873–75. The Sun Building is to the left of the Tribune Tower; the Times Block is to the right. Just visible above the trees is the New Yorker Staats-Zeitung Building. © Collection of The New-York Historical Society, Neg. 396.

position of every stone is dictated by the necessities of construction; and the whole work exhibits the overruling influence of a consistent idea."[14] This emphasis on pragmatic issues, however, seems at odds with the actual design. Hunt's facades featured a subtle use of Ruskinian polychromy in the brick work, Néo-grec details in the piers and stonework, and a touch of the rich three-dimensional quality of the Second Empire in its tower and mansard roof. In other words, it was a design that clearly represented all of the strengths and weaknesses of an eclectic approach.

In contrast to its exuberant exterior, and perhaps more closely fitting Reid's vision, was the building's interior. The final plan of the building resembled a rough "U" shape with one arm extending past the rear of the Sun Building to Frankfort Street. Thus, the building fronted on three streets: Spruce, Nassau, and Frankfort. The first floor consisted of a large office space facing City Hall Park, which Reid referred to as the "bank office," a central hall and circulation core (consisting of a main stair and two passenger elevators), the *Tribune*'s counting room along Spruce, and a series of rental offices along a hall extending to Frankfort. The building's main entry was on Printing House Square through the base of the tower and was intended solely for the use of the commercial tenants, as were the elevators and main stair. Although the client entrance to the counting room was located at the corner of Spruce and Nassau, *Tribune* employees had a separate entrance farther down Spruce. The paper's employees also used a separate elevator that traveled between the cellar, counting room, editorial floor, and composing room. This elevator was one of the first express elevators, providing direct service from the cellar or first floor to the eighth and ninth floors with no stops in between.

The floors bypassed by the *Tribune*'s private elevator housed one of the largest concentrations of rental space in the city. Over 150 offices were available for lease with a combined gross area of over 60,000 square feet. The offices were arranged and outfitted according to standard planning practices. All of the individual offices were linked together by an enfilade, permitting offices to be leased as suites when needed. Reid described the suites facing City Hall Park as especially suitable for lawyers' offices.[15] Each rental space was supplied with steam heat, gas for lighting, and fresh water. The heating and ventilation system was designed so that occupants could independently control the temperature in each office.

In the same fashion that the rental offices were furnished with the latest in building systems, the *Tribune*'s offices represented the state of the art in every aspect of modern newspaper production. The paper occupied the cellar, the basement, and first floor areas on the Spruce Street side of the building, and the entire eighth and ninth floors. Each major functional area was connected by a system of pneumatic tubes, speaking tubes, and electric annunciators. One elevator was also fitted with a special baggage compartment beneath the passenger car, which was used to carry items between floors. A freight hoist, running through one of the main walls, also operated between the ninth floor and the basement.

In its size (over 90,000 gross square feet), its height (260 feet from sidewalk to the top of the clock tower), and its state-of-the-art mechanical systems (interwoven with the building's fabric), the Tribune Building represented the culminating work of the first generation of newspaper/office buildings in New York. The building was labeled "the largest newspaper office in the world" and upon completion of phase one in 1875, it became the tallest commercial building in the city (surpassing the contemporary Western Union Telegraph Company Building by 30 feet). The initial phase also expressed a vertical quality not found in the completed building (the second phase was constructed in 1881, consisting of two addition bays on Spruce and the extension to Frankfort). Here, for the first time, the tall office building as a tower was evident, a form that later became synonymous with New York skyscrapers.

Reid's tower also possessed a broad urban/civic agenda that presaged later works. Like his predecessors, Reid maintained a bulletin board on the exterior where late-breaking news could be posted. At various times during the nineteenth century this area was expanded in a billboard-like manner across the main facade to broadcast critical developments and promote sales of the latest edition. Reid's appropriation of the building's facade as an extension of the newspaper was surpassed by his appropriation of City Hall Park. The Tribune Tower's primary facade, prime rental offices, and editorial spaces were oriented toward City Hall Park. Whereas in the past the Times Block and the Sun Building had served to define Printing House Square and were clearly backdrops to one of the City's oldest green spaces, the Tribune Tower sought to claim the park for itself. This desire was expressed in an 1875 engraving that depicts the Tribune Tower as seen from City Hall Park with the park's main fountain in the foreground (Figure 28). The engraving includes the Times Block and the Sun Building (with the latter partially obscured by a tree), thus also illustrating the Tribune's physical domination of its rivals as well as the architectural richness of Printing House Square.

The Tribune Tower was the last important newspaper building constructed along Printing House Square in the 1870s. By the time its

28. New York Tribune Building, 1875. *Tribune Almanac* (1875).

initial phase was complete, the nation was in the grip of a devastating depression that had begun in the fall of 1873 and lasted the rest of the decade. The economic collapse precluded the possibility of any immediate attempt to rival the Tribune's height and its presence on the city's skyline. However, the die was cast. The next generation of newspaper/office buildings, built between the late 1880s and the early 1900s, followed the path blazed by the Tribune Tower. The *Times* launched the next generation in 1889 with a building constructed on the site of its 1857 home. This was followed in 1890 by Pulitzer's World Building (on the block adjacent to the Sun Building and for a brief moment the tallest building in the world), and the vertical expansion of the Tribune Tower in 1905, which nearly doubled its height. The trio of towers demonstrated the continued importance of the newspaper/office building in the development of the skyscraper. Furthermore, their presence on Printing House Square restated in a dramatic fashion the civic, spacemaking potential of the skyscraper (Figure 29). This critical potential, hinted at in the Times Block, promoted by the Herald, and first realized in the Staats-Zeitung Building and Tribune Tower, coupled with the technological

29. Newspaper Row [Park Row], New York, ca. 1900. From left to right, World Building, Sun Building, Tribune Tower, and the new Times Building, which replaced the earlier Times Building (visible in Figure 27) in 1889. Courtesy of the Library of Congress, Prints and Photographs Div., Detroit Publishing Co. Collection [LC-D4-12492 DLC].

innovations used in these buildings, remains the principal legacy of the newspaper/office building.

NOTES

1. "Our Architects' Advantages," *Real Estate Record and Builders Guide*, 3 (June 19, 1869).

2. The following newspapers constructed buildings housing their operations (date of building completion): *New York Times* (1858), *New York World* (1860), *New York Herald* (1867), *New York Ledger* (1871), *New York Sun* (1872), *New Yorker Staats-Zeitung* (1873), *New York Post* (1875), and the *New York Tribune* (1875, 1881). For a detailed study of the newspaper/office building type in New York City, see Lee Edward Gray, "The Office Building in New York City, 1850–1880" (Ph.D. diss., Cornell Univ., 1993).

3. "The Fire," *New York Tribune*, Feb. 6, 1845.

4. "The Old and the New," *New York Tribune*, May 29, 1845.

5. "The Old and the New," *New York Tribune*.

6. "Mysteries of the Newspaper Press," *New York Sun*, Nov. 14, 1868.

7. Frederic Hudson, *Journalism in the United States from 1690 to 1872* (New York: Harper, 1873):631.

8. "The Times Building," *New York Times*, May 13, 1858.

9. Winston Weisman, "Commercial Palaces," *Art Bulletin* 36 (Dec. 1954):295; Sarah Landau, "The Tall Office Building Artistically Re-considered: Arcaded Buildings of the New York School, c. 1870–1890," in *In Search of Modern Architecture: A Tribute to Henry-Russell Hitchcock*, ed. Helen Searing (New York and Cambridge, MA: Architectural History Foundation and MIT Press, 1982), 141; "The Times Building," *New York Times*, May 13, 1858.

10. "The Times Building," *New York Times*, May 13, 1858.

11. The increase in building activity may be measured by the number of buildings begun each year for the period from 1863 to 1868. These figures derive from the yearly reports of James M. McGregor, the Superintendent of Buildings (as they appeared in the *New Press*). New buildings 1863 – 1,247; 1864 – 733; 1865 – 1,190; 1866 – 1,670; 1867 – 1,736; 1868 – 2,112.

12. "The Fine Arts in America," *New York Herald*, Nov. 17, 1867.

13. "The New Herald Building," *New York Herald*, Nov. 21, 1867.

14. *New York Tribune*, Apr. 10, 1875.

15. "Nearly all the rooms, therefore, can be rented singly, and at the same time they are admirably adapted for law firms and others who require offices in suites. At the north end of the building, especially, the wants of the lawyers have been taken into consideration. The large room in the rear, with a double door opening into the hall, is designed for the clerks and the law library. At the further end it communicates with a room, extending the whole width of the building, with windows front and rear, and on the west side it opens into two fine front rooms. In case it should be determined to rent the front rooms separately, the room in the rear would be used as a hall." *New York Tribune*, Apr. 10, 1875.

5

Chicago's Fraternity Temples

The Origins of Skyscraper Rhetoric and the First of the World's Tallest Office Buildings

Edward W. Wolner

On November 6, 1890, nearly 4,000 Masons from Illinois staged an elaborate cornerstone ceremony in downtown Chicago for the new Masonic Temple at the northeast corner of State and Randolph streets. Celebrating what was to become the highest commercial building in the world, the ceremony involved all the pageantry that had made Masonic cornerstone rituals an American institution.[1] In fact, Freemasons had laid the cornerstones for such notable public structures as the nation's Capitol Building in 1793, the Washington Monument in 1848, and the Statue of Liberty in 1885.[2]

But unlike these national icons or the newer Masonic lodges, the temple, designed by the Chicago firm of Burnham and Root, was neither a fully public nor a fully Masonic building. Instead, the ceremony honored a facility that on its completion in 1892 included not only Masonic parlors but also a greater variety of commercial functions than any previous skyscraper had housed. Among them were a 2,000-seat restaurant in the basement; prestigious shops in the building's three-story granite base; six floors of retail stores and seven of first-class office space in its arcaded midsection; and a roof garden above the four stories of Masonic rooms located within the gabled crown (Figures 30, 31).

To embed Masonic parlors in a skyscraper of profit-making functions was to pursue the commercial values and social status that had

The author expresses his appreciation for the close critical readings this essay received from Carol Herselle Krinsky, Joseph Siry, and Roberta Moudry. Robert Bruegmann and Carol Willis also provided helpful responses. The author is grateful for research funding from the Graham Foundation for Advanced Studies in the Fine Arts and the Ball State University Office of Academic Research.

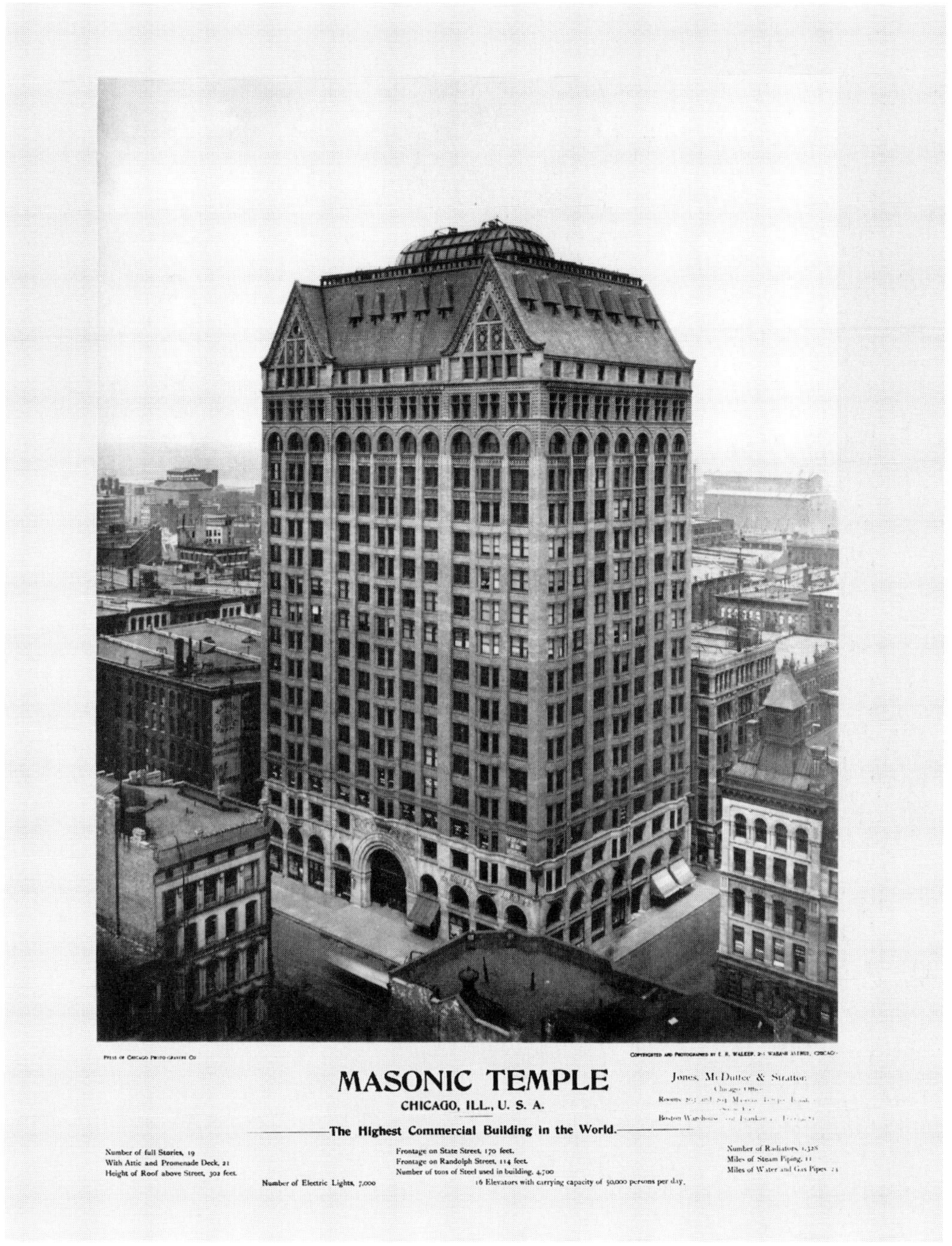

30. Masonic Temple, Chicago, 1890–92. Photograph, 1892. Reprinted with permission of the Chicago Historical Society (ICHi-01023).

begun to dilute the order's moral mission. This change affected other fraternities as well. Just ten months after the temple ceremony, members of the Independent Order of Odd Fellows challenged the Masons by promoting not simply a higher commercial facility but also the first skyscraper to be the tallest building of any kind in the world. Thus groups from the nation's

31. Roof Garden–Observatory, Masonic Temple, 1890–92. *Inland Architect*, December 1892. Reprinted with permission of the Chicago Historical Society (ICHI-30457).

two largest fraternal societies used the novelty of steel-framed buildings to enhance their own status even as this enhancement helped initiate the modern erosion of their spiritual purposes.[3]

So energetically did both groups act on this motive that they developed portions of the skyscraper's commercial might and rhetorical power that no earlier developer had tapped as fully. The Odd Fellows sought to reconfigure Chicago's symbolic identity with the first building high enough to dominate a modern metropolitan region. That it was never built, however, allowed the Masons to make their temple the first of the world's tallest skyscrapers to be systematically promoted and widely recognized as such. Moreover, its sumptuous interiors and ten floors of shops made the temple a prescient example of the resplendent shopping environments that by 1900 embodied America's shift from the vocational, political, and spiritual orientation of agrarian values to the new dominance of market values in modernized cities.[4]

Although architectural histories have closely examined the Masonic Temple and Odd Fellows' project, they have overlooked the many integral and the several spectacular ways in which the two designs embodied this fundamental shift and a newly potent skyscraper rhetoric.[5] The same oversight occurs in the cultural histories that have tracked the intensification of commercial values in the fraternal movement and the largest American cities; these studies neglect both skyscrapers despite how well they confirm the cultural analysis.[6] This essay therefore seeks to close an unacknowledged gap, to recover the lost meanings and rhetoric of two skyscraper projects of much greater historical significance than either type of scholarship has recognized.

Because the Odd Fellows' project was not built, the essay folds it into the longer history of the Masonic Temple's rhetorical power. That power – the sum of the Masons' intentions and the impact on the public of the temple's structural, spatial, functional, symbolic, and promotional features – derived from two factors. First, Masonry enjoyed a highly favorable reputation and a rapidly expanding membership in part because it sustained its charitable works, moral certainties, and craft-based rituals of brotherhood during a period of deeply unsettling urban change. Second, in the increased competition for new members among fraternal orders, the Masonic Temple and its extensive press coverage conferred on Masonry in Chicago during the first half of the 1890s the additional prestige that only a new, distinctly modern kind of publicity could create, and which the Odd Fellows would have enjoyed instead had their project succeeded: the prestige of achieving supreme height at a time when the first group of steel-framed skyscrapers caused widespread public admiration and wonderment. The essay's two parts examine each factor.

Building Rhetoric and Masonry's Public Reputation

Many of the thousands of Chicagoans who witnessed the temple's cornerstone ceremony already had a positive view of Masonry.[7] In fact, it and the other fraternal orders were so important in America that in 1897 an analysis in the *North American Review* estimated that as many as 20 percent of American men belonged to one of the nation's 70,000 lodges. Nearly tripling in size between 1860 and 1890, Masonry was the second largest and the most selective order. Its cornerstone pageants for such national monuments as the Statue of Liberty reflected and augmented its unexcelled prestige, as did its countless ceremonies for local civic and Masonic buildings. Indeed, its public pageants and secret rituals were models for those developed by other fraternal societies such as the Knights of Pythias and the Odd Fellows themselves.[8]

This kind of building rhetoric communicated much of Masonry's public appeal. Sidestepping contemporary sectarian disputes and Darwinist controversies, the Masonic creed integrated the widely shared ideals of equality, fraternity, and charity within an organization able to embody them in highly visible projects. For example, Masonic charity included not only every Mason's oath to aid craft brethren and their families when in need but also the provision of Masonic homes for orphans, the elderly, or the enfeebled; eleven state lodges had erected such homes by 1893. Moreover, Chicago's Masonic Temple was just one among dozens of building campaigns by lodges across the country. These campaigns enhanced the order's public standing and helped attract new members because they demonstrated the efficacy and popularity of Masonic ideals in an age of multiple reform movements.[9]

This was especially true of the construction of new temples that in the late 1880s began to replace the Masons' earlier practice of renovating parts of preexisting buildings for lodge purposes. The Chicago temple's height, its first three stories of hefty granite blocks, its immense neo-Romanesque entrance arch, its soaring arcaded midsection, and its outsized Queen Anne gables epitomized the way in which recent lodge architecture joined Masonry's moral authority to the social prestige of a newly monumental prominence downtown. The unusual bulk of many lodges added to their striking monumentality, and here, too, the Chicago temple was exemplary. It hosted both ordinary lodges and elite Masonic groups in richly decorated suites for 100 to 400 men and in two large galleried halls: a vaulted neoclassical one holding 1,320 people and a 1,300-seat facility for balls, banquets, interlodge conclaves, and parade drills (Figure 32).[10]

Masonry benefited from the prestige of historical associations as well. Chicago's Mayor, D. W. C. Cregier, Past Grand Master of the

Illinois State Lodge and the city's former chief engineer, noted in his speech at the cornerstone ceremony that Masonry "was the fraternity that builded the great temple at Jerusalem." This widely shared Masonic belief enhanced the order's appeal because it associated Masonry with a paradigmatic act of founding and a widely esteemed spiritual summit.

Solomon was not the only prestigious figure whom Cregier and other Masons used to amplify Masonry's mythic history. By noting that "Masonic men have laid the foundation of systems of government," the mayor indirectly referred to George Washington and Benjamin Franklin, known by many Americans to have been Masonic luminaries as well as apostles of democracy. As such, they seemed to reinforce Cregier's claim that Masonry "has within its limits men of all trades and professions, and of all countries and creeds," so that "the cement we place beneath the [corner]stone is that of harmony and brotherly love." With these and other building analogies Creiger claimed that the temple advanced Masonry's "mission of law and order."[11]

His appeals to brotherhood and social order were not rhetorically empty in a city where the problems of crime, alcoholism, labor unrest, unprecedented immigration, uncontrolled urban growth, and the pervasive instability of early modern life generated widespread desire for a reinvigorated moral order.[12] These conditions made Cregier's appeal more resonant even as some Masonic realities contradicted it. In Chicago and other cities with many immigrants from southern and eastern Europe, Masons were often nativists despite the order's claims to universal brotherhood. Moreover, expenses for annual dues, regalia, and building campaigns required middle-class incomes, which automatically excluded many laborers. In an organization dominated by Protestants, there were few Catholics and almost no Jews. Despite Masonry's nonsectarian ideology, the elite order of the Knights Templar was open solely to the few Christians who had attained the rank of Master Mason. Masonry disavowed Negro lodges claiming a Masonic pedigree.[13] Like many other moralists and reformers at the turn of the century, the Masons could only envision a future human brotherhood composed of people who strongly resembled themselves.

But these blinkered practices unwittingly heightened Masonry's public standing and its appeal to prospective members because its cresting popularity partly derived from a desire that disordered cities such as Chicago repeatedly stimulated: the desire to simplify social, political, and economic relations and to counter alarming and often complex urban developments with the uncomplicated Masonic values of temperance, hard work, thrift, and morality.[14] Here the Masons' guildlike structure served them well. Members maintained strict ritual secrecy, addressed one another as "Brother," passed in three clear stages from a moral apprenticeship to the greater enlightenment of "Master Mason," appeared in public pageants wearing the leather aprons of artisans, and contemplated a moral symbolism communicated through masons' tools and building metaphors based on the cornerstone, the compass, the square, the plumb line, the keystone, and a deistlike divinity figured as "the Architect of the Universe." Against the impersonality and complexity of rapidly growing cities, Masonry invoked a face-to-face moral community through the craft and kinship imagery of brotherhood in a simpler preindustrial era, imagery that fit many Masons' experience of growing up in small artisanal towns.[15]

Finally, Masonry's multiple attractions ideally positioned the order in the unfolding status competitions of the early modern city. For men who did not have the wealth, family name, or social connections required to participate in the exclusive club life of traditional elites, Masonic membership and a downtown temple provided an alternative prestige derived

32. Lodge Rooms and Parlors, Masonic Temple, ca. 1892. Reprinted with permission of the Chicago Historical Society (ICHi-30187).

from the many national, state, and local politicians, and the numerous business and professional men of prominence, who belonged to the order.[16]

Skyscraper Rhetoric, the New Commerce, and Chicago's Fraternity Temples

The Masons who backed the temple discovered that they could secure still higher status among the city's proliferating ranks of secondary elites by locating their lodge facilities in what people then experienced as a new kind of downtown building. Around 1890, the structural innovation of steel framing quickly resulted in buildings so tall that the term "skyscraper" was coined for them.[17] Intended to convey the daunting impression made on the people who first encountered these buildings, the term itself was among the first demonstrations of the skyscraper's rhetorical power.[18] As the world's tallest skyscraper, then, the Masons' new Chicago headquarters would be not only a source of profit and Masonic pride, but also a building phenomenon likely to draw widespread attention during the World's Columbian Exposition of 1893.[19]

But the Odd Fellows coveted this attention for themselves as well. While the Masonic Temple was still in construction, a front-page article in the *Tribune* in September 1891 announced plans by the Fraternity Association of the Independent Order of Odd Fellows, Illinois Branch, to erect a much taller facility. Designed by the firm of Adler and Sullivan with two floors of shops, five floors of lodge spaces, and twenty-eight stories of offices, the project's lower portions were as tall as the Masonic Temple, while the tower rose a full fifteen stories higher (Figure 33).[20]

Had it been built, the project – whose ornament, tower, massing, and civic intentions had no skyscraper precedents – would easily have displaced the Masonic Temple as the Loop's most striking image of fraternal and commercial dominance. Vitalist nature motifs wrapped the project's round openings at five lower and upper levels to give the design an ornamental identity distinct from that of all other skyscrapers. Not the flèchelike token affixed to a few earlier office buildings, the tower was the first in skyscraper history to rise from a lower base and hold a significant percentage of the total office space. Yet the tower was slender enough, and the novel setbacks on the two lower portions cut deeply enough into the immense building mass, to ensure that overall bulk and height would not cast nearby buildings into permanent shadow, and that the project's interiors would receive abundant light and air.[21]

Moreover, the design inaugurated a new verticality that magnified the impact of its already immoderate height. Replacing the dominant horizontal lines that tied almost all previous tall buildings to the ground, the accented vertical piers on the twenty-two-story wings and the tower's chamfered corners moved the eye rapidly upward. The crown was not a weighty gabled roof, as on the Masonic Temple, but a steeply sloped faceted cone on the setback portion of the tower. Rather than efface the sky with a flat cornice, the crown addressed it by diminishing the powerful tower and its formidable base to a single point.[22]

The next day, the *Tribune* published the Fraternity Temple Building Association's prospectus. It sought, in the words of an early Chicago historian, to assure investors that "the great project was far removed from the region of dreamland." Thus, most of the document emphasized the project's integrated functional and formal advantages, and its exceptionally high percentage of more profitable corner offices.[23] It even assured readers that the building association had excluded from the anticipated profits such variable sources of income as the tower observatory and an unspecified basement function.

But the novel prospect of free publicity generated by a building of unprecedented height transformed a single sentence in a prospectus otherwise marked by sober prose and prudent banker's arguments into an effusion over "the *unusual and almost phenomenal additional value* which will accrue to business premises [as] *self-advertising* as these... containing within their inclosing [sic] walls a business population equal to that of cities of over 100,000 inhabitants [emphasis added]." To the many Odd Fellows whom the building association needed as investors, this declaration, and two others emphasizing how "enormous" the building's stock dividends and "possible earnings" would be, tendered profits otherwise inaccessible to the largely middle-class brotherhood. Among the earliest statements by developers about how the tallest buildings generated free publicity and unusually fast rates of return, the declarations also revealed the association's excitement over its imminent social ascent as the sponsor of a first-class office building serving a city's worth of people and companies.[24]

Such effusiveness was not merely developer's bluster. Although tall office buildings had been advertising themselves and their tenants for at least twenty years, the Fraternity Temple's extraordinary height embodied a new kind of preeminence on the skyline and a corresponding amplification of the skyscraper's self-advertising power. The tower, the prospectus declared, would be nothing less than a "landmark [visible within] sixty miles around Chicago," and would possess "the utmost artistic and symbolic significance" for the fraternity and the city. The architects and clients thus understood that the tower's visual and symbolic dominance would be of a new order of magnitude, greater by far than that of the Masonic Temple and all other skyscrapers to date.

In fact, the dominance on the skyline of the 556-foot Fraternity Temple would have

33. Proposed Odd Fellows' Fraternity Temple, 1891. *The Graphic*, July-December 1891. Reprinted with permission of the Chicago Historical Society (ICHi-30102).

surpassed in several ways that of such eminent urban landmarks as St. Peter's Basilica (452 feet) in Rome and St. Paul's Cathedral (366 feet) in London. In nearby views, their hard domical shells soared free of their surroundings. But viewed from the middle distance and beyond, they softened into swelling forms firmly tied to the lower city by a churchly array of subordinate domes or steeples. Compared to the Fraternity Temple's tower, no spire or minaret, no religious or civic dome anywhere pushed so abruptly upward or broke so forcefully with the skyline below and around it. Only St. Paul's dominated a city of Chicago's size; but views of the cathedral, just two-thirds the height of the temple, could not have extended as far into London's hinterland as the temple would have into Chicago's. The tower, the prospectus stated, was to be seen from "Michigan City, La Porte, Aurora, Elgin, [and] Waukegan," Indiana and Illinois towns lying along an arc struck on a 38-mile radius centered in the Loop. The temple's astonishing height and stark profile, seen across level terrain and the flat expanse of Lake Michigan, would have given it an unprecedented metropolitan omnipresence.

Its potential rhetorical power throughout a sprawling region broadcast the fraternity's desire to become more than Chicago's preeminent fraternal society. The Odd Fellows asserted that with the first skyscraper to be "the tallest building in the world," Chicago, transformed in two brief decades from the ashes of the 1871 fire to the most technologically modern city on earth, would "outrival all its previous wonders."[25] In a city that had always lacked a definitive landmark, and in the booming Loop whose competing signs often cancelled each other out, the Fraternity Temple promised to be Chicago's indelible signifier, the skyscraper still-point around which much of the visible region and the city's symbolic identity would rotate.

The Masonic Temple, the Odd Fellows' tower, and several building proposals in New York City marked a new skyscraper sensationalism.[26] Taller, larger, and more publicized than the comparatively modest buildings and promotions of the 1870s and 1880s, this cohort of skyscrapers embodied the increasingly pervasive reach of commerce in America's largest cities. So did the fact that fraternal orders backed both projects in Chicago rather than the newspapers, insurance companies, and full-time promoters of downtown commercial development normally associated with major building enterprises. That Masons and Odd Fellows pursued profits and status as avidly as the most ambitious real estate developers showed how far Chicago lodges had moved from an important fraternal aim, that of providing asylum from commercialism.[27] Equally revealing was the Masons' purchase of one of the most expensive and potentially lucrative sites in the nation's most prosperous city. The northeast corner of State and Randolph streets, an intersection served by trains from the north, west, and south sides, seemed to ensure for the temple high office rents and a constant flow of shoppers, because the Loop's principal retailing and entertainment districts converged there.[28]

The Masons' worldly tradeoff resulted in an international publicity windfall between 1890 and 1895 that exceeded even the self-advertising boon that the Odd Fellows had hoped their project would precipitate. Architectural historian Thomas Tallmadge recalled that the Masonic Temple "fired the imagination and enthusiasm, not only of our citizens but of the world." Francisco Mujica, an early historian of skyscrapers, more pointedly noted that "designs and photographs of this building were reproduced in all countries of the world announcing that the birth of the skyscraper had taken place."[29]

In the United States, laudatory articles appeared in widely circulated publications such as *Harper's Weekly*, for which Julian Ralph wrote an essay in September 1892. On the eve of the World's Columbian Exposition, Ralph ranked the Masonic Temple first among Chicago's taller buildings, and these buildings first among the city's attractions for fairgoers. More than the "throngs in the [Loop's] broad but crowded streets," or the excursion steamers plying between the shore and "the water-supply cribs" well out in the lake, or "the great government breakwaters" turned into fishing piers by "many thousands of persons," the tall office buildings, Ralph declared, "will seem the greatest novelties."[30]

ROTUNDA.
INTERIOR VIEWS, THE MASONIC TEMPLE, CHICAGO.
BURNHAM & ROOT, ARCHITECTS.

34. Lobby, Masonic Temple, 1890–92. *Inland Architect*, December 1892. Reprinted with permission of the Chicago Historical Society (ICHi-30456).

For him and many other people, these buildings constituted a technological and social turning point for which the Masonic Temple was the paradigm. In its lobby, Ralph confronted an "imposing battery" of fourteen elevators, a military phrase that aptly evoked the impressive technological armature required to move 45,000 people in and out of the temple daily (Figures 34, 35). "Swift express elevators" invited visitors "to flit up and down" the twenty stories of the temple's skylit court, where visibility through transparent elevator screens heightened the fairylike kinesthesia of mechanized ascension and descent. At the top was "the highest of all roof gardens," Chicago's sight of sights, a "great... chamber" holding 2,000 people and outfitted with sliding windows, a ferrovitreous vault, and vistas comprehending "practically all of Chicago": the city's new parks, the "T-shaped river and its compressed activity," and "the magnificent lake, with its breakwaters... its cribs and its changing collections of shipping."

Set down in enchanted language, Ralph's observations depicted a Chicago that displayed much of the ad hoc pageantry of traditional cities, with their continuously recombining settings, activities, movements, and colors. Yet there were fundamental differences. Whereas all cities subjugated the natural world, Chicago did so on a scale that was immense, mechanical, and modern. The steamers and ships tamed a once formidable inland sea, the breakwaters channeled its shoreline movements, and the cribs secured an inexhaustible water supply that downtown development had otherwise poisoned.

In Chicago's technological pageantry, however, Ralph thought that the novel phenomenon of machine aggregation in buildings like the Masonic Temple constituted the city's and the era's most absolute conquest of nature. This mechanical modernity was best dramatized by the temple's "altitudinous" roof garden. There the city seemed to be a glorious man-made nature, a collocation of panoramas that might rival or surpass sublime and pastoral landscapes, as when a Masonic Temple handbook described the views northward from the Loop: "the life of the great rumbling city rolls like a mighty ocean beneath, and the comparatively quiet and elegant North Side stretches out like a beautiful picture."[31] That the temple and its observatory conferred on Ralph and many others the momentary innocence of marveling over a suddenly modernized city helped gauge the temple's impact and the Masons' social gain.

A brochure published shortly after the close of the exposition noted that the observatory drew 3,000 to 5,000 daily visitors, a number that "has far exceeded the expectations of the management... although [the roof garden] has never been advertised."[32] The management, however, had already capitalized on the innocent wonder that observatories could stir by instituting a 25-cent admission fee, issuing the brochure, using the initial lack of advertising as a type of advertisement, and providing entertainments that built on the spectacle of the world's tallest commercial building. Two "Bijou Edifices" – also called "Scenic Theatoriums" or small theaters (20 by 52 feet) – offered visitors "elegant Opera Chairs" in which to observe the enactment of other spectacular subjugations of nature. A lantern show in one theater highlighted the beauty of mountains under changing light with "'A Day in the Alps,'" in which the "mutations" included "many surprising and beautiful effects produced by Electric Lighting."

The exhibit was built upon the public's recent fascination with the lighting spectacles at the exposition's Court of Honor, shows that had astonished fairgoers with the still novel uses of electric illumination.[33] In fact, the second theater housed a large model of the court itself, billed in the brochure as "the artistic masterpiece of the 19th century." Constructed "with absolute fidelity," the model reproduced the "water effects" of the three court fountains, employing the charm of the miniature to reawaken what for many fairgoers had been the dreamlike beauty of the colossal court and the fountains illuminated at night. The model fleshed out memories stirred by the observatory's southward views to Jackson Park itself, to the "gold tipped domes of the White City, now silent and still."[34] Together with the other views, both theaters sought to stimulate and prolong oneiric or ecstatic states by conflating technological and natural sublimities.

Both sublimities were folded into another kind of miniaturization. Two pages in the brochure outlined Chicago's development as a series of significant moments – ten from the past, eighteen from the present – that began with the city's origins in a swamp and culminated in the Masonic Temple and the exposition. With its drumroll progress, the flier obviously sought to enhance Masonic status. But triumphalist history composed for profits and the palm of one's hand should not obscure a simple truth – that the Temple, Chicago's other technological developments, and an exposition that stunned much of the nation were exceptional enough to precipitate excited commentary in the first place. By emphasizing the number, speed, and superlative nature of the city's modern transformations, the Masons' publicity unmistakably revealed their authors' own sense of wonder and created in

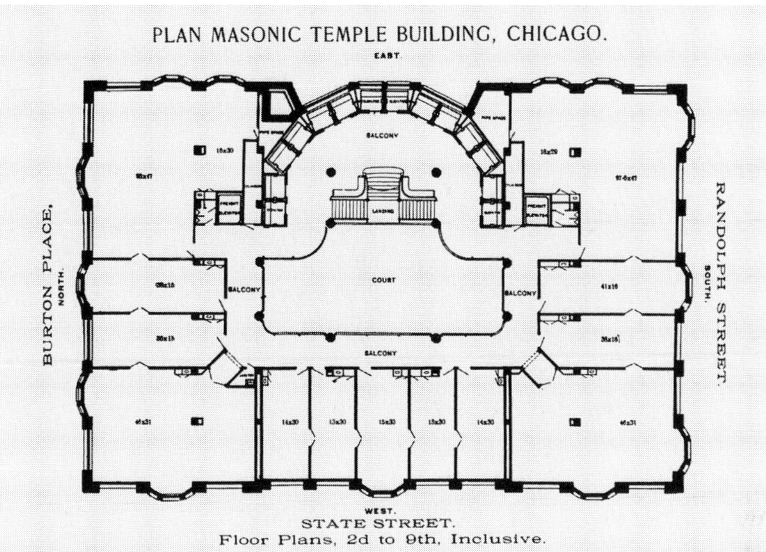

35. Floor plans, second through ninth, Masonic Temple, 1890–92. *Inland Architect*, December 1892. Reprinted with permission of the Chicago Historical Society (ICHi-30453).

the pamphlet one of the first – if hyperbolic – expressions of the skyscraper's power as synecdoche: As "the World's Greatest Architectural Achievement," the temple climaxed the history of what had become "Architecturally the most Modern City in the world."

This and similar publications extended the temple's rhetorical force once visitors left the building. In the self-reinforcing loops of modern publicity, spoken and written accounts used items from this or other pamphlets to communicate wonder-filled responses to the temple's self-advertising power. Ralph himself repeated the Masons' claim that the parlors atop their building "form the most elegant and well-devised headquarters at the disposal of any fraternal organization in Christendom." He and other journalists and visitors also cited the Masons' statistics, which pointed out, for example, that in one year the temple's elevators traveled "123,136 miles" on cables "16 miles" long.[35] Such objective numbers actually augmented nonobjective responses to the temple, for to many people elevators and other machines seemed to work magic, to suspend the law of gravity, to yield results out of all proportion to the effort expended. For engineers such facts were the logical products of machine aggregation or specifications that had nothing to do with a cab's quasimagical capacity "to flit up and down" effortlessly. For the uninitiated, however, statistics heightened the atmosphere of the marvelous that often enveloped modern technologies in the infancy of their public reception.

So did illustrations in non-Masonic publications. Among the best examples was a drawing comparing the temple to other well-known structures for a front-page article in an early 1894 issue of *Scientific American*, which extolled the temple as "one of the unique buildings of the world" (Figure 36). The drawing placed the temple not beside other skyscrapers but next to the nation's most prestigious public building (the Capitol), its most famous statue (Liberty), and New York City's Trinity Church, whose spire ruled Manhattan's skyline from 1846 to 1890. With all objects drawn to the same scale and rendered without perspective diminution, the drawing fully registered the

36. "A City Under One Roof – The Masonic Temple, Chicago." *Scientific American*, February 10, 1894. Courtesy of the Chicago Historical Society (ICHi-30460).

visual shock packed by the temple's formidable mass and height, affirming the text's declaration that "the mammoth pile dwarfs everything shown."[36]

When the article noted the temple's "union of freemasonry and commerce," however, it understated the extent to which the building embodied commercial values even as the drawing underlined their new pervasiveness. The confrontation of three public monuments with one "mammoth" skyscraper underscored the symbolic and spatial displacement of civic and religious institutions by the accelerating commerce of the late nineteenth century.[37] In William Leach's account in *Land of Desire*, the new dominance of urban capital and corporate efficiency over agricultural wealth and agrarian individualism was dramatically evident in the nation's first sophisticated consumer environments.

In fact, the consumer portion of the Masonic Temple, which occupied more than half the building, was a prescient example of what Leach terms the new commercial "strategies of

STAIRWAY AND GALLERIES FROM ELEVATORS.

37. Stairway and Galleries, Masonic Temple, 1890–92. *Inland Architect*, December 1892. Reprinted with permission of the Chicago Historical Society (ICHi-30455).

enticement," which sought to stimulate consumer longing through novel settings. Nearly a decade before the first consumerist "pleasure palaces" achieved maturity in such designs for department stores as Louis Sullivan's for Schlesinger and Mayer (1898), and D.H. Burnham & Company's for Marshall Field's (1902) and Wanamaker's (1909), the Masons and their architects planned a consumer spectacle that deployed the same sumptuous esthetic of color, glass, light, and luxurious materials used in the later development of the department store and the shop window.[38]

For the Masonic Temple's nine stories of shops, the luxurious materials included columns encased in alabaster, balcony soffits paneled in marble, rotunda and gallery floors laid in multicolored mosaics, railings finished in bronze, and the grilles for them and for the open-work elevators cast in delicate ornamental iron.[39] The novelty of electric light in 7,000 bulbs enhanced the luxurious setting, as did the "entrancing" lights in the observatory, which the Masons' brochure described as "thickly hung with beautifully designed Jeweled Lanterns" (Figures 32, 37). To counter low wattage, the windowed back wall of the elevator shaft, the large shop windows of the central court, and the glass canopy over it maximized the amount of natural light bounced off materials whose polished surfaces and creamy colors were chosen to do just that.

The extent of the temple's lustrous materials, the use of large expanses of glass for interior as well as exterior walls, and the intensity of both artificial and natural illumination were all exceptional features even among the many well-appointed commercial buildings of the time. Making the temple the costliest building in Chicago, these accoutrements gave a muted resplendence to an unequaled variety of high-toned shopping attractions in a singular setting.[40] In addition to stores and basement restaurants intended to serve different income groups, the roof garden tempted visitors with flower displays, musical events, and commemorations that supplemented the views, the fresh air, the theatoriums, and the thrilling ascent to the top of the building.[41]

The novelty of nine floors of shops was particularly striking. One German visitor compared these floors favorably to the elegant ambience of the toplit, bazaarlike Bon Marche department store in Paris. The temple's shops, *Scientific American* noted, opened to their balconies through "show windows, exactly as in a street," the balconies themselves carrying street names rather than floor numbers. In 1890 the *Economist*, Chicago's real estate journal of record, deemed this arrangement an "ideal plan" because it avoided "the inconveniences of having to pass along . . . crowded streets by slow and uncertain means of locomotion in heat, or wet, or cold," and because the temple's shopping attractions would not be equaled anywhere in the Loop "in the magnificence of the ensemble and the grandeur of the architectural effect."[42]

That most stores failed by 1897 does not belie their importance for the later development of the department store.[43] Their variety and novel setting were an experiment in newly systematized consumer enticements. Their economically compatible uses exploited the commercial advantages of proximity, efficiency, choice, exclusivity, urbanity, and the inherently theatrical character of people moving about the rotunda, observatory, elevators, and balconies. Removed from downtown's grittier realities – its noise and dirt, its vehicular and pedestrian congestion, its street peddlers, proselytizers, news hawkers, pickpockets, and shoe shiners – the temple was to function better than the city itself by stacking streets in the sky and imbuing them with the aura of resplendent self-containment required in the consumerist fantasy of self-remaking.[44]

Within the walls of their own temple, the city's Masons reenacted the Loop's recent commercial intensification, in which the multiplying number of new and much larger office and retail buildings displaced or dwarfed the downtown's few public institutions. Unlike their brethren elsewhere, Chicago brothers, after passing under the immense granite arch inscribed with the Masonic symbols that often adorned a lodge threshold, had to rise through sixteen stories of a highly rationalized commercial environment before arriving at their parlors. This spatial sequence compromised Masonry's claim that lodge life provided a retreat from the outside world, as did the presence of "the loftiest barber shop in the world" amidst the parlors on the nineteenth floor.[45] In making the order more attractive to potential recruits, the temple's fame and luxurious Masonic suites could only have reinforced nascent tendencies in Masonry to confuse morality with social prominence, to downplay the order's religious rites, or to remain indifferent to its spiritual aims in order to profit from Masonic status.[46]

But moral liabilities offered material advantages. Crowning a skyscraper with fraternal parlors heightened the temple's uniqueness and conferred the Masons' imprimatur on the era's most diverse concentration of profit-making functions within a single structure. As the world's highest commercial building for the country's most prestigious fraternity, the temple was the site for the managed confluence of sumptuous retail, office, public, and Masonic spaces. It was also the site of urban spectacle, consumer enticements, and status aspirations pitched at a modern intensity by the thoroughness of skyscraper planning, design, and publicity and by the retail experimentation in which Chicago excelled in the 1890s. The temple and the unbuilt but more titanic Odd Fellows project were thus the two most dramatic examples of Daniel Bluestone's observation that turn-of-the-century skyscrapers "monumentalized Mammon as never before."[47]

Francisco Mujica pronounced the Masonic Temple to be "the first really important skyscraper in history." In relation to the record of widespread public awareness of individual tall buildings and to the historical development of the skyscraper's rhetorical power, Mujica's claim was accurate.[48]

In addition to its height, several other factors conferred on the temple a renown far larger than that of any earlier skyscraper. Many among the millions of fairgoers and the legions of journalists who spoke and wrote about the Exposition and Chicago itself in the 1890s generated an incalculable amount of free publicity for the temple. More diverse in function than other mixed-use buildings of the time, the temple's urban microcosm – what *Scientific American* termed "a city under one roof" – dramatized for a fascinated public how the largest skyscrapers tended to convert the intensely instrumental variety of downtown commercial activities into the consumer novelties of rationalized pageants and panoramas, as in the light court's simulacrum of city streets and shops, or the observatory's "scenic theatoriums" and kaleidoscopic views.[49]

The roof garden – a world apart from the much smaller observatories of other tall buildings – was another of the temple's singular attractions. Its size, ambience, and variety of entertainments suggested origins in the earlier roof gardens on New York City's Casino Theater (1882) and Madison Square Garden (1890), but the temple observatory was free of their louche associations, and its wrap-around operable windows and steam heat accommodated both open-air and winter functions well before these features appeared elsewhere.[50] Coupled with the ride up a light court of an astonishing height, the roof garden made a visit to the temple altogether more memorable than visits to other observatories in buildings only marginally shorter.

The temple's managers were not the first in the history of the skyscraper to exploit observatory views, choreograph dedication ceremonies, tout building attractions in pocket-size pamphlets, hymn mechanical wonders in a statistical litany, dilate on them in lyrical prose, or play upon the skyscraper's powers of synecdoche.[51] The observatory model of the Court of Honor was certainly not the first instance in which skyscraper developers borrowed architectural forms from the public realm to help legitimate and maximize outsized private gain. But the temple's management was the first to bring together in systematic ways and polished forms all these distinct publicity techniques, whose interlocking with one another and the building design greatly enlarged the temple's windfall of unsolicited public responses.

The building rivalry between the Odd Fellows and the Masons was not the first such contest in skyscraper history, but the Odd Fellows did join the first battle to achieve supreme height in which each party grasped complementary and as yet unexploited portions of the immense rhetorical field opened up by the steel-framed skyscraper. The Odd Fellows and their architects discovered the unparalleled self-advertising reach of a sentinel tower with metropolitan visibility. The temple managers codified those promotional axioms and established that coveted category – world's tallest skyscraper – which developers in each of the twentieth century's four major building booms exploited to publicize their companies, cities, nations, and entrepreneurial world views.[52]

All these factors helped the temple become the first of the world's tallest skyscrapers to accumulate a storied past. The roof garden inspired much of it, whether as the setting for elite society and social climbers memorably limned in George Ade's short story "In the Roof Garden," or as the promontory whose height was so astonishing that, as in Edgar Lee Masters' account, some people believed they could see "Council Bluffs, Iowa, some 230 miles distant." In fact, from the first newspaper and historical accounts onward, observers consistently misidentified the temple as the tallest building in the world. Although the Masonic handbooks accurately called it the world's tallest *commercial* building since its height was still well below that of St. Peter's Basilica, the temple's twenty-one stories were still shocking enough to create in many beholders an afterimage of exaggerated proportions.[53]

In both calculated and unpremeditated ways, the temple became the first skyscraper experienced by multitudes as the "wonder of wonders," as the object "observed [by] all observers."[54] In thus summing up the temple's public impact, Thomas Tallmadge unknowingly identified the rhetorical gold standard that all subsequent skyscrapers aspiring to be the world's tallest now had to meet in order to capture the public imagination in a world of ever higher buildings, more aggressive commercial expansion, and increasingly potent demonstrations of technological "magic."

NOTES

1. "Plumb, Level, Square," *Chicago Tribune*, Nov. 7, 1890, 1–2. The article has a detailed description of the Masons' pageant in the Loop and the elaborate cornerstone ritual. All subsequent information and quotations about the cornerstone ceremony come from this article.

2. Lynn Dumenil, *Freemasonry and American Culture 1880–1930* (Princeton, NJ: Princeton Univ. Press, 1984), 8, 235 n.6; Allen E. Roberts, *Freemasonry in American History* (Richmond, VA: Macoy Publishing & Masonic Supply Co., 1985), 192, 210, 266, 287, 305.

3. In her nuanced and scrupulous study, to which I owe much debt, Dumenil maintains that by 1920, Masonry completed a shift from a religious, ritualistic, and morally oriented fraternity to a social, secular, and status-oriented one. This essay argues that the fraternity temples built or proposed in Chicago in the early 1890s inaugurated this shift much earlier for a significant number of Masons and Odd Fellows. On the importance of the initiatory, ritualistic, mystical, and gender-based appeals of nineteenth-century Masonry and other fraternal orders, see Mark Carnes, *Secret Ritual and Manhood in Victorian Society* (New Haven, CT: Yale Univ. Press, 1989).

4. William Leach, *Land of Desire* (New York: Pantheon, 1993), 3–14. On intensified commercialism's effect on the architectural treatment and social perception of commercial buildings in Chicago's Loop in the late 1880s and 1890s, see Daniel Bluestone, *Constructing Chicago* (New Haven, CT: Yale Univ. Press, 1991), 104–51; and Joseph Siry, *Carson Pirie Scott* (Chicago: University of Chicago Press, 1988), 3–64. On the reactions of foreigners to the Loop's unprecedented commercial concentration, see Arnold Lewis, *An Early Encounter with Tomorrow: Europeans, Chicago's Loop, and the World's Columbian Exposition* (Urbana, IL: Univ. of Illinois Press, 1997), 135–51.

5. The principal sources on the design of the Masonic Temple are Carl Condit, *The Chicago School of Architecture* (Chicago: Univ. of Chicago Press, 1964), 104–7; Donald Hoffmann, *The Architecture of John Wellborn Root* (Baltimore: Johns Hopkins Univ. Press, 1973), 196–204; and Bluestone, 109, 115, 119, 128, 135, 141, 149, 181. For brief critical judgments on the aesthetics of the building, see Hoffmann and Harriet Monroe, *John Wellborn Root* (Park Forest, IL: Prairie School Press, 1896), 140; and Thomas S. Hines, *Burnham of Chicago* (Chicago: Univ. of Chicago Press, 1974), 65, 67. The principal sources for the Odd Fellows project are Hugh Morrison, *Louis Sullivan: Prophet of Modern Architecture* (New York: Norton, 1935), 162–5; Robert Twombly, *Louis Sullivan: His Life and Work* (New York: Viking, 1986), 300–4; and William Jordy, "The Tall Buildings," in *Louis Sullivan: The Function of Ornament*, ed. Wim de Wit (New York: Norton, 1986), 54, 77, 80–1, 90, 120–1.

6. The two principal studies are Dumenil, *Freemasonry and American Culture*, and Mary Ann Clawson, *Constructing Brotherhood* (Princeton, NJ: Princeton Univ. Press, 1989). Clawson shows that by the 1890s, secularizing and commodifying tendencies had begun to appear in aspects of fraternal ritual and public pageants, among other areas of fraternal life. As described in the *Tribune* article cited in n.1 above, the Masons' parade in the Loop and their cornerstone ceremony were good examples of the tendencies Clawson analyzes in "The Business of Brotherhood," Chap. 7 in *Constructing Brotherhood*, 211–42.

7. Chicagoans often read about Masonry in the *Chicago Tribune*, which, like many other American newspapers, offered fraternal columns and generally favorable coverage of Masonic activities (Dumenil, *Freemasonry and American Culture*, 8). An early Chicago historian's view of fraternalism in 1892 was a common

one: "Great Secret Societies [such as the] Free Masons [and] Odd Fellows... have their favorite field in Chicago. Here they exercise all their benevolent and ennobling influence, and mould and sway an innumerable host of the bone and sinew of the land." Joseph Kirkland, *The Story of Chicago* (Chicago: Dibble Publishing Co., 1892), 346. The Odd Fellows viewed Chicago as the future geographical center of its membership, and at least once considered relocating its national headquarters there from Baltimore. See "Another Huge Building," *Chicago Tribune*, Feb. 13, 1886, 8. In the 1870s and 1880s, the Masons who backed the Masonic Temple regarded "the future Chicago as the pivotal center of the continent and the metropolis of the world." See "The Masonic Temple," *Graphic* (Nov. 15, 1890):930.

8. Carnes, *Secret Ritual and Manhood*, 1; he also refers to a 1946 study which estimated that by the early 1900s the lodges of the different fraternal orders outnumbered churches in all large cities (see 89, n.113). Clawson, *Constructing Brotherhood*, 125.

9. Dumenil, *Freemasonry and American Culture*, 18–20. In form, new lodge buildings deliberately resembled courthouses or other kinds of public architecture rather than churches in order to dissociate Masonry from organized religion.

10. *Masonic Temple Hand Book*, n.p., n.d., unpaginated; in Folder 38JGM3z, "Masonic Temple, Chicago, Miscellaneous," Chicago Historical Society. The architectural firm of Flanders & Zimmerman and the interior decorator John C. W. Rhodes, both of Chicago, designed the Masonic rooms in "Grecian," "Gothic," and "Oriental" styles. For plans of these spaces, see in the same folder a second *Masonic Temple Hand Book*, 8, 10, 12, 14, 16.

The Odd Fellows projected their lodge rooms on the same generous scale. For a plan of their drill hall and meeting halls on the tenth floor, see Jordy, "The Tall Buildings," 120, Fig. 104c (corrected caption on errata sheet). To the best of my knowledge, Jordy is the only architectural historian to note one of the most salient features of this project, that in it "the Odd Fellows meant to outdo Burnham and Root... Masonic Temple... in combining boastful visibility and business acumen" (121).

11. On the analogies for cement and the artisanal objects used in Masonic rituals, see Barbara Franco's essay in *Masonic Symbols in American Decorative Arts* (Lexington, MA: Scottish Rite Masonic Museum of Our National Heritage, 1975), 19–52. For a view of Masonry that clearly distinguished, as Cregier's speech did not, between the legendary and the actual history of the order, see "The Masonic Temple," *Graphic* (Nov. 15, 1890):928, 930, which presents the Chicago Masons' history of their own order. See Clawson, *Constructing Brotherhood*, 248, on the need for an origin myth.

12. See, for example, Paul Boyer, *Urban Masses and Moral Order 1820–1920* (Cambridge, MA: Harvard Univ. Press, 1992).

13. Dumenil, *Freemasonry and American Culture*, 11–13; Carnes, *Secret Ritual and Manhood*, 4; Clawson, *Constructing Brotherhood*, 129–35.

14. Dumenil, *Freemasonry and American Culture*, 111. For many other examples of single-cause and single-solution thinking in this era, see Robert Wiebe, *The Search for Order 1877–1920* (New York: Hill and Wang, 1966).

15. Masonry's idealized picture of artisanal values and forms of interaction constituted one of its strongest appeals; see Clawson, *Constructing Brotherhood*, 145–177, 181, 212; and 77–83 for a summary of the ritual content for the degree of Master Mason. Carnes, *Secret Ritual and Manhood*, closely examines the social and psychological appeals of this and other fraternal rituals throughout his book. He emphasizes that in uncertain times, lodge life provided men with substantial certainty about ways to achieve responsible adulthood. Emotionally charged rituals countered the rationalized and instrumental workplace, the lack of dramatic religious expression in many Protestant denominations, and the emotional deficits of Victorian households in which fathers were frequently absent or withdrawn. Ranked initiations for the different levels of instruction and office-holding promised to confer on the initiate the guidance of surrogate father and authority figures and to help reconcile him to new hierarchies of subordination and deference in work and social life. Just as domestic ideologies enshrined women in domestic work and the suburbs, Masonry and the fraternal movement affirmed male emotional and moral self-sufficiency in the gender-segregated world of the downtown lodge.

16. Dumenil, *Freemasonry and American Culture*, 7–8. Carter H. Harrison, another Mason, preceded Cregier as mayor of Chicago, and was elected to an unprecedented four successive terms (1879–87); Kirkland, *The Story of Chicago*, 360–1. For architectural manifestations around 1890 of Chicago's expanding club life, see the numerous commissions for club space in the work of Adler and Sullivan in Jordy, "Tall Buildings," 120–2.

17. On the origins of the word skyscraper, used with some frequency in Chicago, see Sarah Bradford Landau and Carl Condit, *Rise of the New York Skyscraper 1865–1913* (New Haven: Yale Univ. Press, 1996), ix–x; and Bluestone, *Constructing Chicago*, 221, n.16.

18. An early conjoining of the word "sky-scrapers" with the Masonic Temple occurs in Kirkland, *The Story*

of Chicago, 448, in a passage where the word still retains some sense of the emotional impact exerted on observers by such suddenly large buildings. The best example of a foreigner's response to the skyscraper's rhetorical impact is Paul Bourget, *Outre-Mer: Impressions of America* (New York: Charles Scribner's Sons, 1895), 117–19.

19. Siry, *Carson Pirie Scott*, 41; "The Masonic Temple," *Graphic*, (Nov. 15, 1890):930. The Masonic Temple was first to have been 15, then 18, then 20 stories. Hoffman (*The Architecture of John Wellborn Root*, 196) avers that the $830,000 cost of the site may have been the reason the temple's height kept increasing in order to generate the income necessary for debt service. The *Graphic* reported the cost of the site at $1 million, which strengthens Hoffman's argument. The prospect of still higher profits from the building boom and the international attention from fairgoers may also have contributed to the height increases.

20. "Higher than Others," *Chicago Tribune*, Sept. 5, 1891, 1. Only the Eiffel Tower, at 985 feet, would have been taller than the Odd Fellows project, which was as high as the Washington Monument.

21. Louis Sullivan developed ways to prevent increasingly tall and bulky office buildings from darkening streets and neighboring offices in "The High Building Question," *Graphic* (Dec. 19, 1891):405; reprinted in Donald Hoffmann, "The Setback Skyscraper of 1891: An Unknown Essay by Louis H. Sullivan," *Journal of the Society of Architectural Historians* 29 (May 1970):181–7. Adler analyzed ways to provide adequate natural light to offices in large office buildings during a time when electric light bulbs were weak. See Dankmar Adler, "Light in Tall Office Buildings," *Engineering Magazine* 4 (Nov. 1892):176–86. On the importance of light in the social construction of white-collar work in the new office environment of the skyscraper, see Bluestone, *Constructing Chicago*, 140–1.

22. A reference and a drawing in the *Tribune* article suggest that for the tower and its steeply sloping crown the architects may have taken as their point of departure a famous obelisk, the Washington Monument, completed only seven years earlier. Perhaps cued by the Odd Fellows Building Association, the *Tribune* reporter stated in the opening paragraph that the building would be "as high as the Washington Monument [556 feet]." An unattributed schematic drawing of the project in the middle of this paragraph shows a tower and pyramidal crown that suggest a bulkier version of the monument. In the presentation drawing of the project, however, this clear similarity disappears because the observation deck just below the crown is much larger, the tower is set back just above the deck, and the now chamfered angles of the pyramid have changed it to a faceted cone. But the pyramid, like the monument's, retains its steep slope to read tellingly from a distance.

The reporter's reference is an early example of a motif often repeated in later skyscraper publicity. A height equal to that of the famous obelisk could have amplified the tower's potential prominence by borrowing prestige from a public monument and by suggesting that the temple itself would be a kind of public monument. The suggestion was plausible, for the project possessed some of the same physical attributes as public monuments: magnitude, central location, and a capacity to shape a city's image. The *Tribune*'s reference to the Washington Monument showed how associations to public structures could help dignify or even legitimate profit motives and status ambitions. The Odd Fellows may have planned a tower as tall as the Washington Monument for just these reasons, making it no higher in order to not violate their own militant patriotism or that of many other Americans by upstaging a revered public monument.

A much closer adaptation of a skyscraper to the form of a prestigious public structure is Bruce Price's 1891 unbuilt design for the New York Sun Building. Landau and Condit point out that it was the first skyscraper whose architect used Venice's Campanile to create a tower silhouette, thereby conflating "expressions of both the civic and the business worlds," Landau and Condit, *Rise of the New York Skyscraper*, 201–3. Price's major and minor horizontal emphases did not exploit the inherent vertical thrust of a tower silhouette as fully as the Odd Fellows tower did.

23. "Plans for Odd-Fellows' Temple," *Chicago Tribune*, Sept. 6, 1891, 29. All subsequent quotations of the prospectus are from this article.

24. For the Odd Fellows' middle-class status, see Carnes, *Secret Ritual and Manhood*, 25–9. The two articles in the *Chicago Tribune* were examples of the status enhancement and the self-advertising that the statement limned. In financial terms, the quoted statement implied that a building of this kind would produce higher rents and faster building appreciation than other first-class but lower office buildings. The newspaper, long an ardent supporter of all enterprises that increased the city's chances for greatness, hailed the project as "the highest and most costly building... in the world."

25. "Will Build the Temple," *Chicago Tribune*, Sept. 19, 1891, 2. Twombly attributes the ultimate failure to build this project to insufficient funds, the difficulties of finding a site, and new municipal limits on building height. See Twombly, *Louis Sullivan*, 304.

26. Landau and Condit, *Rise of the New York Skyscraper*, 90. In New York and Chicago, the more declamatory buildings and unexecuted projects of the

1890s were often much larger and taller than the more modest commercial buildings of the 1880s. For New York buildings and projects, see Landau and Condit, 78–90, 201–3, 211–12; see 197–201 for the World Building (1890), the tallest building in the U.S. until the Masonic Temple exceeded it in height. For a project for Lower Broadway, see Lewis, *An Early Encounter with Tomorrow*, 119–21.

27. On Masonry's hostility to materialism and commercialism, see Dumenil, *Freemasonry and American Culture*, 94–101. Masons condoned moderate or "respectable" worldly success but only if tempered by the virtues and character building that Masonry sought to instill.

28. On the cost of the site, see "The Masonic Temple," *Graphic*, (Nov. 15, 1890):930; and Hoffman, *The Architecture of John Wellborn Root*, 196. For an overview of the Loop's building boom, profits, and the resulting advances in building construction speed, see 58–66 and n.38. One of Chicago's real estate publications noted of the temple's site on the northwest corner of the intersection that "at all hours of the day, and late into the evening, throngs of people congregate about it." *Economist* 3 (June 21, 1890):807. State Street was the Loop's retail artery and Randolph Street its entertainment spine. For an overview of the architectural consequences of intensified commercialism in New York, see Robert A. M. Stern, Gregory Gilmartin, and John Massengale, *New York 1900* (New York: Rizzoli International, 1987), 144–272.

29. Thomas Tallmadge, *Architecture in Old Chicago* (Chicago: The Univ. of Chicago Press, 1941), 203. Tallmadge was a Chicago resident and architect in his early twenties when the Temple opened, and thus a witness to the Temple's first years of fame. Francisco Mujica, *History of the Skyscraper* (1930; repr., Ann Arbor, MI: Xerox Univ. Microfilms, 1975), 56.

30. Julian Ralph, "The Highest of All Roof Gardens," *Harper's Weekly Magazine* (Sept. 3, 1892):855. All subsequent quotations from Ralph are from this short essay. There was some criticism of aspects of the temple's design in the architectural press, but this seems not to have affected the favorable lay response. For a summary of the criticism, see Condit, *Chicago School*, 107; Hoffmann, *Architecture of John Wellborn Root*, 202, 204; and Robert Bruegmann, *The Architects and the City: Holabird & Roche of Chicago 1880–1918* (Chicago: Univ. of Chicago Press, 1997), 106.

31. *Masonic Temple Hand Book*, third page of the unpaginated text.

32. *Masonic Temple Observatory and Roof Garden*, n.p., n.d., unpaginated six-page foldout brochure. Folder 38JGM3z, "Masonic Temple, Chicago, Miscellaneous," Chicago Historical Society. All subsequent quotations on the observatory's facilities and exhibits are from this brochure.

33. David E. Nye, *American Technological Sublime* (Cambridge, MA: MIT Press, 1994), 147–9.

34. *Masonic Temple Hand Book*, second page. The Masons also sought to reinforce the Masonic identity of the building by incising large Masonic symbols in the granite blocks of the blind arcade above the entrance arch (Hoffmann, *Architecture of John Wellborn Root*, 202), and by naming the seven shopping "streets" "in honor of distinguished members of the order." Quoted from "The Masonic Temple," *Graphic* (Nov. 15, 1890):930.

35. *Masonic Temple Hand Book*, third page.

36. "A City Under One Roof – The Masonic Temple," *Scientific American* 10 (Feb. 1894):1, 82.

37. Unlike the centers of most American and European cities, the Loop's commercial development in the 1870s and 1880s crowded out public squares, displaced churches from the Loop, compromised the eastward views from its narrow lakefront park with a long train trestle, and dwarfed its four public structures with dozens of increasingly tall commercial buildings. Even the public functions of the Auditorium and Schiller theaters were housed in two of the Loop's largest new skyscrapers. This commercial concentration provided one important motive for rebuilding and strengthening the civic identity of Chicago from the mid-1890s onward. See Lewis, *An Early Encounter with Tomorrow*, Chap. 6; and Bluestone, *Constructing Chicago*, 152–204.

38. Leach, *Land of Desire*, 15–90. For a detailed examination of the interrelated design and commercial rationales for one department store at the turn of the century, see Siry, *Carson Pirie Scott*, 119–204.

39. Hoffmann, *Architecture of John Wellborn Root*, 202; "City Under One Roof," 1, 82; *Masonic Temple Hand Book*, second and third pages.

40. On the extent to which rich materials appeared in office buildings see Bluestone, *Constructing Chicago*, 104–51. Tallmadge, *Architecture in Old Chicago*, 203, gives the figure of 31 per square foot for Burnham and Root's Rookery (1886), Chicago's "most expensive building" prior to the temple's 35 per square foot.

41. Lewis, *An Early Encounter with Tomorrow*, 144; "The Masonic Temple," *Graphic* (Nov. 15, 1890):930; *Scientific American*, "City Under One Roof," 82.

42. The German visitor's comparison appears in Lewis, *An Early Encounter with Tomorrow*, 144; the comment on show windows is from *Scientific American*, "City Under One Roof," 82. The balcony street

names were to allow "Mrs. Browne to be shot up to Smith Street, instead of starting with the idea of going up to" a perhaps discouragingly high floor like the ninth to shop; see "Chicago," *American Architect* 30 (Nov. 1890):120. The balcony streets were named for prominent Masons backing the temple; see "The Masonic Temple," *Graphic* (Nov. 15, 1890):930. The *Economist* 3 (June 21, 1890):807 commended the commercial savvy of the floor plan and the exceptionally large store windows facing the balconies: "Standing in the large space about which the elevators are grouped, the front of every shop... is plainly visible, and these fronts are arranged with great plate glass show windows, similar to the most attractive of street facades."

43. The temple's nine floors of shops – a translation of the horizontal iron-and-glass gallerias in European and American cities into the vertical confines of a steel-framed skyscraper – were probably the precedents for similar spaces in department stores developed by D.H. Burnham and Co. over the next 18 years. The firm's later design for the Marshall Field Department Store included a twelve-story balconied light court whose dimensions approximated those for the temple. The court did much to make shopping there more theatrical and spatially arresting, as did the store's Tiffany-domed five-story atrium, and the seven-story atrium for the firm's Wanamaker's store. Typologically, the temple's light court of shops is also the precedent for shopping atria in late modern and postmodern skyscraper complexes.

44. For an examination of the consumer fantasy of self-remaking, see Leach, *Land of Desire*, 3–90.

45. The barber shop advertisement appears in *Masonic Temple Hand Book*, 23 (the second of the two handbooks). The Masonic parlors were not complete when this and the other handbook were published, but both indicate that, in addition to all of the seventeenth and eighteenth floors, "two thirds of the nineteenth and one third of the twentieth floors are to be fitted up for the exclusive accommodation of Masonic bodies" (p. 17).

46. On these tendencies in Masonry, see Dumenil, *Freemasonry and American Culture*, 87–8, 101. Consistent with them and the location of prestigious clubs in skyscrapers (see, for example, Jordy, "Tall Buildings," 120–2) was the Masons' intention to place a "club-room" in the middle of the State Street frontage on the seventeenth floor; it was described as "a beautiful large room... that can be used for a reading room or place of public resort for Masons to meet during the day time, for large committees to meet in, or for a small banquet of less than a hundred persons. The walls and ceiling will be elaborately decorated and the furniture rich and substantial." *Masonic Temple Hand Book*, fifth page.

47. Bluestone, *Constructing Chicago*, 151.

48. Mujica, *History of the Skyscraper*, 56–7. Mujica also called the temple "the first skyscraper of great importance" (caption for Plate 25). The question of the first skyscrapers is distinct from the question of which ones were the first to be recognized as the world's tallest commercial buildings. The best treatments of the technological and formal developments in the earliest skyscrapers (1870s) are Winston Weisman, "New York and the Problem of the First Skyscraper," *Journal of the Society of Architectural Historians* 12 (Mar. 1953):13–21; and Landau and Condit, *Rise of the New York Skyscraper*, 62–107, 120–1.

49. Adler and Sullivan's Auditorium (1887–89) housed a hotel, a recital hall, an opera house and offices; similarly, their Schiller Theater (1891–92) contained an auditorium and office space. On later mixed-use skyscrapers, see my "The Skyscraper, City-Within-a-City and the Myth of the Self-Made Man in the 1920s," *Journal of Architectural Education* 42 (Winter 1989):10–23; and "Design and Civic Identity in Cincinnati's Carew Tower Complex," *Journal of the Society of Architectural Historians* 51 (Mar. 1992):35–47.

50. On roof gardens in New York, see Stern et al., *New York 1900*, 220–2. Burnham and Root also designed a roof garden for the Great Northern Hotel, a nearly exact contemporary of the Masonic Temple; see Bluestone, *Constructing Chicago*, 141. For a photograph of the small, utilitarian observation deck on the Auditorium, see Jordy "The Tall Buildings," 101; for illustrations of the even smaller observatory in the lantern atop the dome on the New York World (Pulitzer) Building, see Landau & Condit, *Rise of the New York Skyscraper*, 198, 201.

51. Perhaps the most elaborate opening or dedication celebrations for skyscrapers in this period of time were those for the Auditorium, with President Benjamin Harrison, Vice-President Levi Morton, and operatic idol Adelina Patti in attendance (see Twombly, *Louis Sullivan*, 175–7); and for the World Building (1890), its management invited numerous state governors, transported many senators and representatives from Washington, DC, on a special train, and staged a fireworks spectacle (see *World*, Dec. 10, 1890, 1, and the souvenir issue, Dec. 11, 1890, 1–7).

52. The first attempt to best a rival skyscraper in height may have involved New York's Tribune (1873–75) and Western Union (1872–75) buildings; see Landau & Condit, *Rise of the New York Skyscraper*, 78–9, 85.

The owner of the World Building in New York claimed that at 309 feet (7 feet higher than the Masonic Temple) it was "the loftiest business building in existence." However, this height was taken from the narrow Frankfort Street side of the building, where the site slopes markedly downward, rather than from the main frontage on Park Row overlooking City Hall Park (see Landau & Condit, *Rise of the New York Skyscraper*, 197–9). Moreover, in three separate issues on the building in two days, with twelve full pages of coverage that mentioned some of the building's noteworthy features several times, the newspaper made its claim about height only once, as the sixth of eight headlines in the souvenir issue. Other newspapers did not mention this claim (see, for example, *New York Times*, Dec. 11, 1890, 3; and *Chicago Tribune*, Dec. 12, 1890, editorial page). I have been unable to discover any evidence that Joseph Pulitzer, the World's owner, or anyone else, ever disputed the Masons' claim that their temple was the world's tallest commercial building. Pulitzer clearly wanted his building to dominate other New York buildings, especially those of rival newspapers in the immediate vicinity, but he appears never to have touted the World as the highest business building on earth.

If built, architect Bruce Price's thirty-two-story campanile design for the *Sun* (1891), another New York City newspaper, would have exerted the kind of regional dominance the backers of the Odd Fellows' tower sought. But neither the architect nor the newspaper recognized this possibility in the *Sun*'s long text on the project (Feb. 8, 1891, 16).

The four boom periods and their most important rivalries for supreme skyscraper height are those of the Singer, Metropolitan, and Woolworth buildings (1900–13); the Chrysler and Empire State buildings (1928–31); the World Trade Center and Chicago's Hancock and Sears towers (1965–73); and four buildings and unbuilt projects in Chicago, Tokyo, Hong Kong, Kuala Lumpur, and Sao Paulo in the 1980s and 1990s.

53. George Ade, "In the Roof Garden," *Chicago Stories* (Chicago: Regnery, 1963), 243–7; Edgar Lee Masters, *Across Spoon River* (New York: Farrar & Rinehart, 1936), 145. The height of St. Peter's Basilica, from the floor to the top of the cross on the dome's lantern, is 452 feet; Bannister Fletcher, *A History of Architecture* (London: Butterworths, 1987), 870. "Plumb, Level, Square," *Chicago Tribune*, Nov. 7, 1890, 1–2, contains the first erroneous identification of the temple as "the highest building in the world." Although the Masonic handbooks qualified the temple's height correctly, the hand-sized pamphlet termed it "the tallest building in the world," as have nearly all the historians who have written on the Masonic Temple since then.

54. Tallmadge, *Architecture in Old Chicago*, 205.

6

The Corporate and the Civic

Metropolitan Life's Home Office Building

Roberta Moudry

Financial institutions, among them life insurance companies, are prominent builders and owners of skyscrapers. Serving as corporate headquarters, these skyscrapers are symbolic markers on the skyline – one thinks of the TransAmerica Building in San Francisco, the John Hancock Building in Chicago, or the Wall Street skyscrapers of the 1920s and 1930s described in Daniel Abramson's recent text *Skyscraper Rivals*.[1] They are also operational centers of corporate activity and important visual totems for an industry lacking a tangible product. Whereas the imprint of these powerhouses of capital on the urban landscape is more extensive than any singular architectural event – their mortgages, bonds, and philanthropic activities are conduits for the financial sector's urban investments – the form and function of the skyscraper headquarters comprise the institution's constructed identity, serving as a public explication of business goals and corporate culture.

This essay focuses on the corporate headquarters of one such institution, the Metropolitan Life Insurance Company. In 1890, Met Life made a surprising break from the financial district of downtown Manhattan and built an eleven-story home office uptown at the

I extend my thanks to Dan May, MetLife's company archivist for facilitating numerous research visits and email requests. Earlier versions of this essay were presented at the College Art Association Annual Conference, Feb. 2000, New York City; the Gotham History Festival, Oct. 2001, Gotham Center, New York City; and the Hagley Research Seminar Series, the Hagley Museum and Library, Feb. 2003. I am grateful to those who offered ideas and critique at these presentations, and who posed questions that prompted refinements, including Sarah Landau, Carol Willis, Roger Horowitz and Angel Kwolek-Folland. Special thanks to Edward K. Muller for his detailed, critical reading.

southeastern edge of Madison Square, then a fashionable social center. Over the next half-century, Met Life's headquarters kept pace with its rapidly growing business, filling two city blocks in over a dozen building campaigns, with a complex that served multiple functions as a public relations device, a highly efficient nerve center for a dispersed, paper-intensive industry, and the cornerstone of the company's welfare program. Just as the complex changed form and internal arrangements multiple times over its fifty-plus years of construction, the accretive building process also altered its immediate urban context, displacing neighboring buildings and their institutions, and affecting the usage of Madison Square Park.

As an insurer of millions of working-class Americans' lives, Met Life profited directly from the health and longevity of its employees and clients. Thus the company sought to transform all dimensions of the workers' city – the home, workplace, and public zones – into healthy and systematized spaces through investment, a welfare program, and construction of large-scale housing projects for the middle class, coupled with educational programming. The home office served simultaneously as a powerful urban symbol of corporate ideology and a site where welfare initiatives were tested and packaged for public consumption.[2]

Met Life both expressed and accommodated its specific blend of corporate and civic identities through the physical aspect of its home office – its site and design, its uses and meanings. Examination of the home office's physical qualities and operation, and its presentation to the public through texts, artifacts, and photographs indicate how Met Life conveyed both corporate and civic identities by three means: architectural design, image-making, and the promotion of behavioral models. As a functioning office building, as well as a widely disseminated model of spatial and social organization, the home office stood as Met Life's most potent urban explication of a corporate ideology with implications for the office, the home, and the public spaces of streets and parks.

By highlighting the connection between Met Life's skyscraper headquarters and the built and cultural landscape of the city, this essay endeavors, in David Harvey's vernacular, to spatialize a corporate history – to trace the three-dimensional impact of a corporation and its culture on the spaces of the city and the ways those spaces were experienced and valued.[3]

The Life Insurance Enterprise

Achieving popular acceptance only in the mid-nineteenth century, life insurance was both modern and urban. It offered industrial workers and capitalists financial security upon the death of the breadwinner, replacing a matter once managed by church or extended family with an impersonal business contract based on mortality statistics and administered with scientific efficiency.[4]

Met Life, established in 1868 as a life insurance concern, was a newcomer to an industry already well established in New York City's financial markets. An industrial or working-class insurance program, introduced in 1879, produced phenomenal growth, and Met Life soon rivaled the size and public position of "The Big Three," industry giants Equitable Life Assurance Association, Mutual Life Insurance, and New York Life Insurance companies.[5]

The physical world of New York City life insurance into which Met Life emerged was geographically clustered on Lower Broadway. A boom in the insurance industry following the Civil War gave rise to a series of home office buildings in the vicinity of City Hall Park. Their monumental size and aesthetics were driven by industry-wide needs for buildings that would serve as investments, house large quantities of clerks and records, and convey positive attributes: wealth tempered by conservative business practice; religious and secular morality; and allegiance to civic and family values. Equitable, Mutual, and New York Life built opulent home offices on Broadway between 1865 and 1870, and all three expanded these structures shortly after their completion. New York Life and Mutual expanded upward, adding floors, elevators, and mansard roofs. Equitable expanded laterally, and by 1887, filled nearly the full city block bounded by Broadway and Cedar, Pine and Nassau streets.[6]

In the years between the company's founding in 1868 and 1893, Met Life occupied three different offices: the first two were rental spaces in the four- to five-story storefront buildings that lined lower Broadway in the last half of the nineteenth century. In December 1875, the still-young company purchased the Constant Building, a five-story loft building on the southwest corner of Church Street and Park Place, just one block to the west of the 200 block of Broadway, City Hall Park, and the insurance strip. Architect Napoleon LeBrun transformed the exterior with a domed corner tower and created office and rental floors on the interior, a commission that marked the beginning of a protracted relationship with the LeBrun firm, and the company's development of business practices, including the hiring of a largely female workforce, which had spatial and organizational implications.[7]

By the late 1880s, undesirable changes to the area and the northward drift of business prompted the company to consider a move to uptown. Committed to a location with unobstructed views and expansion potential, Met Life purchased a site fronting Madison Square Park, situated along Broadway's angling spine at the northern edge of Ladies' Mile.

At this time the park's eastern edge was lined with residences, interrupted only by the spiky brownstone form of the Madison Square Presbyterian Church, famous as the home of Rev. Charles Parkhurst's war against crime and political corruption. Hotels, restaurants, and theaters gradually moved into the area; and in 1890, architect Stanford White designed a full-block sports and entertainment arena, Madison Square Garden, at the square's northeastern corner. The Garden quickly became a prominent social destination, and its towered roofscape, particularly its singular 340-foot tower, topped with a statue of Diana, placed Madison Square on the urban skyline.[8]

One Madison Avenue

Built between 1891 and 1893 at the northeast corner of Madison Avenue and Twenty-third Street, Met Life's original Madison Square structure was an eleven-story white marble Renaissance palazzo. Although aesthetically unremarkable as an office building, its cubic mass stood white and imposing among its dark, smaller-scaled neighbors. Its two richly detailed facades fronted Madison and Twenty-third, and the building's main entrance fronted the park. The structure's design directed focus to the building corner at Madison and Twenty-third – architect and company executives fully grasped the value of impressive views to and from Broadway and the park (Figure 38). Structure and aesthetics were conservative, as one would expect of a conservative business, and the desired impression was one of solidity and traditional values.[9]

The public areas of the new building were spacious and detailed in rich materials. The main entrance opened into a marble corridor and an elaborate stair hall capped with a coved mosaic ceiling and a stained glass dome 70 feet above the floor. Fashioned after the famous Paris Opera staircase, the marble staircase served as a theatrical set piece and as access to the cashiers' department and executive offices – two areas much photographed for, but closed to, the public.[10]

38. Metropolitan Life Home Office, ca. 1898. Courtesy of the Library of Congress, Prints and Photographs Div., Detroit Publishing Co. Collection [LC-D4-10555-R].

Upper floors of the building (floors two through five) were intended for company use, and the remaining space was divided into rental offices for professionals or small companies. Early tenants included brick, glass, and mosaic concerns, insurance and real estate companies, and the company architect, N. LeBrun & Sons. However, by December 1893, less than six months after occupying the new building, Met Life had expanded to fill portions of the first, sixth, and ninth floors. In need of more space, the company constructed a 115- by 100-foot addition, fronting on Twenty-fourth Street and situated diagonally behind the original building. Due to its practical use and less prominent site, the addition was given a relatively plain facade, although its marble veneer, simple details, and cornice complemented the original office block. When the annex was completed late in 1895, the company vacated the original home office except for the second floor, whose custom design for executive and cashiers' offices made it unsuitable for office rental. In this manner, the company retained its monumental corner building for advertisement and income, while easing its management tasks by containing all employees within a single-use, purpose-built structure.[11]

From 1894 until 1906, the company engaged in land acquisition and building expansion, using the LeBrun firm to design building segments identical in height, surface material, and articulation to the original cube-like structure. In 1898, the company built a two-story taxpayer along much of the Twenty-third Street frontage; and in three building campaigns (1901, 1902, and 1905), the LeBrun firm extended the form, rhythm, and detailing of the original structure around the Twenty-third Street corner, along the Fourth Avenue frontage, and along Twenty-fourth Street, finally meeting the 1896 addition. The result was an aesthetically seamless, nearly full-block construction, a horizontal and vertical giant, whose uniform facade and cornice line increasingly placed the building at odds with its four- to five-story brownstone neighbors (Figure 39).[12]

The complex was linked by circulation spaces and communication technologies, including a grand marble arcade – a public thoroughfare lined with shops – that ran the full length of the Twenty-third Street facade (425 feet), opening onto Fourth Avenue (Park Avenue South) to the east and connecting to the original block's grand stair hall and its main Madison Avenue entrance to the west. At this time, Met Life also expanded on the northern side of Twenty-fourth Street, constructing a sixteen-story annex in 1905 to house the Printing Department and other support services.[13]

As Met Life worked with the LeBruns to shape a public face, the company interacted with its commercial and institutional neighbors, negotiating their moves and consuming their building sites. The company stated publicly two reasons for acquiring adjoining properties: to clear the way for future expansion, and to prevent the construction of structures "detrimental to the interests" of the company by virtue of function *or* appearance: the company felt that adjacent red brick or terra-cotta-faced buildings would detract from the upscale appearance of their white marble headquarters.[14] Both of these motivations fueled negotiations with the National Academy of Design, whose highly ornamented, polychromatic brick facades enlivened the corner of Twenty-third Street and Fourth Avenue. Designed in 1863 by P. B. Wight, the academy's headquarters housed exhibition galleries and studio space for art classes. Met Life's purchase offer in 1894 foreshadowed impending home office expansions, and served to emphasize what academy members had already observed: that the residential district was moving uptown away from their exhibition space, and the current bulk of the home office had already darkened the upstairs studios, which were filled to capacity with a new female constituency.[15] Selling their headquarters and two adjacent brownstones, the National Academy left Madison Square in 1899 for the Upper West Side.[16]

The sale and demise of the Academy building was an indication of the transformation of Madison Square by Met Life, the effect of the northward march of business on existing institutions, and the increase in urban real estate acquisition by large corporations.[17] Following Met Life, others built increasingly vertical commercial structures on the square: the Flatiron, a speculative office building turned icon of the modern age, was raised on a narrow triangle of land at the southern edge of the square in 1902, and in 1908, the sixteen-story Fifth Avenue Building replaced the once-bustling Fifth Avenue Hotel.[18]

Displacement of another prominent institution, the Madison Square Presbyterian Church, made possible the final, most dramatic and publicized addition to the office block, a 700-foot campanile. The brownstone gothic sanctuary built in 1854, the home of political reformer Rev. Charles Parkhurst, was completely surrounded by the white monolith of the home office when the congregation agreed to relocate across the street and build a new sanctuary on a site secured by Met Life.[19] Secured as the church architect, prominent architect Stanford White, designer of Madison Square Garden just two blocks to the north, took his design cues from Met Life's white marble complex – the full-block construction, the anticipated tower, and the sixteen-story annex on Twenty-fourth Street, located directly behind the new church site.[20] Composing a structure "in which delicacy and beauty of detail would be combined with a scale which could not be crushed by the surrounding skyscrapers," the architect packaged the church's needs into a domed, centralized structure of yellow buff brick fronted by a projecting portico of highly polished, green granite columns.[21] This church,

39. Metropolitan Life Home Office, ca. 1905. Reprinted with permission of the MetLife Archives.

however, fell to the same fate as its predecessor just ten years later, consumed by the last of Met Life's incremental additions, the 1919 New Annex.

Finally completing the building block bounded by Madison and Fourth avenues and by Twenty-third and Twenty-fourth streets, the fifty-story, 700-foot campanile, built between 1907 and 1909, fulfilled Company President Hegeman's long-standing wish for a home office tower. The tower provided office space for the company and for rental, but was intended primarily as a timely public declaration of civic stature and ethical responsibility (Figure 40).[22] Following the Armstrong Commission Investigation of 1905, which uncovered widespread corruption in the New York State life insurance industry, companies including Met Life visibly positioned themselves as public institutions, shifting from private stock to mutual ownership, and involving themselves in civic activities such as public health campaigns. Met Life's assertion that it was a civic institution was emphatic and architectural: the tower stood as the tallest inhabited building in the world, until surpassed by the Woolworth Building in 1913.[23]

Using the Campanile of San Marco in Venice, a well-known civic monument, for a model, the LeBruns designed a tower that echoed materials and detailing of the office block's base, carrying the line of the lower building's cornice with semi-octagonal balconies.[24] Yet the tower appeared from the park as a complete entity, rising from the sidewalk as an independent tower, unlike its contemporaries, such as the Singer Tower, which protruded from, or were embedded in, an office block and visible as "merely an emergence, a peak in a mountain chain."[25] At the top of the simply detailed shaft, four elaborately framed clock faces, balconies, and a loggia were topped by a gilded tower and an octagonal lantern.[26] These details gave the tower visual prominence, and they offered to the city a range of public amenities: timekeeping, an observation deck, and a geographical locator.

40. The Metropolitan Life Tower and Madison Square, ca. 1910. Collection of the author.

The tower was widely acclaimed in the popular, insurance, and architectural press. Manufacturers like the Otis Elevator Company, whose products were used in the tower, featured it prominently in their advertisements, publicizing the tower's cutting edge technologies – high-speed elevators, concrete and wire gauze floors, and elaborate wind bracing – and precluding any embarrassing comparison of the tower to its Venetian model, which had collapsed into a heap of rubble in 1902 (Figure 41).[27] The New York Chapter of the American Institute of Architects gave the building and its designers the 1909 award of merit for its significant contribution to the solution of the skyscraper problem. The company itself focused attention on the architects, turning a banquet celebrating the tower's completion into a testimonial for the retiring architect brothers.[28]

Part of the tremendous public attention surrounding American skyscraper design and construction, the Met Life tower received considerable attention in the popular press and was used as the advertising backdrop to an inexplicable collection of products ranging from sports coupes to corn flakes, chocolate, and coffee beans.[29] Fiske's assertion that "we do not have to advertise, for the tower advertises itself" was borne out by six months of newspaper coverage worldwide that garnered for the unfinished tower over $440,000 of free advertising.[30]

Also flooding the market were photographic views of and from the tower, the property of commercial photographers and postcard companies, who marketed the images as a part of an outpouring of skyscraper ephemera. These generic cityscapes, as well as the company's promotional photography, positioned the home office complex and tower in relationship to Madison Square Park and the urban landscape beyond, locking the tower to the city in a reciprocal act that made the park appear corporate and the tower appear civic. From stereographic cards documenting unimaginable technological

SCIENTIFIC AMERICAN

[Entered at the Post Office of New York, N. Y., as Second Class Matter. Copyright, 1908, by Munn & Co.]

Vol. XCVIII.—No. 18. Established 1845. | NEW YORK, MAY 2, 1908. | [10 CENTS A COPY $3.00 A YEAR.

The Finishing Coat of Waterproof Paint.

Swinging the Sledge, Five Hundred Feet in Midair.

On the Top of the Topmost Column.

Erection of the Great Tower, with the Marble at 324 Feet, and the Steelwork at 500 Feet Above the Sidewalk.

Photographs copyrighted 1908 by H. C. White Company.

Bird's-eye View of Madison Square.

A NEW YORK CAMPANILE 700 FEET HIGH.—[See page 310.]

41. "A New York Campanile 700 Feet High." Metropolitan Life Tower. Cover, *Scientific American* 98, no. 18 (May 2, 1908).

feats to the pictorialist portraits of the tower and its environment, most notably those of Alfred Stieglitz and Alvin Langdon Coburn, the tower entered into the urban vernacular.

"The Light that Never Fails"

The tower was successful in attracting publicity and conveying a host of positive attributes – permanence and stability, civic and corporate responsibility, the traditional values of religion, home, and country – and it rapidly became Met Life's corporate symbol, known to staff, policyholders, and the public as "The Light that Never Fails." The major insurance companies were heavily dependent on symbols or logos that conveyed desirable institutional qualities. Prudential, a major player in the industrial insurance field, acquired the Rock of Gibraltar logo in 1895.[31] Both New York Life and Equitable developed figural sculptures for their home offices that summarized intentions and goals: Equitable's 11-foot-high marble group, entitled "Protection," showed a widow and orphan under the protective shield of the allegorical figure of insurance, and New York Life chose a globe guarded by an eagle to portray its ambitions to both protect and expand.[32]

In contrast, Met Life used the actual architecture of its home office as its symbolic logo, thereby interlocking the company's daily work, corporate ideals, and urban presence. With the completion of the tower in 1909, the home office and its setting became the company's primary advertising tool, and its image was affixed to all company literature, policies, and canvassing material.[33] Line drawings of the tower with its beacon aglow marked policies and the thousands of booklets on health, business, and design the company wrote and distributed through the 1950s (Figure 42).

The tower's role as the company's public face – how it met the city and the urban everyman it sought to reform and insure – was extensive and profound. Through a company-generated flood of text and images, and specific building uses, the tower functioned as an iconographic billboard that featured overlapping religious, civic, and familial themes. The tower was depicted on everything from coloring books to drinking cups, from fly swatters to picture puzzles, and large tin models of the tower accompanied exhibits to county fairs and international expositions.[34]

The tower provided a bountiful range of historical and religious references to church towers and the New Jerusalem. Company Vice-President Haley Fiske, a deeply religious man, repeatedly cited parallels between Met Life's corporate ideals and religion-based morality, and he noted the fusion of the two in the symbolic architecture of the tower. In a 1909 address to company field workers, Fiske likened the tower's visual representation of Met Life's quasireligious goals to the cross's symbolic embodiment of Christianity. The tower, pointing to Heaven, denoted righteousness, and its white surfaces bespoke honesty and openness of character. The clock represented the systemization that ensured policyholders fair treatment; and the chimes symbolized the harmony and respect that the company advocated internally and toward its policyholders. Finally, the evening beacon atop the tower, "the light that never fails," recalled that the company never failed in meeting its obligations, offering assistance to its policyholders and workers beyond its contractual requirements.[35]

The tower struck a civic pose in a number of ways. The completion of the tower coincided almost precisely with a major shift in the company's identity and allocation of its energies. In 1909, Fiske hired Lee K. Frankel, a scientist turned social scientist and reformer, to initiate for the company a welfare program to educate policyholders about preventable diseases. Fiske's claim that "insurance, not merely as a business proposition, but as a social program,

42. "A War Upon Consumption." Cover, health booklet published by Metropolitan Life, 1909. This publication was printed in twelve languages, and over 11 million copies were distributed free to policyholders. Reprinted with permission of MetLife Archives.

will be the future policy of the Company" was not exaggerated. When industrial policyholders and company staff showed measurable benefits from the program, the company expanded its welfare efforts to support large-scale environmental and social reform in collaboration with organizations such as the Red Cross and the American Tuberculosis Society.[36] The tower presented such civic involvement in architectural language, taking the form of an Italian civic campanile, and more generally of the family towers of medieval Italian settlements such as San Gimingano, raised as assertions of dynastic and defensive strength. Like them, the Met Life tower represented the company's powerful position in the industry and the city, and symbolized refuge for policyholders, who could "fly to [the] Tower from the dangers of industrial life, from the enemies of civilization, disease, crime, from all the vicissitudes and uncertainties of life."[37]

As the tallest building in the world, the tower's technological feats were linked by such periodicals as *Scientific American* to national accomplishments in the areas of architecture and engineering (Figure 41).[38] Its public spaces and functions also contributed to its civic cast. Its four clock faces, daytime chimes, and nighttime beacon served the surrounding city, and the observation deck offered views of the larger metropolitan area.[39] The company used the tower repeatedly to make visible its programmatic links to the city below, inviting groups such as the Charity Organization Society to use its observation deck to introduce interns to the city where they would study social work.[40]

A symbol of civic responsibility and quasireligious morality, the tower was also embedded within a larger symbolic context of the home and family, recurrent themes in insurance advertising. Life insurance protected the living family, promising that after the death of the male head, they would help the survivors construct "a house of protection."[41] The tower was the ever-present reminder that Met Life *itself* was ever present, to honor its contractual obligations, to aid the worker in making a stable and healthy home for his family, and to guide mother and children in homemaking and good citizenship.

Like the policyholder, Met Life possessed an actual and figurative home, in the form of the office block and tower. Lending a second meaning to the term "home office," this long-lived promotional construction rendered the office building as a figurative home for a family that included the larger spread of policyholders (in 1920, one out of every five North Americans), the inner network of employees, the father figure of the company president, and of course, the benevolent and protecting Mother Metropolitan.[42] Emanating from the home office's tower, the beacon represented the company's offer of stability, security, and enlightenment to its extended, geographically dispersed family.[43]

The home and family metaphors, on the grand scale of the corporation, utilized the same gender constructs that defined the work and social life of the home office and its agency counterparts. All company employees were regarded as "older siblings" to the larger family of policyholders; but only the agents (overwhelmingly male) functioned as "the big brothers," whose task was to guide the masses, and to carry "among these people that Light that Never Fails."[44] As the men of the family, agents were "guardians of the light," as stated in the final verses of the company anthem, sung at all field conferences:

> We're the guardians of "The Tower,"
> And the light which it enveils;
> It's the symbol of our power
> To its height no other scales.
>
> For its grandeur and beauty
> Will teach to each his duty
> To be steadfast and loyal
> To "The Light That Never Fails."[45]

Binding the agent yet closer to the company and its physical symbol, Fiske emphasized that each agent was not only a guardian, but also a human light himself, a small but essential part of the great symbolic beacon atop the tower. The assertion that the worker was literally *part* of the building, "a stone ... carefully chosen, unblemished, well-chiseled, cemented with devotion to a common cause, placed ... to rear up a proud and noble organization founded on the corner-stones of loyalty and obedience," was a particularly useful symbolic strategy to keep those in the field, primarily agents, connected to the home office and the goals of the corporation.[46] With these suggestions, an agent on the West Coast could visualize his relationship to fellow East Coast agents and home office clerks, and to the ideals of honesty and service that the tower beacon represented.

The Insurance Factory

Congruent with the symbolic functions of the home office was the operation of the insurance "factory," the network of elevators, corridors, and workrooms, tightly regulated and closed to the public.[47] For hundreds of agencies dispersed throughout the country, the home office served as a supply warehouse, records processing center and repository, and nerve center through which all communication flowed. In addition, it was the central office for company officers, who were responsible for all decision making. Although the working interior of the home office, from its 1893 kernel to the massive complex of the 1920s, underwent spatial rearrangement roughly every five years, the interior form and function were consistently customized to accommodate these tasks by scientific office management, new technologies, and welfare imperatives.[48]

Met Life developed standardized procedures and work-flow-related spatial organization beginning in the 1880s, as a necessary step in management of an increasing volume of work; and the company was lent external expertise after about 1910 from the developing field of office management. The home office interior space was arranged to facilitate movement of paper and people. Public spaces at the ground floor level of the 1909 full-block home office linked the original stair hall and a 400-foot-long marble arcade lined with shops with elevator banks servicing the entire complex, access to all boundary streets, and access to the subway system. Beyond this richly ornamented zone of shopping and movement from building to city street, the building was off limits to the public, a restriction enforced by the Bureau of Information, elevator operators, and hallway monitors. Interior corridors, recreation spaces including the roof, elevators, and even ground-floor entrances were designated for use on the basis of workers' gender, floor, or division; and employees' movements were closely monitored.[49]

On upper floors, open, unornamented spaces housing dozens of clerks placed a premium on natural light and ventilation, and permitted instruction and supervision of a large number of workers performing similar tasks (Figure 43). Departments were situated in relation to each other to facilitate the paper flow from one site to the next and to provide workers with access to toilet facilities.[50] This "factory layout," advocated by office management expert J. William Schulze, was used by many paper-intensive insurance companies at a time when smaller enclosures still characterized the clerical zone of other businesses. Some functions required specially outfitted and located spaces. For example, the filing section featured the largest steel case system in the country; to maintain order and efficiency, it was closed to all workers except those assigned there. Coexisting within the full-block home office wrapper were company workspaces and small rented office spaces, further complicating the regulation of space and workers.[51]

These systemized spaces were served by time-saving technologies, such as the typewriter, telephone, and pneumatic tubes, which were always partnered with company-wide protocols. An integrated system of company clocks and gongs linked to a master clock in the president's office maintained efficiency and coordinated work and circulation schedules. There was a symbolic subtext as well. In the field of life insurance, the clock symbolized the passage of one's lifetime and the need for hard work, and Met Life's integrated timekeeping system symbolized the efficiency, loyalty, and mutual interdependence of an ideal home office staff.[52] Office systems, like their architectural container, had both practical and symbolic functions: they were critical to maintaining production and order, and at the same time they denoted an efficient and resourceful enterprise to policyholders, whose investments, held in trust, capitalized the business.[53]

Home office space and activities were also substantially shaped by Met Life's employee welfare efforts, which were developed into a coordinated program in 1909 by scientist-reformers Frankel and his assistant, statistician Louis I. Dublin. Within the home office, a library, auditorium, medical and dental examination rooms, and a gymnasium offered space and services as an employee benefit. A portion of the 1893 roof was tiled for employee use and became part of lunchtime recreational space, supplementing an equipped gym, while the auditorium doubled as a studio for ballroom dance instruction. A lunchroom serving coffee and tea was provided for women as early as 1893, and between 1908 and 1994, the company's substantial kitchens, bakeries, and dining rooms supplied free lunches to all employees.[54] Workrooms were welfare-inflected as well: layout and seating met lighting and ventilation parameters, and deskside five-minute exercise periods were conducted at midmorning and afternoon, with open windows and gramophone.[55]

Not all nonwork activities were delegated separate space within the home office, but their existence changed employees' uses and perceptions of the building. Free after-hours classes covering topics relevant to work and home, such as typing, actuarial science, sewing, and first aid, as well as clubs, placed the home office at the center of many workers' lives. Unlike the skyscraper offices described by C. Wright Mills and Carl Sandburg, beehives of clerical activity left silent and empty after working hours, Met Life's home office was fashioned by company officials, and by workers themselves, as a place that demanded more than work and gave back more than a paycheck.[56]

While worker welfare programs at industrial plants nationwide peaked after the turn of the century and declined dramatically by the late 1920s,[57] Met Life embarked on its white-collar welfare program in the 1890s and continued to expand it through the 1930s, folding it after 1909 into a larger welfare program for policyholders and the general public. It is this connection between worker and policyholder welfare that again brought the home office and its internal workings and culture in contact with the city beyond its walls. Health programs initiated within the home office were shared with policyholders and the public after assessment by company officials. Conversely, major projects and exhibitions for the public were previewed for staff in the home office. In a more literal fashion, Met Life offered its operation as a model, a laboratory for the development of corporate best practices, through publications of the Policyholders' Service Bureau. A corporate subdivision, the bureau undertook and published studies for group policyholders in office design, employee management and benefits, safety measures, and community relations, frequently citing home office practices.[58]

The company's home office spaces and practices were showcased to agents, policyholders, and the public through descriptive texts and photographs that took the form of postcards, pamphlets, magazine articles, and exhibitions. Central to the company's imagemaking were three oversized monographs published by the company in 1897, 1908, and 1914, lavishly illustrated with photographs of the building, its interiors, and its staff – images that were reproduced by the millions in the form of postcards. Photographs depicted the home office's ornate public spaces, executive offices, workspaces, auxiliary spaces such as the gymnasium and

Metropolitan Life Insurance Co.'s Home Office Bldg., N. Y. City. Part of the Actuarial Division. Nearly all records here are kept on cards, of which more than ten millions are filed in this room.

43. Large workroom at the Metropolitan Life Home Office, ca. 1910. This was one of a series of postcards showing interior and exterior details of the home office, produced by the millions and distributed by company agents nationwide to promote insurance and investment products. Collection of the author.

dining rooms, and the printing and supply divisions. History and symbolism were amply covered, but statistics and system prevailed: the textual and photographic tour of the building was not conducted floor by floor, but followed the efficiency-tested path of a policy from division to division. The monographs asserted Met Life's primacy in the insurance field, and granted to the two-dimensional home office a transparency and publicness that the actual home office, largely closed to the public, did not possess.[59]

The Social Landscape

Efficiency and ideology drove the physical design and prescribed usage of the corporate home office, and its architectural presence and photographic portrait served as the visual and virtual interface with passersby, tourists, and policyholders. Likewise, company officers, an army of white-collar women and men, and a largely immigrant support staff were the company's social interface with the larger urban setting, helping to shape spatial and behavioral practices at work and transporting behaviors and expectations about lifestyle from city to office and back again.

Beginning with its quick growth in the 1880s, Met Life's ever-expanding offices were populated by a large clerical force and support staff. Met Life moved 650 workers into its 1893 home office: by 1908, the staff of the expanded complex numbered just shy of 3,000, and grew to 14,500 by 1938. Replicating the social hierarchies and spatial borders of the city beyond the company's elaborate revolving doors, Met Life created and enforced separate spheres of immigrants, native-born women, and upwardly mobile white men. Immigrants and unschooled members of the working class occupied service positions such as elevator operator, carpenter, cleaner, and commissary staff. Most service positions were male; only seamstresses and the evening staff of cleaners were female. Commissary workers, who operated the free lunch program, were the only mixed-gender group in the service sector. Blacks were not hired in any capacity. White-collar jobs, which included clerks, telephone operators, accountants, and actuarial assistants, were held by native-born, predominantly young men and women.[60]

The corporate mandate of personal health and education urged self-improvement within each "caste." Immigrant service workers were nudged toward Americanization with free company-directed English and citizenship classes, women clerks toward better business and homemaking skills, and male white-collars toward a life insurance career.[61] These programs, however, were not intended to move one to a different class: as in the urban world, the class system and one's place in it were largely unmovable.

At the same time, Met Life's paternalistic social engineering mandated respect and cooperation between groups of home office workers. Subsuming all work and staff in the rhetoric of the Metropolitan Family, the *Daily Bulletin* made known special efforts of various groups, and the *Home Office* regularly ran features on the service staff and the range of white-collar positions and their important roles in sustaining the company's work and welfare efforts.[62] "Every Division, and in fact, every person in the Home Office, is a necessary part of a well assembled but complicated business and humanitarian institution," a company publication asserted.[63] An antidote to the anonymity of a modern, "industrial civilization," the idea of a corporate family could be expanded to subsume all policyholders and the urban population as well, suggesting a civic culture in which difference could be ordered to serve a larger purpose.

White-collar men and women were the largest work groups Met Life managed, and their job paths and social and spatial patterns were significant shapers of corporate culture. Men were channeled into positions that required more technical and analytical skills and were encouraged to engage in actuarial or other insurance studies that would enable advancement to supervisory, administrative, and perhaps executive roles. Women worked in clerical positions that required only limited training, performing tasks that were considered "feminine" by business manuals and women's career guides. These jobs placed women in the service of male supervisors and executives as "housekeepers" of the office, and were thus not completely divergent from what society perceived women's true profession to be.[64]

Within the home office, women could rise to a supervisory position in a section of women clerks, but they had no further opportunity for advancement. The expectation of the company and of the women themselves was that their tenure at Met Life was only temporary, a waystation on their path to becoming wives and mothers.[65] After-work classes in typing and stenography enabled women to advance in the clerical areas open to them, but sewing, millinery, and first aid foreshadowed the domestic life that was their presumed destination. According to one Met Life officer, office work prepared women to be more intelligent and financially prudent wives and mothers, and would serve them later, should widowhood or hardship direct them back to work outside of the home. In pure financial terms, office work represented a considerable improvement in pay and status from teaching, domestic, or factory jobs, which were the typical acceptable job choices for young women.[66]

If Met Life's women clerks were distinguished by their repetitious tasks in service of a male bureaucracy, they were distinguished as well by their overwhelming numbers. In 1893, at a time when women were just beginning to enter offices nationwide, Met Life's office staff was already 60 percent female. By 1911, women accounted for about 66 percent, or two-thirds of the 3,000 home office employees, a ratio that remained relatively constant through the 1930s. In contrast, women nationwide held only 2.5 percent of clerical jobs in 1870; but they continued to enter this area and by 1930 held more than half of these positions.[67]

Earlier than many corporations, then, Met Life was compelled to devise spatial restrictions and codes of conduct to manage their mixed-gender workforce. For example, dining rooms and hours were gender specific, and use of the company gymnasium alternated between the two sexes. Actual workspaces were frequently single sex (because of the gendered job system), although women were often overseen by a male supervisor. When cohabitation was necessary, photographs indicate that men and women worked on opposite sides of the room, or were situated in groups. While spatial segregation instituted to keep the sexes apart was influenced by contemporary social codes and office management manuals, it was also the explicit and spatial expression of the gender-based hierarchy of jobs and salaries within the company: just as women and men rode on different elevators, so they moved on different career ladders.[68]

Beliefs concerning the nature of men and women permeated all aspects of the home office. Some benefits such as the company lunch program, the provision of clothes lockers, and the lending of company umbrellas on rainy days grew specifically from the presence of women in the office, but in time they were extended to all workers. Cleanliness standards for company offices also accommodated the gentler sex: smoking and spitting were managed by regulations and spatial restrictions out of concern for health and tidiness as well as from a perceived need to shield women from inappropriate masculine behaviors.[69] And although Met Life issued few regulations concerning dress code, the company issued aprons and cuffs to protect women's garments, and stipulated that long hair remain rolled during work hours.[70]

At the same time, company-sponsored and monitored recreational activities provided young women and men with interaction that was not always possible or permitted in the larger arena of the city.[71] Lunchtime recreation, dances, and athletic association excursions offered ample opportunities for men and women clerks who may have met in the arcade to pursue their acquaintances (Figure 44). Seeking primarily to uphold morality within the office, the company did not discourage romance or marriage within the ranks.[72]

It is undeniable that Met Life's social dimension, its work culture, was shaped largely by corporate values and widely held contemporary social norms. A constantly expanding workforce signaled the need for high levels of organization and control, and Met Life's management team was highly skilled in manipulating the boundary between beneficence and control. However, workers, both white-collars and the service sector that supported them, also contributed to the social form of their work environment, forging a community that provided emotional support and companionship, entertainment, and economic benefits. Workers formed clubs and organized social events and a cooperative buying club. On a more incremental scale, the daily movements and choices of workers also shaped and at times reversed corporate practices and policies. These events and struggles are recorded on the pages of company publications and house organs, from struggles over ice cream consumption to the use of desks as celebratory tableaux.[73]

44. Women and men on the roof of the Metropolitan Life Home Office, ca. 1910. Reprinted with permission of MetLife Archives.

The North Building

The home office functioned at once as a corporate advertisement and symbol; a factory of paper work and a testing ground for modern office technologies; and an arena where female and male workers could aspire to a controlled change in economic and social status. These functions, accommodated in the incremental expansions of the original office block, ultimately shaped the program for the company's North Building, a full-block structure to the north of the original home office that would subsume the company's 1919 and 1905 annexes.

Unlike the accretion of buildings and additions that comprised the mid-1920s home office complex, the North Building was designed as a single, monolithic structure, solely for company use, with built-in expansion potential. Constructed in three stages over two decades, the North Building's form and function demonstrate the company's continued quest for environmental control and an appropriate architectural expression of its corporate ideology for both internal and public consumption. It also stands as a built product of parallel discussions in life insurance trade groups and among prominent architects in the 1920s and 1930s, which concluded that commercial architecture should be shaped by modern conditions (technologies and functional needs) rather than by arbitrary decorative and style choices.[74]

Met Life entered the 1920s with the pressing task of accommodating rapid growth, an industry-wide phenomenon that ceased only in the 1930s. The resultant reorganization and expansion of office space in 1924 and 1925, some to rental space in adjacent buildings, was prelude to a press release in late September 1929 that made public a comprehensive master plan for a full-block skyscraper solely for company use. With the hubris that raised the 1909 campanile, the 12,000-employee company announced plans for the world's tallest building that would house up to 30,000 workers. On November 3, 1929, the front page of the *New York Times* featured a description and sketch of the proposed building, designed by prominent designer Harvey Wiley Corbett with interior design by company architect Dan Everett Waid (Figure 45).[75]

45. The North Building, the 100-story addition to the home office complex, as proposed by architects Harvey Wiley Corbett and Dan Everett Waid, 1929. Reprinted with permission of MetLife Archives.

Unlike the campanile and office block, the new tower, or North Building, was fashioned on no historical precedent; in the words of its architects, it was "a creation of this age and time" and "unhampered by archaeological precedent."[76] Sleek and stunning, the 100-story building moved upward from its massive marble base containing a continuous pedestrian arcade in tiers of angled glass panels, creating a telescoping structure of glass and steel. Although its forms were drawn largely from the building envelope specified by the city's 1916 zoning ordinance and reflected a current trend toward sheer unornamented surfaces, setbacks, and vertical articulation, the building's obelisk-like tower was unusual; its bowed Madison and Fourth Avenue facades and recessed flanks created a distinctive figure-eight-shaped plan that became increasingly pronounced in the upper floors.[77]

The interior design employed the latest technologies – central air conditioning, soundproof tile, indirect lighting, and a central utility core – creating open floor workspaces required by the company and used in their headquarters since the 1870s. Circulation was carefully orchestrated. Entrances at the center of the four facades, three for pedestrians and one for delivery vehicles (later changed to recessed corner entrances), provided access from all directions. From the main floor lobby, escalators would service lower floors and the dining rooms at the two basement levels to ensure a steady movement of persons, and high-speed local and express elevators would service the upper floors.

As planned, the 100-story building – the tallest in the world – would dwarf the company's signature tower to its south and everything else on Madison Square, much as the campanile and its full-block appendage had dwarfed much of its surroundings just twenty years before. Custom-fit for insurance work, at the cutting edge of architectural design, and civic in scale – an urban spectacle – the design thrilled company officials.

It was neither aesthetics nor height but rather the North Building's extravagance in a time of economic uncertainty that drew sharp public criticism. On November 16, a company press release stated emphatically that the preliminary design was "a rather interesting and entirely hypothetical discussion of what the future trend in business architecture may be as worked out by architects employed to study the problem in detail." It explained that the company would construct only the thirty-two-story base of the proposed monolith, and that would be in stages; any future expansion would be made possible by the retention of substantial foundations and a sizeable vertical circulation core. Met Life's second great tower was to remain a vision, truncated quite literally by the Depression.[78]

The North Building was completed in three phases. Unit One, built between 1930 and 1932, filled the eastern half of the site; Unit Two, situated in the northwestern quadrant of the block, was built between 1938 and 1941; and the southwestern quadrant, which comprised Unit Three, was completed in 1950, its construction delayed by World War II. Rising thirty-two stories, with four levels below grade, the finished building was clad entirely in limestone, a much-subdued version of the widely published marble, metal, and glass tower, a base without its tower (Figure 46).[79]

Nonetheless, the building, as well as its ground floor public area, appeared modern and monumental: entrances and ground floor arcade were detailed in an abstracted classicism. However, the figural ornamentation in the elevator lobby – floodlit, silver-leaf panels of allegorical male and female figures representing the life insurance principles of security, health, thrift, recreation, and industry – acknowledged the persistent role of gender within Met Life, the insurance industry, and the world it tried to shape beyond its home office arcade.[80] But the North Building itself never acquired the campanile's status as both corporate icon and urban monument. As something of a headless horseman riding rough economic and war times, it failed to inspire.

Met Life's home office demonstrated in built, urban-scaled form a complex interweaving of forces: trends in architectural design; legal and financial requirements; symbolic and advertising goals; office management practices and new technologies; and the social strictures that shaped the management of a gendered workforce. Another force, one less easy to document, was the collective impact of the goals, behaviors, and beliefs of those essential members of the Metropolitan family, the women and men who drove the machines of the insurance factory. Observation of the building's life – its siting, design, imagery, and usage – is suggestive of the multiple meanings and experiences harbored by the monumental complex. It also documents Met Life's practice of partnering architectural and spatial design with social design, or directives concerning the use of those spaces, a practice replicated in subsequent company endeavors involving architecture and the city.

Through its functional, visual, and symbolic qualities, the home office served as the site where Met Life engaged the challenge of reconciling sets of binaries at times in conflict: the personal and professional roles of women and men; the efficiencies of modernity with the traditional values of the family; and the profitmaking initiatives of business with public welfare, benevolence, and civic responsibility. Each of these pairs were central to the life insurance enterprise and to Met Life in particular. The paper-intensive insurance industry was early to introduce a female workforce to a male work environment, and the family and home were primary objects of insurance protection. Met Life, as an insurer of the working class, asserted that

46. The North Building as completed, 1950. Reprinted with permission of MetLife Archives.

profitability was linked to and in fact dependent upon public health and welfare, and by extension, the design and use of home, work, and city spaces. In the company's other major endeavors in public welfare and housing, chapters of the Met Life story not detailed here, architecture and spatial control again played a major role. Related by this complex corporate ideology, Met Life's architectural endeavors, from skyscraper to rooftop tuberculosis shed, were enlisted to guide behavior, improve health, and inspire belief, all to the profit of the corporation.

Finally, it is to the home office's dual identity as a corporate and civic architecture that we return. Declaring itself a public institution, Met Life crafted an architecture that spoke that language. In scale and detailing and in its siting on a centrally located public square, the home office assumed the stature of a civic building such as City Hall or the Municipal Building situated on City Hall Park in Lower Manhattan. Between 1906 and 1909 alone, Met Life ordered over 8 million postcards of the home office – its exterior as well as workrooms, mechanical facilities, and public spaces – and this does not account for the commercial photographers and postcard companies whose images and products lent the company standing among the skyscraper wonders of New York City. As one writer observed, the tower served as a symbol, not only of the company, but of the working world. This "steeple of the business of this world" chimed "the religion of business – of the real and daily things, the seriousness of the mighty street, and the faces of the men and the women."[81]

Collectively, the imagery and reality of the home office knit together the work world of greater New York (which could view the tower as part of the skyline), the internal world of the company, and the millions of geographically dispersed policyholders into a community unified by corporate beliefs cast in civic language. As a corporation, it defined space not simply by creating architectural boundaries that contained and controlled, but by ascribing meanings and values to spaces, rendering them at once public, because they were presented for popular consumption, and private, because they bore the imprimatur of the corporation and its specific agenda. Quite simply, in architecture, Met Life found its single, most powerful means of shaping not only its corporate offices, but also the urban landscape and its public culture, which it so desired to configure in its own image.

NOTES

1. Daniel Abramson, *Skyscraper Rivals: The AIG Building and the Architecture of Wall Street* (New York: Princeton Architectural Press, 2001).

2. For general study of Met Life's corporate structure as well as the home office see Olivier Zunz, *Making America Corporate, 1870–1920* (Chicago: Univ. of Chicago Press, 1990); Angel Kwolek-Folland, *Engendering Business: Men and Women in the Corporate Office, 1870–1930* (Baltimore: Johns Hopkins Univ. Press, 1994); Gail Fenske and Deryck Holdsworth, "Corporate Identity and the New York Office Building: 1895–1915," in *The Landscape of Modernity: Essays on New York City, 1900–1940*, ed. Olivier Zunz and David Ward (New York: Russell Sage, 1992), 129–59. This paper is drawn from a project entitled "Met Life's Metropolis," a revision of my dissertation "Architecture as Cultural Design: The Architecture and Urbanism of the Metropolitan Life Insurance Company" (Ph.D. diss., Cornell Univ., 1995).

3. For an overview of David Harvey's work, see his text *The Urban Condition* (Baltimore: Johns Hopkins Univ. Press, 1989).

4. The best general surveys of the American life insurance industry and culture are Burton J. Hendrick, *The Story of Life Insurance* (New York: McClure, Philips, 1907); Morton Keller, *The Life Insurance Enterprise, 1885–1910: A Story in the Limits of Corporate Power* (Cambridge: Belknap Press, 1963); Viviana A. Rotman Zelizer, *Morals and Markets: The Development of Life Insurance in the United States* (New York: Columbia Univ. Press, 1979).

5. The standard corporate histories of Met Life are Louis I. Dublin, *A Family of Thirty Million: The Story of the Metropolitan Life Insurance Company* (New York: The Company, 1943); and Marquis James, *The Metropolitan Life: A Study in Business Growth* (New York: Viking Press, 1947).

6. In 1875, 22 of 29 life insurance companies active in New York City kept offices between 92 and 409 Broadway. *New York City Register, 1875* (New York: Trow City Directory Co., 1875). Douglass North, "Capital Accumulation in Life Insurance between the Civil War and the Investigation of 1905," Chap. 9 in *Men in Business: Essays in the History of Entrepreneurship*, ed. William Miller (Cambridge: Harvard Univ. Press, 1952); Kenneth Turney Gibbs, "Insurance Rivalry and Business Architecture," Chap. 3 in *Business Architectural Imagery in America, 1870–1930* (Ann Arbor: UMI Research Press, 1984), 21–40. Both Equitable and New York Life used engravings of their buildings in advertisements: see *Insurance Times* 9, nos. 2, 3 (Feb. and March 1876). Comparative analysis and view of nineteenth-century life insurance home offices may be found in "Life Insurance," in *King's Handbook of New York City*, ed. Moses King (Boston: Moses King, 1892), 615–34; Sarah Bradford Landau and Carl W. Condit, *Rise of the New York Skyscraper, 1865–1913* (New Haven: Yale Univ. Press, 1996), 62–7.

7. *Plans of the New Building of the Metropolitan Life Insurance Co.*, oversized pamphlet [1876], MetLife Archives; Norman F. Cushman, "Reminiscence of an Audit Clerk of the Home Office at Park Place during 1892–1893," typescript, Vertical File-Home Office, MetLife Archives; Montgomery Schuyler, "The Work of N. LeBrun and Sons," *Architectural Record*, 27, no. 5 (May 1910): 365–81.

8. Charles Lockwood, *Bricks and Brownstones: The New York Row House, 1783–1929* (New York: McGraw-Hill, 1972), 167–206; "23rd Street District – East," in *25th Anniversary Journal* (New York: 23rd Street Assn., April 1954), 48.

9. Barnett Phillips, "A Mercantile Palace," *Harper's Weekly*, 38, no. 1951 (May 12, 1894):453. Sketch and plans were published in "The Metropolitan Life Insurance Building," *American Architect and Building News (AABN)* 38 (Oct. 15, 1892): pl. 877. Three company monographs celebrated the company and its home office: *Souvenir Number of the Weekly Bulletin, 1893–1897* (New York: The Company, 1897); and *The Metropolitan Life Insurance Company: Its History, Its Present Position in the Insurance World, Its Home Office Building and Its Work Carried on Therein* (New York: The Company, 1908, rev. ed., 1914).

10. This arrangement of elaborate marble entrance hall, and second- and third- floor company offices, including a two-story cashiers' department with a balcony followed the pattern of Equitable (1870) and Mutual Life's (1884) home office interiors. See R. Carlyle Buley, *The Equitable Life Assurance Society of the United States, 1859*, vol. 1 (New York: Appleton-Century-Crofts, 1967) 102–3; Shepard B. Clough, *A Century of American Life Insurance: A History of the Mutual Life Insurance Company of New York, 1843–1943* (New York: Columbia Univ. Press, 1946), 210, 362–3.

11. George Kellock Letterbook, ca. 1893. MetLife Archives. The *Souvenir Number of the Weekly Bulletin, 1893–1897.*

12. A taxpayer is a one- or two-story building that yields rent to cover real estate taxes until a larger and more profitable structure can be built on the lot. "Metropolitan Tower Building," *Indicator* (published by the Otis Elevator Co.) 2, no. 6 (June 1909):41–2. Once completed, the nearly full-block structure covered what once had been twenty-eight individual lots (Vertical File-Home Office, MetLife Archives).

13. The arcade, a public thoroughfare between Fourth and Madison avenues, also provided access to elevator banks and stairways up to workspaces and, after 1904, down to the subway. "The Metropolitan Building, New York City," *Architects' and Builders' Magazine* 6, no. 4 (Jan. 1905):145–56; *Architecture* 10, no. 58 (Oct. 15, 1904):152–7, pl. 76–80 (photographs and drawings only); N. LeBrun & Sons, "The Building," in *The Metropolitan Life Insurance Company* (1908), 23–30.

14. "National Academy's Sale," *New York Herald*, n.d. [1894]; Clipping Scrapbook, MetLife Archives.

15. Eliot Clark, *History of the National Academy of Design, 1825–1953* (New York: Columbia Univ. Press, 1954), 38–9; National Academy of Design President's Report, May 9, 1894; Oct. 15, 1895, National Academy of Design Archives. Comment of artist Seymour Joseph Guy cited in "Thinking of a New Home," *New York Tribune*, undated clipping; Clipping Scrapbook, MetLife Archives.

16. Letters, M. Whittredge(?), Aug. 16, 1894; Samuel Coleman, Aug. 2, 1894; Thomas W. Woods, Aug. 12, 1894. Folder 2: "23rd St. Building Sale – NA's Responses," National Academy of Design Archives. The academy moved to temporary quarters at 109th St., on the Upper West Side, where they planned to build a permanent home designed by Carrere and Hastings. The permanent building was never raised, and the galleries, administration, and school are now located in the vicinity of Ninetieth St. and Fifth Ave.

17. "Big Corporations Getting Control of Valuable Parcels," *New York Tribune*, n.d. [1894]; "Positive Evidence of Improvement," *New York Post*, n.d. [1894]; "Our New Moving Day," *New York Recorder*, n.d. [Oct.1894]; Clipping Scrapbook, MetLife Archives.

18. "Changes in Madison Square," *Sun* (Nov. 12, 1911):14; "23rd Street – East," 46–52.

19. Agreement between the church and Met Life was reported in the *Weekly Underwriter* 68, no. 6 (Feb. 7, 1903):92, and was signed on Feb. 6, 1903, as reported in the Madison Square Presbyterian Church Trustee Minutes, May 20, 1903. Like its dealings with the National Academy of Design, Met Life arranged the purchase well in advance of its anticipated use of the property. Met Life paid for the building in installments from Feb. 1903 to Apr. 1905 and leased the building back to the church for $1 until July 1906; Madison Square Presbyterian Church Trustee Minutes, Jan. 1903–Oct. 1906.

20. Rev. Charles H. Parkhurst, "The Erection of the New Church," *A Brief History of the Madison Square Presbyterian Church and Its Activities* (New York: Printed by request, 1906), 62; Madison Square Church "Report of Subcommittee on Selection of Architect &C. to the Building Committee," n.d.[1903?]. McKim, Mead & White Papers, New-York Historical Society.

21. White abstracted his forms from the early Christian church, and defended his style choice by asserting that the Gothic had a Roman Catholic pedigree, and that the early Christian aesthetic was in fact more appropriate historically to Protestant sects. Stanford White, "The Madison Square Presbyterian Church," 2pp. typescript, and untitled 3pp. typescript, both in McKim, Mead & White Papers, New-York Historical Society. Christian Brinton, "A Departure in Church Building," *Century Magazine* (Sept. 1905):718–19.

22. The tower functioned as a multiuse structure. Rental office space was arranged on four sides of the tower around a circulation and utility core. The company retained space on the lower floors, but advertised office space from the fourteenth to the twenty-fourth floors. *The Metropolitan Life Building, New York* (New York: The Company, 1910), MetLife Archives. The forty-fifth floor was used as a public observation deck, visited by thousands for 50¢ admission, Vertical File-Tower, MetLife Archives; *Tower 75* (New York: The Company, 1984).

23. The tower height was originally set at 560 feet; *The Weekly Underwriter* 72, no. 25 (June 24, 1905):589. Press notices in 1907 state a projected height of 658 feet, but the design was modified in April 1908 to extend the tower to 700 feet for advertising purposes. Met Life hoped to claim the tallest skyscraper for a decade, but the tower was surpassed in 1913 by the 760-foot Woolworth Building. Tower Scrapbook, Vertical File-Tower, MetLife Archives.

24. Architect Richard E. Schmidt had also used the well-known campanile as the prototype for a Chicago skyscraper, the Montgomery Ward Building (1897–99), and a San Marco look-alike anchored the corner of Denver's Daniels and Fisher Department Store. For information concerning the Montgomery Ward Building, see Carl W. Condit, *The Chicago School of Architecture* (Chicago: Univ. of Chicago Press, 1964), 186–93. The composition of the tower also drew from an earlier LeBrun tall building, the Home Life Insurance Building (1893–94) on Lower Broadway. Schuyler, "The Work of N. LeBrun & Sons," 378–80.

25. Schuyler, "The Work of N. LeBrun & Sons," 380.

26. N. LeBrun & Sons, "The Building," 25–6.

27. John L. Hall, "Description of the Structural Steel Framework for the Tower of the Metropolitan Life Insurance Building, New York City," *American Architect* 96, no. 1763 (Oct. 6, 1909):130–4; "Solving Problems in Tower Construction," *American Industries* (Jan. 15, 1908). Tower Scrapbook, MetLife Archives.

28. Vertical File-Tower, MetLife Archives. Also "The Metropolitan Life Building," *The New York Architect* 3, no. 7 (July 1909); "Architectural Criticism," *Architecture* 20, no. 3 (Sept. 15, 1909):129–30; Schuyler, "The Work of N. LeBrun & Sons," 365–81. See the *Weekly Underwriter*, 1906–10, especially its coverage of the company's Jan. 1910 banquet honoring the architects and celebrating the completion of the tower: "The Metropolitan Life Insurance Company Celebrates the Completion of Its Great Home Office Building," *Weekly Underwriter* 82, no. 5 (Jan. 29, 1910):103–12.

29. Huyler's produced a chocolate bar called "Metropolitan Sweet Chocolate," whose wrapper bore an image of the tower; Washington Crisps ads depicted a giant box of their corn flakes next to the tower, "the two biggest things of their kind in the world." Stores that lined the arcade added the tower to their letterhead; and such varied products as the Flanders "20" Coupé and Coca-Cola used the Met Life office block and tower as the backdrop for their promotions, with Coca-Cola substituting a glass of soda for the tower's beacon. "Tower Advertises Itself," *New York Herald*, Aug. 4, 1907. Tower Scrapbook and Vertical File-Tower, MetLife Archives.

30. Haley Fiske, "The Light that Never Fails," address given at the Triennial Conventions of 1909–10, in *Addresses Delivered at the Triennial Conventions and Managers' Annual Banquets of the Metropolitan Life Insurance Company*, vol. 1 (New York: The Company, 1923), 9–10. Fiske was quick to point out that the tower was not built for advertising purposes primarily, but as an investment that would earn 3.5 to 4% interest as required by state insurance regulations.

31. Earl Chapin May and Will Oursler, *The Prudential: A Story of Human Security* (Garden City, NY: Doubleday, 1950), 119–21.

32. Buley, *The Equitable Life Assurance Society*, vol.1, 106–9; Gibbs, *Business Architectural Imagery*, 102. New York Life added its sculpture in 1895–96, as part of a remodeling by McKim, Mead & White.

33. *Tower 75*, which commemorated the tower's 75th anniversary, collects a number of images that indicate the range of materials on which the tower was emblazoned.

34. For information concerning the development of the tower logo and slogan see Internal Memorandum 3/10/39 in Vertical File-Slogans, MetLife Archives; "More Light On: The Light That Never Fails," *Home Office* (Aug. 1956): 6–9; *Tower 75*.

35. Fiske, "The Light that Never Fails," 24–6. For examples of Fiske's rhetoric, see his speeches in *Addresses Delivered at the Triennial Conventions*, 3 vols.; William Henry Atherton, *The Metropolitan Tower: A Symbol of Refuge, Warning, Love, Inspiration, Beauty, Strength* (New York: The Company, 1915), 4–6.

36. Dublin, *A Family of Thirty Million*, 62. For a detailed account of the origins and expansion of Met Life's welfare program, see the quasiautobiographical account by Louis I. Dublin, *After Eighty Years: The Impact of Life Insurance on the Public Health* (Gainesville, FL: Univ. of Florida Press, 1966).

37. Atherton, *The Metropolitan Tower*, 3–4.

38. *Scientific American* 96, no. 13 (Mar. 30, 1907): cover, 270; and *Scientific American* 99, no. 23 (Dec. 5, 1908), 400–3.

39. The *Herald Tribune* furthered the tower's civic position by flashing election returns from its pinnacle with a powerful searchlight beginning in 1908, when the tower was still partially skeletal. Tower Scrapbook, MetLife Archives.

40. "College Juniors Visit Met Tower," *Home Office* 11, no. 2 (July 1929).

41. Griffin Lovelace, *The House of Protection* (New York: Harper, 1921). This book, endorsed by the National Association of Life Underwriters, promoted annuity or income plans, using the house as a metaphor for a family's financial security. The biblical construction referred to is cited in Matthew 7:24–27. See also "The Metropolitan Clock: How It Symbolizes and Effectively Defines to Metropolitan Life Policyholders the Value of Time and Money, the Saving of Both and the Ultimate Protection of the Home," *The Expositor* (Dec. 1908). Vertical File-Tower, MetLife Archives.

42. Haley Fiske, *The Metropolitan Family at Home and Abroad: The Substance of Addresses Delivered at Five Meetings in May 1914, to the Home Office Staff* (New York: The Company, 1914) 6–11, 27–9.

43. "The Light That Never Fails," *The Metropolitan* 25, no. 5 (ca. 1910), back cover advertisement. Also published as a leaflet, ca. 1920.

44. Haley Fiske, "A Mother's Beauty in Metropolitan Business," *Addresses Delivered at the Triennial Conventions*, vol. 1, 297–318.

45. For the origin of the company anthem, see "Company's Song Inspired by Kipling's 'Light That Failed,' " *Pacific Coaster* (July 1940). Vertical File-Songs, MetLife Archives.

46. Atherton, *The Metropolitan Tower*, 7.

47. Met Life President John R. Hegeman referred to the home office as a factory, an allusion to insurance companies' use of large open workrooms to facilitate efficient processing of applications and claims.

48. For a general discussion of office technologies and work, see Thomas J. Schlereth, "The World and Workers of the Paper Empire," Chap. 5 in *Cultural History & Material Culture: Everyday Life, Landscapes,*

Museums (Charlottesville, VA: Univ. Press of Virginia, 1990), 144–78.

49. At the time, restriction of office building access was not uncommon, and a 1895 guide to New York City noted that these structures "are like municipalities with laws of their own.... [Each] is a separate community with its own police, its own servants and with laws that must be respected.... The duties of the guardians in ordinary times are confined to saving the tenants from annoyances and theft," *New York 1895 Illustrated*, 2nd ed. (New York: A.F. Parsons, 1895), 55. Various editions of the company's *Rules and Regulations;* the *Daily Bulletin*; and the memos of Third Vice-President George B. Woodward offer excellent documentation of daily life and problems in the home office. MetLife Archives.

50. A typical floor plan of the 1909 home office published in *The American Architect* shows large workspaces located around light courts and fronting Twenty-fifth Street. Smaller offices, presumably for rental, were located along Twenty-third Street, Madison Ave., and Fourth Ave. frontages, with the exception of space on the second floor, which was used by Met Life executive offices. "Wasted Opportunities: A Critique on Planning and Construction," *Architectural Record* 3, no. 1 (July–Sept. 1893):72–84, 169–74, 436–40; Barr Ferree, "The Modern Office Building," *Journal of the Franklin Institute* 141, nos. 1 and 2 (Jan. and Feb. 1896):47–71, 115–40. For a discussion of small office plans, see Carol Willis, *Form Follows Finance: Skyscrapers and Skylines in New York and Chicago* (New York: Princeton Architectural Press, 1995), 24–47.

51. J. William Schultze, "Office Layout," Chap.10 in *Office Administration* (New York: McGraw-Hill, 1919), 145–69. See esp. Fig. 21-Detailed layout, 159; *A Tour of the Home Office Building* (New York: The Company, 1914); *Rules and Regulations Governing the Office Employees of the Metropolitan Life Insurance Company* (1895), 3.

52. A number of manufacturers whose products were used in the home office, including Otis Elevators, Jno. Williams Bronze Foundry and Iron Works, and the Art Metal Construction Co., manufacturers of the steel filing system, advertised adjacent to a large article on the newly expanded home office in *Architecture* 10, no. 58 (Oct. 1904). The gong is mentioned in *The Metropolitan Life Insurance Company* (1908), 33; "Metropolitan Clocks," *Home Office* 20, nos. 2 and 3 (July–Aug. 1938):2, 19.

53. J. William Schulze, *The American Office: Its Organization, Management and Records* (New York: Key Publishing Co., 1913) and the subsequent *Office Administration*; and William Henry Leffingwell, *Office Management: Principles and Practice* (New York: A.W. Shaw, 1925) were widely used office management texts. These studies were tailored to the American life insurance industry by Harry A. Hopf of Guardian Life. See his "Home Office Organization," *Proceedings of the American Life Convention* (1917), 26–46, and "Office Administration," *Proceedings of the Twelfth Annual Meeting of the Medical Section, American Life Convention* (1922), 83–97.

54. Notice, *Daily Bulletin*, Nov. 18, 1908; Dublin, *A Family of Thirty Million*, 246–7. Efficient use of segregated lunchrooms is described in *A Wonderful Village* (New York: The Company, n.d.[1911]), 3.

55. See Fiske, "Welfare Work for Employees," in *An Epoch in Life Insurance*; *The Metropolitan Life Insurance Company* (1914), 140–67; and Lee K. Frankel, "Welfare Work of the Metropolitan Life Insurance Company for Its Employees," *New York State Journal of Medicine* (Jan. 1917) for details of employee welfare. Met Life was of course not unique in its enactment of an employee welfare program. Various historical interpretations of welfare capitalism are summarized in Stuart D. Brandes, *Welfare Capitalism, 1880–1940* (Chicago: Univ. of Chicago Press, 1970), 5–8, 135–40; Andrea Tone, *The Business of Benevolence* (Ithaca, NY: Cornell Univ. Press, 1997); and Nikki Mandell, *The Corporation as Family: The Gendering of Corporate Welfare, 1890–1930* (Chapel Hill, NC: Univ. of North Carolina Press, 2002). Zunz views the welfare activities of life insurance companies, and Met Life specifically, as closely related to philanthropic agencies. He calls Met Life a "reforming" corporate model. Zunz, *Making America Corporate*, 90–2, 100–1.

56. C. Wright Mills, *White Collar* (New York: Oxford Univ. Press, 1951), 189–212; Carl Sandburg, "Skyscraper," in *Chicago Poems* (New York: Holt, Rinehart and Winston, 1916).

57. Brandes, *Welfare Capitalism*, 135–42.

58. Vertical File-Policyholders Service Bureau, MetLife Archives. There is a large body of research and reports written by the PSB published and available in typescript form.

59. Pamphlets include *All in a Day's Work*, n.d., and *Number One Madison Avenue: The Business of a Life Insurance Company* (rev. ed., 1927). The three monographs are titled *Souvenir Edition of the Weekly Bulletin, 1983–1987*; and *The Metropolitan Life Insurance Company* (1908; rev. ed., 1914). Photographs of workrooms, dining room, and machine shop from the 1908 and 1914 monographs, the work of the famous commercial photography firm of Byron, were made into millions of postcards and distributed by the home office and the far-flung agency force.

60. "An Echo from Sarajevo," *Home Office* 6, no. 9 (Feb. 1925):5–6. The 97 immigrants described in this

article were all home office porters. The company overwhelmingly classified jobs by gender and ethnicity: native-born status presumed a facility with English that was essential for tasks of handling correspondence, filing, and answering the telephone. Memo JEM to D. E. Waid, architect, July 11, 1930, shows a breakdown of the maintenance staff by classification (job) and gender. See also Home Office Study, 1924 (looseleaf binder). The official explanation of exclusion of Blacks from the workforce was that it was "not because of any prejudice on the part of the company, but because there would be very serious objection on the part of our white employees," statement of Met Life Vice President Leroy A. Lincoln in "Metropolitan Life Official Tells Why Company Does Not Hire Negroes," *New York Age* 43, no. 33 (Apr. 26, 1930):1. In addition to discriminatory employment policies, Met Life had a long history of ambivalence toward Blacks as policyholders. See Circular Letters files, MetLife Archives.

61. *The Metropolitan Life Insurance Company* (1914), 142–3, 143–51. All clerks were encouraged to take the correspondence course, "The Principles of Life Insurance," a requirement for all agent trainees, which was later published: see Lee K. Frankel and Louis I. Dublin, *The Principles of Life Insurance* (New York: The Company, 1915); "An Echo from Sarajevo."

62. "The Home Office 'Village'," *Home Office* 5, no. 11 (Apr. 1924):1–4; "The Carpenter Shop," *Home Office* 6, no. 11 (Apr. 1925):16–17; "There's Even a Modern Laundry to Be Found in This Home Office City of Ours," *Home Office* (Oct. 1938): "The Work We Do: The Secretary," *Home Office* 41, no. 4 (Oct. 1959): 1–4.

63. "The Home Office 'Village'," 4.

64. For example, in the Actuarial Division, where women clerks outnumbered men six to one, the "male sections" collected data, operated multiplication and adding machines, and prepared "difficult classifications" and "detailed calculations," which demanded "not only technical knowledge, but often the most searching analysis." Women clerks in the division handled the cards on which information was recorded about each policy. *The Metropolitan Life Insurance Company* (1914), 66–7. Met Life used the term housekeeping in relation to a secretary's job as late as 1959, in a description of an inhouse Secretarial Practice Course, see "Course Outlines Secretarial Fine Points," *Home Office* 41, no. 4 (Oct. 1959):4. One women's career guide is Mrs. M. L. Rayne, *What Can A Woman Do: Or Her Position in the Business and Literary World* (Petersburgh, NY: Eagle Publishing Co., 1893); see also Davies, *Woman's Place Is at the Typewriter*, 154–8.

65. There is no evidence of a written rule mandating that a female clerk resign upon marriage, although it appears it was either a verbal rule or that most did in the decades surrounding the turn of the century. However, there is evidence in the *Home Office* that by the late 1920s, some women remained at Met Life after marriage. Policies at other insurance companies were not so liberal: New York Life maintained a policy between World War I and ca. 1950 that prohibited married women from working for the company. The industry at large discussed gender in clerical hiring and the significance of a woman's marital status in the 1930s. At that time, 90 of the 139 institutions surveyed by the Life Office Management Association (LOMA) retained female clerks who married after hire, but 135 of those companies had rules restricting or forbidding hire of already married women. See issues of the *Home Office*; D. M. Stevenson, "Some Social Aspects and Trends in Clerical Employment – Women vs. Men," *Proceedings of the Annual Conference of LOMA* (1935), 90–7; *Special Report No. 13, LOMA, Questionnaire Summaries: Personnel Policies. Part 2: Employment of Married Women* (Fort Wayne, IN: LOMA, 1930).

66. Fiske, *An Epoch in Life Insurance*, 245–57; "Metropolitan University Tuition Free," *Home Office* 6, no. 4 (Sept. 1924):8.

67. Statistics calculated from *A Wonderful Village; The Metropolitan Life Insurance Company* (1908 and 1914), 33 and 66, respectively; *Number One Madison Avenue: The Business of a Life Insurance Company* (New York: The Company, 1927). For general information about women in the clerical force, see Elyce J. Rotella, *From Home to Office: U.S. Women at Work, 1870–1930* (Ann Arbor, MI: UMI Research Press, 1981), 2, 65–103; Sharon Hartman Strom, *Beyond the Typewriter:Gender, Class, and the Origins of Modern American Office Work, 1900–1930* (Urbana, IL: Univ. of Illinois Press, 1992), 197.

68. See photographs in *The Metropolitan Life Insurance Company* (1908 and 1914). Etiquette books for the working girl cautioned clerical workers about improprieties that could occur within the office because of the unsupervised mixing of the sexes. Ruth Ashmore of the *Ladies' Home Journal* warned young working women to guard against sexual and financial temptation, to wear modest clothing, to not speak socially to male clerks, and to avoid familiarity with the boss. The intrigue of the mixed-gender office was further elaborated in office novels and short stories. See Lisa M. Fine, *The Souls of the Skyscraper: Female Clerical Workers in Chicago, 1870–1930* (Philadelphia: Temple Univ. Press, 1990), 145–51.

69. For example, women were given lockers by 1895; all workers were given lockers by 1915. Umbrellas, lent to women beginning in 1909, became a privilege extended

to male clerks in 1917 and to printing and bindery employees in 1921. For details of these services and the gendered nature of housekeeping and company-mandated hygiene standards, see various editions of *Rules and Regulations* and the *Daily Bulletin*; George Kellock Letterbook (Kellock was the facility manager of the home office in the 1890s); H. E. Coffin, "The Housekeeping of a Skyscraper," *Book-Keeper Magazine* (June 1909):535–43. MetLife Archives.

70. Met Life required only that all employees be neatly and practically clothed. Photographs indicate that fashion and an unwritten code of business etiquette provided clear and narrow guidelines concerning appropriate dress, yet another indication that the world of Met Life was a controlled and business-driven extension of the urban social environment beyond its doors. Men wore suits and ties; women of the 1890s through the 1910s wore dark skirts, light-colored shirtwaists, stiff collars, and occasionally, bows at the throat – a feminized version of male business dress. The company did mandate that women's hair remain rolled during business hours to avoid sexual innuendo and a diversion from work tasks for time-consuming coiffing in the bathrooms. *Rules and Regulations*, revised periodically, contains no mention of a dress code for either men or women, save for the stipulation in the 1895 edition (p. 5) that men must wear their suit coats during office hours. For general advice in business girls' guides concerning work attire, see Ruth Ashmore, *The Business Girl in Every Phase of Her Life*, Ladies' Home Journal Library (Philadelphia: Curtis Publishing Co, 1895), 16–17.

71. *Rules and Regulations*, editions 1895–1936, MetLife Archives; Angel Kwolek-Folland, "Gender, Self and Work in the Life Insurance Industry, 1880–1930," in *Work Engendered: Toward a New History of American Labor*, ed. Ava Baron (Ithaca: Cornell Univ. Press, 1991), 168–90. Zunz, *Making America Corporate*, 120–1.

72. In 1930, the overwhelming majority of 139 life insurance companies surveyed stated that they did not discourage association between their female and male clerks. *Special Report No.* 13, LOMA, 24–25. *Home Office*, June 1923, reported the marriage of two Statistical Bureau employees and noted that it was the fourth wedding of people within the bureau. "Statistical Facts and Fancies," *Home Office* 5, no. 1 (June 1923):3.

73. An excellent, if fragmented, view of life at the home office is gleaned from the *Daily Bulletin*, published beginning in 1905, where company commentary, directives, and reprimands documented employees' daily activities, particularly those that diverged from the company's behavioral guidelines. The *Home Office*, published monthly beginning in 1919, featured longer articles about various divisions and their work and about employee activities, and carried announcements of events, employee marriages, deaths, and other personal occasions. Although written by employees, the *Home Office* was published by the company and thus clearly reflected corporate policies and goals. It provides a record, if selective, of everyday practices and issues within the home office and the company at large.

74. Insurance trade groups include LOMA and the American Life Convention, which formed committees on home office design and sponsored publications and conference papers on the subject. For example, see Henry W. Cook, "The New Life Insurance Home Office," and C. E. Johnston, "Home Office Buildings," *Proceedings of the American Life Convention* (1923), 125–59 and 160–9, respectively; *Life Insurance Home Office Buildings: A Study of the Problems of Building Construction* (Fort Wayne, IN: LOMA, 1933); and Arthur O. Angilly, "Insurance Building Design Trends," *Proceedings of the Annual Conference of LOMA* (1945), 9–16. Advertising, efficiency, and uplift as general goals of life insurance companies are explicitly discussed in Benjamin Wistar Morris, "The Home Office Building as the Expression of the Activities of the Life Insurance Company," *Proceedings of the Annual Conference of LOMA* 1924), 54–61.

75. Home Office Study, 1924. Looseleaf binder. Memos, Nov. 1929–Sept. 1930. MetLife Archives; "Metropolitan Life to Buiid New Tower," *The New York Times*, Sept. 25, 1929; unidentified clippings, Oct. 23 and Oct. 31, 1929; "Madison Square Tower to Rise 100 Stories," *New York Times*, Nov. 3, 1929, 1. Vertical File-Home Office, MetLife Archives.

76. "Madison Square Tower to Rise 100 Stories"; "Metropolitan to Build 100 Story Home Office," *Weekly Underwriter* 121, no. 19 (1929):1062. Notices and photographs appeared in many trade, popular, and architecture publications. Vertical File-Home Office, MetLife Archives.

77. The current trend toward sheer unornamented surfaces, setbacks, and vertical articulation was seen in the work of such prominent architects as Ralph Walker, Ely Jacques Kahn, and Holabird and Roche. See R. W. Sexton, "The Design of Commercial Buildings of Today," and "Skyscraper Office Buildings," Chaps. 1 and 2 in *American Commercial Buildings of Today* (New York: Architectural Book Publishing Co., 1928), 1–108, esp. 9–11, 14; and Abramson, "Exterior Expresion," Chap. 7 in *Skyscraper Rivals*, 94–119.

78. Press release, Nov. 15, 1929, Metropolitan Information Service, Vertical File-Home Office, MetLife Archives. My speculation that the company came under fire about the 100-story building is based on their

speedy retraction of the proposal, the defensive nature of their press release, and details of press coverage. For articles heavily based on this press release, see "32-Story Building for Metropolitan," *Spectator* 123, no. 21 (Nov. 21, 1929); "Metropolitan Building to Be 32 Stories High," *Weekly Underwriter* 121, no. 20 (1929): 1119; "Metropolitan to Erect New Building," *Life Insurance Courant* 34, no. 11 (Nov. 1929). Vertical File-Home Office, MetLife Archives.

79. The press paid little heed to the aesthetic modifications, and instead lauded the downscaled project for its employment of some 2,000 trade workers and others engaged in production of the required materials. Miscellaneous clippings, Vertical File-Home Office, MetLife Archives. For details of the building as constructed, see Harvey Wiley Corbett, "Metropolitan Life Insurance Company: New Home Office Building in New York," *Architectural Record* 74, no. 3 (Sept. 1933):175–83; "The Last Word in Office Buildings," *System and Business Management* (Jan. 1934):11–13; "The Editor's Diary," *Architecture* 64, no. 4 (Apr. 1933):213.

80. For the full and unexecuted scheme of decoration proposed for the North Building see "Synopsis of Decoration: For the New Home Office Building," unsigned and undated typescript by the architects. Vertical File-Home Office, MetLife Archives. See also "Five Goals in Silver Leaf," *Home Office* (Jan. 1952):6–7.

81. Gerald Stanley Lee, "The Metropolitan Tower," excerpted from *Everybody's Magazine* (Feb. 1913) in *The Intelligencer* (Feb. 1, 1913). Vertical File-Tower, MetLife Archives.

7

The Chicago Tribune Tower Competition

Publicity Imagines Community

Katherine Solomonson

On June 10, 1922, Tribune Company celebrated the *Chicago Tribune*'s seventy-fifth anniversary by challenging architects the world over to design no less than the world's most beautiful office building for the "World's Greatest Newspaper." As one of the largest and most influential publishers in the United States if not the world, Tribune Company was in an unusually good position to maximize the competition's publicity value.[1] Through myriad articles and pictorials and a series of public events, the company transformed what might have been a low-profile design competition into a spectacle orchestrated to attract the attention of millions.[2] Two hundred and sixty-three architects responded with entries that revealed widely (and sometimes wildly) divergent concepts of the skyscraper. Conducted during a period of ferment in architectural theory and design, the competition quickly came to be seen as a watershed event, and the relative merits of its entries became the subject of international debate in both popular and professional publications. After the competition was over, the company organized selected entries into a traveling exhibition that opened in twenty-six North American cities in six months, triggering numerous lectures and articles on the future of skyscraper design. When the newly completed Tribune Tower opened to the public in 1925, the newspaper reported that 20,000 people poured into the building, shot up to the top, and gazed through screens of tracery at what the *Tribune* modestly called "Tribune territory" stretching far into the distance (Figure 47).[3]

The sheer amplitude of rhetoric the *Tribune* generated during and after the competition makes this an unusually rich case study for examining the relationships between skyscraper design and the mass media at a time of explosive growth in advertising and consumer culture. As I analyze the rhetorical space the *Tribune* produced for the competition, I will consider how, in the pages of the newspaper, publicity became education, a profitable newspaper company became a civic institution, and a corporate office building designed to be an effective advertisement became a monument to civic ideals. In the process, I will argue, the competition's publicity provided a vehicle for advancing the *Tribune*'s concept of civic and national identity in the turbulent aftermath of World War I. To conclude, I will look at some of the ways this was contested and reaffirmed in the competition's aftermath.

Producing Publicity

The Chicago Tribune Tower competition's publicity potential was a factor from the beginning as Robert McCormick and Joseph Patterson, first cousins who ran Tribune Company together, considered whether to hold a competition for the design of their new office building.[4] The *Chicago Tribune*'s staff was well versed in the techniques of advertising, public relations, and market research, both for the sake of those who used the newspaper as an advertising medium and for the promotion of the newspaper itself. To attract attention, boost circulation, and enhance its public image, the *Tribune* had organized numerous publicity stunts, including contests for everything from growing beautiful lilacs to reassembling pieces of movie stars' faces, often with the incentive of generous cash prizes. A competition for the design of a significant skyscraper was almost guaranteed to attract public interest. Since the emergence of the skyscraper as a building type, countless corporations, organizations, investors, and tenants had derived some measure of publicity from the tall office buildings they commissioned or occupied. Many skyscrapers functioned as recognizable trademarks for those who linked their public identities with them.[5] The press played a significant role in this. Local newspapers across the country covered their planning and construction. People crowded around peepholes in the fences at construction sites hoping to catch a glimpse of them as they rose. And their memorability was enhanced by the circulation of their images on countless postcards, on corporate and individual letterhead, and in advertisements and souvenir booklets.[6]

The *Tribune*, with McCormick and Patterson's direct oversight, developed a program of publicity designed to keep its skyscraper "contest" (as the newspaper often called it) continuously in the public eye.[7] It initiated the competition with a full-page announcement designed with all of the hyperbole and flash of the ads for other *Tribune*-sponsored contests, especially with the inflated black numerals touting $100,000 in cash awards (Figure 48). Although this was clearly an advertisement, most of the publicity that followed took the form of "free advertising," for the competition gave the *Tribune* the opportunity to publish a continuous stream of articles, editorials, and pictorials related to the event. Through these, the *Tribune* restaged the competition as a drama issued in installments, not unlike the newspaper's popular fictional serials – except in this case the *Tribune* could cast itself in a leading role. With a period of buildup, a climax, and a dénouement, it kept its readers informed as architects from many nations enrolled, dropped hints about the designs as they arrived, built up suspense as the jurors agonized over the top awards, and splashed the competition's first-prize winner across the front page at its conclusion. In the pages of the *Tribune*, then, the competition became a compelling public narrative that paralleled (without always strictly resembling) what was happening in the background.

This narrative was structured according to several interrelated strategies. The most obvious is the way the *Tribune*'s articles directed

47. Tribune Tower in 1925. Photograph by E. L. Fowler. Collection of the author.

attention toward the newspaper as they relayed the events of the competition. At the same time, they also imbued both the event and the future building with meaning through a technique akin to what Edward L. Bernays, a leading public relations expert at the time, referred to as "continuous interpretation."[8] Less obvious, but no less significant, is the way the *Tribune* positioned its readers in relation both to the competition and to the newspaper itself. In the process, the *Tribune* also constructed an image of the community to which it belonged – an "imagined community," to use the term Benedict Anderson coined in his 1983 study of nationalism. Community is imagined, according to Anderson, because most of its members never meet or know one another, yet they can imagine that they share common interests and ideals. Newspapers play an instrumental role in the construction of imagined community by reaching large numbers of people on a regular basis. As readers peruse the same edition of the same newspaper at virtually the same time each day, they engage in what becomes a mass ritual that provides regular reassurance that the imagined community exists. Anderson argues that imagined community is fundamental to the definition of the modern nation state. Though its members might differ from one another in various ways, imagined community masks inequality and difference, and the "fiction seeps quietly and continuously into reality, creating that remarkable confidence of community in anonymity which is the hallmark of modern nations."[9]

During the Tribune Tower competition, the *Tribune* not only provided material for simultaneous consumption, it also represented its readers' commonality by incorporating them into the public narrative both as audience and as active participants. Unlike its other contests where readers were cast as consumers competing for prizes, in the context of this competition, the *Tribune* cast them in the role of citizens united in the quest for the design of a corporate office-building-cum-monument that would embody their ideals. In the process, the *Tribune* contributed to the construction of imagined community at both the civic and national levels. To explore this further, we first need to consider how the *Tribune*'s own explicitly nationalist agenda related to broader tensions concerning cultural unity and American identity that emerged in the late nineteenth century and intensified during and after World War I.

Imagining Unity

In the late nineteenth and early twentieth centuries, American cities were transformed by waves of immigration from southern and eastern Europe, the influx of people from small towns and farms, and the northward migration of African Americans from the South. As members of the white middle and upper classes confronted unfamiliar customs and values and a workforce that was increasingly diverse, many grew anxious over what they saw as fragmentation and disorder born of the loss of a common culture binding the nation into a civilized and unified whole.[10] Tensions escalated immediately after World War I with increased labor unrest, "race" riots, and a Red Scare (which the *Tribune* did its part to inflame) that fueled fears that foreign agitators and subversives would replay the Russian Revolution in the United States. A movement to "Americanize" this heterogeneous population, which had gained increased momentum during the war, intensified in its aftermath as federal agencies, state governments, civic and private organizations, and newspapers launched educational programs to persuade potentially traitorous "hyphenated Americans" to embrace American values and ways of life.[11]

In the early 1920s, Chicago School sociologists became interested in the role that newspapers played in recent arrivals' adaptation to the complexity of life in the modern American city. Drawing on the work of Ferdinand Tönnies, they traced the shift from *Gemeinschaft* to *Gesellschaft*, that is, from identification with the relative intimacy of community structured through kinship networks and face-to-face relationships, to identification with social organizations based on rational cooperation, contractual relations, and the bureaucratic anonymity of modern urban society. They believed that newspapers – especially English-language dailies – played a crucial role in this process by

$100,000.00

IN PRIZES TO ARCHITECTS

Seventy-five years old today, The Tribune seeks surpassing beauty in new home on Michigan Boulevard

THE TRIBUNE herewith offers $100,000.00 in prizes for designs for a building to be erected on its vacant lot at North Michigan Boulevard and Austin Avenue. Commemoration of our Seventy-fifth Birthday is made in this manner for three reasons:

—to adorn with a monument of enduring beauty this city, in which The Tribune has prospered so amazingly.

—to create a structure which will be an inspiration and a model for generations of newspaper publishers.

—to provide a new and beautiful home worthy of the world's greatest newspaper.

The contest will be under the rules of the American Institute of Architects. Competition will be open and international. Each competitor will be required to submit drawings showing the west and south elevations and perspective from the southwest, of a new building to be erected on The Tribune's property at the corner of North Michigan Blvd. and Austin Ave. Architects desiring complete information are requested to write to

Robert R. McCormick, Joseph M. Patterson, Editors and Publishers

The Chicago Tribune

The World's Greatest Newspaper

SEVENTY-FIVE YEARS OLD TODAY

48. Advertisement for the Chicago Tribune Tower Competition. *Chicago Tribune*, June 10, 1922. Courtesy of *Chicago Tribune*.

representing the dominant values with which the newcomers' would fuse to form a common culture and by facilitating the formulation of public opinion, which is the basis of community life.[12]

The newspapers Chicago School sociologists studied contributed to the Americanization process in both overt and subtle ways. Among them was the *Chicago Tribune*, a self-styled advocate of "intense and inspiring nationality" and guardian of American democracy.[13] Robert McCormick and Joseph Patterson, both of them former politicians, wielded the newspaper as a powerful political instrument. The *Tribune* issued blazing editorials that railed against threats to American ideals,[14] and it also disseminated values and models for taste, behavior, and consumption through its special features, advice columns, and advertisements. Implicitly present were the readers toward whom these were directed. Through its extensive market research, the *Tribune* was well aware that its readers were ethnically and economically diverse,[15] but it tended to represent them as assimilated and prosperous "men and women who are on the up-grade."[16] (The *Tribune*'s erasure of difference in constructing its ideal reader as a thriving, fully assimilated consumer paralleled strategies used in advertising, which provided Tribune Company's greatest revenues.[17]) The paper invited all of its readers, whatever their background, to identify with and aspire to acquire the tastes, interests, decorum, and shopping habits of the "best classes" whose values the *Tribune* positioned itself as representing and reinforcing.

The Chicago Tribune Tower competition was thus conducted within a rhetorical space that advanced Americanization both explicitly and implicitly. At the same time, the *Tribune*, literally and figuratively, projected its efforts into the space of Daniel Burnham and Edward Bennett's Plan of Chicago. Completed in 1909, the plan featured radiating avenues converging upon a prominent domed civic center – an image of a unified body politic superimposed on a city that was in fact growing increasingly diverse and decentralized. The first page of the book documenting the plan asserted that "the time has come to bring order out of chaos incident to rapid growth, and especially to the influx of people of many nationalities, without common traditions or habits of life."[18] Using techniques devised by a specialist in salesmanship, the Chicago Plan Commission continued to promote the plan heavily during the 1910s, when the Americanization movement was on the upswing.[19] Its publicity abounded with references to "community patriotism," "a great melting pot of ideas of civic advance," and "trained and enlightened citizens" who would be improved by living in a city structured according to such a plan.[20] The Plan of Chicago carried its greatest impact through Jules Guérin's evocative watercolors, which presented a vision of civic spaces orchestrated for the production and performance of citizenship, reinforced through monumental imagery symbolic of civic unity and identity.

As the Chicago Plan Commission promoted the plan (with heavy *Tribune* backing), it called upon Chicagoans to perform a rite of citizenship, quite literally, by casting votes for the bond issues that would finance its realization. Although the domed civic center would never be built, those votes helped bring into being one of the plan's key arteries, North Michigan Avenue, which was developed as a link between the business district in the Loop and the wealthy residential Gold Coast, where McCormick and Patterson had grown up. Property owners took steps to ensure that the street would be limited to what they characterized as "high class" businesses; and in 1918 architects drew up proposals for a monumental bridge plaza flanked by matching towers that provided a gateway to a boulevard lined with lower buildings all of the same height (Figure 49). Like the Plan of Chicago, the new proposals for the bridge plaza presented a vision of civic unity, competition, and individual self-interest subordinated to the larger civic good.

Constructing Monumentality

In 1919, Tribune Company purchased a site opening onto the North Michigan Avenue Bridge Plaza for the construction of its new printing plant and office building. By the time it announced the competition for the office building's design, the new bridge spanned the river, and the Wrigley Company had completed its gleaming new structure, located on the plaza diagonally across from where Tribune Company's building would rise. Hailed as a magnificent contribution to Chicago's beautification, the Wrigley Building formed the first half of the gateway to North Michigan Avenue. The Michigan Avenue Bridge Plaza was thus well on its way toward becoming a major monumental nexus for Chicago.

When the *Tribune* announced the competition for the building that would rise in this location, it built upon the momentum toward civic beautification generated by the Plan of Chicago, casting its own efforts in similar terms. From the beginning, the newspaper played up the event's civic significance. One-upping the chewing-gum manufacturer across the street, Tribune Company emphasized that, being a newspaper company, it could claim the status of a quasicivic institution and a guardian of democracy and the public good.[21] It made its campaign for Chicago's civic improvement part of its ongoing mission; and it periodically published its "Platform for Chicago" – to which the competition contributed a new plank. Underscoring the competition's contribution to this cause, the newspaper announced a list of civic leaders who would serve on an advisory board, and it published testimonials to the importance of Tribune Company's efforts toward the beautification of Chicago.[22]

49. Proposal for North Michigan Avenue, 1918. Drawing by Andrew Rebori. *American Architect* 114 (Dec. 11, 1918):691.

Often during the competition, the newspaper referred to its future building as the Tribune "monument." Its location on the North Michigan Avenue Bridge Plaza helped reinforce its monumental stature. Equally important was the *Tribune's* emphasis on securing "the most beautiful office building in the world." Midway through the competition, the *Tribune* confessed that the competition's real purpose was educational: "to stimulate interest in the establishment of a high standard of architectural beauty not only among architects and their clients but by arousing the general public."[23]

Through the articles and pictorials that facilitated these educational aims (while providing the newspaper remarkably good "free advertising"), the *Tribune* informed its readers about the broader cultural ideals its new building would represent. The pictorials that appeared week after week in the Sunday *Coloroto Magazine* were particularly instructive. In the midst of the clamor of full-page advertisements and photographs of movie stars and sports figures, the *Tribune* produced regular features on what it proclaimed to be some of the most beautiful buildings in the world. The paper explained that any of these buildings, which ranged from the Parthenon and Antwerp Cathedral to the Philadelphia City Hall and the Woolworth Building (Figure 50), might prove a worthy model for its new skyscraper. The *Tribune* implied that its building would soon join them in the pantheon of venerable monuments.

Associating beauty with qualities that transcended both function and the commercial culture that the newspaper thrived on and perpetuated, the *Tribune* rhapsodized over the "inspiration" and "higher values" these monuments embodied. In this regard, the newspaper situated its efforts clearly within the idealist tradition, which emphasized the distinction between high and commercial culture, finding in the fine arts timeless values and the power to elevate the spirit and improve society. Actively promoted by newly founded civic cultural institutions in the late nineteenth century, this definition of the fine arts associated their appreciation with gentility and refinement, upper-class values that also came to be adopted by the middle class. In the late nineteenth and early twentieth centuries, some cultural institutions and publications (including the *Tribune*) developed strategies for disseminating high culture more broadly, targeting the increasing number of recent immigrants, many of whom were perceived as gravitating toward popular, commercialized amusements rather than the genteel, high culture of the art museum and concert hall. These efforts dovetailed with efforts to assimilate them to dominant American values and ways of living. Some proponents argued that the fine arts could thus form a bulwark against cultural fragmentation and anarchy by binding together a heterogeneous society through the highest ideals a community could espouse – a bulwark, built of class-bound values, which served to reinforce the cultural authority of those who constructed it.[24]

In the course of the competition, the *Tribune* invited its readers to embrace and identify with this notion of the ideal and beautiful. Like the great monuments of the past, the *Tribune*'s pictorials implied, its skyscraper would represent "higher values," humanity's best impulses, and universal truths transcending time, place, and cultural difference.

Performing Citizenship

To emphasize that this monument would indeed stand for the ideals of Chicago's citizens, the *Tribune* bound its readers into the competition's public narrative. An audience is implied from the outset in the competition's initial advertisement (Figure 48). Here the new building is already under construction. Cranes hoist steel beams into place beneath a billowing sky while cars whiz by and pedestrians look on. The building becomes part of a city being transformed, and we – spectators, passers-by, and potential tenants – are present, waiting to see what will develop. As the competition progressed, the *Tribune*'s articles represented the newspaper's readers not as passive spectators, but as active players in the competition's process and outcome; not as competitors and consumers (their role in most of the newspaper's promotional contests), but as *citizens* united in the ideals that would be embodied in the new building.

The editors' first intention had been to handle the *Tribune*'s "contest" like any other by opening it up to anyone who cared to sketch out an idea for a skyscraper.[25] When they discovered that the American Institute of Architects (A.I.A.) would not sanction a competition organized this way, they refocused their efforts on getting reader input on what the new building should be like. In less than two months, thousands, according to the paper, had responded.[26] The *Tribune* then reflected readers' responses back to them, creating a picture of community involvement by publishing letters to the editor and an artists' rendering of readers' suggestions (Figure 51). These ranged from a Great Pyramid–office building to the figure of

CAN THE GENIUS OF GREECE CONTRIBUTE TO THE TRIBUNE'S NEW BUILDING?

JAY HAMBIDGE of Yale, one of the greatest authorities on Greek architecture, says of the old Fine Arts building in Jackson park that next to the Parthenon it is the most beautiful building ever done in the classic style. The photograph at the left was taken at the time of the World's Fair, after which the building was used, for a number of years, to house the exhibits of the Field Museum. The building has fallen into decay, and a campaign is now under way for its restoration.

WHILE Pericles was head of the Athenian democracy the Parthenon was built in honor of Athene Parthenos, the protective divinity of Athens. For twenty years the quarries of Attica were plumbed for their most beautiful marbles and these great blocks were joined and adjusted without cement. The sculptor Phidias, who was the counsel of Pericles in matters relating to the embellishment of Athens, superintended and directed the artists and workmen who built the temple. To his unerring judgment is due the perfect proportion of the Parthenon—the height and thickness of the columns, pediments and other proportions of the temple which harmonize to give the impression of perfect symmetry.

THOUGH science has brought us new and better methods of construction since the days of the Parthenon, for sheer architectural beauty that old temple has never been surpassed. The Tribune hopes to build the most beautiful modern building in the world. The best known architects are competing for The Tribune's $100,000 prize. Doubtless, many of them will seek suggestions for The Tribune's new home in the calm, serene strength of the temples of the ancients.

50. Proposed models for Tribune Company's building: the Parthenon and the Fine Arts Building from the World's Columbian Exposition. *Chicago Tribune Coloroto Magazine*, Nov. 12, 1922. Courtesy of *Chicago Tribune*.

a colossal Samson, his body patterned with windows.

Toward the end of the competition, the newspaper proclaimed that the choice of the winning entry would be a "community matter."[27] The *Tribune* had initially planned to publish what it considered the best entries so that the public could vote on them, but it scrapped this idea once it discovered that it would have been too irregular in a competition conducted according to A.I.A. guidelines. Nevertheless, the *Tribune* assured its readers that their views needed to be heard so that "a consensus may determine just what is Chicago's idea of the most beautiful building in the world."[28] Reinforcing its own long-standing claims for the newspaper's role as guardian of democracy, Tribune Company represented the pages of the newspaper as a civic space, a site of deliberation and democratic process; and it reinforced its own image as the facilitator of the free process of negotiation involved in the formulation of public opinion. In the process, it constructed an image of the community to which its readers belonged. But here the "community in anonymity" of which Benedict Anderson speaks was imagined as being produced through direct, active, and personal involvement; *Gesellschaft* (society) blurred into *Gemeinschaft* (community) as "neighbors and fellow townsmen" joined together in the quest for a monument to their highest ideals.[29]

Shaping an Icon

The entries that arrived by the competition's deadline presented the jury with options ranging from Byzantine to Bauhaus. Some designs came in the shape of classical columns, triumphal arches, towers, and obelisks; others bore crowns bursting with Roman mausoleums, over-scaled sculpture, radio antennae, Gothic spires, inflated globes, Greek columns, huge billboards, classical temples, and more. From this scenographic set of designs, the jury selected as the first-prize winner John Mead Howells and Raymond Hood's Gothic tower, its crown bursting with flying buttresses.

To what extent did reader input actually have an impact on the jury's decision? This is as difficult to gauge with any certainty as it is to determine what *Tribune* readers actually thought beyond how their views were represented in the newspaper. The letters the *Tribune* solicited from readers during the competition provided a means of gauging public opinion even as the newspaper attempted to shape it. At the same time, Tribune Company clearly set up the competition to ensure that it got the results it wanted. The jury was stacked with four Tribune Company executives (McCormick, Patterson, and two subordinates who may not have been in much of a position to argue) and only one architect. Moreover, the competition's results may well have been a foregone conclusion. As it happens, John Mead Howells was married to a member of Tribune Company's board of directors.[30]

In the competition's aftermath, the *Chicago Tribune* drew upon a host of texts, images, and ideas in current circulation to articulate the new building's significance and the newspaper's own munificence. The narrative the *Tribune* developed continuously negotiated the tensions between commercialism and idealism, fragmentation and unity, individualism and community; and in the end, opinions differed considerably about how successful it was in reconciling them.

In the stream of articles and pictorials published after the competition closed, the *Tribune* emphasized the ways the tower's beauty transcended utility and commercial expediency. It described how the flying buttresses, the depth of the reveals, and the chamfered corners all cost extra money while serving no purpose other than to enhance the building's beauty. But even though the newspaper chose to downplay it, the expenditure on beauty did serve a distinctly commercial purpose. Although the competition program had made it clear that the future building was to be surpassingly beautiful, it also indicated that it was to be a distinctive representation of the newspaper company's image. Egerton Swartout, in an article in *American Architect*, correctly interpreted this to mean that the *Tribune* "wanted a building which would be of constant commercial value as an advertisement."[31] In response, the jury received numerous eye-catching designs, some featuring elements specifically associated with newspapers, such as globes, radio antennae, and electric bulletin boards. Any of them might have become an even more noticeable corporate trademark for the *Tribune* than a skyscraper crowned with flying buttresses. But

A PYRAMID

" . . . . . . Last night I dreamed that I was designing the new Tribune Building. It took the form of a huge pyramid, a marvelous structure of blue marble. The windows and doors were of the same pyramid shape . . . . . ."

C. H., Kewanee, Ill.

A BELL

" . . . . . . By all means have a tower and don't forget to have a big deep toned bell in it, and not a dinky little one either . . . . . ."

[illegible]. O., Oak Park, Ill.

AN OBELISK

" . . . . . . Let your aim be ruggedness, not nicety! Let it have the appearance of one stone from bottom to top. I suggest this type for your building—rugged simplicity—obelisk type . . . . . ."

B. A. P., Chicago.

A BLOCKHOUSE

" . . . . . . A massive structure should be built, combined with something that would be a monument of remembrance of early Chicago and still be a part of the modern skyscraper. Represent the blockhouse of 'Old Fort Dearborn' . . . . . ."

F. T. L., Chicago.

A CLOCK

" . . . . . . One of its big features to me is an immense clock in the tower, which at its height can be seen for miles away . . . . . ."

E. M. B., Toledo, O.

SAMSON

" . . . . . . Samson was the world's strongest man. Why not erect the new building in the form of a colossal Samson extending as many stories as you desire? In the legs and arms of Samson you may have office space, the body will be occupied by offices and elevators, the head or dome should be a lookout . . . . . ."

B. M. S., Chicago.

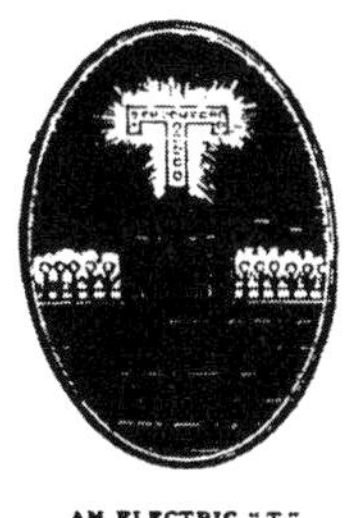

AN ELECTRIC "T"

" . . . . . . One of the features of The Tribune's new building should be a beacon light, a large electrical 'T' . . . . . ."

M. B. M., Danville, Ill.

AN IMMENSE FLAG

" . . . . . . Have a flag pole run up from the center and get out the biggest flag you can find . . . . . ."

B. A. P., Chicago.

EIFFEL TOWER

" . . . . . . I cannot think of anything more appropriate for your building than the Eiffel tower style . . . . . ."

J. H., Dubuque, Ia.

A few suggestions from Tribune readers

The Tribune is planning to build the most beautiful modern building in the world in front of its Plant on upper Michigan avenue. One hundred thousand dollars in prizes has been offered to architects for the best designs.

51. Readers' suggestions for the design of Tribune Company's building. From *Chicago Tribune Coloroto Magazine*, Sept. 10, 1922. Courtesy of *Chicago Tribune*.

these elements were clearly connected with advertising and mass culture and would have been contrary to the high-culture tradition within which the newspaper situated its building. Howells and Hood's design, on the other hand, enhanced the *Tribune*'s claims for its building's status as a monumental work of art and a contribution to Chicago's civic beautification. Nevetheless, as Swartout noted, "The winner, with all its illogical buttresses, will be a remarkably picturesque and noticeable object. It will be popular."[32]

Tribune Tower, once completed, did serve as an effective advertisement for the newspaper, its image appearing on countless postcards, publications, and souvenir items. But, according to the *Tribune*, its Gothic elements heightened its association with higher, noncommercial values. Emphasizing the building's ecclesiastical precedents, especially the Butter Tower of Rouen Cathedral, the newspaper rhapsodized over the ways Tribune Tower's Gothic ornamentation and soaring vertical lines conveyed its inspiring and even spiritual qualities. With language that echoed Henry Adams's popular book, *Mont-Saint-Michel and Chartres*, it extolled the tower's virtues with a host of religious allusions: "There is inspiration in that tremendous sweep upward, and it ends in benediction."[33] The *Tribune* gave no indication that there might be anything contradictory about using such metaphors with reference to a corporate office building. In fact, the newspaper's rhetoric resonated with contemporary corporate public relations materials, which represented business as a public service and even as a spiritual pursuit. If Bruce Barton, author of *The Man Nobody Knows* (which in 1925 reinvented Christ as a businessman), could characterize the corporate system as "not secular but divine" and businessmen as raising peoples' ideals and regenerating whole communities, then the *Tribune* could just as readily transform an office building into a church tower and present it as a source of spiritual inspiration for Chicago.[34]

While reinforcing the newspaper's claims for Tribune Tower's spiritual associations (and by extension, for the company's own high ideals), other meanings associated with the Gothic style also bolstered the image of the cohesive community the *Tribune* constructed during the competition. The belief that Gothic architecture was born of a society that was unified, harmonious, and animated by spiritual values was both long standing and widely held. Among the most vocal American proponents of this view was Ralph Adams Cram, a prolific architect and writer who pictured the Middle Ages as a period when all classes were bound into an organic, democratic social order in which individuality and liberty were balanced with community. For Cram, this vision – the antithesis of anarchy – could provide an antidote to bolshevism and a worthy model for modern America.[35] A similar vision of *Gemeinschaft* – and a similar urge to counter divisiveness in general and bolshevism in particular – informed the *Tribune*'s articles and editorials, as well as its picture of "neighbors and townsmen" come together to shape a Gothic monument to their highest ideals.

The choice of Howells and Hood's Gothic tower drew considerable attention from "neighbors and townsmen" as well as from an array of other publications. Controversy surfaced almost immediately. Some echoed the *Tribune*'s account. Others introduced counter narratives that teased out some of the contractions in the newspaper's account of the competition and the winning design. The most vituperative response came from Louis Sullivan, whose diatribe appeared in *Architectural Record*. Looking beyond the specific historical associations connected with the Gothic style, he framed the competition more broadly as a confrontation between democracy and feudalism. To Sullivan, Eliel Saarinen's design, which earned second place, embodied the values of freedom and democracy, the very "idealism . . . at the core of the American people" – consistent with the idealism the *Tribune* expressed in its competition program. Yet the *Tribune* had rejected this "priceless pearl" in favor of a mere simulacrum. Through such "an act of dominion – of brutal will," it embraced feudalism and the tyranny of moneyed power; it squelched the free expression of the human spirit; and in doing so it betrayed both itself and the American people.[36]

The *Freeman*, which featured articles by leading progressives, asserted that Sullivan's critique was "irrelevant and unduly harsh," and then launched into a critique that turned out to be every bit as biting. The key to the competition's outcome, the *Freeman* argued, lay in the nature of the *Tribune* as a newspaper. Saarinen's mistake was to have read the competition program's idealistic language rather than the newspaper itself. As a highly rated advertising medium, the *Tribune* operated not according to the ideals of freedom and democracy but according to the rules of the marketplace. Even though Saarinen's entry might be the more beautiful and inspiring, it would have made a "manifestly improper" home for a newspaper like the *Tribune*. In this light, the jury had done well in selecting the winning design. "Particularly happy is the symbolism of its ponderous Gothic head-piece with its simulacra of heavy stone supports . . . appropriately reminiscent of mediaeval ways and thought, and of the old feudal order."[37] To the *Freeman*, the Gothic crown, which the *Tribune* presented as an expression of its high, noncommercial ideals, was in fact consistent with the commercial aims that drove it. And to both the *Freeman* and Louis Sullivan, the Gothic style related not to an idealized image of the Middle Ages as unified and democratic, but to a regressive and repressive feudal order.

52. North Michigan Avenue Bridge Plaza, with the Wrigley Building (left), 1919–21, 1924, and Tribune Tower (right), ca. 1933. Collection of the author.

One other significant line of criticism concerned how well Tribune Tower's design advanced the goals of the Plan of Chicago. During the competition, the *Tribune* had made much of the fact that its building would be located adjacent to the North Michigan Avenue Bridge Plaza, which it characterized as becoming "perhaps the most impressive metropolitan group in the history of civic architecture."[38] This enhanced the *Tribune*'s assertion that its new building would become a monument with civic significance. Not long after the competition closed, Edward Bennett, who co-authored the Plan of Chicago with Daniel Burnham, sent a private letter to Robert McCormick calling into question Tribune Tower's appropriateness for its location. To Bennett, the building's individualistic design and its position at a diagonal (rather than across) from the Wrigley Building – with which it did not harmonize – would destroy the chances of ever realizing the well-coordinated, monumental gateway to North Michigan Avenue he and others had planned (Figure 52).[39] Taken in this light, the *Tribune*'s building would thus become a monument to corporate competition rather than the larger civic good.

Even so, Tribune Tower's design received as much if not more praise than condemnation. Some echoed the newspaper's characterization of its goals in terms so similar to the *Tribune*'s that they read like a press release. Others developed their own pithy language. Among the latter, J. B. Carrington, editor of *Architecture*, acclaimed the *Tribune*'s civic-mindedness in terms that would have dismayed the winning design's harsher critics:

> We have too often been prone to think of Chicago as preeminently the embodiment of our so-called national spirit of commercialism, of restless and unmitigated materialism, of the essence of modernism and civic selfishness, indifferent to all but the great god of business and bunk. We doff our hat to . . . the fine, uncontaminated idealism that is expressed in the *Tribune*'s attitude.[40]

Imagining Community

During and after the competition, the *Tribune* enlisted a number of strategies to present its new building as a civic monument. It articulated the ideals the building stood for, it positioned its readers as active participants in shaping a monument to these ideals, and it imagined the community to which they belonged. To conclude, I will discuss an event that gave the *Tribune* the opportunity to orchestrate, in the physical space of the city and in the rhetorical space of the newspaper, the experience of simultaneity and connection that, to Benedict Anderson, provides reassurance of an imagined community's existence.

Crowning Tribune Tower was a 110-foot pole designed to hoist the American flag to what the *Tribune* proclaimed to be the highest point in Chicago. In late September of 1924 the newspaper discovered that a three-foot pulley at the top of the pole was out of its socket. Even so, "Old Glory stood flat against the strong southerly wind yesterday while thousands below gazed with admiration and wonder." To ensure that this inspiring sight could be sustained, the *Tribune* advertised nationally to find a steeplejack who could scale the flagpole and set the pulley aright. This provided an excellent opportunity to turn the process of fixing it into a public drama.

During the daring feat, the *Tribune* trained the eyes of Chicago upon its new building. It published a map showing particularly good vantage points for witnessing the climb, claiming that "more than six square miles of Chicago can watch . . . without eyestrain." Most of the vantage points were other tall buildings, among them some of Chicago's newest (the Temple, Strauss, and Wrigley buildings – the Tribune Tower's competitors in grandeur), which, in this context, were no longer sights to be seen in themselves but grandstands for gazing upon the new Tribune Tower. Uncountable thousands witnessed the climb, the *Tribune* reported; Michigan Avenue was "black with spectators," while at the Wrigley Building "no one did much else than watch," and at the Republican national headquarters, "the candidacy of Calvin Coolidge was forgotten for a time." Time stopped. All eyes focused simultaneously on the building in a shared experience, which, as recounted in the newspaper, forged *Tribune* readers and spectators into a community participating in the proper enshrinement of the Stars and Stripes. Whether or not the event drew the attention the *Tribune* claimed, it provided an opportunity for the paper to present the picture of a community drawn together through its common focus on the Tribune monument, with the American flag flying at its summit (Figure 47).[41]

NOTES

1. Eclipsing many of the foreign-language newspapers that had flourished before World War I, the *Chicago Tribune* led circulation in Chicago and drew a substantial number of readers in the five-state Tribune territory. Through the *New York Daily News*, the European edition of the *Tribune*, and its foreign news service, Tribune Company also extended its reach nationally and internationally. See the Chicago Tribune Business Survey, *The Chicago Tribune's 1919 Book of Facts on Markets and Merchandising* (Chicago, 1919), 28; Business Survey of the Chicago Tribune, *Book of Facts 1920 Edition* (Chicago, 1920), 42; Chicago Tribune, *Pictured Encyclopedia of the World's Greatest Newspaper* (Chicago, Tribune Co., 1928), 112, 227, and passim.

2. Little previous attention has been given to how the competition was publicized. The significant exceptions to this are Merrill Schleier, *The Skyscraper in American Art, 1890–1931* (New York: DaCapo, 1986), 70–1, who recognizes the importance of the competition in disseminating ideas about the skyscraper to the general public; and David Van Zanten, "Twenties Gothic," *New Mexico Studies in the Fine Arts* 8 (1983):19–23, who discusses its dramatization in *Chicago Tribune* articles for advertising purposes. For a more detailed discussion than is possible here, see Katherine Solomonson, *The Chicago Tribune Tower Competition: Skyscraper Design and Cultural Change in the 1920s* (New York: Cambridge Univ. Press, 2001).

3. *Chicago Tribune*, July 7, 1925.

4. Robert McCormick to "Joe," Jan. 4, 1922, photocopy of typescript in Tribune Company Archives, Colonel Robert R. McCormick Research Center of the First Division Museum at Cantigny, Wheaton, IL.

5. This coincided, not surprisingly, with the explosion of advertising in the late nineteenth and early centuries, the establishment of brand names, and the increasing use of slogans and trademarks in advertising and packaging. See, for example, William D. McJunkin, "Pictures in Advertising," in *Advertising Methods and Mediums*, ed. Thomas Herbert Russell (Racine, WI: Whitman, 1916): 209, who included corporate buildings in his list of trademarks. Whether seen in the context of the city or in an advertisement, the tall building's form could be designed and disseminated so that, like a trademark, "just the fleeting glance, almost unconscious . . . sets the name [of the company or brand] vibrating in the mind." George French, *How to Advertise* (New York: Doubleday, Page & Co., 1917), 181.

6. On "Skyscraper Mania" see Schleier, *The Skyscraper in American Art*, 69 ff.

7. "Tentative schedule for publicity leading up to the awarding of a prize for the plans for the Tribune Monument," n.d. Handwritten at top right is "Capt Patterson" and stamped below this is "Please note and return to Colonel McCormick" with "Noted JMP" handwritten. Tribune Archives.

8. According to Bernays, "continuous interpretation" is structured to implant the "desired impression" in the "public mind" often without their being aware of it. Edward L. Bernays, *Biography of an Idea* (New York: Simon and Schuster, 1965), 240.

9. See Benedict Anderson, *Imagined Communities*, rev. ed. (London: Verso, 1991), 6–7, 33–6, and passim.

10. James Gilbert, *Perfect Cities: Chicago's Utopias of 1893* (Chicago: Univ. of Chicago Press, 1991), 48–9, 55, and passim; and Alan Trachtenberg, *The Incorporation of America: Culture and Society in the Gilded Age* (New York: Hill and Wang, 1982), 125–6.

11. See John Higham, *Strangers in the Land: Patterns of American Nativism 1860–1925*, 2nd ed. (New Brunswick: Rutgers Univ. Press, 1988), passim; and Milton M. Gordon, "Assimilation in America: Theory and Reality," in *The National Temper: Readings in American Culture and Society*, eds. Lawrence W. Levine and Robert Middlekauff (New York: Harcourt Brace Jovanovich, 1972), 268–84.

12. Stow Persons, *Ethnic Studies at Chicago, 1905–45* (Urbana and Chicago: Univ. of Illinois Press, 1987), 3, 4–5, 47–8, 53–7, 60–4, 67, and passim; Chicago Commission on Race Relations, *The Negro in Chicago: A Study of Race Relations and a Race Riot in 1919* (1922; repr., New York: Arno Press and the New York Times, 1968), 520; Robert E. Park and Ernest W. Burgess, *Introduction to the Science of Sociology* (Chicago: Univ. of Chicago Press, 1921); and W. I. Thomas, *Old World Traits Transplanted* (New York: Harper, 1921).

13. *Chicago Tribune*, Jan. 11, 1917, cited by Higham, *Strangers in the Land*, 203.

14. Oswald Garrison Villard, "The World's Greatest Newspaper," *Nation* 114 (Feb. 1, 1922):117; and Chicago Commission on Race Relations, *The Negro in Chicago*, 520 ff.

15. See, for example, *Winning a Great Market on Facts* (Chicago, 1916), 1–2, 14.

16. This appeared in an advertisement concerning the Chicago Tribune Tower competition. *Chicago Tribune*, June 12, 1922.

17. Roger Miller, "Selling Mrs. Consumer: Advertising and the Creation of Suburban Socio-Spatial Relations 1910–1930," *Antipode* 23 (July 1991): 263–301.

18. Charles Moore, ed., *Plan of Chicago* (Chicago: Commercial Club, 1909), 1.

19. On the promotion of the Chicago plan, see Chicago Plan Commission, *Ten Years Work of the Chicago Plan Commission* (Chicago: Apr., 1920), Bennett Papers, Ryerson and Burnham Libraries, Art Institute of Chicago; Charles H. Wacker, "The Plan of Chicago – Its Purpose and Development," *Art and Archaeology* 12 (Sept.–Oct. 1921):103–4; Robert P. Akeley, Jr., "Implementing the 1909 Plan of Chicago: An Historical Account of Planning Salesmanship" (Master's thesis, Univ. of Tennessee, 1973), 77, 112 ff.; Thomas J. Schlereth, "Moody's Go-Getter Wacker Manual," *Inland Architect* 24 (Apr. 1980):9–11; and Joan E. Draper, *Edward H. Bennett, Architect and City Planner, 1874–1954* (Chicago: Art Institute of Chicago, 1982), 17.

20. See especially Walter D. Moody, *Wacker's Manual of the Plan of Chicago: Municipal Economy*, 3rd ed. (Chicago: Chicago Plan Commission, 1920), v, vi, 25, 61–3.

21. This was expressed or implied in various *Tribune* articles and editorials, but it comes through particularly pointedly in Robert McCormick, *What Is a Newspaper?* (Chicago: Chicago Tribune, 1924), 32.

22. *Chicago Tribune*, June 11, 1922.

23. *Chicago Tribune*, Sept. 29, 1922.

24. I owe a particular debt to the following works for their analysis of the popularization of "high" culture, its growing distinction from popular culture, and the institutional matrix within which this occurred: Helen Lefkowitz Horowitz, *Culture and the City: Cultural Philanthropy in Chicago from the 1880s to 1917* (Chicago: Univ. of Chicago Press, 1976); Lawrence W. Levine, *Highbrow/Lowbrow: The Emergence of Cultural Hierarchy in America* (Cambridge, MA: Harvard Univ. Press, 1988); Joan Shelley Rubin, *The Making of Middlebrow Culture* (Chapel Hill, NC: Univ. of North Carolina Press, 1992).

25. Holmes Onderdonk, "The Tribune Tower," *Journal of the Western Society of Engineers* 29 (Dec. 1924): 444.

26. The *Tribune* reported that it based its estimate on written and oral communications. *Chicago Tribune*, Aug. 1, 1922.

27. *Chicago Tribune*, Nov. 27, 1922.

28. *Chicago Tribune*, June 18, 1922.

29. *Chicago Tribune*, Dec. 1, 1922.

30. John Mead Howells's wife, Abbey White Howells, was the daughter of Horace White, who was managing editor and part owner of the *Tribune* in the late nineteenth century. Her name appeared in the Statement of Ownership the *Tribune* published on Oct. 5, 1919. See also "The Key to the *Tribune's* Management," *Fortune* 9 (May 1934):108.

31. Egerton Swartout, "Review of Recent Architectural Magazines," *American Architect* 123 (Feb. 28, 1923):209.

32. Swartout, "Review of Recent Architectural Magazines," 209.

33. *Chicago Tribune*, Dec. 3, 1922.

34. Bruce Barton, *The Man Nobody Knows: A Discovery of the Real Jesus* (Grosset & Dunlap, 1924, 1925); and Bruce Barton, "A Few Kind Words for Business," from *More Power to You*, excerpted in *The Literature of Business*, ed. Alta Gwinn Saunders and Herbert LeSourd Creek (New York: Harper, 1928), 70–1.

35. Cram articulated these views in numerous publications, including *The Substance of Gothic* (Boston: Marshall Jones Co., 1917), 38, 108, and passim. See Robert Muccigrosso, "Ralph Adams Cram: The Architect as Communitarian," *Prospects* 1 (1975):166–7.

36. Louis Sullivan, "The Chicago Tribune Competition," *Architectural Record* 53 (Feb. 1923):151–7.

37. "Stately Mansions," *Freeman* (Mar. 14, 1923):5.

38. *Chicago Tribune*, June 10, 1922.

39. Edward H. Bennett to Robert H. [sic] McCormick, Dec. 19, 1922. Patterson Papers, Lake Forest College.

40. "The Chicago Tribune Building Competition," *Architecture* 47 (1923):11.

41. *Chicago Tribune*, Sept. 28, Sept. 30, and Oct. 1–4, 1924. See also Van Zanten, "Twenties Gothic."

PART THREE

URBAN CONTEXTS

8

The Heights and Depths of Urbanism

Fifth Avenue and the Creative Destruction of Manhattan

Max Page

In an image from her book *Changing New York*, the definitive record of New York in the 1930s, photographer Berenice Abbott juxtaposes the small brick houses of South and DePeyster streets with 60 Wall Street, a thin skyscraper that seems of a different world from the waterfront homes and warehouses of early nineteenth-century Manhattan (Figure 53). Time and again Abbott, as well as countless photographers and painters throughout the early twentieth century, used the replacement of old with new, townhouses with skyscrapers, tenements with apartment towers, as a leitmotif in their work. The use of this contrast is telling. For if the tall building transformed, indeed *created*, the "skyline" of the city, so too was its influence felt profoundly on the ground level, and on the historical level, in its radical remaking of the fabric of the city. It is the metaphorical "ground floor" – the urban context of construction – of Manhattan's skyscrapers with which this essay is concerned.

Skyscrapers have come to define how we understand urban growth. Perpetually rising, they suggest a linear process of urban growth, where cities grow always larger, denser, taller. They have literally shaped not only the sites of work and home, but also the way city dwellers understand urban development. However, the process of urban growth belies this simple metaphor of a steadily expanding organism. American cities, especially in the most rapid period of their development from 1870 to 1940, were defined not by steady growth but rather by a tumultuous "creative destruction." To city dwellers of all types, the tearing down and rebuilding of the city's physical landscape posed crucial cultural

This essay is adapted from my book, *The Creative Destruction of Manhattan, 1900–1940*.

dilemmas and thus was at the heart of the experience of urban living.

In this essay, I offer a way of viewing urban development in the early decades of the twentieth century that forces us to reconsider the skyscraper's roots and impacts. I begin by describing the concept of creative destruction and how it offers a new lens for viewing urban development. I then turn to the process of real estate development on Fifth Avenue, the most visible and valuable linear space in all of America, where the impact of the tall building was felt, and in some cases battled, most intensely by New Yorkers. On Fifth Avenue, and throughout Manhattan, the story of skyscrapers was far more than a story of architectural visions or technological innovations. It was equally a story about private real estate development and public controls, visions of the ideal city and practical efforts to cope with development, and the attempts to preserve a physical and social order in the face of unsettling change.

The Concept of Creative Destruction

In 1904, Henry James left his self-imposed exile in Europe and returned to the United States. The journey was partly a nostalgia trip, giving him an opportunity to search out his old haunts and homes in New York and Boston. But like most nostalgia trips, this one was a disappointment, if not a disaster. Expecting to return to the city of his youth, he instead found a radically changed city, where greed and vulgar pursuit of profit manifested itself in gaudy, ostentatious buildings. Returning from Europe, a continent of ancient cities, stretching back several millennia, James found in New York only a "provisional city."[1]

The trope of the "provisional city" has been a persistent metaphor for New York City. Scholars, teachers, novelists, critics, artists, and poets have dipped into the waters of this metaphorical well to explain New York to itself and to the nation. Although historians have quoted the poignant voices of city dwellers to emphasize this quality of urban experience, they have never placed it at the center of the study of the process of citybuilding and the experience of the modern city. Indeed, New York's casual as well as scholarly observers have dipped far more regularly into a different well. They have preferred to perpetuate a view of New York, and by extension all cities, as growing rapidly but steadily, upward and outward. Terms such as "expansive" and "burgeoning" have attached themselves to descriptions of New York's growth at the turn of the century.[2] The classic description of the transformation of cities has been the series of time-lapse photographs, the "then and now" comparisons, showing the city as something akin to a flowering plant. Each time this natural, linear metaphor of city growth is repeated, it further obscures a crucial dynamic of urban life – the intentional destruction and rebuilding of the city.

I argue that American cities are best defined by an urban development process whose central dynamic was not defined by simple expansion and growth but rather by a vibrant and often chaotic process of destruction and rebuilding. The upheavals of New York City were not the result of dramatic, isolated natural disasters or government-sponsored urban renewal projects but rather were necessary episodes in the process of capitalist urbanization.[3] The economist Joseph Schumpeter captured the essential process of capitalism – the never-ending cycle of destroying and inventing new products and methods of production – with his phrase "creative destruction." "Capitalism," wrote Schumpeter in 1942, "is by nature a form or method of economic change and not only never is but never can be stationary. This process of Creative Destruction is the essential fact about capitalism.... To ignore this central fact is like *Hamlet* without the Danish prince."[4] Nearly one hundred years earlier, Karl Marx

53. Berenice Abbott. *South and DePeyster Streets*, November 26, 1935. This image, among hundreds of photographs created by Abbott to document a changing New York, juxtaposes the skyscraper (60 Wall Street at the center, and the Bank of Manhattan to the left) with the four- to five-story city, attempting to capture the visual and spatial changes experienced by the urban everyman. Reprinted with permission of the Museum of the City of New York. Federal Arts Project: "Changing New York," Abbott File 52.

had anticipated Schumpeter. "All that is solid melts into air," Marx wrote in the *Communist Manifesto*, expressing the deeply paradoxical nature of the modern experience. The most concrete objects of capitalist society, the sociologist Marshall Berman wrote in a modern interpretation, "are made to be broken tomorrow, smashed or shredded or pulverized or dissolved, so they can be recycled or replaced next week, and the whole process can go on again and again, hopefully forever, in ever more profitable forms."[5] Schumpeter's phrase succinctly describes the process of development in the city in the first four decades of the century.

By applying Schumpeter's concept of economic creative destruction to the literal, physical destruction and creation of buildings and natural landscapes in Manhattan, I want to suggest the ways in which capitalism inscribed its economic and social processes into the physical landscape of the city, and then into the minds of city people.[6] Marx's pungent phrase – "all that is solid melts into air" – applies to both the transitory physical landscape of New York and the social and cultural dynamism that came to characterize the city. Schumpeter's phrase – but not his celebration of capitalist innovation – suggests how the creative destruction of the physical landscape posed for New Yorkers the fundamental tension between creative possibilities and destructive effects of the modern city.

The broadest methodological goal of the following pages is to suggest that we place the process of creative destruction at the heart of the story of urban development and the story of the development of skyscrapers. It is not a revisionist rejection of urban growth, an analysis which tries to describe the modern city as merely "destructive." The aim is rather to highlight the fundamental tensions – both physical and cultural – at the heart of the urban experience. The literature on cities has either listed toward nostalgia for a better, lost time, or veered sharply toward an embrace of "improvement" and "modernization." In fact, the most accurate and revealing path is at the intersection of these conflicting beliefs. The oxymoron "creative destruction" suggests the tensions that were at the heart of urban life: between stability and change; between the notion of "place" and that of undifferentiated, developable "space"; between market forces and planning controls; between economic value and cultural value; and between what was considered "natural" and "unnatural" in the growth of the city. While some observers celebrated planning by destruction or marveled at the rapid domestication of the natural environment, others decried the devastation of their homes and lamented the passing of the architectural heritage of the city. Celebrated and decried, encouraged and resisted, this process defined the experience of the city. It also posed in the most jarring manner the dilemmas of modernity.

Fifth Avenue's Restless Renewals

It was on Fifth Avenue that Henry James found the soul and source of the destructive spirit he sensed throughout his travels in 1904. For Fifth Avenue spun through cycles of construction and destruction at a rate unmatched in the city. The Avenue, and the city as a whole, had become a "monster of the mere market."[7] In the course of only a hundred years, the Avenue had been transformed from an empty country road into a "millionaire's mile" of estates and then into a densely inhabited line of wealthy apartments, stores, and manufacturing lofts. If we are to locate and understand the essence of the creatively destructive logic of private real estate development – the primary engine of Manhattan's continuous transformation – it is to Fifth Avenue, the "spine of Gotham," we must look.[8] In the first decades of the century, as the entire island was a churning landscape of development, redevelopment, destruction, and construction, few places received the attention Fifth Avenue did. Virtually every demolition, every construction project, and every increase and decrease in property values was recorded and reported. Fifth Avenue captivated writers and citizens of the time because it represented like no other street in New York the forces of capitalist industrialization remaking America (Figure 54). And yet, even as it displayed the "pure" market forces that drove the creative destruction of New York, Fifth Avenue became, in the early years of the twentieth century, the center of intense efforts to resist that market's destructive dynamic and to preserve a particular, tangible sense of place. Indeed, Fifth Avenue, the ultimate market in private property, was also one of the most regulated pieces of land in the nation. The modern

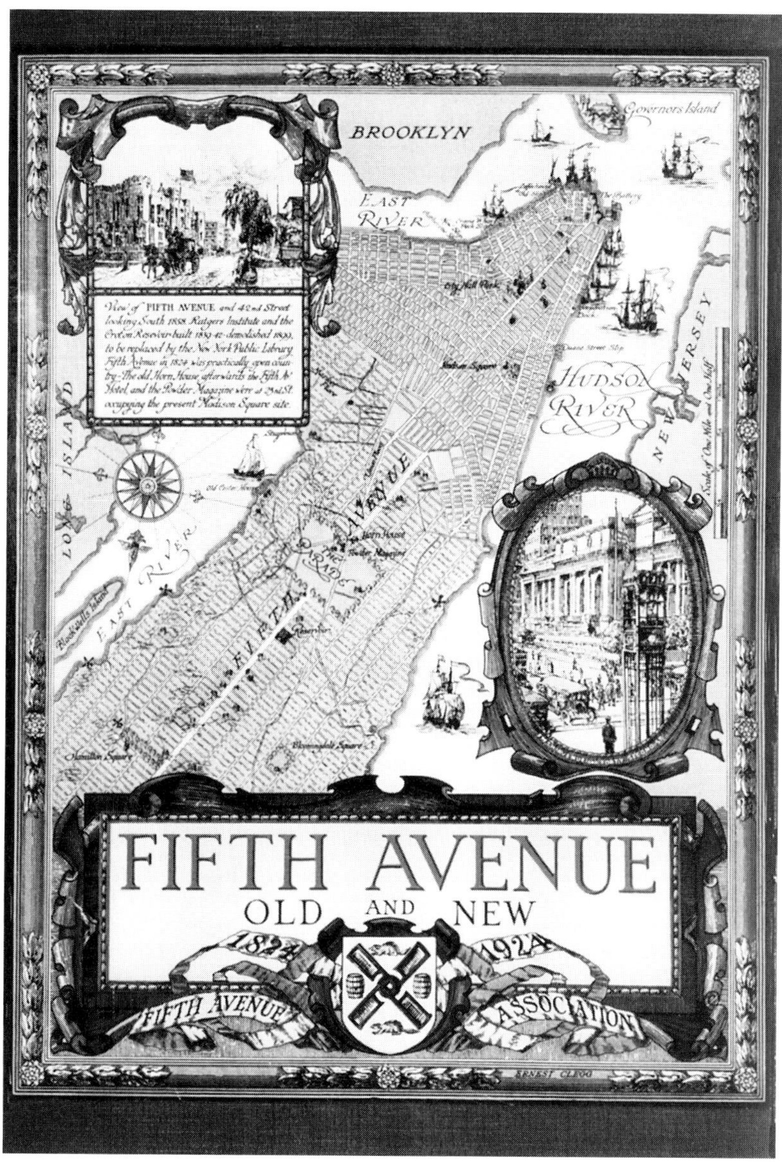

54. Fifth Avenue's transformation from country lane to elite residential street and finally to a prestigious shopping destination is illustrated here on the cover of a Fifth Avenue Association publication. Henry Collins Brown, *Fifth Avenue, Old and New, 1824–1924* (New York: Fifth Avenue Association, 1924).

methods of controlling urban land values, uses, and aesthetics all found some of their first trials on Fifth Avenue. Fifth Avenue was the site of one of the earliest business districts and business district associations; it was influential in the passing of America's first comprehensive zoning law (the 1916 Zoning Resolution), and it was subject to informal as well as legal restrictions on architectural form. Simply put, even as it was seen as a symbol for nothing less than America's wealth generated by "free" capitalistic entrepreneurship, Fifth Avenue was the birthplace of modern city planning and some of the most far-reaching efforts at controlling the capitalist market in space, of which the skyscraper was the most exclamatory demonstration.

Fifth Avenue developed in reaction to the cycle of building and rebuilding in Lower Manhattan. The Commissioners Plan of 1811, which laid down New York's grid of streets, had included Fifth Avenue, but it was not until 1824 that the street was laid out; and it remained undeveloped above Fourteenth Street until the 1850s. After the Panic of 1837, Manhattan resumed its heady growth – especially after 1845, when the Croton Aqueduct was completed. In the following decade, the city's population doubled, and concerns about crowding and disease resulted in the fabled "march uptown" by the wealthier classes.[9] It was to Fifth Avenue that the wealthiest families in America gravitated, to embody their far-flung wealth – in western mining companies, railroad lines, and steel plants – in bricks, mortar, and, more typically, marble (Figure 55).

The development of Fifth Avenue as a residential and elite shopping street slowed by the end of the nineteenth century. The market itself had overheated, creating a lack of lots for building and land prices so high that few could afford to build private mansions along the Avenue. Furthermore, the Depression of 1893 stalled virtually all building projects until the beginning of the new century. The numbers of new private homes along Fifth Avenue (and in Manhattan as a whole) declined precipitously.[10] This, however, did not signal a corresponding decline in Fifth Avenue development. With few individuals willing or able to build private homes, manufacturers – eager to join the elite cadre of Fifth Avenue businesses and be close to the rail and transport centers of the East and West Sides – began to take over space along the Avenue. The image of an elite residential neighborhood was now appropriated by manufacturing and retail firms. Above Fifty-ninth Street, the Avenue remained one of the most elite residential areas in the city, a solid wall of wealth across from the park. But the continued pressures on land values, and the push to squeeze profits out of a finite amount of land, spurred a new wave of destruction and rebuilding. Just as the wave of mansion building crested in the late 1890s, the first luxury apartment buildings were erected on the lots of recently demolished mansions.

The transformation of the Avenue was accelerated by the passage of the 1916 Zoning Resolution. The ordinance, the culmination of a long fight that I will discuss in a following section, subjected all land in Greater New York City to controls on use and development. First, the city was divided into zones, where different types of uses – unrestricted, residential, and business – would be allowed. Second, in order to prevent such notorious structures as Ernest R. Graham's Equitable Building (1912–15) – an immense volume of offices covering an entire block on Lower Broadway near City Hall, which quickly became a touchstone for skyscraper critics – the law restricted the amount of a site that could be built upon. Finally, and most importantly for the Fifth Avenue Association, the law limited heights, using an elaborate formula based on the width of the street, in order to allow more light and air into the city's streets. On most major avenues in Manhattan, the ordinance permitted buildings to rise twice the width of the street – 150 feet on a 75-foot-wide street – before "stepping back" a foot for every two-foot elevation thereafter.[11] The resulting ziggurat-like form of Manhattan's skyscrapers in the 1920s and 1930s – though perhaps not intended by the authors of the 1916 ordinance – was in part a response by architects to develop a skyscraper aesthetic within the setback constraint.

Although World War I delayed the transformation of Fifth Avenue, it was the 1916 zoning ordinance that provided the legislative framework for a rapid development of tall commercial and residential towers along the Avenue,

55. Fifth Avenue north from Fifty-first Street, New York. Among the grandest of the Fifth Avenue residences were the pair of Renaissance palazzi built by William H. Vanderbilt in the 1880s for his daughters, and the French château occupied by his son, William K. Vanderbilt, directly to the north. Courtesy of Library of Congress, Prints and Photographs Div., Detroit Publishing Co. Collection [LC-D4-12528 DLC].

and the elimination of the nineteenth-century brownstones. As I will discuss, although the zoning ordinance inhibited the extreme development of a land lot – a sheer tower 300 feet tall on a narrow lot was impossible under the ordinance – it ultimately sped up development by preventing uses and forms that might have destroyed the allure of Fifth Avenue.

Thus, beginning in the late nineteenth century but exploding after World War I, Fifth Avenue was remade into a line of skyscraping apartment houses for the wealthy. The last inhabitants of the mansions lining the Avenue and the new wealthy class fled for the suburbs or took refuge in the apartment towers. Their former homes were promptly demolished to make way for high-rise apartments or were saved as part of some of the first preservation efforts conducted by organizations such as the Municipal Art Society and the American Scenic and Historic Preservation Societies. Other mansions were converted into museums, beginning the process whereby "Millionaire's Row" became "Museum Mile."

The postwar boom was launched in March 1920, when the Astor estate sold 141 parcels of land in Manhattan for over $5 million, in one of the most successful auctions in the history of the city. The usually sober *Real Estate Record and Building Guide (RERBG)*, and the trade journal of record, allowed itself to be caught up in sentimental observance of the passing of an age. The income tax, economic conditions of wartime, and the postwar economic opportunity for development had "brought about the sale of many pieces of land and numerous buildings to the amazement of old New Yorkers, who would have taken an oath that certain well-known estates would remain intact until the end of time."[12] And indeed, there were other signs that the battle had been relinquished. Even before Cartier's arrival, the end of the Vanderbilt stronghold had been foreseen. The *RERBG* reported that the Vanderbilts' agreement to rescind their restrictive covenant on a site at Fifty-second and Fifth Avenue "must mean that they have agreed to abandon their opposition to the transformation of the district."[13] Although the Vanderbilts remained on the Avenue for more than a decade, the symbolic end of the old society arrived in 1924 when the grand mansion at Fifty-eighth and Fifth was torn down.

Few Fifth Avenue families had simply watched as their neighborhood changed. Their answer to the pressure of development was, finally, to join the real estate boom (Figure 56). In recognition of their impotence before real estate development and retail expansion, the families along the Avenue dove wholeheartedly into the development of upper Fifth Avenue, demolishing, selling, auctioning, and developing their plots, all to the awestruck observation of the press. Led by architect James Edwin Ruthven Carpenter, some of the most strident defenders of the mansion neighborhood now saw great profit in apartment buildings along Central Park, and brought a lawsuit to overturn legislation restricting building heights there (fixing a weakness of the 1916 zoning ordinance that had effectively allowed for the tallest of all buildings to be built opposite open space).[14] The legislation was overturned in 1924, fueling an almost instantaneous demolition spree, which brought down no less than twenty-six mansions above Fifty-ninth Street, most of which were replaced by apartment buildings.[15] For all the incredulity, New York's developers and architects were poised to take advantage of a new real estate boom and legal rulings – as well as a cultural acceptance of apartment living. As Elizabeth Hawes has argued, apartments became more attractive as the costs of maintaining a private house and the required servants escalated, country houses fulfilled the desire for private open space, and growing public forms of entertainment replaced the need for private ballrooms and massive dining rooms.[16]

The 1920s were simply a continuation of the building boom that had begun in the prewar years. In 1925 alone, fifty-three new buildings were completed on the Upper East Side and fifty-four were in progress. Architects like Carpenter, and McKim, Mead & White; real estate brokers like Douglas Elliman; and new developers like the upstart Benjamin Winter were ready and eager to exploit the possibilities of Fifth Avenue and the neighboring, and up-and-coming, Park Avenue.[17] In 1916, Carpenter himself had given a running start to the transformation of upper Fifth Avenue with his apartment building at 906 Fifth Avenue, which marked the first time a mansion was replaced by an apartment block. The lamentations for the noble past of Fifth Avenue on the editorial page of the *RERBG* were matched by reports of developers and architects eager to transform the Avenue.

In 1940, when the *WPA Guide to New York* was published, Fifth Avenue was much transformed. Genteel houses along Lower Fifth Avenue – from Washington Square to Thirty-fourth Street – had been replaced by factories and office towers. But once above Thirty-fourth Street, the *Guide* noted, Fifth Avenue "abruptly emerges from a street of buildings housing wholesale clothing, textile, and bric-a-brac concerns to become the aristocrat of shopping thoroughfares."[18] It was still the most financially and culturally valuable commercial

56. Vanderbilt House, Plaza Hotel, and entrance to Central Park, New York. By the turn of the century, palaces for the social elite, such as the Cornelius Vanderbilt II mansion at Fifty-seventh Street and Fifth Avenue, shared privileged addresses and views with luxury apartment houses and hotels like the Plaza, built in 1907 at the edge of Central Park. Courtesy of Library of Congress, Prints and Photographs Div., Detroit Publishing Co. Collection [LC-D4-36551 DLC].

and residential land on the island. For those who argued that Fifth Avenue should remain residential, the Avenue still was home to the elite of New York even if they were now lifted a hundred feet in the air, perched over Central Park. If the "encroachments of commerce" had effectively amputated Fifth Avenue in the middle, at least its upper reaches retained the key elements of what made the Avenue unique.[19]

"A Compelling Force": The Speculative Market in Space

Fifth Avenue's "restless renewals" must be understood within the larger context of New York's rise as the "capital of capitalism."[20] The tremendous demands for space were not simply due to New York's position as the greatest center for manufacturing in America, but also because it had become the "front office" for America's industrial giants and the country's biggest market for many goods. New York was thus unique in its leadership in industrial management, production, and consumption. It was this role, as the "principal command post of industrial capitalism in the United States," that urged on the cycles of private destruction and rebuilding.[21]

This combination of economic factors made for an incredibly diverse range of land uses. Elite residence areas bordered on the dense acres of the laboring classes, while manufacturing lofts spread quickly through Lower Manhattan, filling increasingly larger and taller buildings. The "compelling force" behind the rapid and continuous rebuilding of the island came from factors in part unique to New York. First, the growth rate of New York's population was unmatched anywhere in the nation. Ellis Island was admitting up to one million people a year, one-third of whom chose to stay, at least for a time, in New York. Thus, the city grew steadily denser, especially in Lower Manhattan residential areas, such as the Lower East Side, that were within walking distance of workplaces.[22]

Second, the unique configuration of New York's economy – as the center of fashion and consumption – made New York fertile economic soil not for large-scale manufacturing enterprises but rather for an incredible diversity of small manufacturing enterprises.[23] New York's was a relatively unstable marketplace, with businesses opening and closing, rapidly expanding and contracting; few industries with apparent permanence demanded homes like Ford had created at his River Rouge plant. To meet the proliferating desires of shoppers, New York manufacturers developed endless small factories and satellite sweatshops that could change styles with ease. This is what drove the explosion of lofts, the small factory enterprises located in Lower Manhattan and increasingly in midtown.[24]

Over time, lofts encroached upon Fifth Avenue and moved northward. Because the garment industry followed the garment fashion center, where the stores went, the garment factories followed. But while these exclusive stores needed the relatively close presence of the garment manufacturers – for designs and alterations – they also wanted to be distant from them, and a game of leapfrog commenced between department stores and their wholesalers and manufacturers.[25] Lofts dominated the development of manufacturing space in Lower Manhattan and became the archenemy, as we shall see, of Fifth Avenue inhabitants and some commercial owners. A post–World War I boom generated 50 to 60 million square feet in industrial loft space in the 1920s, in increasingly taller and wider structures that necessitated the demolition of previous loft structures. Thus on the West Side, where once hundreds of small merchants and factories crowded near the Hudson River, now a few large printing firms were housed in taller and larger buildings. Industrial lofts were soon eclipsed in importance by the growth of corporate headquarters, housed in skyscrapers that would come to dominate the image of New York.[26]

The growth of manufacturing and commerce drove a segregation within Manhattan, whereby downtown and, increasingly, midtown Manhattan was becoming dominated by business. A notice in the *RERBG*, advertising the sale of the Astor midtown properties, declared that "New York, compared to other cities, is like a boy of 18. The characteristics and features of its manhood are now discernible. The Heart of This Great City Is Now Settled for All Time. It is the district from 34th to 59th Sts., 3rd to 10th Avenues."[27] Although this process had begun much earlier in the nineteenth century, the combination of manufacturing and commerce expanded dramatically at the end of the century. Their efforts culminating in the 1916 zoning ordinance, private developers and city government worked in tandem to segregate Manhattan by functions. This process – well-known to urban historians – accelerated the settlement of Upper Manhattan and then its redevelopment with ever-denser housing, and the destruction and rebuilding of Lower Manhattan's residential areas to make way for lofts and, later, office skyscrapers. While the Lower East Side, near the heart of Manhattan's industrial center, remained a primary residence for the poorest of workers, its popularity steadily declined, as many migrated up the avenues to apartments and brownstones on the Upper East and West Sides, and to new tracts of housing in the outer boroughs.[28]

The result was a market for land that was incredibly destructive and profitable in that destruction. As David Scobey has argued, the New York real estate industry did not explode in the post–Civil War era to serve and facilitate the growth of New York's manufacturing and finance might. The trade in space was, in and of itself, a powerful generator of New

York's wealth. The most influential and wealthy families in New York – the Vanderbilts, Astors, and Belmonts – acquired much of their profits from holding and trading land on Manhattan Island.[29] Indeed, New York's private real estate industry was built and depended on the cyclical rebuilding of the city's physical fabric, making it increasingly dense and centered around business. Manhattan was in a constant state of "improvement" – as the *RERBG* liked to call all new building activities. Property values increased so much because private developers never stopped remaking the landscape of the city. With people and wealth flowing into the city, developers found clients for repeated demolition and construction of newer, taller lofts, offices, and, especially after 1920, apartment houses. There seemed to be no end to the need for greater density, both for homes and businesses.

A writer for the *RERBG*, explaining the transformation of Fifth Avenue, noted that "the compelling force is the same which about the year 1845 cleared away the shanties from the ragged edges of the common, smoothed over the potter's field, and built these old dwellings and stores, whose turn it is now to go."[30] In his 1932 essay about 1920s New York, "My Lost City," F. Scott Fitzgerald noted that many of the iconographic sites in Manhattan "had somehow disappeared."[31] The sense of mystery in real estate development had become one of the central elements of Manhattan's folklore of growth. For many, the creative destruction along Fifth Avenue was driven by a "compelling force" – a force attractive but also elusive and incomprehensible, and, some would suggest, uncontrollable.

Commerce without Commercialism: The Fifth Avenue Association and the "Conservation" of the Avenue

The inhabitants of Fifth Avenue – some of the wealthiest families in America, and certainly some of the most powerful actors in city government and business – responded rapidly in the first two decades of the twentieth century to the spin of destruction and rebuilding that threatened their homes and businesses. The story of Fifth Avenue residents' and business owners' efforts to freeze Fifth Avenue in a certain incarnation – that of an elite residential area and exclusive shopping district – is a study in the rise of intervention in the marketplace of space. In essence, Fifth Avenue inhabitants and investors utilized the most modern methods of city development in order to achieve conservative results. For we find not only one of the first and certainly the most influential example of government zoning but a whole range of tools used to mold, manipulate, and control space. These tools ranged from private cajoling and the backroom discussions held at the Century and Metropolitan clubs or at the Fifth Avenue Hotel, to municipal measures of street widening, zoning, and policing. In between were semipublic efforts of the Fifth Avenue Association (FAA), the pressure applied by banks and insurance companies, the aesthetic arguments of the press, and the implementation of private legal measures to restrict land use. The approaches to managing the market for space encompassed the variety of Progressive urban reform efforts, from individual moral control to the large-scale planning of the "technocrats."[32] Beginning well before the turn of the century and ranging from the most personal, informal actions to the most public and radical, inhabitants and businesspeople took concerted steps to intervene in the market and control Fifth Avenue's development, employing a patchwork of methods to shape its physical transformation.

The magnates of Fifth Avenue soon found that the forces that were transforming the grand avenue of mansions and expensive stores were too powerful for any of them individually to hold back. Retail stores as well as hotels and offices crowded up the Avenue, taking over older homes and replacing them quickly with denser developments (Figure 57). In the frenzied developing of early twentieth-century Manhattan, restrictive covenants were no longer powerful enough for the Vanderbilts, Astors, and Belmonts to achieve the spatial security they once enjoyed.

If individual residents along Fifth Avenue could do little to stop development, a union of politically influential commercial investors and retailers could further challenge the "compelling force." The retailers of Fifth Avenue led the movement for shaping development along Fifth Avenue in a new direction – away from flight, restrictive covenants, and land acquisition and toward the new field of city planning. Like the older residents, their goal was preservation of the unique characteristics of the Avenue. But they now defined those characteristics differently: they saw Fifth Avenue not as "Millionaire's Mile" but as America's Bond Street, the country's finest shopping boulevard.

It was out of this extensive public discussion and image-making that the FAA articulated its message for "preserving" the Avenue and developed new methods for regulating space. Founded in April 1907 by a small group of property owners, residents, and retailers with the motto "to conserve at all times the highest and best interests of the Fifth Avenue section," the voluntary organization grew from a founding membership of 37 to 500 just three years later (in 1910) and reached membership as high as 1,000 in the 1950s.[33]

The central idea behind the FAA's advocacy was to retain an exclusive retail and residential area, where immigrants would be scarce and beggars absent, where the more flamboyant popular culture growing on Broadway would be held in check, and where a genteel, controlled commercial culture would hold sway. Assimilation might have been the goal of some Progressives, and New York might have been known within the general culture increasingly as the place where cultures and peoples melded, but on Fifth Avenue the goal was always segregation and exclusion.

What made Fifth Avenue special – and eminently necessary to preserve – was its different idea of commerce, one that provided a serene environment for a limited and exclusive clientele as opposed to the bustling, diverse, and high-volume commerce of neighboring Broadway, where gaudy signs and lures of all types drew a heterogeneous mix of classes. The Fifth Avenue Commission in 1912 stated the case clearly: "If, however, our indifference to its appearance continues, we may expect that Fifth Avenue will cease to retain even its present commercial prominence but will become another and cheaper Broadway, with a garish electric sign display and other undesirable accompaniments."[34] So, even as Fifth Avenue became the resting place of the most revered and expensive of the commercial culture's production, it somehow stood above it, thus adding to its allure. It was this delicate image that was threatened at the turn of the century, thus spurring the FAA reforms.

The FAA would not be the agent of some foreign, radical new future, but instead a logical instrument to strengthen and enhance the existing structure of the Avenue by freezing it in a particular moment of economic organization. Ironically, then, Fifth Avenue would lead the economic prosperity of the city by moving in the opposite direction, away from unregulated loft and office development. Fifth Avenue's property values would be maintained now by regulating what was built and sold there.

The FAA used various means of public and private real estate intervention to mold and resist the changes along the Avenue, including legislative advocacy, policing the streets, awarding architectural honors, and such aesthetic moves as planting trees, placing traffic lights, and fighting the proliferation of garish signage. The association's most far-reaching goal was to stop the construction of loft manufacturing

57. Fifth Avenue and Forty-second Street, New York. Taken between 1900 and 1910, this photograph records the increasing height of Fifth Avenue's retail district and the nature of its clientele. Courtesy of Library of Congress, Prints and Photographs Div., Detroit Publishing Co. Collection [LC-D4-36485 DLC].

buildings on the Avenue. These lofts had already been built in the lower part of the Avenue – between Fourteenth and Twenty-third streets and even around Washington Square. Indeed, the Triangle Shirtwaist Factory, whose devastating fire of 1911 inspired labor reforms and transformed New York City politics, was a classic loft building, located almost on the site where Henry James grew up. The FAA used the fire as a springboard for its campaign to regulate and ultimately eliminate loft buildings from the Avenue, citing their marginal architectural and human qualities and referring to "the loft building and factory employee menace."[35] Like its campaign against beggars, the FAA was concerned about maintaining the "quality" of people inhabiting and using the Avenue.[36]

If the fear of immigrant "hordes" ruining the high-class atmosphere of Fifth Avenue was foremost in the minds of the FAA, this concern pointed to other, even larger dangers. The FAA saw in the orgy of loft construction a debilitating set of changes taking place in the social and physical appearance of the Avenue. Loft construction was particularly volatile: the buildings were often cheap, rapidly built, and financially insecure because of the unstable nature of the garment industry. When they were vacated, often within a few years of construction, the loft buildings could not be easily converted to other uses. Narrow and tall with long, dark interiors, usually built upon one or two 25-foot lots previously occupied by brownstones, the buildings were appropriate only for factories or cheap business ventures. The presence of single, ten-story towers on narrow lots was an ironic product of Fifth Avenue's tradition as the brownstone and marble mansion home to New York's elite families. With city taxes calculated to the full market value of the site, a brownstone lot was "worth" a phenomenal sum, if, as tax policy assumed, the owner could develop his or her land to its fullest extent.[37] But because Fifth Avenue's property was largely held in small parcels by individual landowners – many of whom were willing to "hold out" for years – developers could rarely assemble large lots. Thus, as individual families sold off their brownstones, developers quickly put up individual loft buildings to accommodate burgeoning garment-related industries.

The FAA, through its promotion of zoning, as discussed in the following section, succeeded where so many powerful individuals had failed. It managed to prevent the influx of manufacturing firms and stabilized the Avenue from Forty-second to Ninetieth streets as the most valuable residential and commercial property in the city. To this day, Fifth Avenue in this stretch is the most expensive retail land in the world.[38] As one of the first modern business improvement districts, it anticipated what has become a national trend: the private development and regulation of neighborhoods and even whole towns. Today, business improvement districts (BIDs) and private towns with elaborate aesthetic and land use controls are increasingly the dominant forces in shaping manufactured and even natural landscapes.[39]

The FAA, it should be clear, was not a bastion of antiquarianism, urging – like some preservation advocates – that New York simply hold onto the past. The problem, as it would be for slum clearance advocates and historic preservationists, lay primarily in managing creative destruction (Figure 58). The FAA ardently sought to prevent certain types of destruction while encouraging others. Thus, height rules were meant to preserve upper Fifth Avenue (above Fifty-ninth Street, along Central Park) as an elite row of mansions and low apartment buildings. At the same time, the FAA long advocated street widening, which required extensive destruction of stoops and front yards and walls. The association was happy for taller buildings (except lofts) to replace rows of dull brownstones. Thus, even as the FAA "resisted" the course of creative destruction, it learned how to manipulate it to achieve its own ends.

The work of the FAA was oriented as much toward luring and keeping the elite shopping clientele as it was in raising property values. The association began its work with rather limited campaigns to enhance the appearance and experience of Fifth Avenue. At its first meeting in April 1907, the FAA declared its goals to be the "betterment of trade and traffic conditions on the Avenue by taking up for instance questions relating to heavy trucking, garbage disposal, public nuisances, the proposed widening of the Avenue etc. etc."[40] Much of the FAA's energy, even after the passage of the Zoning Act, was occupied with an extensive array of landscape-policing functions that quietly but powerfully shaped the form and activities of Fifth Avenue. Just as the Charity Organization Society's Tenement House Committee served for years as a semiofficial city housing agency, the Fifth Avenue Association was, for the "Fifth Avenue section" (comprising Fifth to Madison avenues and all cross streets), the police and traffic departments, the public art commission, and the city-planning commission. Through its office, which served as a members' clearinghouse for information and assistance, and aided by a variety of ordinances passed on its behalf, the FAA restricted the types of traffic on the Avenue, forcibly removed beggars and peddlers, eliminated

58. In this advertisement, Father Time oversees the tasteful transformation of Fifth Avenue from a residential street of brownstones and churches to a commercial street of tall buildings served by public transportation. Advertisement for the Fifth Avenue Coach Co., in Henry Collins Brown, *Fifth Avenue, Old and New, 1824–1924* (New York: Fifth Avenue Association, 1924).

certain types of signs, and influenced the architectural design of new buildings.[41]

Zoning the Avenue, Zoning New York

Only a few years after it was formed, the FAA recognized that it had to be more than a beautification agency if it wished to accomplish its goals of protecting the Avenue as an elite retail and residential area. The association's concerted lobbying bore fruit in 1916, when the first comprehensive zoning law was passed, legislation that profoundly changed how cities would be built; governmental regulation of development now became a dominant force in shaping urban form.[42] The FAA was the key force in bringing the zoning movement to fruition in 1916, and it is remarkable that a private organization, advocating primarily the interests of a very particular section of the city, was behind the national movement for citywide zoning. In the name of "preserving" a place with a particular meaning, a perceived social significance, and a distinct, measurable economic value, the FAA proposed to transform city policy concerning urban space.

Historical accounts traditionally trace the origins of the zoning movement to protests concerning the Equitable Building in Lower Manhattan. Predating the Equitable controversy, a wide range of citizen groups and politicians had been urging the city to intervene more significantly to address the problems of light and air, traffic, and aesthetic monstrosities. Subsequently, a number of factors, discussions, and proposals provided the political and intellectual setting for zoning. The writings of key figures in city planning (George Ford, Edward Bassett, Nelson Lewis, and Benjamin Marsh) placed comprehensive city planning at the forefront of policy discussions, while in practice, limited measures related to zoning and height limitations were observed in other cities. And closer to home, a strong borough president, George McAneny (1910–13), championed city planning theory and practice; and a number of massive public works projects (bridges, subways, street widenings) suggested to politicians and the public the benefits of comprehensive planning.[43]

Though adherents to the nascent city planning movement had for years before the zoning ordinance been agitating for land use controls – including height limitations and use segregation – it was only when the FAA pushed for the creation of a quasi-governmental Fifth Avenue Commission that these ideas were brought to the forefront of public debate. The FAA viewed the rapid rebuilding along the Avenue as both a grave threat and a rare opportunity to firmly establish Fifth Avenue; failure to act would mean disaster. "There is probably no street or avenue in this great city to which the question of height limitation is of as much importance as Fifth Avenue," the FAA declared,

> no district whose interests and character are as much affected by it as the Fifth Avenue district. It is now, and for some years to come will be, in a constant, seething turmoil of tearing down and rebuilding, and it is safe to say that a few years from now, with perhaps a few exceptional houses, the busy section of Fifth Avenue will be composed entirely of new buildings.[44]

In their aggressive campaign for height limitations and ultimately citywide zoning, various members of the FAA appealed to the Commission on Building Heights with dramatic statements of the future of Fifth Avenue. Robert Grier Cooke, the founder and long-time president of the FAA, stated simply that without height limitations, "It is not too much to say that the very existence of the Avenue, as New York residents have known it for many years, is threatened."[45] Frank Veiller, a member of the FAA, declared that without legislation halting the increase of loft buildings on the Avenue, "Fifth Avenue, as now known, will be lost to this city forever."[46]

The FAA had begun its efforts to involve city government with its campaigns for street widening and signage regulations. But it took its advocacy for the Avenue further when it successfully lobbied McAneny to establish a Fifth Avenue Commission expressly to deal with the problems faced by Fifth Avenue residents and retailers. The commission, meeting in 1912 and 1913, produced an ordinance proposal on limiting heights, but the Board of Aldermen ultimately rejected it. However, the ideas put forth by the Fifth Avenue Commission were elaborated on a citywide basis in the new Heights of Buildings Commission, formed in 1913. This commission was accompanied by the Commission on Building Districts and Restrictions, and in 1914 the standing Committee on the City Plan.

It was the Commission on Building Districts and Restrictions that ultimately, in 1916, produced its report advocating comprehensive use and building height and mass limitations for New York City.

The focus of the work of these commissions, and of the 1916 zoning ordinance, was strongly shaped by the vision of the FAA for the Avenue and its surrounding elite district. In specific instances, the Avenue was given special treatment by the commissioners. For example, virtually all of Manhattan below Central Park was divided into zones in which buildings could rise to one and one-half or two times the width of a street – except for Fifth Avenue between Thirty-fourth and Fifty-ninth streets, where the FAA managed to procure the lowest of all ratios: buildings could rise no more than one and one-quarter times the width of the street.[47] Many in the FAA leadership had sought even lower height limitations but were satisfied to have at least secured this victory. But in far more fundamental ways, the whole focus of the commissions – on segregating residential and industrial areas, limiting heights, and creating a stable real estate market – was shaped by the FAA's own interests.

The 1916 zoning ordinance was not, in the end, a radical measure; it was only revolutionary through its influence on other cities and as the precedent for future city planning efforts. The ordinance accelerated the demolition of Fifth Avenue's nineteenth-century past by creating an ordered framework in which developers and architects could develop and redevelop the Avenue. Had a more laissez-faire system of real estate prevailed, Fifth Avenue might have become a permanent center for the garment manufacturers and other small businesses, up to and even beyond Central Park.

Conclusion: The "Provisional City"

In 1935, a long-awaited visitor came from Europe to inspect Manhattan. Like Henry James, who had journeyed back to his hometown 30 years previously, the Swiss architect Le Corbusier came to see how well the most modern of cities measured up. In Manhattan he found a perfect soapbox for pontificating about his vision of the modern city, a "radiant city" of skyscraping towers, submerged highways, and wide-open park space. Accompanied by reporters and architects, Le Corbusier toured New York, walking the narrow streets of Lower Manhattan and riding to the top of the Empire State Building.[48] Summarizing the essence of the island, he echoed James, declaring ephemerality to be the city's most defining feature. "New York," wrote Le Corbusier, "is nothing more than a provisional city. A city which will be replaced by another city."[49]

Though they used the same words, there was little similarity between these two men. For Henry James the "restless renewals" of Manhattan were a nightmare. The city's mad, money-hungry speculation had brought down his boyhood home and replaced it with a loft factory, and his genteel Fifth Avenue was filled with garish mansions of the nouveau riche. But what Henry James had offered as an indictment, Le Corbusier now offered as high praise. New York was "a city in the process of becoming." He celebrated the city for being "overwhelming, amazing, exciting, violently alive – a wilderness of stupendous experiment toward the new order that is to replace the current tumult."[50]

Indeed, New York was only a suggestion of what the truly modern city should be. In so many ways, according to Le Corbusier, New York had not gone far enough. The skyscrapers, though the tallest in the world, were "too small" and too appallingly disorganized. There was still far too much of the nineteenth-century fabric still standing. While Le Corbusier found the contrast between old and new, historical and modern intriguing – he called the setting of the early nineteenth-century Subtreasury Building on Wall Street, where Washington had been inaugurated, a charming, "accidental composition" – in general he believed that historic buildings had to go. "Older architecture," Le Corbusier argued on his visit and throughout his writings, "is incompetent to solve" the modern problems of city life.

Le Corbusier journeyed to the top of the Empire State Building, which is anchored at the corner of Thirty-fourth Street and Fifth Avenue, in order to get a view of the city and proclaim the future of Manhattan. Taking the aerial view, as so many planners would do in the postwar era, Le Corbusier declared his faith in future processes of change: "The old city dies and the new city rises on its ruins – not gradually, but in a burst, suddenly – as the butterfly emerges from the cocoon of the caterpillar." At the World's Fair, which opened four years after Le Corbusier's visit, New Yorkers would be offered a chance to view Le Corbusier's vision for the future. In the Perisphere, the white orb which, along with the Trylon, was the symbolic and physical heart of the fair, was General Motors' Democracity exhibit. Looking down from above – taking the aerial view – New Yorkers saw a city of sleek towers and wide highways that would replace the nineteenth-century city. Outside, in the temporary city that was the fair, they could visit model homes of the past and future. When they were finished, they would return to their cars to drive on the highways that had already started to create that vision of the future.

Something remarkable had changed in thirty years. Not only Le Corbusier but also New York's citybuilders, imaginers, developers, and preservationists had come to believe that the remaking of the city along these lines was desirable, possible, and perhaps inevitable.

NOTES

1. Henry James, *New York Revisited* (New York: Franklin Square Press), 1994, reprint of parts of *The American Scene* (New York: Harper and Brothers, 1906), 45.

2. David Ward and Olivier Zunz, "Between Rationalism and Pluralism: Creating the Modern City," in *The Landscape of Modernity: Essays on New York City, 1900–1940*, eds. David Ward and Olivier Zunz (New York, Russell Sage Foundation, 1992), 3.

3. Dramatic examples of destruction – natural and man-made – such as the Chicago fire of 1871 and the San Francisco earthquake of 1906, the radical replanning of Paris under Baron Haussmann, the urban renewal efforts of Robert Moses are highlights in the history of cities and their physical transformation; they have also proven to be fruitful moments for historians to study social change. My focus, however, is on the "ordinary" sources and effects of creative destruction. For examples of some fine works focusing on destruction in the city, see Christine Meisner Rosen, *The Limits of Power: Great Fires and the Process of City Growth in America* (Cambridge: Cambridge Univ. Press, 1986); Karen Sawislak, *Smoldering City: Chicagoans and the Great Fire, 1871–1874* (Chicago: Univ. of Chicago Press, 1995); Ross Miller, *American Apocalypse: The Great Fire and the Myth of Chicago* (Chicago: Univ. of Chicago Press, 1990); David H. Pinkney, *Napoleon III and the Rebuilding of Paris* (Princeton, NJ: Princeton Univ. Press, 1958); Carl Smith, *Urban Disorder and the Shape of Belief* (Chicago: Univ. of Chicago Press, 1994). There is an extensive literature on the San Francisco earthquake, as well as important floods such as those in Galveston, TX, and Johnstown, PA, at the turn of the century.

4. See Joseph A. Schumpeter, "The Process of Creative Destruction," Chap. 7 in *Capitalism, Socialism and Democracy* (1942; repr. New York: Harper and Row, 1976).

5. Marshall Berman, *All That Is Solid Melts into Air: The Experience of Modernity* (New York: Simon and Schuster, 1982), 99.

6. In doing so I am building on a generation of work by urban geographers, mostly notably David Harvey, who have explored "the urban process under capitalism." These scholars have "respatialized" urban studies, showing how urban space itself becomes a reflection and generator of capitalist innovation, and is a powerful engine shaping social and cultural development. I use this theoretical work to explore a particular historical moment in the history of "capitalist urbanization." For an excellent overview of Harvey's work, see David Harvey, *The Urban Experience* (Baltimore: Johns Hopkins Univ. Press, 1989). For an overview of recent Marxist studies of the city, including the work of Harvey and Manuel Castells, see Ira Katznelson, *Marxism and the City* (New York: Oxford Univ. Press, 1993).

7. James, *New York Revisited*, 40.

8. Fred Rothermell, *Fifth Avenue: Twenty-Eight X-Rays of a Street* (New York: Harcourt, Brace and Co.,

1930); "Spine of Gotham" is the title of the frontispiece poem.

9. David Schuyler, *The New Urban Landscape: The Redefinition of City Form in Nineteenth-Century America* (Baltimore: Johns Hopkins Univ. Press, 1986), 78.

10. In 1927, for example, only five new single-family homes were built in Manhattan. Robert A. M. Stern, Gregory Gilmartin, and John Massengale, *New York 1900: Metropolitan Architecture and Urbanism, 1890–1915* (New York: Rizzoli, 1983), 444.

11. Theoretically, a skyscraper could go infinitely high, as long as the tower did not cover more than 25 percent of the lot. This synopsis comes largely from Keith Revell, "Regulating the Landscape: Real Estate Values, City Planning, and the 1916 Zoning Ordinance," in *The Landscape of Modernity: Essays on New York City, 1900–1940*, eds. David Ward and Olivier Zunz (New York: Russell Sage Foundation, 1992), 19–45. The literature on the creation and effects of the 1916 Zoning Resolution is extensive. For a good overview, see S. J. Makielski, Jr., *The Politics of Zoning: The New York Experience* (New York: Columbia Univ. Press, 1966).

12. *RERBG*, Mar. 13, 1920, 340. Just as the rise of Millionaire's Mile was not a steady, linear process, neither was its demise. Even the removal of private homes along Fifth Avenue was not a steady process. For example, after World War I began and the whole real estate market slowed down, pressure on Fifth Avenue residents to convert their mansions into high-rises or office buildings declined. Latecomers to the "age of gold" quickly marched in to gain a foothold on the Avenue.

13. *RERBG*, Jan. 8, 1910, 51.

14. Elizabeth Hawes, *New York, New York: How the Apartment House Transformed the Life of the City, 1869–1930* (New York: Henry Holt and Co., 1993), 222. The lawsuits are discussed in "Upper Fifth Avenue's Future," *RERBG*, Apr. 12, 1924, and in the months thereafter. See also Stern et al., *New York 1900*, 387.

15. James, *New York Revisited*, 242. Several commentators saw this development as a "democratization" of the Avenue. See, for example, *RERBG*, Apr. 12, 1924.

16. Hawes, *New York, New York*, 195.

17. Hawes, *New York, New York*, 199, 222.

18. *The WPA Guide to New York City: The Federal Writers' Project Guide to 1930s New York* (1939; reprint, New York: New Press, 1995).

19. Phrase is from a draft chapter for the *WPA Guide*. See WPA Federal Writers' Project – NYC Unit, "Architecture of New York," ser. 32, roll 117, MN# 21116. Municipal Archives (Box 2, Folder 2, "Miscellaneous").

20. Kenneth T. Jackson, "The Capital of Capitalism: The New York Metropolitan Region," in *Metropolis 1890–1940*, ed. Anthony Sutcliffe (Chicago: Univ. of Chicago Press, 1984).

21. Emanuel Tobier, "Manhattan's Business District in the Industrial Age," in *Power, Culture, and Place*, ed. John Hull Mollenkopf (New York: Russell Sage Foundation, 1988), 85.

22. The peak immigration year was 1907, when just over one million immigrants were processed at Ellis Island (but that number was nearly matched in several other years as well). In 1910 Manhattan had an average density of 166 people per acre, but the Lower East Side averaged 727.9 people per acre – with some areas exceeding 1,000 people per acre. Edward Ewing Pratt, "Industrial Causes of Congestion of Population in New York City," *Columbia Univ. Studies in History, Economics and Public Law* 43 (1910):45.

23. Ironically, however, Manhattan's greatest growth in manufacturing capability occurred in the final decades of the nineteenth century. The first three decades of the twentieth century saw Manhattan gradually lose its manufacturing empire, as the new borough of Brooklyn eclipsed it. In the first few decades of the twentieth century, manufacturing did continue to grow, but at a much slower rate than previously, particularly in comparison to Brooklyn.

24. Lofts had first expanded in the waterfront areas and up along the center of the island beginning in the 1850s – in part because of the invention of cast iron, which allowed the construction of multistory buildings with large interior open spaces. Leybl Kahn, "The Loft Building in the Central Business District of Manhattan" (Ph.D. diss., Pratt Institute, June 1963).

25. The stores' dependence on their factories may explain why the Fifth Avenue Association (FAA) never pushed for an outright ban on factories or a retroactive removal of the industries. The FAA after 1915 was in part led by executives from B. Altman and Best and Co. See Gregory Gilmartin, *Shaping the City: New York and the Municipal Art Society* (New York: Clarkson Potter, 1995), 192.

26. Gail Fenske and Deryck Holdsworth, "Corporate Identity and the New York Office Building, 1895–1915," in *The Landscape of Modernity*, 129–59.

27. *RERBG*, Feb. 21, 1920; 247.

28. Tobier, "Manhattan's Business District," 91.

29. In *Empire City: The Making and Meaning of the New York City Landscape* (Philadelphia: Temple Univ. Press, 2002), David M. Scobey discusses the "market in space" in the post–Civil War period. See "The Rule of Real Estate," Chap. 3, 89–133.

30. "Present and Future of Union Square," *RERBG*, Oct. 8, 1904, 718.

31. F. Scott Fitzgerald, "My Lost City," in *The Crack-Up*, ed. Edmund Wilson (New York: New Directions, 1945), 25.

32. The reformers who have been included in the world of "Progressivism" varied radically in their philosophies and strategies. In the case of Fifth Avenue, reformers followed few rules, utilizing a whole range of strategies. For a discussion of how the term "Progressive" might still have relevance, see Daniel T. Rodgers, "In Search of Progressivism," *Reviews in American History* (Dec. 1982): 112–32.

33. FAA, *Report for the Year* (1916), cover. The FAA is discussed extensively in Toll, *Zoned America* (New York: Grossman, 1969). While seemingly a simple property owners' association organized to preserve the value of real estate investments, a surprising number of FAA members did not own property on Fifth Avenue. Among these "nonresident" members were art dealer Roland Knoedler, piano maker William Knabe; publishers Simon and Brentano, and William Mitchell Kendall of the McKim, Mead & White architecture firm. FAA, *Fifty Years on Fifth, 1907–1957* (New York: International Press, 1957), 36.

34. Fifth Avenue Commission, *Preliminary Report of Fifth Avenue Commission* (New York: R. L. Stillson Co., 1912), 2.

35. The FAA used the tragedy of the Triangle fire to issue the following resolution on April 4, 1911: "Whereas the members of a democratic community are... responsible for the conditions existing in the Washington Place building which made it possible for the recent disaster to occur were deplorable and whereas there are many similar buildings in New York City and particularly in the Fifth Avenue district in which it is possible for similar conditions to exist. Resolved: That we offer our co-operation in the various movements now on foot in the community leading towards better legislation for fire prevention and especially endorsing the Bureau of Fire Prevention recommended by the Fire Commissioner." Minutes of the FAA, Apr. 4, 1911. See also Minutes of the FAA, May 15, 1912. Fifth Avenue Association.

36. At first the FAA used the tactics it had used with beggars – forcibly removing them. With the encouragement of the FAA, police arrested lunching garment workers for loitering on the Avenue. When that provoked outrage from the mayor, the FAA resorted to an education campaign: placards in several languages explained to the workers the detriment to all of loitering and spitting tobacco juice. See Gilmartin, *Shaping the City*, 191.

37. Gilmartin, *Shaping the City*, 194–5: "The city's finances were inextricably tangled up with those high assessments. Eight percent of the city's budget flowed from taxes on property or buildings: the whole architecture of the municipal bond market rested on this foundation."

38. See *New York Times*, Dec. 11, 1994, City Section, 6, for a comparison of the value of the land on Fifth Avenue with elite retail corridors worldwide.

39. For a discussion of the number and powers of BIDs in New York City today, see *New York Times*, Nov. 20, 1994. An almost apocalyptic portrait of America's future, especially the "fortress" mentality of elites, can be found in Mike Davis, *City of Quartz* (New York: Vintage Books, 1990).

40. Minutes of the FAA, Apr. 30, 1907.

41. At times critics attacked the existence of these private police forces, over which the public had no control. These same accusations are made about BIDs today. In 1995, the Grand Central Partnership was found guilty of beating and forcibly removing homeless people from the area of Grand Central Station (see *New York Times*, July 7, 1995, B1).

42. Even as the FAA achieved its most fundamental victory, it continued to use more informal, semipublic means to hasten the elimination of the noxious manufacturing enterprises that had settled on the Avenue. Through the Save Your City Committee, the FAA was able to dispatch with manufacturing and eliminate visual "nuisances." See, for example, *RERBG*, Jan. 3, 1920, 8.

43. McAneny pushed for the formation in 1914 of a permanent city planning committee (instead the standing Committee on the City Plan was created, only to be abolished in 1918 under new Democratic Mayor John Hylan) and initiated a series of important public works projects, including new bridges, street widenings, and subway lines. He was also executive manager of the *New York Times* and director of the Regional Plan Association after 1930. In the FAA's 1912 pamphlet advocating height limitations, the association's counsel, Bruce Falconer, listed 13 cities in 7 European countries and 25 large U.S. cities that enforced some form of height limitations. FAA, *Statement of the Fifth Avenue Association on the Limitation of Building Heights, to the New York City Commission and the Testimony of the Association's Representatives at a Conference, June 19, 1913* (New York, 1913), 22.

44. FAA, *Statement*, 2–3.

45. FAA, *Statement*, 19.

46. FAA, *Statement*, 38.

47. Revell, "Regulating the Landscape," 23.

48. "Le Corbusier Scans Gotham's Towers," *New York Times Magazine*, Nov. 3, 1935.

49. Le Corbusier, *When the Cathedrals Were White* (New York: Reynal and Hitchcock, 1947), 45; Nathan Silver, *Lost New York* (Boston: Houghton Mifflin, 1967), 11.

50. Le Corbusier, *When the Cathedrals Were White*, 45.

9

Built Languages of Class

Skyscrapers and Labor Protest in Victorian Public Space

Sarah Watts

On June 7, 1913, 2,000 members of the nation's preeminent radical, violent labor union, the Industrial Workers of the World (IWW), Local 152, in the midst of a bitter strike against the silk mills of Paterson, New Jersey, journeyed to Manhattan. They were met at a West Side ferry by 5,000 striking silkworkers from the city's garment district, including the Socialist Party of America's shop at Smith & Kaufman, the city's largest silk manufacturer. Singing the *Internationale* and the *Marseillaise*, they marched over to Broadway and up Fifth Avenue to Madison Square where, that night, they staged their strike in Madison Square Garden before a mass audience of 15,000, one of the largest ever assembled in the city for a public event.[1] Playing themselves in "The Pageant of the Paterson Strike," a six-part dramatic reenactment of the strike's precipitating events and its current impasse, militant weavers and dyers repudiated bourgeois society and demanded the overturn of capitalism. They presented what newspapers called "the red tide of anarcho-syndicalism" as for-profit entertainment in the heart of the nation's media and entertainment capital and its largest port city.

The IWW's defiant radicalism played opposite the visions of harmonious commercial life projected by the city's two tallest skyscrapers: the Metropolitan Life Tower, completed in 1909, fronting Madison Square on the same side as the entertainment center of Madison Square Garden; and Frank Woolworth's skyscraper, completed downtown just two months before the pageant. They were the world's tallest for nearly the next

I thank Erica Gottfried, Curator of Nonprint Materials, Tamiment Institute Library, New York University, and Daniel May, Archivist at the MetLife Archives, for their respective archival hospitality.

twenty years. Inscribed dramatically on the skyline, forcing themselves into visions of the modern, they presented immense, extravagant, ornately lit totems to the successes of the world's largest insurer and retailer (Figure 59). They marked successive public relations coups in a city that had begun to prize elegant tallness as it had come to fear labor radicalism in its developing collective imagination. Skyscraper and pageant spoke different social languages inferring different meanings and uses of urban space, different versions of the American dream, and different views of the proper role of labor and capital in society.

Class polarization, the increasing maldistribution of wealth, and unrest among workers had grown after the turn of the century. Membership in the American Federation of Labor (A.F. of L.) had grown from a little over a half million to 1.5 million between 1900 and 1910. Of American cities, New York had perhaps the most fully formed and articulated working-class consciousness; it was no less than the "cradle of the American labor movement" to Samuel Gompers, who lived on the Lower East Side. Though city businessmen tolerated moderate affiliates of Gompers' A.F. of L., radical unions like the IWW were deeply linked in the public mind with the assassination of Idaho's exgovernor, for which IWW member Bill Haywood had been recently charged and acquitted, and the 1910 bombing of the *Los Angeles Times* building, for which radical unionists were convicted. John Reed, one of a group of Greenwich Village radicals who, with Bill Haywood, had organized "The Pageant of the Paterson Strike," raised public fears when he announced in 1913, "I have become an IWW, and am now in favor of dynamiting."[2] Referring to the IWW as a "Godless, anarchistic, red flag organization," New York's mainstream newspapers raised the public's fears of the political violence, social leveling, and property redistribution inherent in the union's philosophy.[3] "We have as much to fight for as they have... and we must be as determined as they," said former city comptroller William Ivins, citing the IWW "menace" in the *New York Tribune* the week of the pageant. Presently, the public "stands by helpless," he said, but "sooner or later it will be forced to line up on one side or the other."[4]

Paterson, N.J., was the nation's silk manufacturing center, where 25,000 workers, more than half of them German and Italian immigrants, had closed all 300 of the city's mills in January 1913. As the strike spread to an additional 50,000 silkworkers in New York City, New Jersey, Pennsylvania, and Connecticut, the IWW took credit and sent a who's who of the extreme left – William D. "Bill" Haywood, Elizabeth Gurley Flynn, Carlo Tresca, and Adolph Lessi – to Paterson to lead it. The IWW demanded a 40-hour work week instead of the typical 55 to 66 hours, reduction of a worker's responsibility from four looms to two, and higher piecework rates. Behind these extraordinary demands, strikers presented a solid front – "an injury to one is an injury to all" in IWW parlance – pledging not to settle with individual manufacturers. Under New Jersey's law prohibiting incitement to riot, over 2,300 were arrested and 100 sentenced to imprisonment. As the strike stretched into the summer of 1913, New York unions raised relief funds to feed the strikers, took in their children, and raised money to fund a pageant.

Founded by Bill Haywood in 1905, the IWW included locals of the Western Federation of Miners, eastern immigrants, Populists, and migratory workers, and was organized across race and gender. Widely scattered throughout the United States, the heterogeneous and usually leaderless IWW locals were based in small communities rather than in industry, where they undertook employment counseling, education, and political activity. Through these loosely

59. Madison Square Garden, 1908, view from its northeast corner, Fourth Avenue (Park Avenue South) and East Twenty-seventh Street. In the background, Madison Square Garden Tower is to the right; the Metropolitan Life Tower is to the left. Reprinted with permission of Culver Pictures.

connected locals, the IWW provided a national network for the rise of a new revolutionary culture expressed in camp songs, poems, cartoons, newspapers, and "The Pageant of the Paterson Strike." Its national umbrella union organized locals by industry, paralleling not the skilled craft organization of the A.F. of L., but the trust organizations of large businesses.[5]

"It is the historic mission of the working class to do away with capitalism. There is a class struggle in society with workers on one side and capitalists on the other," said Bill Haywood explaining the IWW's syndicalist views, on May 12, 1915, before the U.S. Senate Industrial Commission investigating the Paterson strike. "Workers have nothing but their labor power – while capitalists have control of government, all forces of the law, the police, the militia, [and] the Regular Army." Concentrated capital in the hands of men like Rockefeller created cities; at the same time, it destroyed local communities; for this reason, such "unproductive" forces should not control society. Instead, Haywood argued, let workers run factories and factory towns, the very places that brought them together *as workers*. Keep towns below 50,000 inhabitants. Abolish private in favor of communal property; abolish the state, eliminating the need for "lawyers, preachers, or stockholders." "Do you suppose," Haywood asked the commission, "under *normal* conditions there would *be* communities like New York or Chicago with great skyscrapers sticking up in the air?" "What would you do with the city of New York?" the astonished senate commissioner asked. "Tear it down," Haywood replied, "or leave it as a monument to the foolishness of the present day."[6]

The pageant, performed on a Saturday evening in June, reenacted the strike's key events: the growing anger, the walkout, the police killing of a silkworker, his martyr's funeral, a May Day parade, and mass meetings. With the actors, the audience sang the *Internationale*, the *Marseillaise*, and the *Red Flag*, in German, Italian, and English. On Saturday, the *Call*, New York's largest socialist paper, ran a series of large ads, one of which read, "Hail the new pageantry! Hail the red pageant with red blood in its veins" (Figure 60).[7] Everywhere inside the Garden, the color red signified social revolution, as volunteers sold syndicalist, socialist, and anarchist publications. Red brightened sashes, ribbons, and flowers worn by the crowd.[8] Red banners on the interior walls flaunted "the dread flag," as Elizabeth Gurley Flynn's favorite poem called it. "Tis the flag of the barricade, the flag of the blood-run street; the red flag waves and the red cock crows as the blazing palaces crash . . . and a trampled folk fight free."[9] In the funeral scene, strikers covered the coffin with red carnations, "crimson symbols of the workers' blood."[10] Red appeared nowhere more prominently than on the outdoor, 10-foot-tall, red-lighted IWW initials emblazoned on Madison Square Tower, "the first time that the significant letters had

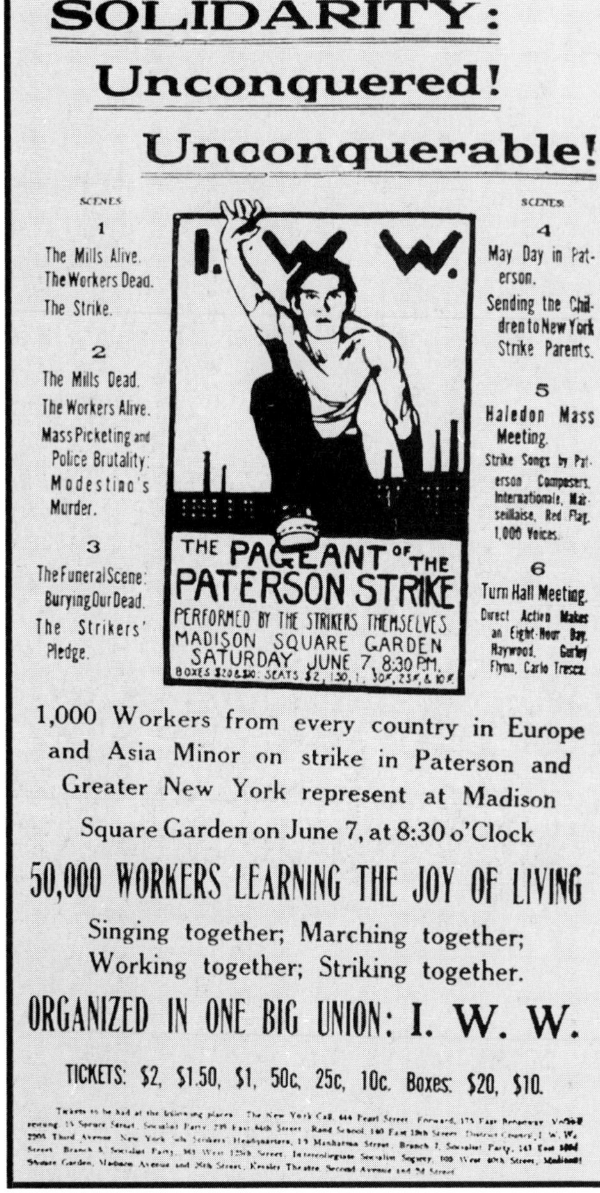

60. The official program handed out the night of the pageant was bright red. It appeared in ads on successive days before the pageant in the *New York Call*, the city's largest socialist newspaper. *New York Call* (June 4, 1913), 2. Reprinted with permission of Tamiment Institute Library, New York University.

61. Madison Square Garden. No picture of the 10-foot-tall IWW sign in red lightbulbs is known. It was roughly equivalent in height to these letters appearing on the Tower in an unrelated sign. Reprinted with permission of Culver Pictures.

ever been given so conspicuous a place," an observer noted (Figure 61).[11] After a panicked search, the police were unable to find the switch to turn off what Mabel Dodge Luhan, one of the Greenwich Village radicals, glowingly termed the "Seditious Blaze."[12] The *New York Times* duly reported the specter: "there were red IWW emblems every where.... Everything was red but a single sign, which read 'No God, no master.' There was not an American flag in the whole scheme."[13]

The pageant brought the spectacle of unified, defiant labor to the city's heart. "For a few electric moments there was a terrible unity between all those people," said Mabel Dodge. "I have never felt such a high pulsing vibration in any gathering before or since."[14] "It was not a pageant of the past; but of the present – a new thing in our drama," the *Independent* reported.[15] "Here is a pageant...that presents history fresh from the hands of its makers," a *New York Call* observer echoed.[16] With such moments, the pageant brought the historical immediacy of lives in struggle in contrast to the skyscraper's timeless aloofness and universalizing spectacle.

In the matrix of mass culture and public opinion emerging at the turn of the century, New York City's parks, squares, and streets offered dramatic public spaces for staging, framing, and relating ideas. Rising to new possibilities, labor and capital expanded the forms and venues of their own social representations in a city whose terrain was already diverse, egalitarian, fluid, and contestable, elite interests and political machines notwithstanding. People, streets, building facades, and entertainments inscribed in the city's public spaces mediated one another, thereby changing how people saw themselves and interacted with one another and with their physical surroundings. City dwellers read and decoded those languages of class according to their own class, gender, race, religion, or ethnic culture.[17]

Although apparently "public," streets and squares were not ideologically neutral, but scripted by the intent of their designers and builders. An established culture had produced New York City's street grid, its formally landscaped squares, and its commercial buildings, connecting "public" space to the world view of capital wealth. Within competing class and ethnic notions of propriety, bourgeois society sought to "master" this space through every means, from establishing manners and policing conduct to creating zoning laws. Presumably, all city dwellers used public space. Yet in the latter half of the century, worker presence was increasingly marginalized in many areas of city life through the increasing differentiation of class-based residential and shopping areas, for example. After 1900, as city fathers gradually eliminated union representation from official parades and celebrations commemorating bridges, canals, and city events, workers increasingly staged their own events in traditional working-class space or in union halls. Such attempts to contain the working-class presence reduced the visibility of labor protests, leaving the established culture with its dramatic skyscrapers to reap the benefits of the "neutrality" of public space.[18]

Madison Square was just such a public crossroads in the heart of uptown Manhattan, where Broadway intersected with Fifth Avenue. Bounded by Madison and Fifth Avenues and Twenty-third and Twenty-sixth Streets, the square was privileged by trees and fountains, sacralized as the burial place of a Civil War general, and vertically bounded by two skyscraper landmarks, the Flatiron Building and the Metropolitan Life Tower. Farther north, on the eastern edge of the square, Madison Square Garden covered the whole block bounded by Fourth and Madison avenues and by Twenty-sixth and Twenty-seventh streets. It sported a Spanish Renaissance tower, and its 300 by 200-foot amphitheater where the pageant was performed was the city's largest public arena, which hosted everything from chicken shows to political rallies. By 1913, these buildings helped convert the square from a fashionable hotel and residential area to an entertainment and commercial district. The square provided a matrix for mostly bourgeois activity – office workers crossing to jobs, genteel ladies with nurses and baby carriages, men in suits reading newspapers.[19]

The Metropolitan Life and Woolworth skyscrapers came to influence their urban audience through their display of status and immense scale. Through publicity campaigns from the press, city promoters, and the companies themselves, the public followed every detail of each skyscrapers' planning and construction, comparing their size, weight, and monumental presence with other dramatic objects of greatness: zeppelins, pyramids, ocean liners, cathedrals, and the Panama Canal.[20] Using stunning representations of Renaissance and Gothic styles, the Metropolitan Life Tower and the Woolworth Tower appropriated, respectively, traditional architectural forms to promote a business image. The Woolworth Building served in the eyes of one observer as "a giant sign-board" advertising five-and-tens "around the world."[21] Extravagant electrification was the showpiece of dramatic opening nights; as David Nye has pointed out, owners used lighting "as a weapon in the struggle to define the business center of the city."[22] Woolworth's ceremony began at 7:30 p.m. on April 24, 1913, when President Woodrow Wilson, standing in the White House, pressed a telegraph signal that instantly illuminated the new building's 80,000 bulbs, including red and white flashing lights on its top. Played as sensory appeal to a large outdoor crowd, the lighted skyscraper resembled, to one observer, "an immense ball of fire, giving the effect of a gorgeous jewel resplendent in its setting of rich gold."[23]

Each skyscraper was designed to be the tallest building on earth. The Metropolitan Life Tower at 700 feet enjoyed this distinction for only four years and was "overtopped," to use Frank Woolworth's term, by his skyline queen in 1913. Both were designed to be seen in the round from near and distant points, requiring people to update city images to include its newest skyline trophies.[24] Met Life had moved uptown, where its campanile "captured the view of the pedestrian... uncluttered by any nearby tall buildings."[25] Likewise, Woolworth chose a site opposite the Fifth Avenue public library next to City Hall Park, where his building could, he said, be seen "all at once." From the Hudson River, immigrants coming to Ellis Island could see both the Woolworth and Metropolitan Life towers, symbols perhaps for what they sought in America.

Both skyscrapers played on growing public fascination with the transformative power of the elevated gaze, as New Yorkers and tourists saw the city from viewing platforms 700 feet in the air. Woolworth made $200,000 a year from sightseers who crowded the fifty-fourth floor observation gallery.[26] The view from the top of Metropolitan Life Tower of a "new New York," said a reporter, also drew coins from the pockets of the tantalized.[27] The gush of news articles and postcards that pictured the new vistas of Manhattan helped summon a more coherent vision of the city as they elevated both companies' prestige, extended ideas about progress, and made easier the modernization and gentrification of the city.[28] The skyscrapers expressed their owners' accrual of capital, technology, and public awe. Compared to capital's ability to position dramatic events or icons in public space, labor strikes, union halls, street protests, and boycotts presented little in the manner of grand sublime spectacle. Although labor experienced their own events as grand, increasingly middle- and upper-class folk did not. This is what makes the pageant unique in the history of strikes in the United States.

Although New York's skyscrapers were seemingly above the fray, they were deeply implicated in the city's class relations. They represented capital amassed in commercial life. As such, skyscrapers scripted commercial bourgeois requirements for a cosmopolitan mercantile city – its streets functioning as arteries for business traffic, its department stores cultivating refined consumer desires, its public squares providing places to see and to be seen, and, most of all, its white-collar workers remaining polite, clean, and unorganized.

Implicit in the bourgeois perception of society was the notion of a shared, classless ideal. Although political satirists vilified greedy capitalists, they hardly ever targeted skyscrapers, leaving them to fulfill their self-appointed aesthetic roles as heralds of corporations' twentieth-century modern face, seemingly anonymous and politically inert. Met Life Tower's imitation of Venice's Renaissance campanile, intended by company directors to "echo the qualities of past centuries," and Woolworth's Gothic design sought to codify this vision. Properly stylized in formal architectural detail and seemingly cleansed of class associations, the skyscrapers ascended to a silent plane of civic generosity, stability, and progress that, by default, branded contention, diversity, and critique as its antithesis. Middle-class New Yorkers looked out with great anxiety over a chaotic city where three-quarters of its residents were immigrants or their children. They "read" social crisis in immigrant crowds, tenements, disease, dirt, and defiant workers. Using the new medical language of social pathology, Progressives confronted working-class culture with laws against drinking, gambling, prostitution, vagrancy, and even in 1913, attempts to ban the "evil" of street vendors, who represented unwanted competition for more respectable indoor shopping.[29] New York City's workers fought an uphill battle against such attempts to eliminate their activities, a fight made more difficult as the country's labor wars increased toward the end of the century. By 1901, President Theodore Roosevelt could brand the city's strikers as "undesirable citizens."[30] Thus, the IWW brought its pageant into a space already infused with class tension yet dominated by gleaming skyscrapers projecting images of order.[31]

Because it saw such orderliness as enforcing an unacceptable status quo, the IWW used the pageant to mark streets, parks, and buildings as arenas for confrontational political activity. In contrast to the Metropolitan Life Tower's unified social vision, the pageant depicted workers trying to exercise control over deeply contested issues in manufacturing, a "battle," the official program proclaimed, "between two social forces – the force of labor and the force of capital."[32] But the pageant put this battle on a new plane, bringing labor activity previously found in union halls – street picketing, harassing scabs, and distributing labor newspapers – to the performing arts in genteel Madison Square. By replaying the battle as public theater, Paterson's strikers turned the strategy of gentility upon itself and challenged evolving middle-class notions of what constituted proper behavior in public space.[33] Most importantly, the strikers successfully posed radicalism opposite commercial capitalism as evidenced by the reaction of city editors. The pageant intended to "inspire hatred, to induce violence," warned the *New York Times*, "which may lead to the tearing down of the civil state and the institution of anarchy."[34] Yet newsmen hoped that the power of Madison Square's *public* space to prescribe behavior might bring the IWW's dangerous tendencies back in line with business-approved uses of space. "Energies that have kept Paterson on the verge of anarchy the last fifteen weeks, rising at times to scenes of riot and bloodshed," the *New York Tribune* reported, "were concentrated in the orderly rehearsal of those scenes set to music and restrained by the discipline of dramatic form."[35] Here, the *Tribune* writer discerned the essence of the pageant's challenge, its co-opting of middle-class values of reserve and self-control for radical ends (Figure 62).

Languages of class posed competing visions of the American dream. For Paterson's workers, more than half of whom were recent immigrants from Germany and Italy, personal identity was

Photograph by Paul Thompson, N. Y.
CHILDREN OF PATERSON STRIKERS ON WAY TO NEW YORK CITY TO BE CARED FOR BY COMRADES

62. Truckloads of strikers' children, sent to New York City for safekeeping and feeding "by comrades" during the strike, became a plea for public sympathy. *International Socialist Review* 13 (June 1913):847. Reprinted with permission of Tamiment Institute Library, New York University.

found largely in artisanal and agricultural traditions that saw economic security best attained collectively as producers. But the events of 1913 took place in a commercial world that was changing the relation of the self to just about everything that surrounded it regarding time, leisure, work, and community. The consumer "culture of impersonality" joined people in temporary and unequal associations, as strangers who shopped, ate, or partook of amusements in an impersonal market. Such dislocations weakened collective mentalities and made individuals more malleable and subject to the commercial market's intrusion into domains of life formerly structured by community and place.[36] Against the pageant's affirmation of collective working-class purpose, skyscrapers represented the corporate society of thriving commercial enterprise. Their presence accelerated the domination of cosmopolitan culture as they replaced neighborhoods with masses of concrete and steel.[37]

Consumer culture elevated the importance of individual identity over the collective by linking purchased goods to creating and satisfying personal desire. Identity in goods, as Mark Seltzer observed, becomes "the perfect unity of persons and things." As purchased items became "prosthetic extensions of the self-possessed self," they contributed to the general "fall from things to representations, from substance to shadow, from production to consumption, from use to exchange."[38] They created what T. J. Jackson Lears called "weightless" selves, bound only by desire for ever-shifting fashions, and prey to modern "weakness" that allows for the entry of not just goods, but, by extension, modernism's giant urban icons. Thus, for city folk, especially new immigrants eager to assimilate and become acceptable, personal identity was increasingly found through owning manufactured items and being entertained in the city's lighted stores and signboards. The commerce in goods and images focused on the entertained and ornamented individual self for whom displays of stylish goods were acts whose meanings at best differed, and at worst conflicted, with their worker ethos, shifting attention from their role in production to their identities as consumers.[39]

As purveyors of mass-marketed goods and services, both Metropolitan Life and Woolworth were deeply implicated in workers' lives. Skyscrapers represented the class of people most invested in the hope that the city's complex cultural life would overwhelm workers' class loyalties and replace them with the promises of free enterprise. Woolworth's Manhattan store, opened in 1896 on Sixth Avenue near Seventeenth Street, resonated with its parent skyscraper farther downtown by placing Woolworth's five-and-tens squarely in competitive consumer culture. Spurred by a burgeoning advertising business, increased marketing sophistication, raised consumer expectation, expanded newspaper and magazine circulation, and a proliferation of foreign and domestic goods, Woolworth's and other retailers rode the crest of the consumer revolution that began in the 1890s. In such stores, shoppers were enticed with a myriad of brightly lighted, affordable, mass-produced goods, which could be handled on open tables, and they tarried long enough to, in the words of Woolworth's biographer, "surrender to the impulse to buy something, anything."[40]

Woolworth's stores in Paterson and Manhattan rested on a 684-store empire with 2,250,000 customers nationwide, part of a national network of mass-marketing chain stores opened by such companies as S. S. Kresge (1897), S. H. Kress (1896), Kroger Grocery and Baking (1882), J. C. Penney Co. (1902), Liggett Drug Co. (1907), Walgreen Drug Co. (1906), and Safeway Stores (1915). It sold five- and ten-cent items in towns and cities where, in Paterson's case, half the workers were low-wage immigrants. Despite his sale of Horatio Alger novels, Woolworth's policy of paying workers was an outgrowth of his merchandising philosophy: "we must have cheap help or we cannot sell cheap goods."[41] Even the poor could afford cheap items, he thought, and made them the target consumers of his empire. "As the curve of immigration rose, so did the curve of [Woolworth's] ambition," wrote his biographer.[42] Such an ambition paid handsomely. In 1913, sales of $66,228,072, which returned a profit of 10 percent, included 50 million pairs of hosiery, 89 million pounds of candy, 20 million toys, 42 million boxes of matches, 15 million cakes of soap, and 100 million picture postcards. He was the first to popularize cheap Christmas decorations and target children with toys and candy, which he sold in such volume – 90 million pounds annually by 1907– that his primary supplier had to build a new factory on Canal Street.[43] "Was there ever such a romance of nickels and dimes?" B. C. Forbes asked Frank Woolworth.[44]

Perhaps not, as the 1895 opening of the Brooklyn Woolworth's suggested. A "near riot" erupted, as thousands of shoppers at nine in the morning caused "such a crush" trying to enter the store that police had "more than their hands full in keeping the crowd in something like order." Even then, shoppers "threatened . . . to go through the big plate glass windows" in their desperate haste to "see what a big concern . . . could sell for five and ten cents." Few were disappointed, as the store, stocked "from floor to ceiling," sold by day's end $3,139 worth of "useful and ornamental objects of almost every conceivable kind." Averaging five- and ten-cent sales, this represents 47,090 individual items purchased on opening day in one store.[45] Through high turnover and low unit profits on just such millions of small items sold at volume, Woolworth amassed $13.5 million in cash.

New York's workers perceived how their own lives were inextricably linked to the building. A reporter recounted the following exchange one evening, allegedly between two cleaning women looking up "awestruck" at the brightly lit Gothic tower. "How is it that any man can build a buildin' like that?" one asked. "'Tis easy explained," the other replied, "your ten cents and my ten cents."[46]

It is within the interplay of the city's overlapping cultures of work, family, consumer, spectator, class, gender, and ethnicity, Thomas Bender argues, that the city's business elite "define[d] for themselves *and for others* a public culture that looked like their group values writ large."[47] By comparison, William Taylor sees workers, at least before the 1920s, relatively uninfluenced by commercial culture, which, having no "strong didactic form," was less important in a worker's life than home or job. Yet commercial culture's very provision of viable public spaces, where worker-consumers "could find genuine, if partial, representation of their experiences," may have displaced labor activism. This displacement "limited the scope for a separate, politically adversarial culture rooted in New York's new working class."[48] Bender and Taylor both see the penetration of class by commercial culture, though each arrives from a different point, Bender citing the more directly exercised power of hegemonic elite agency and Taylor citing a more nebulous and gradual displacement of one class culture by another.

One example of this displacement lies in what David Nye has called the technological sublime, an emotional "enthusiasm for technology" that inscribes great bridges, monuments, or skyscrapers with a transcendent, almost religious significance. Sublime experiences encountered *en masse* are not based on one's social antecedents or even on the relations to production; instead, they tend to *displace* historical experience with that of immediate, emotional sensation. Brought together simply by the extravaganza before them, people have cross-class and cross-cultural, yet common, experiences that dissociate them from their ordinary class and culturally diverse lives and summon uniform, ritualized responses, if not belief.[49] Electrification was an integral feature of the turn-of-the-century urban sublime, nowhere more dramatic than with skyscrapers like Woolworth's and the Met Life Tower, whose lighted, colored facades were especially reflective and luminous. No building stood apart, Nye said, from the "overwhelming impression produced by the constellation of city lights," as the towers reaped the awe inspired by their brilliance. Skyscraper subliminity may also have, as H. G. Wells observed in 1906, reinserted the idea of great class-based wealth: "New York is lavish of light, it is full of the sense of spending from an inexhaustible supply. For a time one is drawn irresistibly into the universal belief in that inexhaustible supply."[50]

If Woolworth and Metropolitan Life's resplendent, illuminated towers did indeed provide sublime experiences for ordinary citizens, did they do so for pageant-goers? This September 1913 image from the *International Socialist Review* comparing the size of the world's largest man-made objects, in which the two skyscrapers are outdistanced only by an ocean liner, seemed to indicate a sublime gaze (Figure 63). Did others, however, see monuments, as Elizabeth Gurley Flynn insisted of the Statue of Liberty, "personified by the policeman and his club"?[51] Did they claim, as Louis Fraina, a founder of the Communist Party of the U.S.A., wrote in 1913, that socialists could not "support" the "aggressive and brutal power" of skyscrapers, avant-garde art, or the urban landscape "because they try to mechanize man"?[52] Did Paterson's strikers project their red-lighted IWW sign on the Garden's tower intentionally, defying, if but for one night, the awesome image of the skyscraper's illuminated facade? If so, the pageant marked one of labor's rare sublime technological displays, since working people's influence in public space more commonly took the form of strikes and associated violence, acts the public increasingly saw not as sublime, but as deeply threatening.[53] The police were unsuccessful in turning off the IWW sign that night, but we may be certain that city elites would have resisted its permanent inclusion in the commercial community's illuminated skyline.

Modern time consciousness was another part of modern industrialism's rationalizing project. In 1913 New York City, Metropolitan Life was the only skyscraper bearing a clock. Not even the building that most signified time – the Times Tower, the home of *The New York Times* from 1908 to 1913 in Times Square at Forty-second Street and Broadway – had a clock. Four 26-foot-diameter lighted clocks marked time on each side of the Metropolitan Life Tower and four "mastodonic bells" sounded four notes on the quarter, eight on the half, twelve on the three-quarter, and sixteen on the hour. "No bells or chimes are mounted even half as high; either in Europe or America," claimed a reporter, referring to London's Big Ben, which was larger but not taller. The clocks sat 334 feet above the street, 50 feet higher than the roof of the Flatiron Building across the square. Each note, heard 30 miles away, was accompanied by a flash from the world's largest searchlight, visible 100 miles away. Its "exalted position" and "immense size" made timekeeping "easy...from a great distance," a newsman reported. The clock could be read from 25 miles away at night and thus operated within earshot and view of 5 million people. Tower architects Michel and Pierre LeBrun predicted that with its "colored lights for artistic effect the clock will be the greatest thing of its kind ever devised."[54]

What did this singular emphasis on time signify and to whom? In the political economy of modern industrial relations, time discipline became the universal standard of expectation, reinforcing the "rational" spatial organization, management techniques, and habituated work patterns that accompanied the spread of modern production. As productivity was calculated in terms of hours, modern time-economy made time into money spent or wasted. Clocks posed these demands against the more slowly paced agrarian and artisanal time consciousness of recent migrants from domestic and foreign farms.[55] Modern time-consciousness created a universalizing frame of reference, placing "our" city and civilization in the present and locating immigrant workers further back in evolutionary time, not yet modern, not yet acculturated to time discipline but in need of it.[56] In factory towns like Paterson, the clock was the most powerful symbol of that need.

In New York's metropolis, many city dwellers lacked household or pocket timepieces and depended on prominently displayed clocks. Metropolitan Life's clock underwrote the manufacturing workday *and* commercial time that extended across twenty-four hours, making time "public," there for everyone to use. Eliciting time consciousness throughout the day with sight and sound, Metropolitan's clock reinforced such habits as timely rent or insurance payments and habits of thrift. And nobody had an excuse for "clocking in" late at work. The clock also identified off-duty time for leisure activities or shopping, the sort of activities reinforced by Progressive reformers.[57] Perhaps the greatest value of positioning clock-time on a modern skyscraper, however, came from setting *in historical time* the corporation's own vision of progress with its raised expectations for performance and profitability.

In editorial policy, most Manhattan newspapers were open enemies not only of the strike and boycott, but also of unionism and collective bargaining.[58] Yet, the *New York Times* conceded that the pageant was a "spectacular production" that had "given new hope to the agitator and fresh courage to the strikers."[59] Nevertheless, the *Times* continued, the "strikers lost the sympathy of practical people when they lent themselves to the plans of the IWW,"

63. The White Star Liner *Olympic*, sister ship of the *Titanic*, compared with the Metropolitan Life Tower (4) and the Woolworth Building (5). *International Socialist Review* 14 (July 1913):155. Reprinted with permission of Tamiment Institute Library, New York University.

plans that aimed not for the "improvement of the condition of laborers, but . . . the destruction of the State and the extinction of law." The whole nation, the *Times* said, should applaud Paterson's businessmen for their "firm stand."[60]

Stand firm they did. The strike was broken ten days after the pageant when ribbon workers at New York City's Smith and Kaufman settled with their bosses for a nine-hour day and 10 percent pay increase, half their original demand. After the New York unions settled, Paterson weavers reluctantly returned to their shops without a settlement, accepting the same hours, wages, and conditions as before. Most Paterson silkworkers claimed the pageant provided emotional benefits even though it made no money for depleted strike funds. The defeat lost the IWW the national influence achieved during its victorious strike the previous year in Lawrence, Massachusetts. New Jersey's silkworkers continued to seek unionization for another quarter century.[61]

The pageant prompted middle-class New Yorkers to confront the reality of radical unionism in their midst, as the *New York Times* claimed, and forced them to choose between it and their immaculate skyscrapers. The pageant and the skyscrapers presented conflicting languages of American urban life, one of working-class, largely immigrant, social change and the other of rationally prescribed consensus in the form of monumental architecture. The respective languages of class confronted one another materially and spatially that night in 1913 as Paterson's silkworkers deftly appropriated the corporate physical landscape for radical ends and forced the city to acknowledge their presence in public culture. Labor protests continued nationwide throughout the decade of the teens, reaching a high point of strike activity in 1919 in which 4 million workers, roughly 20 percent of the nation's workforce, caused 2,600 work stoppages. Then, in the immediate post-World War I climate, antilabor sentiment swept the land. The IWW and the Socialist party retreated in the face of nativism, anti-Bolshevism, and the Red Scare of 1918–22 that included the mass arrest and deportation of radicals. The New York State legislature expelled its Socialist members, labor retreated from politics, and radical unionism declined dramatically throughout the 1920s. In labor historian David Montgomery's words, the house of labor had fallen.[62]

On the skyscrapers' side of the dialogue, it was business as usual. New York City's 1916 zoning ordinance sprang in part from the desire to legally separate the working class from the upper class in city space. Madison Square Garden moved farther uptown and continued as a successful commercial enterprise and high-style amusement venue. The Garden building on the square was razed in 1925 and replaced by 1928 with New York Life's forty-story skyscraper, marking the square's final bounding, if you will, by commerce. It was, in the languages of class, as if the New York Life skyscraper's presence, by its sheer weight, held down the red tide, at least until labor militancy reappeared in the 1930s in the form of sitdown strikes. By 1929, the *New York Times* was able to report that "deep red is easily the favorite [color] in the lighted advertising signs" lining the commercial and entertainment stretch of Broadway.[63] No longer symbolizing the presence of radical labor, red had become neutralized in the imagery of commercial capitalism, part of the ultimate conversion of the modern city into a "corporate campus" in which public spaces were seldom politically contested but were given over almost entirely to the business of America.

NOTES

1. Accounts of the strike include Anne H. Tripp, *The I.W.W. and the Paterson Silk Strike of 1913* (Urbana, IL: Univ. of Illinois Press), 145; Steve Golin, "The Paterson Pageant: Success or Failure?," *Socialist Review* 69 (May–June, 1983):45–78; and Martin Green, *New York 1913: The Armory Show and the Paterson Strike Pageant* (New York: Scribner, 1988), 195. Theodore Roosevelt's Oct. 30, 1912, address at the close of his Progressive Party presidential bid was said to have attracted 16,000 to Madison Square Garden. See William Roscoe Thayer, *Theodore Roosevelt: An Intimate Biography* (New York: Grosset & Dunlap, 1919), 381.

2. Quoted in Green, *New York 1913*, 94.

3. Bill Haywood, "On the Paterson Picket Line," *International Socialist Review* 13 (June 1913): 847–51, 854.

4. "The Paterson Strike," *New York Tribune*, June 1, 1913, 9.

5. Melvin Dubofsky, *We Shall Be All: A History of the I.W.W.* (Chicago: Univ. of Chicago Press, 1969); Salvatore Salerno, *Red November, Black November: Culture and Community in the Industrial Workers of the World* (Albany, NY: State Univ. of New York Press, 1989), 8, 157.

6. U.S. Commission on Industrial Relations, *Final Report and Testimony on Industrial Relations*, vols. 2 and 3, 64th Congress, 1st Session, Senate Doc. # 451 (Washington: GPO, 1916), 2:10584; my italics.

7. "Tonight's Red Pageant at Garden," *New York Call*, June 7, 1913, 1. In 1874, the violent riot in Tompkins Square had begun when the unemployed provoked the police with the red flag of the Paris Commune. See M. J. Heale, *American Anticommunism: Combating the Enemy Within, 1830–1970* (Baltimore: Johns Hopkins Univ. Press, 1990), 27.

8. "Strike Realism Staged in Pageant," *New York Tribune*, June 8, 1913, 1; "Paterson Strikers Now Become Actors," *New York Times*, June 8, 1913, 2; Tripp, *The IWW*, 145.

9. Elizabeth Gurley Flynn papers, scrapbook clipping of "The Red Flag" by Wex Jones, printed in the *International Socialist Review*, n.d. but ca. 1905, and written of the 1905 Russian Revolution; scrapbook clipping of "Red Flag in Broadway Causes Five Arrests," *New York Times*, Aug. 23, 1906, n.p., Tamiment Institute Library, New York University.

10. Strike Program; *Independent* 74; *New York Times*, June 8, 1913, 2.

11. Phillips Russell, "The World's Greatest Labor Play: The Paterson Strike Pageant," *International Socialist Review* 14 (July 1913):7.

12. Richard O'Connor and Dale Walker, *The Lost Revolutionary: A Biography of John Reed* (New York: Harcourt, Brace and World, 1967), 74.

13. *New York Times*, June 8, 1913, 2.

14. Quoted in Linda Nochlin, "The Paterson Strike Pageant of 1913," *Art in America* 62 (May–June 1974): 67.

15. *Independent* 74 (June 19, 1913): 1407.

16. "Tonight's Red Pageant at Garden," *New York Call*, June 7, 1913, 1.

17. See Henri Lefebvre, *The Production of Space*, trans. Donald Nicholson-Smith (Oxford: Basil Blackwell, 1991); David C. Hammack, *Power and Society: Greater New York at the Turn of the Century* (New York: Russell Sage, 1982); and esp., William R. Taylor, *In Pursuit of Gotham: Culture and Commerce in New York* (New York: Oxford Univ. Press, 1992).

18. See Susan G. Davis, *Parades and Power: Street Theatre in Nineteenth-Century Philadelphia* (Philadelphia: Temple Univ. Press, 1986).

19. William R. Taylor, "The Evolution of Public Space in New York City," in *Consuming Visions: Accumulation and Display of Goods in America, 1880–1920*, ed. Simon J. Bronner (New York: Norton, 1989), 287–309.

20. "The Tallest Tower," *New York Sun*, Jan. 5, 1907; Gerald Stanley Lee, "The Metropolitan Tower," *Everybody's Magazine*, Feb. 1, 1913. Clippings. Vertical File-Home Office-Tower, 1906–09. Box 18-02-03. MetLife Archives.

21. David Nye, *American Technological Sublime* (Cambridge, MA: MIT Press, 1994), 315; Mona Domosh, "The Symbolism of the Skyscraper: Case Studies of New York's First Tall Buildings," *Journal of Urban History* 14 (May 1988):320–45; quote from Nichols, *Skyline Queen and Merchant Prince*, 86.

22. Nye, *American Technological Sublime*, 178.

23. Sarah B. Landau and Carl W. Condit, *Rise of the New York Skyscraper, 1865–1913* (New Haven, CT: Yale Univ. Press, 1996), 390, 446.

24. Nye, *American Technological Sublime*, 96.

25. Gail Fenske and Deryck Holdsworth, "Corporate Identity and the New York Office Building, 1895–1915," in *The Landscape of Modernity: New York City, 1900–1914*, eds. David Ward and Oliver Zunz (Baltimore: Johns Hopkins Univ. Press, 1992), 132, 129–59.

26. John Winkler, *Five and Ten: The Fabulous Life of F. W. Woolworth* (Babson Park, MA: Spear and Staff, 1951), 190.

27. "The Singer Tower to Be in Second Place," undated article. Vertical File-Home Office-Tower, 1906–09. Box 18-02-03. MetLife Archives.

28. Peter Bacon Hales, *Silver Cities: The Photography of American Urbanization, 1839–1915* (Philadelphia: Temple Univ. Press, 1984).

29. Daniel Bluestone, "The Pushcart 'Evil'," in *The Landscape of Modernity*, 287–312.

30. "Undesirable Citizens Jeer at President," *New York Herald*, May 2, 1907, 1.

31. Daniel Pick, *Faces of Degeneration: A European Disorder* (Cambridge: Cambridge Univ. Press, 1989), 89.

32. *The Pageant of the Paterson Strike: Madison Square Garden, Saturday, June 7th, 8:30 p.m.*, official pageant program (New York: Success Press, 1913), 16.

33. Taylor, *In Pursuit of Gotham*, 35.

34. "Two Pageants: A Contrast," *New York Times*, June 9, 1913, cited in Tripp, *The IWW*, 147.

35. "Heavy Penalty for Paterson Editor," *New York Tribune*, June 7, 1913, 2.

36. T. J. Jackson Lears, *No Place of Grace: Antimodernism and the Transformation of American Culture 1880–1920* (New York: Pantheon, 1981), 37.

37. Nochlin, "Paterson Strike Pageant," 67.

38. Mark Seltzer, *Bodies and Machines* (New York: Routledge, 1992), 75, 184.

39. William Leach, *Land of Desire: Merchants, Power, and the Rise of a New American Culture* (New York: Vintage, 1993), 190.

40. James Brough, *The Woolworths* (New York: McGraw-Hill, 1982), 215.

41. Winkler, *Five and Ten*, 109.

42. Winkler, *Five and Ten*, 102.

43. John P. Nichols, *Skyline Queen and Merchant Prince: The Woolworth Story* (New York: Trident Press, 1973), 50–2, 58.

44. B. C. Forbes, *Men Who Are Making America* (New York: B.C. Forbes Publishing Co., 1916), 420, 424; *Woolworth's First 75 Years* (New York: F.W. Woolworth Co., 1954), 14.

45. Winkler, *Five and Ten*, 115–16.

46. Brough, *The Woolworths*, 150.

47. Thomas Bender, "Metropolitan Life and the Making of Public Culture," in *Power, Culture, and Place: Essays on New York City*, ed. John Mollenkopf (New York: Russell Sage, 1988), 262–4.

48. William R. Taylor, "The Launching of a Commercial Culture: New York City 1860–1930," in *Power, Culture and Place*, 129–30.

49. Nye, *American Technological Sublime*, xiii, xiv.

50. Quoted in Nye, *American Technological Sublime*, 195, 197.

51. Untitled newspaper clipping, Elizabeth Gurley Flynn paper clipping file, Tamiment Institute Library, New York Univ.

52. Daniel Aaron, *Writers on the Left* (New York: Harcourt, Brace & World, 1961), 15; quoted in Green, *New York 1913*, 183–4.

53. Sarah Watts, *Order Against Chaos: Business Culture and Labor Ideology in America, 1880–1915* (New York: Greenwood Press, 1991).

54. "Biggest Clock to Flash the Time," and "The Highest Chimes on Earth," Vertical File, Tower Scrapbook, 1907–20. MetLife Archives.

55. Donna Gabaccia, *From Sicily to Elizabeth Street: Housing and Social Change among Italian Immigrants, 1880–1930* (Albany, NY: State Univ. of New York Press, 1984).

56. Johannes Fabian, *Time and the Other: How Anthropology Makes Its Object* (New York: Columbia Univ. Press, 1983).

57. Gareth Stedman Jones, *Languages of Class: Studies in English Working Class History, 1832–1982* (Cambridge: Cambridge Univ. Press, 1983), 192.

58. Irwin Yellowitz, *Labor and the Progressive Movement in New York State, 1897–1916* (Ithaca, NY: Cornell Univ. Press, 1965), 257.

59. *New York Times*, June 8, 1913, 2, 3.

60. *New York Times*, July 25, 1913, 6.

61. Tripp, *The IWW*, 167, 186, 203–8; Green, *New York 1913*, 215.

62. David Montgomery, *The Fall of the House of Labor: The Workplace, the State, and American Labor Activism* (New York: Cambridge Univ. Press, 1987).

63. Leach, "Introductory Essay," 239.

10

The Skyscraper Ensemble in Its Urban Context

Rockefeller Center

Carol Herselle Krinsky

A group of buildings – a cultural center, a government complex, an ensemble of commercial buildings – almost inevitably creates a different urbanistic situation from that generated by a single building, however remarkable the one may be. The ensemble interrupts the urban promenade for a longer period in the journey of those who walk past or through it. If the ensemble is visually coordinated, it creates a zone of color, texture, form, and often style that differentiates it from its surroundings and becomes a focal point in the cityscape. Ideally, however, impenetrable walls will not segregate it from its surroundings. If agreeably designed and functionally successful, it may help to shift property development to its immediate vicinity, which is precisely what planners in Los Angeles, Atlanta, New York City, and elsewhere have hoped to accomplish when inaugurating cultural enclaves and stimulating large-scale commercial developments. Few of these ensembles are wholly public or wholly private, as public enterprises are often planned in the expectation that private development will support the newly renovated area and that tax revenue will increase in the long run, while private projects are often supported by temporary tax abatement, provision of public transportation, and other measures.

At Rockefeller Center (1929–40 and later additions, Figure 64), we will see this interaction and we will learn how long it took for one private investor to reap a profit and for the city to develop around it. The length of time was affected by the Great Depression's brake on property development and by the near absence of civilian office construction during and immediately after the Second World War. But between 1940, the end of the first stage of building at Rockefeller Center, and 1960, only two buildings were added to the complex, no buildings were added across Sixth Avenue although it was freed in 1940 from the gloomy and noisy presence of an elevated railway, and no significant buildings were erected in its immediate vicinity. This suggests that vigorous urban building requires substantial governmental participation through condemnation procedures for urban renewal, rezoning, rehabilitation of nearby public spaces, tax abatements, and other measures. By the late 1960s to 1973, when development adjacent to and then extending Rockefeller Center occurred, the zoning rules had been changed, the city had built a subway line, and even the name Sixth Avenue had been officially eliminated in favor of the Avenue of the Americas.

To understand all this, we must examine Rockefeller Center from several perspectives – geographic and economic first, because it is a commercial enterprise; it is not primarily a work of art, but John D. Rockefeller, Jr., insisted from the start that the project be handsome.[1] Beyond money and beauty, historic, urbanistic, and architectural matters form part of the story. Aspects of social interaction including labor relations and networks of personal acquaintance affected the outcome, which was shaped significantly by the original owner's character. Even aspects of art patronage in two generations – modernistically representational before and abstract after the Second World War – affected the buildings' popular and commercial success. This essay summarizes these matters, allowing the center to exemplify ways in which money, law, planning, personal character, taste, public relations, and other factors help to determine skyscraper design. Although there was nothing else built like Rockefeller Center in the 1930s, it has been the model for other coordinated urban complexes built a generation or more later, such as Peachtree Center in Atlanta, Embarcadero Center in San Francisco, and Canary Wharf in London; few developers would not hope to duplicate its best and most enduringly profitable aspects.

As for geography, money, and law, one must realize that Rockefeller Center, stretching originally from Fifth to Sixth avenues, Forty-eighth to Fifty-first streets, was built in an undesirable location. That seems hard to believe, because it is now in what is considered the heart of midtown Manhattan, between the imposing New York Public Library at Forty-second Street and the delightful Central Park at Fifty-ninth Street. Across Fifth Avenue are St. Patrick's Roman Catholic Cathedral and an elegant department store. Nevertheless, the original three blocks were poorly located in the eyes of developers and real estate experts because they were not near the major railway facilities, the Pennsylvania Railroad Station at Seventh to Eighth avenues, Thirty-first to Thirty-third streets, or Grand Central Terminal at Forty-second Street and Park (Fourth) Avenue. Clusters of hotels, clubs, shops, and office towers focused on those facilities because suburban-dwelling business executives preferred to rent office space that was convenient for commuters. As several subway lines met at each railway station, employees, too, could reach the offices easily from the outer boroughs of the city. A great deal of office space had been built during the 1920s, so that business owners had choices more easily accessible than sites on Fifth Avenue around Fiftieth Street.

Another problem was that on the Sixth Avenue side of the center, an elevated mass transit railway blighted the street by darkening it and creating noise. Saloons and pawnshops there reduced the prestige of all properties that faced the avenue. Both property owners and the city hoped to remove the "el" so that the owners could demand higher rents and the city could exact higher real estate taxes from more elegant businesses or new buildings.

Fifth Avenue, though remote from railways, did attract development, primarily of the kind that did not demand rail access at two peak periods per day. Buses and taxis brought

64. Rockefeller Center, air view looking west, ca. 1974. The tallest building is the RCA (now GE) Building. Reprinted with permission of Rockefeller Center Archive Center.

customers to expensive department stores, luxurious shops, and art galleries. Against these, tall skyscrapers would stand out prominently, attracting notice and renters who would enjoy – and pay more for – broad views of the city. Investors interested in office towers would understand that the three blocks at issue, covered mainly with low-rise row houses on which the ground leases would expire within a short period, would be ideal for comprehensive and conspicuous development.

John D. Rockefeller, Jr., son of the robber baron who created the family's fortune, owned a house three blocks north, on part of the present site of the Museum of Modern Art, in a small zone preserved for low-rise building. Believing that the three blocks to the south might be profitable especially if the elevated were replaced by a subway, and given the business boom of the 1920s, he negotiated with the landowner, Columbia University, which was eager to find a single developer to provide an integrated, prestigious complex of buildings. Columbia envisioned a group of structures more closely akin to plans for Washington, D.C.'s Federal Triangle, or New York's museum complex at 155th Street and Broadway than to customarily isolated skyscrapers. The principal goad to renters was to be a new Metropolitan Opera House toward the west (Sixth Avenue) side of the property but insulated from noise of the elevated trains by its thick, windowless walls. The opera house's private owners wanted to move north of their Thirty-third Street site, and "Metropolitan Square" would be an excellent office address for the opera and its neighbors.

Despite the stock market crash in 1929, Rockefeller optimistically signed a lease with Columbia; but by the end of 1929, he understood that the opera was unlikely to move to the site because several of its owners had been ruined financially. Moreover, hardly anyone else was in a position to move to a new office either. Rockefeller's only escape from paying high rents for land that was producing only low rents lay in forgetting about near-term profitability and building exceptionally well for the long term. He, unlike many other investors, had funds in reserve to make this strategy possible.

In his efforts to plan well, he had the advice of experienced developers Todd, Robertson & Todd, and their associated engineers, Todd & Brown; the first two Todds were brothers, the more important one being John R., whose son was the engineer, Webster Todd. They had worked on such prominent projects as the Cunard Building on lower Broadway, and – more important for our story – on several office buildings and hotels on railway air rights around Grand Central Terminal.[2] These structures formed a recognizable but monotonous group, their coordination produced merely by juxtaposition. One beside another, exteriors of tan brick trimmed with stone on the lower floors lined up on the blocks bordering the terminal, each built only high enough to maximize the return on the investment. A few elaborate exceptions, such as the New York Central Building astride Park Avenue, emphasized by contrast the dullness of the others. The Todds entrusted interior space planning in several office buildings to a firm of young architects, L. Andrew Reinhard and Henry Hofmeister, but they could not have produced adequate building models for the development that Rockefeller required.

For those, the Todds and Rockefeller turned to architects who had won acclaim for handsomer designs. The first was Harvey Wiley Corbett, a senior member of the profession who had such admirably massed high-rises to his credit as the Master Apartments and One Fifth Avenue. A man who could get along well with fellow professionals and who respected a client's budget, he was the principal in a firm that had recently elevated to partnership a younger architect, Wallace K. Harrison, whose wife's brother was then married to Rockefeller's only daughter. The other architects added to the team were the prominent designer Raymond Hood and his partner, J. Andre Fouilhoux, who took charge of the office; following his prize-winning design for the *Chicago Tribune*, executed under the direction of John Mead Howells, Hood had designed the black, gold-trimmed American Radiator Building and was at work on the Daily News and McGraw-Hill buildings, all in midtown Manhattan.

Personal connections led to a meeting in December 1929 between the Rockefeller group and officers of the National Broadcasting Company (NBC). Here was a potential tenant that, almost uniquely at the time, was expanding its business, thanks to the introduction of commercials on radio programs in 1927. Rockefeller's group proposed to solve NBC's needs for a long time to come by tailoring spaces for the radio corporation in the new development. NBC was under the umbrella of the Radio Corporation of America (RCA), which also owned RKO cinemas and other communications interests. Suddenly, the Rockefeller group could proclaim that instead of the older art of opera, the new development would feature the modern arts of radio and film. The architects conceived a plan focused upon a central office tower named for RCA and including at the west end two theaters for variety shows and film. They could be soundproofed against the noise of the "el" trains on Sixth Avenue.

The former Metropolitan Square now became Rockefeller Center, and the plan, occupying all but small parts of three blocks, became loosely symmetrical on either side of the focal tower in the middle block. The high commercial tower replaced the low opera house, making a plan that now descended outward from a central peak, abandoning a plan in which taller buildings created a frame for a smaller jewel-like focus. Flexibility had to be built into the planning because at this stage, there were tenants only for some floors in the tower and for the theaters; everything else would have to await the needs of people who expressed an interest in renting space – or who could be enticed into doing so.

The central block drew the most attention and its design was established within a few months. On Fifth Avenue, two low buildings flank a central promenade that leads pedestrians westward to a central plaza in front of the tower; later, matching low wings were attached to another tower on the north block. The focal tower extends westward as a long office building that includes soundproof broadcasting studios in hard-to-rent windowless spaces in some of the lower floors. Between the plaza and the tower runs a private street added to the city grid, starting at Forty-eighth Street and continuing northward for three blocks but imagined, at some stages, as extending to the family property on Fifty-fourth Street.[3] At the Sixth Avenue end of the property, where the Rockefeller group had added land to the original Columbia site, rises a lower office building, known informally as RCA West. One great advantage of focusing height on the center block is that the planners knew where later buildings should be made high or low, both to concentrate attention on the RCA Building and to assure rent-enhancing light, air, and views in offices and in other structures on the side blocks. Another advantage is urbanistic: The project descends toward other buildings in the area instead of forming its own fortress focused inward. Because these are business buildings, they are accessible through many entrances as well as openings to shops and restaurants at street level.

The architects, developers, Rockefeller, and his legal and real estate advisers refined the design but their proposals were always constrained by the comprehensive zoning ordinance that has determined much about New York City's architecture since its passage in 1916. This measure, carrying the force of law, determines the types of buildings permissible in various districts of the city, as well as their square footage and its arrangement. The most famous aspect of the rules safeguards some light and air in high-rise areas, simultaneously keeping land values – and tax revenues – safe from rapacious neighbors who might build so as to overwhelm smaller structures. A building in midtown could rise to a certain multiple of the street width but would then have to step higher floors back in what people called a Mesopotamian ziggurat silhouette until the building contracted to 25 percent of its lot; at that point, a tower could rise to any desired height – hence the famous Empire State and Chrysler towers. At Rockefeller Center, each block was treated as a separate zoning unit, requiring complicated adjustments of height and bulk within a single block and then within the three-block ensemble. The low-rise buildings on Fifth Avenue, the open promenade, the plaza, and the private street kept the zoning configuration low enough to permit the enormous RCA building. On either side of it, the planners avoided placing other high-rise towers. They calculated that a tall building on one part of a block required low ones in other parts, but they always held enough space in reserve to accommodate a desirable tenant later. The private street helps concentrate permissible bulk, but it also provides street frontage considered desirable by tenants, who always pay more for corner offices and who prefer internal corridors less than several hundred feet long.

The plaza reveals the economic and legal constraints upon the project. At first envisioned as a spacious approach to the Metropolitan Opera, it proved too strong a publicity feature to drop when the opera bowed out. It shrank, however, to dimensions slightly larger than those required in exchange for height and bulk on the RCA Building. This generosity is surely due to artistic discretion, but it is also due to the character of John D. Rockefeller, Jr., a religious man who strove to do the right thing if virtue did not cause financial ruin. Zoning rules prevented the plaza rim from rising above grade level if the RCA Building were to reach the desired height and bulk. There could not, then, be shops around the plaza unless they were placed below grade. But because commercial rentals are higher than office rentals, owners want to build as many shops as possible, and some had to be provided. The plaza was therefore relocated to a subterranean level so that shops could be installed around it (Figure 65). To entice pedestrians into the plaza, and thus into the shops that would then earn enough income to pay their rent, the central promenade path to it from Fifth Avenue was made to slope downward as it went westward, so that the sunken plaza would appear to be easily approachable. Low steps originally led down from the west end of the promenade, gently seducing those who wondered whether or not to descend; the steps have since been modified. Developers knew that once below street level, most people would seek an exit that did not require them to reverse course and climb up, so the architects designed doorways leading even farther westward, under about half the length of the RCA Building. Along the exit corridors are shops and services for tourists and office tenants. In this way, Rockefeller Center, following the model of internal shopping streets given by arcades within buildings and by railway stations, created a predecessor for the multi-level indoor mall of the future. No urbanistic or antiurbanistic theories crossed the planners' minds; they simply tried to cram as many shops into the project as they could for the sake of the rents to be earned.

While the planners took psychology into account when designing the sloping promenade, the low, descending steps, and the exits from the plaza, they ignored it when designing a sunken plaza. Too late, they discovered common wisdom: most people do not like to put themselves into holes.[4] In addition, the owners charged substantial rents for shops in this unusual location. With few customers during the Depression, the shops soon failed. While restaurant tables could enliven the plaza during the summer months, the empty plaza looked bleak in wintertime, a problem for the public relations staff as well as for the investors. In December 1936, they allowed an inventor to display his technology that prevented ice in skating rinks from melting in the sunshine, which in any case reaches the sunken plaza for only a limited period each day. The resulting ice rink proved so popular that it inspired owners of commercial premises in other cities to add this delightful bit of recreation – and this public attention-getter – to their developments. This change meant that the doors from the plaza had to be closed, lest people sneak onto the skating rink without paying. As a result, since 1937, the public has been largely unaware that underground shops and services are conveniently available under most buildings of Rockefeller Center. Consequently, businesses there continue to fail, although some have survived. The building owners have tried installing directive signs at street level, constructing conspicuous glass elevators down to the restaurants, remodeling the shop fronts, and using other expedients to remind people to patronize the shops. Later builders who have tried to reap profit from shops around sunken plazas – such as the one in front of the General Motors Building farther north on Fifth Avenue – have had, rumor says, to subsidize the shops; at 9 West Fifty-seventh Street, subterranean space remained empty for a long time. Successful subterranean shops are often attached to corridors

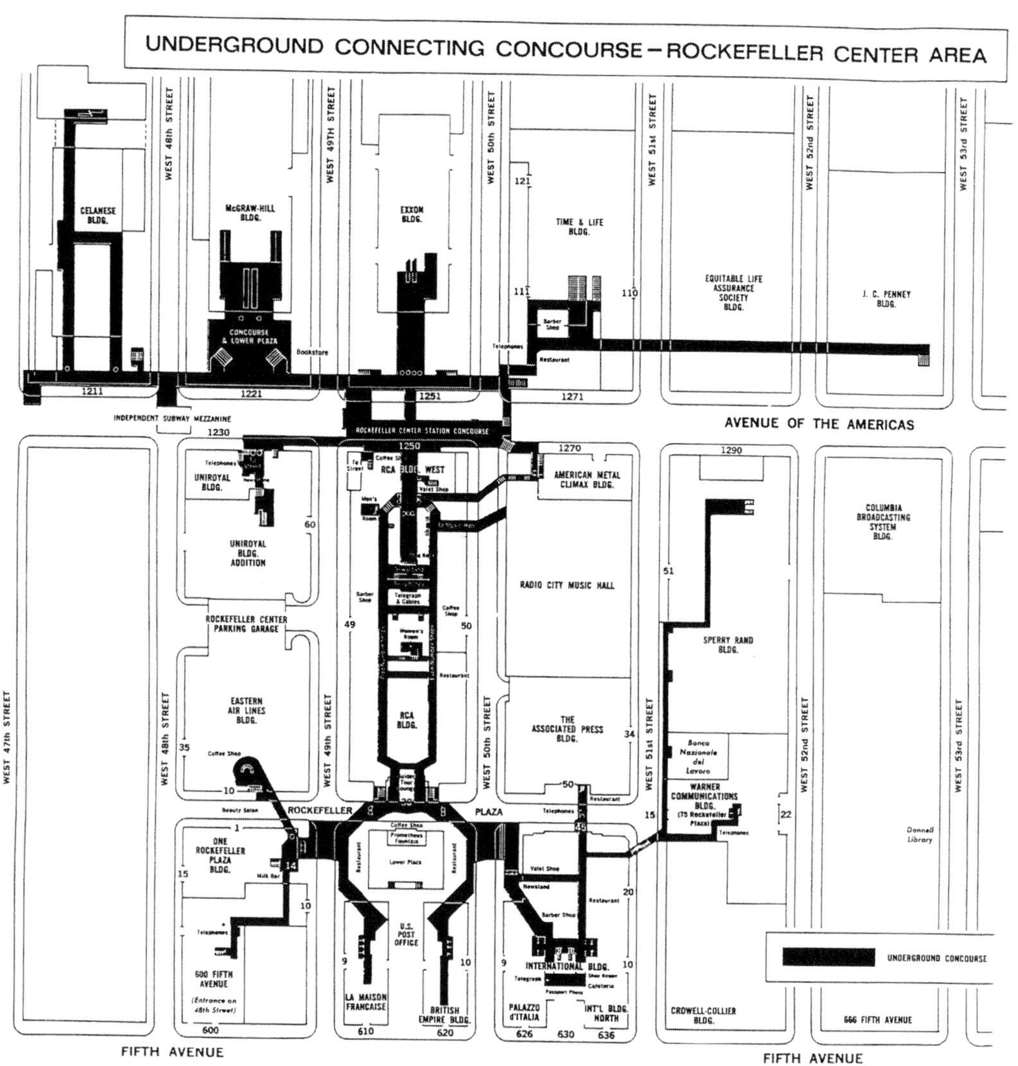

65. Rockefeller Center, plan of buildings and underground concourse since 1974. Reprinted with permission of Rockefeller Center Archive Center.

that lead to mass transportation facilities, and while Rockefeller Center can be reached from the subway that replaced the "el," pedestrians can easily ignore its shopping halls.

All year long, however, Rockefeller Center's outdoor plaza is lively, featuring the skaters in winter, attractive restaurants in summer, flags of the United Nations, and at Christmas, an immense and well-publicized Christmas tree at the focal point of the plaza as seen from Fifth Avenue. The public has always been pleased to see a private owner offer attractive and meticulously maintained public space. The axis leading from Fifth Avenue to the sunken plaza on the central block has planting beds and fountains with sculpture by Rene Chambellan along the center of the path so as to keep pedestrians near the shops. The plants types vary with the seasons; they are changed about eight times each year and thus provide a constantly changing attraction; topiary displays and Easter lilies are among the most popular, but novelty and ingenuity in design draw the public to this privately maintained public garden. At one time, plantings on the setbacks of the RCA Building offered additional pleasures; after commercially operated roof gardens on several buildings ceased operation, the lower rooftops retained more modest vegetation to enhance the desirability of adjacent offices.

On the plaza, at entrances, over former entrances now remodeled, in lobbies, and especially in the two theaters (one later replaced by an office tower), the sponsors commissioned works of painting and sculpture. A prestigious office building had to have artistic embellishment; one without it was seen as stingy, not sleek. Most of the artists customarily worked to order, executing thematic programs for religious, civic, and commercial premises. One exceptional independent artist, Paul Manship, executed a gilt statue of Prometheus bringing fire to mankind as part of an initial program, subsequently altered beyond coherence, intended to praise technological progress that might lead to the construction of skyscrapers as improved workplaces. In addition, a gilt statue in this location was meant to attract notice from Fifth Avenue, pulling pedestrians down the promenade and past the shops that lined it, then farther toward the less desirable western part of the property, where additional shops could be found. The famous destruction of Diego Rivera's unfinished mural in the RCA Building came about because the artist altered the terms of his contract and introduced the face of Lenin and red flags, which surely would have deterred capitalists from renting space upstairs.[5]

By 1940, all the lots had been filled, creating an ensemble attractive primarily from Fifth Avenue but offering pleasant features in most parts. The two theaters, especially Radio City Music Hall, drew customers from Broadway to the west. Depression prices made shot-sawn limestone facades affordable instead of cheaper brick. Stone gives the impression of dignity and of generous expenditure for the sake of high quality. Interior lobbies and corridors, featuring murals, sculpture, and admirable details of vents, light fixtures, and stairway rails support this impression. And while the low labor and materials costs during the Depression account for some of the liberality, it was motivated by the dignified image that John D. Rockefeller, Jr. hoped to project of himself as sponsor of this unprecedented commercial and artistic complex. The idea that a private developer was offering the public a plaza, plantings, seats and fountains along the central promenade, a brilliant Christmas tree, entertainment, restaurants, businesses, and both private and governmental offices in one compact, visually coordinated area was impressive then and remains so today.[6]

Additional tenants gradually rented offices and shops, especially during World War II, when civilian construction stopped. When the war ended and prosperity increased, new and growing enterprises needed space, preferably in the newest buildings then available. Having covered most of three blocks with handsome architecture and open spaces, and having made itself the locus of patriotic rallies during the war, Rockefeller Center was able to proclaim itself as a focal point in the city, using design and modernity to overcome its disadvantageous location. At least the new municipally sponsored subway (1940) provided a pleasanter way than the "el" had offered for employees to reach their workplaces. It need hardly be said that the Rockefellers had been prominent lobbyists for the new mass transit line.

With the increased demand for office space, it made sense for the Rockefeller organization to abandon plans for an extended private street lined with cultural institutions and concentrate on using land it owned for an office tower – hence, the thirty-three-story Esso tower, planned during the war for land that Rockefeller controlled directly north of the private street.[7] The building benefited in height from the purchase of unused zoning rights from adjacent properties, a device now frequently used to increase the size of buildings in Manhattan and to save smaller, often historically significant, properties next door. By emphasizing the cross-axis of the center and by blocking views northward, the Esso tower prevented anything farther north from being visually incorporated into the center.

There remained, however, land across Sixth Avenue, where the center could be extended. With the advent of air-conditioning and fluorescent lighting that made deep interior spaces habitable, property owners and architects advocated straight-sided buildings of pristine geometric form rather than the setbacks that suited a period when no worker was likely to be seated more than thirty feet from a window. The ideal of a glass and steel tower, still seen as modern in the 1950s, led Rockefeller Center, in partnership with Time, Inc., to plan a building of this form across Sixth Avenue. The only survivor of the center's original architectural team, Wallace Harrison, now with a new partner, Max Abramovitz, designed the Time–Life Building with a diagrammatic expression of the supports and utility risers on the facades. In order to attain the desired height, the center had to buy air rights from an adjacent theater, and the architects had to leave open a small plaza. They embellished it with wavelike designs in the pavement, a low fountain, and an abstract sculpture over the entrance to the Sixth Avenue subway station. By this time, the sculpture was as abstract and antipicturesque as the building form, reflecting the architect's modernist taste rather than the earlier representational taste of Rockefeller and his wife.

Geometric glass-walled office buildings with uniform structural frames and broader work floors had risen to popular acclaim in the 1950s; one thinks of Lever House and the Seagram Building. Architects and property owners lobbied successfully for revised zoning rules that would make more of them possible. The revised rules of 1961 allowed straight-sided towers of great but no longer infinite heights in exchange for street-level plazas, although the open spaces could be entirely bare. A prosperous economy in the 1960s stimulated further construction along Sixth Avenue, once Time–Life broke the invisible barrier along that street. The artistically mediocre Hilton Hotel and Sperry–Rand buildings were partly financed by and then incorporated within Rockefeller Center, the latter connected to an expanded subway-access concourse. Few people recognize that the two relate to the center at all, given their varied cladding and the stingy open spaces they left within a densely built area.

In about 1963, Esso made known its need for more space, and within several months a plan was conceived for a new office tower for that corporation just south of the Time–Life Building. In addition, two more were to be built on the blocks south of that, so that four postwar towers would form a group extending Rockefeller Center westward (Figure 66). Harrison, Abramovitz, and a younger partner, Michael Harris, conceived of the two at the end with protruding wings bracketing the two central towers occupied by Esso (now Exxon) and the McGraw–Hill publishing company; these would have deeper plazas along the eastern – Sixth Avenue – sides. Accustomed to planning formal, classicistic ensembles, as at Lincoln Center for the Performing Arts, the architects created open spaces to mitigate the height and the near monotony of the three new vertically articulated facades and to counteract the density of the original center's Sixth Avenue fronts – the only ones to create an exclusionary wall, against the "el" but inadvertently, therefore, against the city. Exxon's open space features a raised pool flanked by trees, while McGraw–Hill's sunken plaza, meant

66. Rockefeller Center, three buildings completed in 1973. Exxon Building at right, McGraw-Hill Building in center. Photograph by H. W. Janson. Collection of the author.

originally as the entrance to a subterranean commercial planetarium, accommodated an astronomically inspired sculpture and a small pool, as well as shop windows of the company's bookstore.

The plazas are present in part because of zoning rules and in part to create space to mark a second visual focus for the center. Broader-than-usual plazas may make people aware that the new buildings belong to the prestigious older complex, although the broad barrier of Sixth Avenue makes the connection difficult to perceive. Moreover, the buildings of the original center stop the eye at the east because they rise in a phalanx straight from the sidewalk, with few setbacks to give visual relief.[8] A new central plaza across the avenue was out of the question because the owners needed rental income and no longer needed a distinctive plaza to enhance their already internationally famous reputation. A respectable but not exceptional amount of open space, enhanced by plants, sculpture, and changes in grade, sufficed around 1970. Rockefeller Center's public relations department pays musicians and entertainers to perform on some of the plazas in summertime. Additional plazas at the rear of the Exxon and McGraw–Hill buildings, provided to satisfy other zoning rules, serve as lessons in the design of public spaces. Provided with trees and benches so as to highlight the customary public-spiritedness of the Rockefeller enterprise, the plazas nevertheless differed markedly in their effects. At the Exxon plaza, seats curving around widely spaced circular planters discouraged socialization. A waterfall placed perpendicular to the street merely added noise and did not cover it. At the other plaza, movable seats and tables and a tunnel through a waterfall combined the elements more delightfully

67. Rockefeller Center, mini-park west of McGraw-Hill Building. Photograph by H. W. Janson. Collection of the author.

and allowed for individual rearrangement (Figure 67). Faced with sneering criticisms and frequented by fewer people, the Exxon plaza was remodeled, thereafter attracting enough office workers to stave off vagrants and drug dealers.

Overall, this part of the center has never been considered the aesthetic or urbanistic equal of the original complex, much of which was designated by the city's Landmarks Preservation Commission in 1985 as deserving preservation. Some of the least significant parts have already been replaced: The handsome Center Theater on the south block failed as a business and was replaced in 1955 by the U.S. Rubber (now Uniroyal) Addition; its lobby was remodeled a generation later. The International Building lobby at Fifth Avenue between Fiftieth and Fifty-first streets gained new sculpture to replace confused advertising images. Other interior and exterior spaces have been modified, especially on the south block where the center never owned the frontage on Fifth Avenue.

In 2001, Rockefeller Center expanded farther west, with an office tower designed by Kohn Pedersen Fox. Its glass façade, illuminated moving sign on its lower floors, and apparent orientation to Seventh Avenue have no visual relation to, and therefore no effect on, the new or the old clusters of the center. In 1999, Christie's auction house opened new premises on the original south block, replacing part of a parking garage; designed by Beyer, Blinder, Belle with Gensler Associates, it harmonizes with Harrison's elevations of 1935–40 and looks much like them. By contrast, inappropriate alterations were made to the Fifth Avenue facades in 1999, approved by the Landmarks Preservation Commission in 1998. This occurred at the instigation of the original center buildings' new owners and managers, especially the Tishman-Speyer Realty

Corporation. At that time, many chain merchandisers demanded tall plate glass windows providing vistas into shop interiors. The landmarked facades had smaller horizontal windows surrounded by limestone walls, creating human-scale openings on each of the four low buildings on Fifth Avenue. For pedestrians, the low windows had established the identity of the center as a distinctive urban destination, but Gabellini Associates, architects, removed a meter-high course of stone above each window. They thereby altered the proportions and made the facades less memorable without adding usefully to the display area; clothes and cosmetics do not need high windows. Moreover, the new vertical windows clash with any remaining horizontal ones, and have less elegant frames. At this time, Beyer, Blinder, Belle remodeled and enlarged the sunken plaza's openings to the underground concourse, where the former dark marble was replaced by upscale shopping mall white, eliminating the remaining period character of the subterranean halls and shops. Around the plaza, tourists can now rest on new polygonal benches, but their style clashes with that of the buildings. Other alterations are less significant, but the result is the new owners' obvious commercialization of a business complex that had maintained its prestige for sixty years because it managed to cast itself also as an artistic and civic institution. The consequences for historic preservation remain to be seen: Will small property owners be able to cite these large alterations to one of the city's leading landmarks as precedents for now-forbidden smaller modifications to less conspicuous properties?

Rarely does a commercial complex reach the level of architectural artistry that can be seen at Rockefeller Center. Even less often does a group of office buildings maintain its prestige and even touristic appeal for two generations. Much of this is due to careful planning that resulted in skyscrapers of staggered heights within exceptional amounts of well-kept open space. Urban amenities such as an additional street within the city's dense grid, subway entrances, off-street truck loading areas, and two layers of internal corridors that relieve sidewalk traffic were combined earlier only at Grand Central. Any city center benefits from a mix of tenants, and Rockefeller Center's were remarkable and unusual, from the long-gone seller of supplies for bird-owners to a shop for books in French, from stationers to restaurants, from a passport photographer to the government's passport agency.

This mix of facilities is likelier to occur in a multiple-building complex than in a single building, however distinguished. It is easy for potential customers to move among connected buildings and corridors. People linger in outdoor meeting places, among plants and fountains, pause to admire the extensive art program, and visit as tourists who buy merchandise and dine in the center's restaurants. All this keeps tenants in business and enhances the prestige of the center as a focal point in the city. A group of buildings is likelier, too, to affect its neighborhood. In this case, responsible planning that mixed aesthetic with commercial considerations raised the desirability and prestige of its originally disadvantageous site, and helped to raise the standing of Sixth Avenue. Rockefeller Center was one of the city's riskiest developments for its original owner, but his far-sighted prudence created the one most urbanistically successful for the public.

NOTES

1. Winston Weisman made clear how architecture is affected by finance and law; see his Ph.D. dissertation, "The Architectural Significance of Rockefeller Center" (Ohio State Univ., 1942), and his "Towards a New Environment: The Way of the Price Mechanism," *Architectural Review* 108 (Dec. 1950):398–404. See also "A Phenomenon of Exploitation," *Architectural Forum* 61 (Oct. 1934):292–8; "Rockefeller Center Now Threatens to Climb Out of the Red: A View of Its Changing Reputation," *Fortune* 14 (Dec. 1936):139–53. For a history of Rockefeller Center to 1975, see Carol Herselle Krinsky,

Rockefeller Center (New York: Oxford Univ. Press, 1978). The *New York Times Index* provides a convenient chronicle of the center's development. Documents pertaining to the center are in the archives of Columbia Univ. in New York City, and in those of the Rockefeller Family at Pocantico Hills, in suburban Westchester County. Secondary sources and some primary sources formed the basis for the designation report of the New York City Landmarks Preservation Commission (1978). Alterations proposed in 1998–99 and hearings before the Landmarks Preservation Commission are recorded in *Village Views* 8, 1 (1998) and 2 (1999), a publication of the Cityscape Foundation, Inc. in New York City.

2. For the Todds, see John R.'s autobiography, *Living a Life*, ed. William Vogel, (New York, 1947), and additional references cited in Krinsky, *Rockefeller Center*, 202 n.35. Webster Todd later became prominent in Republican politics, and his daughter, Christine Todd Whitman, was elected governor of New Jersey.

3. Grand Central Terminal had adjacent to it a new street, Vanderbilt Avenue, to provide convenient access and to ensure street frontage for offices on the adjacent blocks.

4. For plaza design, including popular distaste for sunken plazas, see William H. Whyte, *The Social Life of Small Urban Spaces*, (Washington, DC: Conservation Foundation, 1980) or the 60-min. videorecording with the same title (Los Angeles, Project for Public Spaces, 1988).

5. Art lovers and people with left-of-center political opinions have always lamented the destruction, but many others, and especially businessmen, considered Lenin and revolution as threatening as they later saw Hitler and Nazism. How many art lovers would have protested the removal of Hitler's face and swastikas? For Rivera's views, see his *Portrait of America* (with Bertram Wolfe) (New York: Covici Friede, 1934), 21–32, 40–7.

6. U.S. government offices included the passport agency and a post office branch. Foreign governments located their tourist offices, airline and railway offices, and some consulates within Rockefeller Center. The center's rental office wanted these tenants so as to make the complex an international hub, and then to market the center as a hub to commercial tenants.

7. Esso was the name then used for the Standard Oil Co., the source of much of the Rockefeller family's wealth; it is now Exxon Corp. When Exxon moved to its present office building, its former home became the Warner Communications Building.

8. Land use here is intense because the Rockefellers, not Columbia, owned the lots along Sixth Avenue, and Rockefeller wanted to maximize rental income from the sites he owned. Nelson A. Rockefeller, the owner's son, who was active in the family's oil interests in Venezuela and also was in charge of renting at Rockefeller Center for a decade, was among those who urged the city in the 1940s to change the name of Sixth Avenue to Avenue of the Americas, although native New Yorkers usually use the original name.

9. After Hood died in 1934, Harrison became the principal designer. He was responsible for the International Building and Associated Press buildings on the north block, the U.S. Rubber (now Uniroyal) Building and its western extension on the south block, and the Eastern Air Lines Building on the south block. Having secured a reputation for sponsoring high-quality design in 1929–33, the owner could save money later by accommodating Harrison's more austere architectural taste.

PART FOUR

POPULAR CULTURE

11

The Shadow of the Skyscraper

Urban Photography and Metropolitan Irrationalism in the Stieglitz Circle

Antonello Frongia

This essay is about the counterimage of 1920s New York as the quintessential American city of modernism – its dialectical opposite, a negative shadow-city that both nourishes and contradicts the daily functioning of the visible metropolis. This particular image of New York in the 1920s – an abstracted, formalist space where aesthetic values and economic forces seem to be so perfectly integrated that they in fact efface each other – is not just another metaphor in a long chain of figures that comprise the discursive history of New York. Rather it is a specific cultural projection, the psychological substitute for a collective inability to cope with the contradictions of change generated by massive immigration and the radical loss of the sense of totality in the late nineteenth century.

The attempt to sublimate an inarticulated, mythical unity from metropolitan difference and alterity is the focus of this study. It will be clear that the shadow of the skyscraper I refer to is not the neat, measurable shadow cast by the new architecture of New York onto the city's gridlock, which the 1916 zoning ordinance could pragmatically assess and regulate as an economic externality.[1] In fact, the shadow I call into question stands for the denial of any assessment based on rationalist foundations: rather, it calls for an absence, for the erasure of another city, namely the city of the Other. As a dialectical image, it allows us to reconsider urban transformations – what was hailed as a new

This essay began as a project in the graduate seminar "City as Text" at Cornell University in fall 2000, directed by Prof. Joan Ramon Resina. A version of this work was presented as "Picturing Public Space: Photography and the Towers of Madison Square" at the Gotham History Festival at the Gotham Center, New York City, on Oct. 7, 2001. I thank Christian F. Otto for his critical reading of this text.

urban landscape, or the city as a work of art – in terms of a dynamic tension between the stability of common sense and the flow of interpretation, or between the structure and the subtext of historical events. This image of the metropolis implies memory and loss in a culture where the governing principle of action is the hopeful expectation of a brighter future; it belies a conflicted state of affairs in a setting where agreement seems to regulate social intercourse. Paradoxically, it highlights an abyss of uncertainty where pragmatic behavior seems to take its normal course.

The historical framework of this conceptual turn is the decade preceding the First World War. Suddenly, between the invention of the "Greater New York" in 1898 and the outburst of a "new New York" in the 1920s, the unsettled (and unsettling) question of immigration, social order, and Americanness that had haunted social reformers and capitalists alike in the 1890s was reversed into a linear discourse of progress and rational growth. The city of the slums was incorporated into the "metropolis of tomorrow," to quote a successful slogan coined by Hugh Ferriss in the 1920s.[2]

As Freud wrote in *Civilization and Its Discontents*, "There is certainly not a little that is ancient still buried in the soil of the city or beneath its modern buildings."[3] Yet what I address here is not the immediate *content* of that substructure but the very fact that another city exists where everything seems to be offered to the sight of the beholder. What I consider to be crucial – and indeed inherent to the idea of the modern metropolis – is the slippery ground where visuality and textuality conflate to generate this "doublure."

Photography has played a crucial role in the development of this middle ground. Although it is eminently an apparatus of vision, it has been characterized simultaneously (by its own inventors) as "light writing" and as "the art of fixing a shadow." Throughout the nineteenth century, the medium has done more than just perpetuate a given image of its own technical and aesthetic environment. In fact it has reinforced the paradoxical status of modernism as an accelerated "creative destruction": for photography shares with the city both the panoptic structure rooted in Renaissance *perspective*, distancing, and order, and its conceptual counterpart, the experiential domain of *expectation*, which implies time – the creation, fixation, and modification of memory that the modern city problematizes (in Benjamin's terms, the Diltheian distinction between *Erlebnis* and *Erfahrung*) (Figure 68).[4] The photographic trace of the city is both document and text, fact and fiction, in every instance the objective record of reality *and* one of its possible, time-ridden interpretations.

The end of the century, with its technical acceleration and the physical growth of the metropolis, is the time when this paradox explodes, first with the recognition of the interpretive power offered to the city by this double nature of photography's *Traumdeutung*, and soon thereafter with its erasure and the sublimation of its form as chart and diagram of an abstracted space.

By the 1920s this cultural process was complete: the image of the city had been reshaped from within, the eye of the beholder definitely uplifted and diverted from the street-level, nitty-gritty, day-to-day sequence of urban fragments. In 1930, Margaret Bourke-White's skyscraper photographs inaugurated the visual boldness of *Fortune*, Henry Luce's willful attempt to foster a culture of economic efficiency and optimism in the midst of the Great Depression; in 1932, Lewis Hine's documentation of the Empire State Building – another capitalist enterprise that seemed to be totally blind to the effects of the economic crisis – first appeared in book form (Figure 69). By that time, there was literally no space for the city of the shadow that photography had helped visualize

68. Alvin Langdon Coburn. *The Octopus*, 1912. Gelatin silver print. Reprinted with permission of George Eastman House.

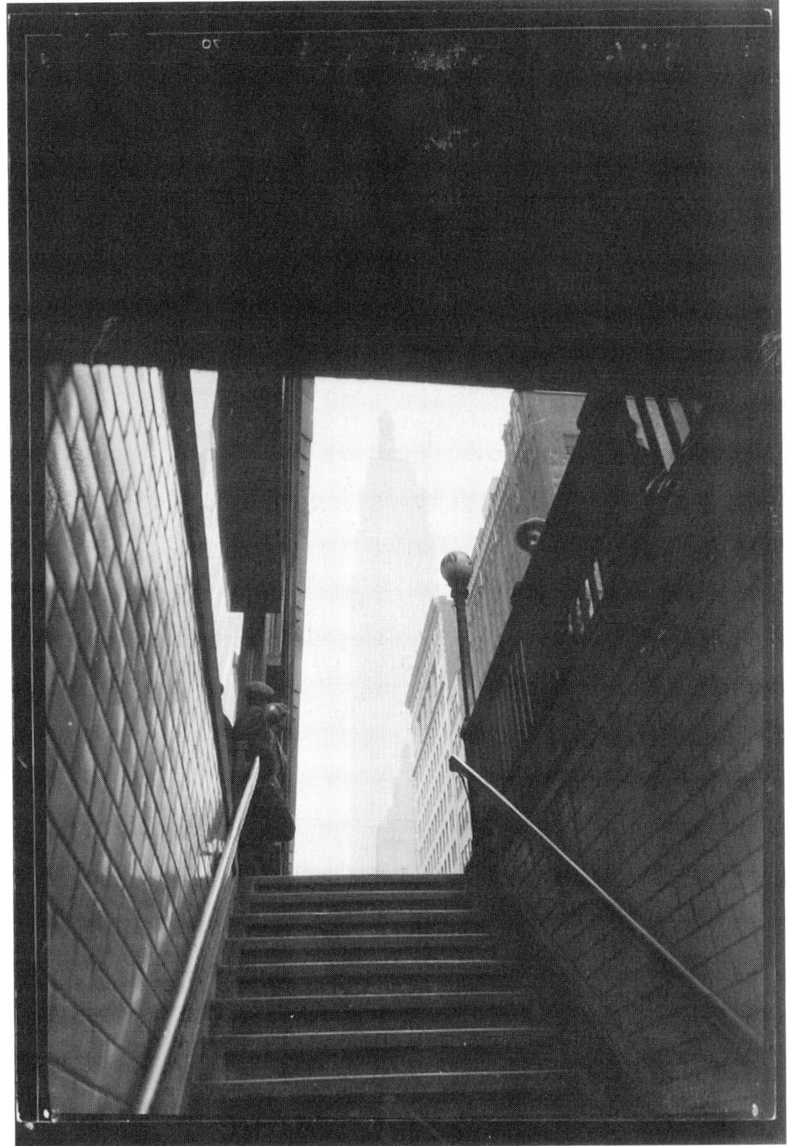

69. Lewis W. Hine. *View of Empire State Building from Subway*, 1930–31. Reprinted with permission of George Eastman House.

in the preceding decades, although there were still some traces of it left in the discourse of metropolitan modernism. Here I set out to recover these traces.

To contemporary observers at the turn of the twentieth century, the visible form of New York seemed to materialize the values of progress and self-confidence of society at large. Never before, since Walt Whitman, had the power of seeing aroused such a soothing feeling of cohesiveness. Describing the view "from the Flatiron" at Broadway and Twenty-third Street in 1905, one writer commented: "Evolution may be slow, but it is sure.... It is demonstrable that small rooms breed small thoughts. It will be demonstrable that as buildings ascend so do ideas. It is mental progress that skyscrapers engender."[5]

For once, the advancement of civilization was not a matter of intellectual refinement but the consequence of material growth. Or, to put it another way, the urban nation had finally managed to construct and recognize its own identity, and it did so by simply observing itself in the mirror of modernity. The Flatiron (Fuller) Building the writer was speaking from – designed in 1902 by the same Burnham of Chicago who had planned the majestic White City of 1893 – was the apt metaphor for such an act of self-recognition (Figure 70). Architecturally, it stood as a massive, yet somehow gracious urban object at an intersection where only ten years before it would have been inconceivable to build anything but a small, empty square.[6] An unsigned article in *Architectural Record* maintained that the Flatiron was one of the few buildings in New York that "can be seen all around, can be seen all at once, can be seen from a distance that allows them to be taken in by the eye as a whole."[7] And yet, despite the enthusiastic prose that seemed to adhere without reserve to the visual experience of the building, the anonymous reviewer could detect more than one flaw in it. He deemed inconsistent the regular, apparently rational rhythm of the facade, maintaining that the diminishing size of the rooms within the triangular plan should have commanded a similar variation in the layout of the windows. By the same token, the corner solution, where the continuous fenestration subtracted from the building's monumentality and created a space almost unusable, was dubbed a "*productio ad absurdum.*" Finally, by criticizing the identical treatment of the facade on both Broadway and Seventh Avenue, the article touched upon a crucial aspect of metropolitan visibility:

70. Flatiron Building, 1903. Keystone Stereoview. Collection of the editor.

> Either of the principal elevations, taken in conjunction with the edge upon which they converge, has not the aspect of an enclosing wall, so much as of a huge screen, a vast theatrical 'wing,' which conceivably rests upon Titanic castors and is meant to be pushed about, instead of being rooted to the spot.[8]

Here the reviewer seemed to attack precisely what Burnham – who was trained at the Beaux-Arts and had given proof in Chicago of his bias for urban décor – had intended to create: a piece of urban architecture that functioned as a decorated background for the unpredictable animation of the metropolis (Figure 71). This fact appears to be confirmed by the presentation of the building in the *American Architect and Building News*, which included renderings from Burnham's office of the Broadway façade, but none of the corner.[9] By highlighting the contradictions of the Flatiron, the architectural critic exposed the double standard of New York's cityscape: a presence that was supposed to contain all the varieties of the fragmented city, a modernistic set piece that had given up the task of educating or instructing a metropolis that was all too busy to be interested in a built narrative.

71. Fuller Building (Flatiron), ca. 1903. Irving Underhill, photographer. Courtesy of the Library of Congress, Prints and Photographs Div. [LC-USZ62-127124].

From its appearance, then, the Flatiron posed a problem that urban architecture seemed to share with other artistic expressions that were not just representing but indeed were also staging New York as a modern metropolis – namely, the relationship between fact and fiction, between the city represented by painting, poetry, literature, or photography and the city as a representation of itself. What the Flatiron pointed at was the discrepancy between the "natural" spectacle that instinctively caught the eye of the beholder and the multiplication of perspectives that laid bare the deep recesses of subjectivity and imagination. In fact, what was at stake here was not only the interpretation of the Flatiron Building as either object or scene, but also and perhaps more crucial, the status of the artist as citizen and his legitimacy as producer of both forms and meanings for the larger public. In the age of naturalism and under the influence of Herbert Spencer, most critics seemed to imply that effective forms – the spirit of the age – could be achieved by merely imposing on the creative act some kind of internal rationality. Architectural critic H. D. Desmond, for example, proposed the Singer Building of Ernest Flagg (1906–08) as the prototypical "rational skyscraper," arguing that with it "the architect clearly has endeavored to permit the structure to design itself, confining his own role as much as possible to making the structural features as good looking as lay within his power."[10] On the other hand, the doubt that the anonymous commentator of the *Architectural Record* raised only incidentally – the

72. Alvin Langdon Coburn. *The Flat Iron Building, Evening*, 1912. Platinum print. Reprinted with permission of George Eastman House.

interpretation of the Flatiron plan as "*productio ad absurdum*" – disclosed a radically different perspective. For the recognition of even a minor inconsistency in the holistic idea of the designer as master builder in fact undermined the very structure of reality as the domain of objective rationality.

The untenable status of the city as both practical object and moveable scene was already implicit in the comment quoted earlier, where the sweeping description *from* the Flatiron was suddenly interrupted by a self-reflective countermovement that displaced the observer and exposed the building in all its alterity: "indifferently, the Flatiron looms. Semi-animate as the motor is, superhuman, vibrant with a life of its own, from its hundred eyes it stares."[11] Here a beast-like, animated Flatiron unexpectedly turned its eyes toward the city and questioned the ability of the viewer to understand, largely anticipating the theme of Fritz Lang's *Metropolis*.

In a similar vein, in 1903 Montgomery Schuyler characterized the technology of the new skyscraper-city as both alluring and repulsive, the paroxism of a civilization that was constantly exceeding itself: "Like Frankenstein, we stand appalled before the monster of our own creation, literally *Monstrum horrendum, informe, ingens, cui lumen ademptum.*"[12] The skyscraper was presented here as a Polypheme, a one-eyed Cyclops, a half-blind shadow-eater (Figure 72). What even architectural journals surmised, then, was a mixed feeling ranging from the rational recognition of the development of technology to the almost fearful disdain of the animistic life of a city that was irrational and ungovernable.

This ambiguous reaction to American modernism in the first decade of the twentieth century was even more explicit beyond the limited domain of architectural criticism. Indeed, it was by way of *Camera Work*, the art journal founded and directed in New York by Alfred Stieglitz from 1903 to 1917, that modernism made its first, polemical appearance in the United States. Literary critics, art historians, artists, and photographers gathered on the pages of Stieglitz's journal to celebrate the double status of the modernist metropolis: for modernism occurred in New York both as physical space where ideas were generated and exchanged (the notorious 291 gallery on Fifth Avenue) and as representation, as works of art (as such, it was the subject of so many contributions, either visual or written, to *Camera Work*).

Yet behind the lines of this outspokenly modernist credo lurked a counterdiscourse of irrationality and discomfort that has rarely been critiqued. At best, recent scholarship has downplayed the modernism of Stieglitz and his circle by maintaining that at the basis of their interest in a new art stood economic profit rather than cultural radicalism. Ulrich Keller, for instance, has argued that the iconography absorbed and reproduced by Stieglitz himself, let alone his less known colleagues, was heavily drawn from the popular press rather than from European modernism, and was supposed to appease a less than sophisticated audience.[13] But if Keller's polemical argument serves the purpose of dismissing Stieglitz as a producer of innovative art, it does not fully explain the contradictory relationship he was entertaining with the unsettling modernism of the metropolis.

In fact, Stieglitz's first photographs were not so much a refined repetition of popular themes as a presentation of issues that the new urban culture was in the process of recognizing as problematic. Stieglitz's imagery of this period – ideally circumscribed by his work on the Lower East Side and on the Flatiron Building – responded to a personal process of adaptation to the metropolis: the psychological labor of assimilation to a place that he had deemed dry and sterile, but that finally came to be his living environment (Figure 73).[14]

Back from Europe in the 1890s, where he had spent years studying at a technical institute and apprehending the basics of photography, Stieglitz had perceived New York as a dreary environment, both culturally and visually. His first attempts to work on the Lower East Side, he suggested, were an antidote to such dissatisfaction:

> Nothing charms me so much as walking among the lower classes, studying them carefully and making mental notes. They are interesting from every point of view. I dislike the superficial and artificial, and I find less of it among the lower classes. That is the reason they are more sympathetic to me as subjects.[15]

Cautious as we should be in reading these retrospective remarks, and problematic as they are in their definition of urban *subjects*, we can at least recognize that Stieglitz's words shared much with an epoch's understanding of the metropolis as a world of appearances. His tentative reaction to the insincerity of the urban scene was to roam the streets where the "human character" could be caught unawares and from

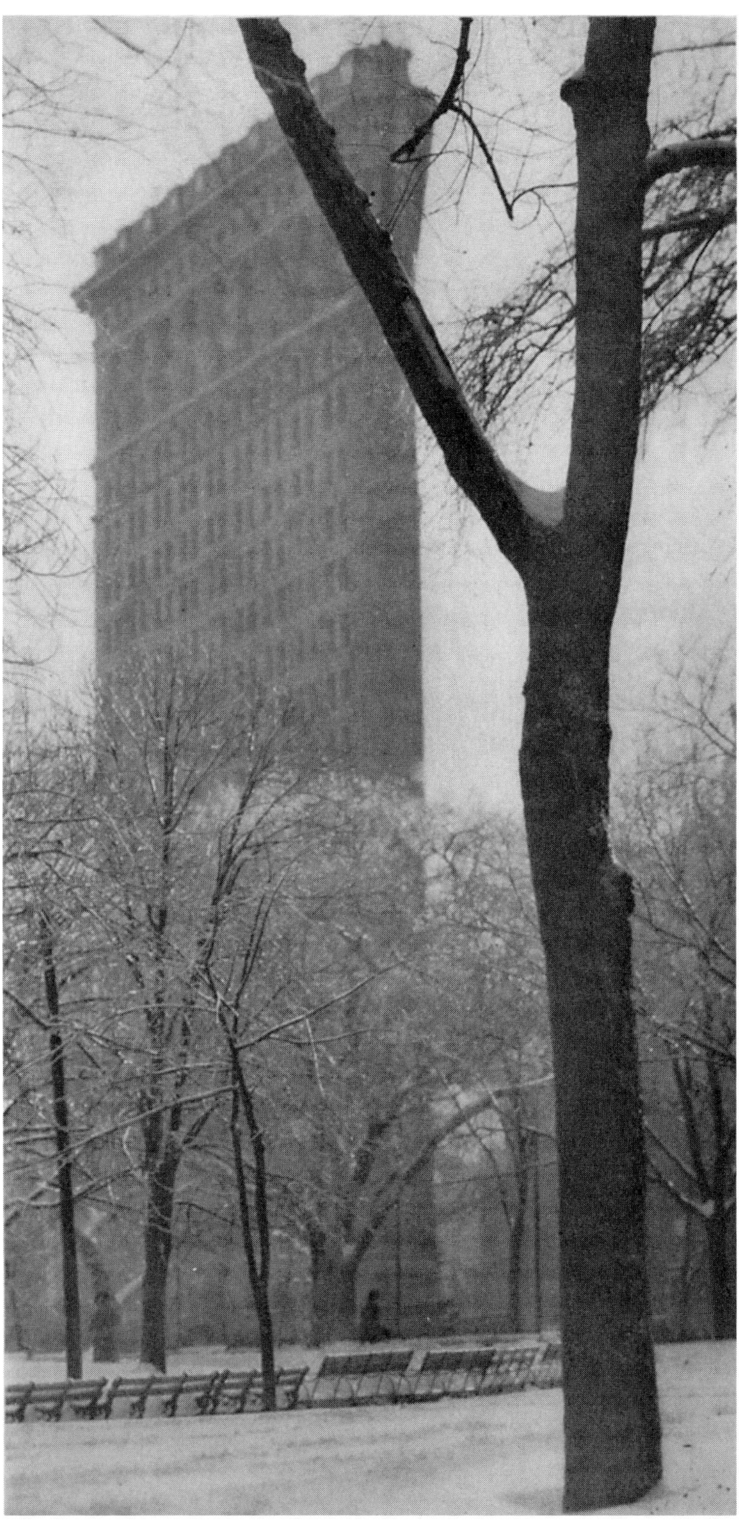

73. Alfred Stieglitz. *The Flat Iron – New York*, 1902. Photogravure. Bequest of William P. Chapman, Jr. (Class of 1895). Courtesy of the Herbert F. Johnson Museum of Art, Cornell University. ©2004 The Georgia O'Keeffe Foundation/Artists Rights Society (ARS), New York.

a distance in snapshots that recorded the momentary grace of an act of labor – both of the photographer and of his subjects.

To find a similar notion of the city as a theater of mystification that it is the task of the photographer to inhabit, we should turn to a photographer who was still active when Stieglitz made his first attempts on the Lower East Side, but had come to be known as a journalist and a reformer rather than an artist – Jacob Riis. Riis had been the author in 1890 of the successful *How the Other Half Lives: Studies among the Tenements of New York*, and was undoubtedly a major public figure by 1901, when he published his autobiography, *The Making of an American*. Riis was born Danish and in a way had experienced beforehand Stieglitz's estranged view of New York as a scene where the eye of the observer could easily be misled. One of the most quoted passages of Riis's first book sets the stage for his entire career as urban explorer and social philanthropist:

> My route from the office lay through the Fourth and the Sixth wards, the worst of the city, and for years I walked every morning between two and four o'clock the whole length of Mulberry Street, through the Bend and across the Five Points down to Fulton Ferry. There were cars on the Bowery, but I liked to walk, for so I saw the slum when off its guard. The instinct to pose is as strong there as it is on Fifth Avenue. It is a human impulse, I suppose. We all like to be thought well of by our fellows. But at 3. A.M. the veneering is off and you see the true grain of a thing.[16]

Although a generation older and with a totally different agenda, then, Riis had in common with Stieglitz a measured appreciation for the "other side" of the city as the locus, if not of sincerity, at least of a potential truth of the human condition. For both Stieglitz and Riis, distant as they now seem in the history of the medium, the task of photographic work was to make sense of the imperfect self-evidence of the city, of the subtle trick it plays upon the eyes of the observer. What is striking when we consider Stieglitz and Riis side by side is precisely the symbolism of their respective cities, a surplus of meaning that exceeds what the eye can normally see. For Riis, it was a seduction, perhaps unconscious, with an anthropomorphic city whose behavior is not fully predictable: the darkness of the slum not only as a material condition of the city's lack of light and air, but as the image of moral decay, much as Hobbes, in the *Leviathan*, had identified immorality with "the children of the shadow"[17] (Figure 74). For Stieglitz, it was a more elaborate aesthetic, one that had made him strive, as a student in Germany, for a technical solution that might allow his camera to record every fold of a black robe or the shape of a dynamo in the pitch-black darkness of the school basement. Curiously enough, Stieglitz seemed to be very proud of his first night photographs in 1897 – repeatedly published as both a technical achievement and an artistic endeavor, for "a certain degree of halation naturally belongs to these night-pictures" – just as Riis, almost ten years earlier, had marveled in front of his very first negatives, whose unintended overexposure "added a gloom to the show more realistic than any the utmost art of professional skill might have attained."[18]

In a sense, Riis and Stieglitz shared the same preoccupation with the material conditions of the photographer's work. For them, the interpretive power of the medium was not intrinsic, but depended on the ability of the operator to overcome the dumbing spectacularization of the city. Lincoln Steffens, who published a series of articles on the "face" of New York in the same year as Stieglitz's night experiments, claimed confidently that "it is time to read this writing of the walls."[19] Yet photographers and visual artists alike knew that such writing was not as easily readable as muckraking journalists were inclined to believe. For the photographer concerned with the physical face and space of the metropolis, the discourse of citizenship required a more subtle mediation between what was visible and what was desirable, a transformation that was not so much material and pragmatic as it was ideal and rhetorical. The urban topology of "darkness and daylight" or "shadows and sunshine" that had forged the minds of bourgeois readers through mystery novels and city guides during the second half of the nineteenth century had to be restructured into a less picturesque and more problematic image, a symbolic field where the traditional oppositions of the city could be faced and hopefully transcended.

74. Richard Hoe Lawrence. *Gotham Court*, ca. 1890. Reprinted with permission of the Museum of the City of New York. The Jacob A. Riis Collection (#452). Lawrence and Henry G. Piffard, two members of the Society of Amateur Photographers of New York, often accompanied Jacob Riis on his 1890s photographing ventures on the Lower East Side. A line drawing based on this photograph was the frontispiece of the 1892 edition of Jacob Riis's *How the Other Half Lives*.

That the aesthetic treatment had to respond to certain standards of taste was a principle that the major spokesman of the Pictorialist movement, Sadakichi Hartmann, expressed repeatedly in his articles for *Camera Work*. Hartmann charted the American city as the realm of unfettered creativity, but once again his battle for the autonomy of art carried within itself reminders of the nineteenth-century debate on the slums. Even transposed into the domain of art criticism – here in the form of a comment on Raffaelli's visit to New York – the same problematic relationship to the contested past came to the fore:

> Rafaelli [*sic*], the French painter, once asked me to show him the poorest quarters. I took him through Stanton, Cherry, Baxter, and Essex Streets. I could not satisfy him. But when he saw a row of dilapidated red brick houses with black fire-escapes covered all over with bedding, clothes lines, and all sorts of truck, he exclaimed: *"C'est fort curieux!"* and like a ferret ran from one side to the other to take a number of snap-shots.[20]

Slumming is used here by Hartmann as an example of the encompassing task of art, whose social relevance lies in the ability to overcome, not to reproduce, the material conditions of the city. What Riis saw conservatively as a lack of humanism in the metropolis and Raffaelli saw politically as a space for civic action was for Hartmann basically another picturesque bit of curiosity. Art for him was not supposed to entertain any relationship with the nominal value of the city's surface, let alone the city's "problems." Even with this scornful critique of Realism, however, Hartmann was forced to come to terms with the compelling subtext of the city:

True enough we have not such scenes of extreme poverty as Rafaelli found in the outskirts of Paris, at least not so open; but one only needs to leave the big thoroughfares and go to the downtown back alleys, to Jewtown, to the village (East Twenty-ninth Street), or Frog Hollow, to prove sufficiently that many a portfolio could be filled with pictures of our slums, which would teach us better than any book 'how the other half lives.'[21]

Just as Hartmann placed Raffaelli, not without irony, among "the lovers of proletarian socialism," so he derogatorily downplayed Riis's representation of the "other half" as a trivial exposé of urban decay. It is interesting to notice, in this respect, that despite Hartmann's polemical stance toward Riis's documentary approach, ten years earlier the same institution that now published his article (*Camera Notes*, the journal that Stieglitz founded and edited for the New York Society of Amateur Photographers before he moved on to create his own *Camera Work*) had hosted a presentation of Riis's first experiments with artificial light. Yet it is undeniable that Hartmann was confident in the redemptive powers of art. For him the spectacle of dawn from the "el" platform was comparable to the picturesqueness of Venetian canals; Madison Square, the place, could be described as having the same tones of a colored gouache. Hartmann went so far as to suggest that the only experience of the new metropolis was in fact the panorama one could enjoy from the top of a tall building overlooking the "sea of lights":

Have you ever dined in one of the roof-garden restaurants and watched twilight descending on the sea of roofs, and seen light after light flame out, until all the distant windows began to glimmer like sparks, and the whole city seemed to be strewn with stars? If you have not, you are not yet acquainted with New York.[22]

Despite such a manifestation of turn-of-the-century elitism, this passage is crucial because it introduces the viewer to a domain of obscurity and shadow in a way that was unheard of at that time. Here we have one of the first examples of the transmutation of the metropolitan shadow from menacing mystery to aestheticized spectacle. As with the *Architectural Record*'s assessment of the Flatiron Building, here the process is best viewed through the apparently objectifying lenses of technical explanation. Writing on the advancements of night photography nine years later, Hartmann expanded on the theme of the city's animism:

Out of the darkness, like some magical effulgence, merges a dazzling shower of light, a myriad of beaming sparks. Buildings and objects, that were of no pictorial consequence in the daylight may assume quite the first place in our favor. . . . Everywhere loom large bulky forms shrouded in mystery, suggestive, conducive to poetical imagining. Emerging from the gloom are weird shapes like outstretched limbs against a confused glare of light, and beyond an impenetrable depth of shadows.[23]

Quite literally, the modernist art critic was grappling with the same "lights and shadows of a large city, and the joys and sorrows of its inhabitants" that filled the pages of sensationalistic books forty years before.[24] Consciously or not, Hartmann's "expressive drama of conflicts" was in fact an attempt to recast by way of modernistic detachment what Riis had sympathetically characterized as the "human drama" of the metropolis, which it was the task of the journalist to unravel.[25] What remained unvaried, or perhaps was even reinforced, was the subtext of the order and surveillance still associated with artificial illumination. Although for Riis the notorious Captain Byrnes (the New York Police Commissioner who had adopted photography as a scientific device for mapping criminal behavior) was a positivist hunter with no understanding for the complex life of

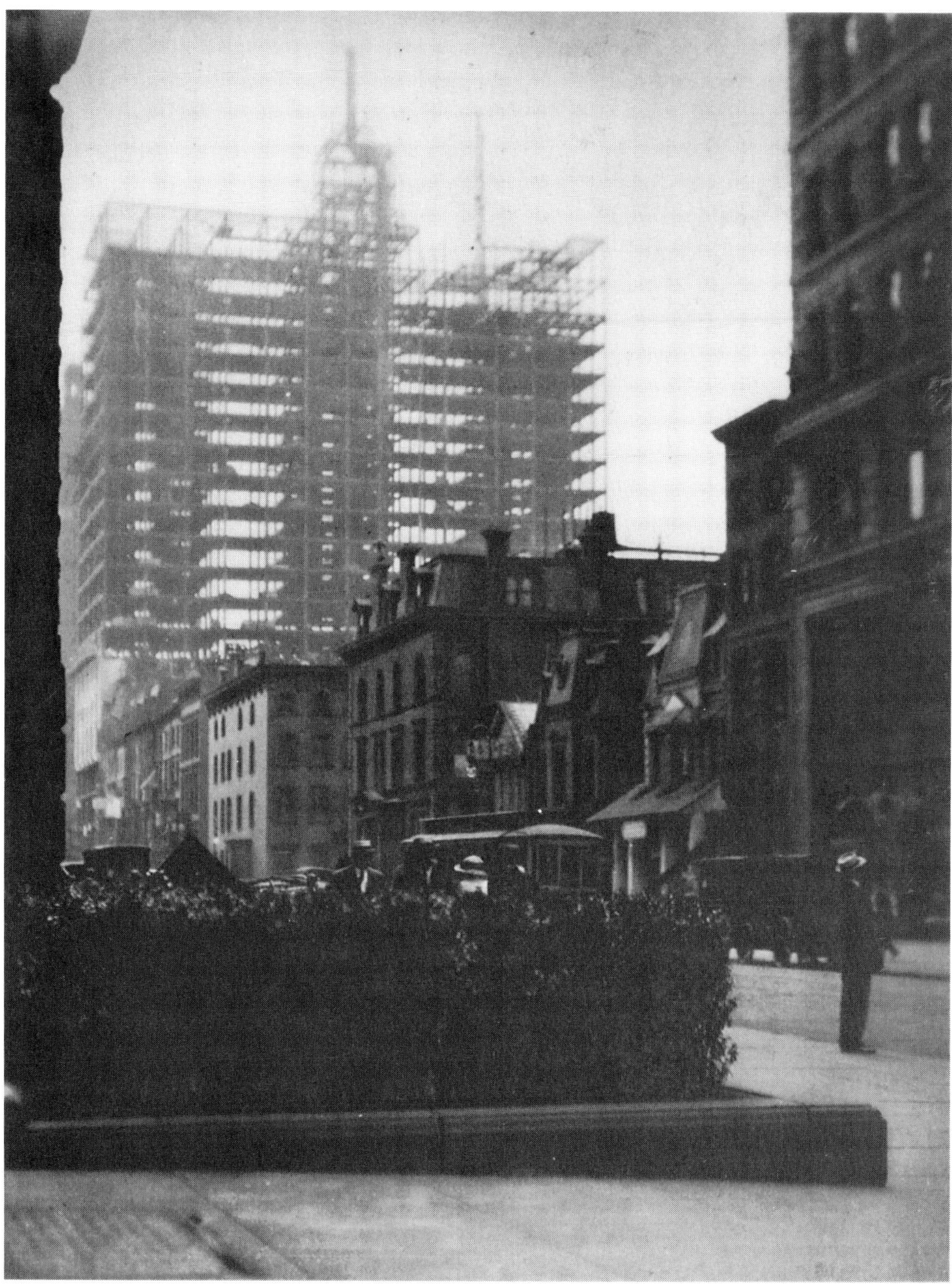

75. Alfred Stieglitz. *Old and New New York*, 1910. Photogravure. Reprinted with permission of George Eastman House. ©2004 The Georgia O'Keeffe Foundation/Artists Rights Society (ARS), New York.

the city, the policing power of light was still hailed well into the new century as a welcome contribution to the technological order of the metropolis:

Regarding street lighting as a preventative of crime, there comes to mind an old saying that 'a light is as good as a policeman.'... A criminologist of worldwide fame, and one who is considered an authority, says that he would rather have plenty of electric lights and clean streets than all the law and order societies in existence.[26]

In fact the electrification of the night brought about more than just a rational device for the maintenance of urban order. Subtler minds, like Hartmann's, realized early on that the consequences of night illumination meant more than just the extension of daytime order. By materializing the opposition between darkness and daylight that in the past had been posited in rhetorical terms, electricity redefined the urban spectacle as inherently "present" to the citizen's eye. The old living environment was now understood as an ever-visible subject in its own right, to the point of being recognized as intrinsically active, even violent. Hartmann recognized the aggressiveness of a city endowed with "beauty in virile and individual emotions," much like the first critics of cinema saw a potential cause of disease for the moviegoer in what was considered the unrelenting rhythm of light projected at fifteen frames per second. But what Hartmann confidently expected from the photographer was a method that could engage the city's aggressiveness on aesthetic grounds: "The lighted objects issue painfully out of shadow, they surprise us with their vehemence of lustre, and the eye is startled from them to noticing gradations of obscurity in the universal duskiness that surrounds them. We have to discipline our eyes for these surprising contrasts."[27]

Thus it was the task of "the modern mind" to adapt itself and educate the eye to this new phantasmagoria, socially as well as physiologically. Optical sensations were both pleasurable and discomforting, for they created "a new world of solemnity, beauty, and mystery [that] lies *before our gaze*," while they also hit "*the very depth*" of the spectator, thus questioning the cohesiveness of his or her identity.[28]

Finally, Hartmann's plea "for the picturesqueness of New York" was not just an invitation to look at the city as it was, or as it was rapidly changing. In fact, it was the call for a new vision, an aesthetic turn that would cohere into a single method the parallel paths of art, technics, and culture (Figure 75):

Wherever some large building is being constructed, the photographer should appear. It would be so easy to procure an interesting picture, and yet I have never had the pleasure to see a good picture of an excavation or an iron skeleton framework. I think there is something wonderful in iron architecture, which as if guided by magic, weaves its networks with scientific precision over the rivers or straight into the air. They create, by the very absence of unnecessary ornamentation, new laws of beauty, which have not yet been determined and are perhaps not even realized by the originators. I am weary of the everlasting complaint that we have no modern style of architecture.... The iron architecture is our style.[29]

Hartmann's view – which is crucial when we consider the development of Stieglitz's art out of the narrow streets of the Lower East Side – implies more than just a generic *Gesamtkunstwerk*: it implies a reconnection between magic and technology that can dispel the shadows of irrationalism of the nineteenth century, such as they had been evident in the Haymarket riots of 1886 in Chicago, in repeated economic crises, and in the progressive destruction of the familiar notions of urbanity. In the twentieth-century city, the "characteristic American sky is clear and pure. The genius of light prevails," and although colored shadows may occasionally animate the scene, "we are the children of this high-spirited, shadowless sky."[30]

The menace of Riis's (and Hobbes's, for that matter) "children of the shadow" was now explicitly erased from the transparent screen of the city. By 1909, the political implications of any Realist aesthetics were clear to anybody in New York. John Van Dyke's *The New York* (1909), lavishly illustrated by Joseph Pennell's drawings of picturesque urban scenes, addressed the "other half" in a voice that had come to assume the same somber tone it attempted to dispel:

> There is nothing discreditable about commercialism. Material prosperity is what the world, in all times and all places, has been struggling for. The necessities of life are the prerequisites of the luxuries. No city ever did much with art and literature until it had solved the fiscal question.... To the cry of Mr Riis, "Abolish the tenements!" there may be suggested an alternative. Why not abolish the tenants?[31]

The modernist "final solution" proposed by Van Dyke was not literally put into action, although in the same years the Fifth Avenue Association was arguing that the traffic of laborers who invaded the commercial sector at the end of each shift damaged their enterprise and had to be moved elsewhere – a debate that would finally lead to the 1916 zoning ordinance. It is irrelevant to this argument, however, that zoning did not manage to wipe out the slums from the fabric of New York: indeed they were still much a part of the debate in the 1930s, when a new notion of collectivity seemed to emerge and, significantly, the first biography of Jacob Riis was published. What is crucial is rather the conviction that a new New York could emerge by erasing an entire social class from the tableau of the metropolis, a notion that was at least partially grounded in the belief that commercialism was the specific character of American civilization and had to be nourished and preserved in all its manifestations. The elevation of Sadakichi Hartmann's ode "To the Flatiron" echoed a common faith among architectural critics and culture at large about the moral edification provided by the new city, and stands as the manifesto of a modernism whose consequences for the political arena were soon to become apparent with the development of scientific management and Taylorism:

> Iron structure of the time,
> Rich, in showing no pretence,
> Fair, in frugalness sublime,
> Emblem staunch of common sense,
> Well may you smile over Gotham's vast
> domain
> As dawn greets your pillars with roseate
> flame,
> For future ages will proclaim
> Your beauty
> Boldly, without shame.[32]

Finally, one cannot but think of this "roseate flame" without remembering Schiller's lines from *The Diver* quoted by Freud in *Civilization and Its Discontents*, where he summarizes his argument against the idea of an unrelated totality of the unconscious: "Let him rejoice who breathes up here in the roseate light!"[33]

NOTES

1. As Seymour I. Toll has written with reference to the Equitable Building of 1914: "Its noon shadow enveloped some six times its own area. Stretching almost a fifth of a mile, it cut off direct sunlight from the Broadway fronts of buildings as tall as twenty-one stories. The darkened area extended some four blocks to the north": *Zoned American* (New York: Grossman, 1959), 71.

2. Hugh Ferriss, *The Metropolis of Tomorrow* (1929; repr. Princeton, NJ: Princeton Architectural Press, 1986).

3. Sigmund Freud, *Civilization and Its Discontents*, trans. James Strachey (1930; New York: Norton, 1961), 18.

4. Walter Benjamin, *Illuminations*, ed. Hannah Arendt (New York: Schoken Books, 1985), esp. "On

Some Motifs in Baudelaire," 155–200; and "The Work of Art in the Age of Mechanical Reproduction," 217–52.

5. Edgar Saltus, "New York from the Flatiron," *Munsey's Magazine* (July 1905):389. Saltus (1855–1921) introduced Oscar Wilde to the American public and was the author of such novels as *Mr. Incoul's Misadventure*, *Truth about Tristram Varick*, *Eden*, and *Transactions in Hearts*. Optimist as he seemed to be in his 1905 article about the fate of American civilization, Saltus, as one contemporary critic noticed, "has established his position as the foremost literary exponent of pessimism in America, and that he is a worthy disciple of Schopenhauer is proved by his two striking works, *The Anatomy of Negation* and *The Philosophy of Disenchantment*." William Sharp, ed., *American Sonnets* (London: Walter Scott, 1889), xx.

6. "The small squares – set about the city like little girls dressed for company and told not to stir lest they muss their stiff white skirts – have for function in the city's topography to look well ordered and pleasant. They, practically, are sitting for photographs." Charles Mulford Robinson, *The Improvement of Towns and Cities or The Practical Basis of Civic Aesthetics* (New York: Putnam, 1901), 179–80. For an anticipation, see "Improvement in City Life," *Atlantic Monthly* 83 (Apr. 1889):533–4.

7. Anon., "Architectural Appreciations – No. II. The 'Flatiron' or Fuller Building," *Architectural Record* 12, no. 5 (Oct. 1902):526.

8. Anon., "Architectural Appreciations – No. II," 535.

9. See *The American Architect and Building News* 77, no. 1396 (Sept. 27, 1902):103 ff.

10. H. W. Desmond, "A Rational Skyscraper," *Architectural Record* 15, no. 3 (Mar. 1904):279.

11. Saltus, "New York from the Flatiron," 389.

12. Montgomery Schuyler, "The Field of Art – The Skyscraper Problem," *Scribner's Magazine* 34, no. 2 (Aug. 1903):254. The lines "A monster horrendous, hideous and vast, deprived of sight" are from Vergil's *Aeneid* (Book 3, line 658).

13. Ulrich Keller, "The Myth of Art Photography: A Sociological Analysis," *History of Photography* 8, no. 4 (Oct.–Dec. 1984):249–75 and "The Myth of Art Photography: An Iconographic Analysis," *History of Photography* 9, no. 1 (Jan.–Mar. 1985):1–38.

14. For an overview of Stieglitz's life and work in New York City as well as the work of Jacob Riis, see "Camera Work/Social Work," Chap. 4 in Alan Trachtenberg, *Reading American Photographs: Images as History, Mathew Brady to Walker Evans* (New York: Hill and Wang, 1989), 164–230.

15. Stieglitz quoted by W. E. Woodbury, "Alfred Stieglitz and His Latest Work," *Photographic Times* (Apr. 1896):161.

16. Jacob A. Riis, *The Making of an American* (New York: MacMillan, 1901), 236.

17. Thomas Hobbes, *Leviathan*, eds. Richard E. Flathman and David Johnston (1651; repr. New York: Norton, 1997).

18. The quotation regarding Stieglitz is in James B. Carrington, "Unusual Uses of Photography – Night Photography," *Scribner's Magazine* 22, no. 5 (Nov. 1897):626; Riis's words are from *The Making of an American*, 271.

19. Lincoln Steffens, "The Modern Business Building," *Scribner's Magazine* 22, no. 1 (July 1897):37.

20. Sadakichi Hartmann, "A Plea for the Picturesqueness of New York," *Camera Notes* 4 (Oct. 1900):91–7, reprinted in Sadakichi Hartmann, *The Valiant Knights of Daguerre: Selected Critical Essays on Photography and Profiles of Photographic Pioneers*, eds. Harry W. Lawton and George Knox (Berkeley, CA: Univ. of California Press, 1978), 60–1. Other writings of Hartmann are collected in *Sadakichi Hartmann, Critical Modernist: Collected Art Writings*, ed. Jane Calhoun Weaver (Berkeley, CA: University of California Press, 1991).

21. Hartmann, "A Plea for the Picturesqueness of New York," 61.

22. Hartmann, "A Plea for the Picturesqueness of New York," 57. It is perhaps of some significance that Hartmann posthumously celebrated Edgar Saltus by comparing him to the Parisian writer and *flâneur* Gerard de Nerval: "The Edgar Saltus I Knew," *Bookman* 58, no. 1 (Sept. 1923):19.

23. Hartmann, "Recent Conquests in Night Photography," *Photographic Times* 41 (Nov. 1909):441–50, reprinted in *The Valiant Knights of Daguerre*, 127.

24. Among the many possible examples of this genre, see James D. McCabe, *Lights and Shadows of New York Life; Or, the Sights and Sensations of the Great City* (Philadelphia: National Publishing Co., 1872); and Helen Campbell, Thomas W. Knox, and Thomas Byrnes, *Darkness and Daylight, or Lights and Shadows of New York Life* (Hartford, CT: Hartford Publishing Co., 1892). For an interesting overview, see Stewart M. Blumin, "George G. Foster and the Emerging Metropolis," in George G. Foster, *New York by Gas-Light and Other Urban Sketches* (Berkeley, CA: Univ. of California Press, 1990), 1–61.

25. Riis, *The Making of an American*, 204.

26. John Allen Corcoran, "The City Light and Beautiful," *American City* 7, no. 1 (July 1912):108–9, quoted by David Nasaw, "Cities of Light, Landscapes of Pleasure," in *The Landscape of Modernity: Essays on New York City, 1900–1940*, eds. David Ward and Olivier Zunz (New York: Russell Sage, 1992), 276.

27. Hartmann, "Recent Conquests in Night Photography," 130.

28. Hartmann, "Recent Conquests in Night Photography," 130. The emphasis is mine.

29. Hartmann, "A Plea for the Picturesqueness of New York," 62–3.

30. John Corbin, "The Twentieth Century City," *Scribner's Magazine* 33, no.1 (Mar. 1903):260.

31. John C. Van Dyke, *The New New York* (1909), 147, 261, quoted in Mike Weaver, *Alvin Langdon Coburn: Symbolist Photographer 1882–1966* (New York: Aperture, 1986), 42.

32. S[adakichi] H[artmann], "To the 'Flat-Iron'," *Camera Work* 4 (Oct. 1903):40. See also the essay that directly preceded the poem: Sidney Allan [Sadakichi Hartmann], "The 'Flat-Iron' Building – an Esthetical Dissertation, *Camera Work* 4 (Oct. 1903):36–40.

33. "... Es freue sich, / Wer da atmet im rosigten Licht," Freud, *Civilization and Its Discontents*, 21. But the entire stanza is remarkable in this context: "Long live the king! He rejoices / who can breathe in this rosy light! / For below, in contrast, it is horrible, / and man should not test the gods; / nor should he desire to see / what they mercifully conceal in night and terror."

12

The Skyscraper, Gender, and Mental Life

Sophie Treadwell's Play *Machinal* of 1928

Merrill Schleier

The skyscraper assumed a dominant position in American Machine Age discourse in part because of the post–World War I building boom. In New York City alone, skyscrapers were no longer relegated to the downtown business district, and they increasingly pushed their way toward midtown. Seemingly omnipresent derricks and beams prompted a 1925 *New York Times* headline "Titanic Forces Rear a New Skyline," which reported that workers were striving to complete 350 buildings by 1925, while 900 additional structures were being rehabilitated.[1] Between 1918 and 1925 alone, office use in skyscrapers had increased tenfold throughout the country.[2] This led to heated debates on the future of the tall building that ran the gamut from the support of unchecked expansion to passionate renunciation.[3]

A multitude of cultural and artistic productions also sought to respond to the proliferation of the skyscraper. Painters, playwrights,

Portions of this paper were presented at the Society of Architectural Historians annual conference in St. Louis (1996) in a session entitled "The Internal World of the Skyscraper," chaired by Prof. Lee Gray, and at the American Psychological Association, Division 39 conference in Denver (1997) in a session entitled "Metaphors of Medical Discourse: Gender and Psychoanalysis in Film, Drama, Poetry," which was chaired by Prof. Diane Borden. Appreciation is extended to the University of the Pacific for providing the funding for the presentation of my research and for enabling me to visit the University of Arizona, Tucson, to examine the Sophie Treadwell Papers. I would also like to express my appreciation to Prof. Jerry Dickey of the University of Arizona for alerting me to visual materials that enhanced this study and for his thoughtful comments. Thanks also to Roberta Moudry, Ph.D., for providing the necessary leadership that has prompted skyscraper scholarship to expand its boundaries. Lastly, I thank the members of the Critical Theory reading group and the faculty of the Gender Studies Program at the University of the Pacific.

filmmakers, composers, and novelists depicted the skyscraper's impact on work, sexuality, creativity, and the transformation of American physical and psychic life. Although fictional and frequently hyperbolized, these skyscraper "constructions" were instrumental in formulating popular attitudes toward the tall building, often expanding upon the concerns of architects, politicians, sociologists, and city planners. John Alden Carpenter's ballet *Skyscrapers* (1926), Elmer Rice's play *The Adding Machine* (1923), Edgar Selwyn's film *Skyscraper Souls* (1932), and King Vidor's film *The Fountainhead* (1949), an adaptation of Ayn Rand's earlier best-selling novel, disseminated these ideas in prevailing entertainment genres. These visualizations and enactments afforded the public a more experiential and vicarious encounter with city dwelling.

This study seeks to expand upon previous skyscraper scholarship by exploring how gender, mental health, and the metropolis are imbricated in Sophie Treadwell's play *Machinal* (1928).[4] Drawing upon material culture, architectural history, gender theory, and the historiography of nervous disorders, I examine Treadwell's rendition of the skyscraper as both a physical and ideological construct, instrumental in forging female office workers' subjectivities. In contrast to previous studies on the effects of modernity, I explore the singular effects of skyscraper space and its concomitant office machinery on metropolitan dwellers and workers in Treadwell's fictional account. More importantly, and in concert with Treadwell, the effects of skyscraper modernity are not simply explored in a generic manner, or as a uniform response to overstimulation; rather, they are gauged in terms of their impact on the city's gendered and classed inhabitants.[5] That is, overstimulation was experienced differently by men and women and was also mediated by their economic statuses. Recognizing these subtleties, Treadwell combined her own knowledge of working conditions in the recently mechanized office with research on the origins and treatment of nervous disorders to create a dystopian environment where the female body and its internal processes are severely compromised.

In *Machinal*, the skyscraper extends beyond the boundaries of the physical office space to encompass living quarters, leisure activities, and modes of travel, resulting in the virtual "skyscraperization" of the life of the main character, Young Woman. Mediation and regulation by the skyscraper also occurs at the bodily level, infiltrating her comportment, gestures, speech patterns, sexuality, and, finally, her psyche. As Treadwell portrayed, women's subjectivities were more adversely affected than men's because of their status as the lowest paid members of the newly mechanized office, occasioned, in part, by the advent of scientific office management.[6] In response to routinized work, a whirling congerie of machines, and surveillance by superiors and peers alike, Young Woman suffers from a host of psychiatric symptoms caused by her lowly class and gender position in a skyscraper office. Resembling Foucault's later description of the eighteenth-century panopticon tower employed in prisons to control inmates by the sheer power of the gaze, Treadwell's rendering of the skyscraper makes it an icon of patriarchy and phallic authority, the perpetrator of both the actual and ideological rape of women.[7] Yet the play's generic Young Woman does not simply conform to the spatial regimentation and the administration of her person; rather, she transgresses the skyscraper's boundaries and subverts its influence in an elusive quest for autonomy and creative expression.

A self-avowed feminist, Treadwell was an accomplished newspaper journalist, an actress, and a playwright. As a college student and an aspiring writer, she herself suffered from bouts of neurasthenia or nervous disorder, and in accord with Young Woman, Treadwell supplemented

76. "At Seven" (New York production title: "At Home") scene set for 1934 Russian production of *Machinal*. In M. A. Zelikson, comp., *Kamernyi teatr I ego Khudozhniki: 1914–1934* (Moscow: Izd., Vserossiiskoe teatral'noe obschchestvo, 1934).

her income with mind-numbing clerical labor.[8] *Machinal* reveals that the author had an abiding interest in, and well-informed knowledge of, the gender-inflected character of contemporary psychiatric views on feminine psychology, including the most up-to-date beliefs concerning the effects of metropolitan life on the psyche. Thus *Machinal* may be read as a fictional case study in which Treadwell, as both experiencing and observing self, tried to plumb the psyche of her unrealized double, Young Woman, a stenographer who served as the skyscraper's least creative, ill-paid worker. Traditionally a young female amanuensis to an older male superior, deprived of her creativity and voice, the stenographer represented, for Treadwell, the counterpart of herself, the artist.

The topical springboard for *Machinal* was the much publicized New York murder trial of Ruth Snyder and Judd Gray, which Treadwell attended unofficially. After Snyder and her paramour were convicted of bludgeoning the former's husband to death, Snyder was sentenced to death and executed by electrocution in January 1928.[9] The case held a special fascination for Treadwell who held a dim view of conventional marriage, which she saw as oppressive and stifling. She and her mother were themselves abandoned by her prominent father, a San Francisco judge who left them financially and emotionally ill equipped. Treadwell's mother also suffered from neurasthenia, which the author believed was due, in part, to her powerlessness in a patriarchal society. Thus many of her plays are peopled with characters in unsatisfactory marriages who long for escape.

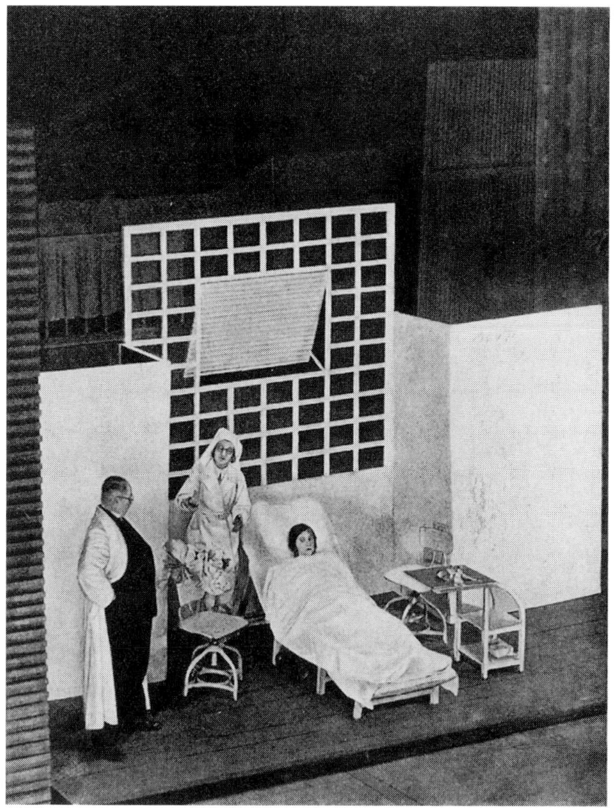

77. "Maternity" (New York production title: "Maternal") scene set for 1934 Russian production of *Machinal.* In M. A. Zelikson, comp., *Kamernyi teatr I ego Khudozhniki: 1914–1934* (Moscow: Izd., Vserossiiskoe teatral'noe obschchestvo, 1934).

Treadwell felt a kinship with the condemned Ruth Snyder, whom she viewed as an example of thwarted female creativity. Moreover, she may have identified her mother's and her own childhood rage, and their potential for decompensation, with Snyder's. As Burns Mantle, a journalist and the first publisher of *Machinal,* reported, Treadwell "left the courtroom finally deeply resentful of the mechanical set reactions of humanity. She . . . read into the soul of the condemned woman, the revolt of a seeker after beauty, and built her crime from that basis."[10] However, Young Woman's personality was not based on the passionate, spirited Snyder with whom she identified. Rather, Treadwell created a repressed, passive counterpart, similar to her mother, who was unable to seek release in a mechanomorphic world controlled by men.[11] Skyscraperization was employed as a material and symbolic presence, which thwarted Young Woman's efforts to express herself in a healthy, creative manner.

Directed by Arthur Hopkins, the play is divided into nine episodes or "life situations," which were originally accompanied by the stage sets of Robert Edmond Jones, who had previously designed the malevolent backdrops for the dystopian ballet *Skyscrapers* (1926).[12] These may have served as the inspiration for the Russian sets by Vadim Ryndin that Treadwell claimed most closely reflected her aims.[13] In both Jones's and Ryndin's designs, the skyscraper served as a dominant, destructive presence, which regimented existence. Ryndin's stage sets created architectural and spatial counterparts to Young Woman's experiences at the office, hospital, speakeasy, court room, and prison. Both dialogue and action were intersected by overpowering skyscraper imagery, from the opening scene in a crowded office, to a metaphorical rape by a skyscraper frame in a hospital, culminating in the metal bars of a prison cell, an analogue to the office building's steel cage. Young Woman is positioned high atop apartment, office, or hospital, or below in an infernoesque speakeasy, perennially unable to achieve mental or physical equilibrium (Figures 76, 77). Geometric cells and grids created entrapment and precluded organic expression. As Treadwell explained, she wished *Machinal* to serve as an antifunctionalist manifesto, "by showing the different flat surfaces and hard edges of life that the woman comes up against," disclosing her "inner reactions" to this mechanized environment.[14]

Treadwell's original instructions for the scenography specified that Episodes 1 to 4 were to take place in a business office with an entrance, a back door, and a large window. From the window, clerical workers and audience members saw another office, an apartment court, a dance casino, and steel girders.[15] Thus characters were circumscribed by a skyscraper existence, which encompassed their work environment, visual scenery, home life, and hopes for the future. Theater critic Richard Watts, who saw both the American and Soviet versions of the play, commented on how the Moscow stage designs best achieved this effect. He observed, "the curtain rises against a backdrop of skyscrapers in a silver and black sky. Then across this background is thrown an ever-shifting succession of light forms and pictorial symbols of metropolitan life."[16] In spite of the spaces of conformity signified by the skyscraper and its geometric analogues, Treadwell underscored that workers' needs for sexuality and creative expression could be neither contained nor repressed without consequences.

Machinal opened to rave reviews at New York's Plymouth Theater in September of 1928, starring Zita Johann and the young Clark Gable. It subsequently enjoyed a brief revival in London in 1931, and a successful two-year engagement at Moscow's Kamerny Theater beginning in 1933. The moribund drama's main character is a stenographer who cannot conform to the skyscraper office's regimentation, resulting in her neurasthenic or nervous condition, which is manifested by diverse symptomatology including loss of appetite, inability to breathe, obsessive-compulsive gestures, dissociation, and claustrophobia. To escape her mechanized existence and a dependent mother, Young Woman marries her Babbitt-like boss and has a child she does not want. Yet she finds that life with Boss-Husband Jones is as stultifying as her office routine and she seeks release in an illicit affair. After she is rejected by her lover and forced back to the oppressive marriage, she, like the infamous Ruth Snyder, snaps and murders Jones, only to be executed at the play's denouement in an electric chair, a retribution enacted by the mechanical forces from which she sought release.

Treadwell's creation of a nervous stenographer was in accord with the psychiatric community's belief that neurasthenia was caused by the accelerated pace of modern urban existence. According to Dr. George Beard who first coined the term in 1869 and elaborated on his findings in subsequent writings, neurasthenia or "brain sprain" resulted from America's modernity, its steam power, the periodical press, the telegraph, and the sciences.[17] Had Beard written a generation later, he most certainly would have included the skyscraper in his list of material causes for mental exhaustion and overstimulation. Since men were the first inhabitants of the commercial sphere, they were designated as the primary sufferers of neurasthenia, replaced in subsequent generations by women who were entering professional life.

Herman Melville's characters Turkey and Nippers in his short story "Bartleby the Scrivener: A Story of Wall Street" (1853) were perhaps the first American literary victims of neurasthenia. In accord with Treadwell's Young Woman in *Machinal*, their confinement in a cubical office recording the words of others resulted in dyspepsia, indigestion, mercurial moods, and flighty tempers. The fate of Bartleby was more extreme. His refusal to conform to the office routine led to mental decompensation and ultimately death. Although Melville's story was written before the advent of scientific office management, it demonstrated that routinized, bureaucratic office labor was associated with psychic decline and even death.[18]

Intellectual, autonomous, and creative women, as Beard asserted, could also be fixed with the neurasthenic label. But unlike neurasthenic men whose condition was deemed situational and environmental and thus easily ameliorated by exercise and regeneration in the outdoors, nineteenth- and early twentieth-century female neurasthenics were thought to suffer from faulty reproductive functions often exacerbated by mental overstimulation, which might include reading, writing, or academic study. Treatment included confinement to bed, a heavy diet to foster lassitude, and a prohibition against the aforementioned activities. Prominent physicians such as Dr. S. Weir Mitchell regarded female neurasthenics as conniving malingerers in need of masculine supervision.[19] One of Treadwell's aims in *Machinal* was to assert that an oppressive material and ideological environment rather than an imperfect female physiognomy was the cause of Young Woman's nervous condition. To buttress her case, Treadwell relied on the most progressive views on the subject by the psychiatric establishment.

The somatic view of female neurasthenia began to change in psychiatric circles with the publication of Freud's pioneer essay " 'Civilized' Sexual Morality and Modern Nervousness" (1908).[20] While acknowledging Beard's recognition of modern urban life's demands on mental functions, Freud regarded it as inadequate to explain neurasthenia. It was not simply developments in material culture that mediated mental functions, but also social expectations to conform to these conditions, which led to the repression of natural instincts such as sexuality and aggression. Freud recognized that the external manifestations of neurasthenia were gendered; hence the perverted man and the neurotic woman, yet he disagreed that its causes were biologically based. As the dialogue in several of her plays illustrates, Treadwell concurred with his belief that repression created by overindustrialized civilization resulted in the impossibility of healthy sublimation, leading frequently to sexual neurosis and violence, and that women like men could suffer from situational nervousness.[21]

The sociologist Georg Simmel's "The Metropolis and Mental Life" (1903) was also an effort to delineate the effects of the city on its inhabitants' internal world, devoid of the earlier gendered divisions identified by Beard and Mitchell. In accord with the psychiatric community, Simmel pointed to the "intensification of emotional life due to the swift and continuous shift of external and internal stimuli," where the individual must protect against being swallowed up in the "social–technological mechanism." A veritable battle ensued in which city dwellers fought to maintain their individuality against continual expectations for conformity. The result was a new personality or "metropolitan type" that Simmel described variously as calculating and "matter-of-fact," the product of a rational money economy. Simmel also noted another adaptation to the overabundance of stimuli, which he termed the "blasé" outlook. Characterized by seeming indifference, this personality type seemed as bland and colorless as the exchange of paper commodities, which neutralized all diversity between things.[22] Simmel's personality characterizations are particularly useful for understanding Boss Jones and his employees who, at the outset of the play, shout numbers and advertising slogans in a rote fashion devoid of affect.

Episode 1 of *Machinal* commences in the offices of the George H. Jones Company, which a critic described as "a hive of a place in which telephone girls, stenographers, filing clerks and adding clerks are jumbled together in a kind of orderliness that may promote efficiency but does not make for comfort or concentration."[23] "Orderliness" and "efficiency" and the segregation of the largely female clerical staff were references to the current effort to regulate office work by employing the strategies of scientific office management. Its promoter, William Henry Leffingwell, who began his career as a stenographer, believed that one of the most useful ways to maximize production was to separate cerebral from manual labor. The latter was increasingly segmentalized so that workers frequently did not understand the full significance of their routinized tasks, resulting in alienation and mental fragmentation. As feminist historian Angel Kwolek-Folland has argued, greater specialization and its accompanying spatial arrangements were thought to promote greater efficiency by expunging work of all superfluous gestures, detail, and distractions. Because women were more frequently relegated to habitual and automated labor while their male bosses were entrusted with management, supervision, and the power to scrutinize their female subordinates, this division assumed a gendered character. To ensure maximum control, managers often seated women at flat-topped desks in community rooms, which afforded little personal space and privacy from either the probing eyes of their supervisors or co-workers.[24]

Treadwell simulates the auditory and phenomenological experience of a typical skyscraper office created by the cacophony of numerous indoor and outdoor machines, which compete with the clipped, accelerated jargon of the office staff. Steel riveting, an airplane engine, jazz music, and the sound of telegraph instruments heard from offstage add to the clamor. In addition, Treadwell underscores the increasingly mechanical nature of feminine labor by linking each character with either a typewriter, a switchboard, or an adding machine, which serves as prosthetic extension of her body. After a tardy entrance, Young Woman is met in Episode 1 with a barrage of punitive voices and implicit threats, which are delivered in a rapid fire, robotic manner. Al Jolson, who attended the play, believed that "machinal," which means machine-like in French, also sounds like the German "mach schnell" or hurry up.[25] The stychomachic dialogue was also meant to simulate "the rhythm of common city speech, its brassy sound" and "its trick of repetition," according to Treadwell.[26]

Stenographer – You'll lose your job
Young Woman – No!
Stenographer – No?
Young woman – I can't
Stenographer – Can't?
Filing clerk – Rent – bills – installments – miscellaneous.
Adding clerk – A dollar ten – ninety-five – 3.40 – 35 – 12.60
Stenographer – Then why are you late?
Young Woman – Why?
Stenographer – Excuse!
Adding Clerk – Excuse!
Filing Clerk – Excuse.
Telephone Girl – Excuse it, please.
Stenographer – Why?
Young Woman – The subway?
Telephone Girl – Long distance?
Filing Clerk – Old stuff!
Adding Clerk – That stall!
Stenographer – Stalled?
Young Woman – No—
Stenographer – What?
Young Woman – I had to get out![27]

Although she is ostensibly describing her claustrophobia in the subway, the skyscraper's horizontal and subterranean counterpart, and her repulsion to all the pressing bodies, Young Woman's co-workers' speech underscores the office's lack of personal space. Unfortunately her plea for freedom is met with the imperious command, "Mr. J. wants you."[28] As so much of Treadwell's dialogue, these words carry multiple meanings: Boss Jones covets her both as a productive and a sexualized body. Male bosses and their colleagues viewed female clerical workers, including stenographers, file clerks, and secretaries, as manifestations of the private in public space. As Elizabeth Wilson has noted, the office was seen as an intermediate zone where "the relation of boss and secretary was a pale replica of marriage."[29] Thus Young Woman's eventual transition from stenographer to boss's wife reflected current social expectations of female advancement.

Young Woman's loss of self is evinced by her persistent calls throughout the play for somebody. Her dissociative episodes in the form of dreamlike states may be viewed as her strategy for salvaging her imagination from the mindlessness of her stultifying job. These flights of reverie are also indicative of her thwarted creativity, which is reinforced by the Adding Clerk's exclamation, "She's artistic," and the other Stenographer's reply, "She's inefficient."[30] Treadwell's delineation of Young Woman's creative mental adaptations to her job were probably gleaned from the theories of the prominent philosopher and psychologist Karl Jaspers who asserted, in his magisterial *General Psychopathology*, that the "increasing mechanization of modern life" resulted in compulsive thoughts, behaviors, and phobias where the sufferer is prone to endless daydreaming.[31]

Young Woman's body also enacts the effects of mechanized and depersonalized environment given over to rationality and patriarchal control. Despite her loss of selfhood, evidenced by her call for "somebody," she exhibits a maniacal concern for the beautification of her hands, which may represent her resistance to manual labor and her class aspirations. We learn at the play's outset that Young Woman's typewriter, the contemporary term for clerks using these machines, is broken, which announces her lack of instrumentality in the office. Yet her lovely hands attract Boss Jones despite their ineffectualness, pointing to her value as an aestheticized object or bodily part in the office hierarchy rather than a productive, respected member of the staff. Her hands will ultimately serve as her ticket out of the office, enabling her to shift from one of the clerical masses to boss's wife, her only hope for material advancement.

Typical advice literature and fictional accounts of office work encouraged female clerical staff to take special care of their physical appearance rather than offering them suggestions for professional promotion. In *What Girls Can Do* (1926), a book offering vocational advice, Ruth Wanger directed her young readers to such gender-specific fields as social work, teaching, and clerical work. In addition, Wanger devoted an inordinate amount of attention to demeanor and physical appearance rather than skill. In a chapter entitled "Fundamental Qualities for Success," Wanger's subheadings included "Fluffy Hair, Cold Cream vs. Water," "War Paint for Pale Faces," and "The Right Kind of Clothes," which rehearsed the popular belief that a crucial aspect of a woman's business identity was as an aestheticized object.[32]

By the 1920s, the typical clerical worker was usually a white, unmarried woman in her 20s who earned between $12.00 and $50.00 per week, while bosses were older, well-remunerated men. By 1930, 96 percent of all stenographers were women, one of the most ill-paid, mechanical jobs in the office hierarchy. This power dynamic encouraged sexual liaisons between wealthy older bosses and youthful clerical subordinates.[33]

Obsessive–compulsive hair grooming further illustrates Young Woman's maniacal concern for the beautification of her physical person.

These repetitive gestures may also be viewed as the outward manifestation of her exploited state, what gender theorist and philosopher Susan Bordo and a number of scholars have referred to as "body talk." By exaggerating or performing her hyperbolized feminine role, Treadwell suggests that she is both colluding with and resisting patriarchal domination. Caricaturing her femininity underscores that it is a culturally constructed affectation, which she unconsciously adopts as her only means of success. The repetitive gesture also doubles as an echo of her mechanical job, a robotic adaptation to a work environment given over to scientific office management. Yet as Bordo argues in her discussion of gender-specific syndromes, symbolic protest through the body reinforces the established order and female docility, thereby reproducing the sexual division of labor and capitalism.[34]

In spite of efforts to ensure efficiency, the office is rife with sexual innuendo in Episode 1, echoing Freud's earlier caveats. Young Woman's colleagues gossip about her future with Boss Jones and her apparent sexual dysfunction, all the while using the switchboard to arrange dates and social events, which points to scientific office management's failure to ensure efficiency by repressing the organic and the sexual. Office dialogue is frequently punctuated with the snappy "hot dog," a phrase with obvious phallic overtones, which refer to the skyscraper's omnipresence.[35]

78. Husband's costume, sketch for 1934 Russian production of *Machinal*. In M. A. Zelikson, comp., *Kamernyi teatr I ego Khudozhniki: 1914–1934* (Moscow: Izd., Vserossiiskoe teatral'noe obschchestvo, 1934).

When the slogan-spewing Boss Jones emerges from his office and places a proprietary hand on her shoulder, she recoils from the advance. In a monologue, which simulates a stream of consciousness, Young Woman verbalizes aloud her confusion at the thought of marrying Jones. Although he can provide the material support to liberate her from the office, his body repulses her. She laments, "Fat hands – flabby hands – don't touch me – please – fat hands are never weary – please don't – married – all girls – most girls – married – babies – a baby – curls – little curls all over his head – George H. Jones – straight – thin – bald – don't touch me – please."[36] Just as Young Woman's hands are rendered nonfunctional, so are Boss Jones's, which are as effeminate as those of an old woman. Their lack of instrumentality and their softness are representations of his impotence and emasculation by the office environment. His hair is also thin and straight, echoing the hard-edged lines of the functional, efficient environment. Likewise in the Moscow adaptation of *Machinal*, his suit pattern is a skyscraper grid rather than the organic curls or waves that signify the passion that she seeks (Figure 78).

79. "Domestic Hearth" (New York production title: "At Home") scene set for 1934 Russian production of *Machinal*. In M. A. Zelikson, comp., *Kamerny I teatr I ego Khudozhniki: 1914–1934* (Moscow: Izd., Vserossiiskoe teatral'noe obschchestvo, 1934).

Young Woman's "touch phobia" emerges from her repulsion to Jones, and a view of marriage gleaned from her mother, who unintentionally likens conjugal relations to filth and garbage in Episode 2. There is evidence to suggest that Treadwell consulted Freud's *Totem and Taboo* (1919) in her delineation of Young Woman's repulsion reaction.[37] Freud argued that there was a similarity between the cultural taboos of so-called primitive societies and the private ones of the modern neurotic. Had he not already characterized these syndromes as obsessional, he claimed that he would have referred to them as "taboo sickness." Freud identified the "touching phobia" as the core obsessional neurosis, which applied to overt physical contact as well as anything that reminded the patient of the forbidden object. Young Woman's avoidance of Jones's touch and her own obsessive touching of herself reveal the "continuing conflict between prohibition and instinct" noted by Freud.[38] Later in the play, Treadwell's protagonist violates the societal taboo against sexual expression by initiating an extramarital affair.

Episode 2 depicts Young Woman's relationship with a domineering mother who inculcates guilt about sex, expects monetary support, and is incapable of listening to her daughter's doubts and frustrations, a characterization that mirrors Treadwell's own relationship with her mother. Ryndin's stage designs underscore that skyscraperization has extended to the domestic realm and augur her future unhappiness with Jones. Vicariously experiencing Young Woman's present and subsequent entrapment, the audience observes cubical story upon story of fighting couples that extend interminably upward in the pattern of a modern setback skyscraper (Figure 79).

Her confinement continues during her honeymoon in Episode 3 in a hotel room devoid of scenery, where she tries to ward off the overzealous advances of Jones. Foucault referred to the honeymoon hotel as a marked-off space or heterotopia where the ritual defloration of the wife occurs in patriarchal marriage.[39] Her husband's legal right to "claim" her body occurs in a room devoid of adequate exits or liberating viewpoints where she might enjoy either psychic or physical escape, reinforced by the proprietary fling of his hat on the bed. His reminder that the room costs "twelve bucks a day" underlines her commodity status in the marriage, and his subsequent joke about the Pullman porter and the tart underscores that he intends to assume the role of a train and proceed to his destination. Young Woman responds with mortal terror and retreats to the bathroom, her only hope of a temporary reprieve. Finally emerging in a virginal white gown, she weeps uncontrollably in a state of "helpless animal terror," as she reluctantly submits to the inevitable marital rape.[40]

The legitimized rape of the honeymoon leads seamlessly to Young Woman's metaphorical rape by the skyscraper in Episode 4, which is dubbed "Maternal" (Figure 77). Riveting, which began at the end of the previous episode during the marital rape, continues, with deafening regularity. The steel skeleton of an office building under construction is seen from her hospital bed, as its incessant pounding is now inserted forcibly into her consciousness. Her response to the visual and auditory intrusion, coupled with her new maternal role and her continued aversion to her husband, prompts gagging, choking, and her refusal to eat. Her resistance is countered by the commands of a supercilious doctor who tries to force-feed her while intoning about these "modern neurotic women."[41]

Treadwell associates the skyscraper rape with the continued abuse by the medical establishment whose prescriptions for neurasthenic women included a regimented eating plan administered by a nurse under the strict supervision of the attending physician. Nervous women were also forbidden to read or write since intellectual activity would tax their supposedly already overstimulated brains, which, in turn, would interfere with their natural female roles of reproducing and nurturing. When the doctor inquires if Young Woman is unable to speak, Treadwell implies that she has been deprived of both her body and voice. Meanwhile, her husband insists she "face the music," but the only sound she continues to hear is the metallic riveting of an emergent skyscraper.[42] In her delirium, the doctor, her husband, and God serve as tripartite manifestations of patriarchal authority. At the end of Episode 4, which marks a turning point in the play, she asserts repeatedly that she will no longer submit.[43]

Hence she ventures into a speakeasy where transgression is tacitly sanctioned, the antithesis of the skyscraper office where behavior is controlled and sexuality repressed. Episode 5 is titled "Prohibited," which pertains to both the legal taboo on alcohol and the strictures imposed by "civilized" society on instinctual behavior noted earlier by Freud. In Foucauldian terms, the speakeasy may be regarded as a heterotopia of deviance where illicit behavior is accepted so as not to disrupt the rationalized world above. Concretely, the speakeasy serves as the skyscraper's inverted double or repressed mirror. One ascends the tall building while one must descend physically and morally into the infernoesque speakeasy, which sports steel-barred windows. While skyscrapers attempt to brazenly traverse space in a skyward reach for the sun, the speakeasy is shielded in darkness where it is difficult to gaze and patrol behavior. The skyscraper is given over to human labor and production; conversely, the speakeasy is reserved for entertainments and forbidden pleasures. Yet those who control the tall building may be said to allow the subterranean speakeasy to exist, thereby relegating certain activities "underground."

80. "Prohibited." Photograph of Clark Gable and Zita Johann from the 1928 New York production of *Machinal*. Clipping, The Sophie Treadwell Papers, MS 318. Special Collections. Reprinted with permission of the University of Arizona Library.

Here Young Woman meets her bohemian lover, a playboy with coarse, wavy hair unlike Jones's functional variety, who has escaped from Mexican banditos by killing one with a pebble-filled bottle.[44] Seeking release in alternative male companionship, Young Woman comes to realize that her options are either the pragmatic, boosterish masculinity of her husband or the primeval, outlaw masculinity offered by Richard (Dick) Roe. The latter's last name, which means both fish sperm and "the reproductive organs of a male fish when filled with seminal fluid," and his wavy, sealike hair underscore his primitive virility.[45] As she will ultimately conclude, both models of masculinity regard her as nothing more than a sexualized body.

Treadwell's choice of objects and spatial references in the Prohibition episode provide a plausible explanation for Young Woman's subsequent murder of her husband. The glass-filled bottle is an overdetermined symbol of illicit activity, liberation, and revenge. Resembling a vertical tower, it is filled with inanimate stone or dead weight much like the glass-curtain-walled skyscraper, which contains the trapped, lifeless bodies of workers. Moreover, the bottle has additional phallic significance. Clark Gable as Richard Roe in the New York version of *Machinal* points the bottle insinuatingly at Young Woman, accentuating its signification as both erect penis and weapon (Figure 80). Her later smashing of the bottle over Jones's head simultaneously represents explosive orgasmic release, the liberation of pent-up aggressions, and the metaphorical destruction of the skyscraper, which is also fabricated of glass and stone.

Poe's "Cask of the Amontillado" provides further insight into Young Woman's seemingly senseless act of violence, and suggested to Treadwell parallels for the entrapping nature of her skyscraper existence.[46] In the speakeasy, one occupant offers another

81. "At Court" (New York production title: "The Law") scene set for 1934 Russian production of *Machinal.* In M. A. Zelikson, comp., *Kamernyi teatr I ego Khudozhniki: 1914–1934* (Moscow: Izd., Vserossiiskoe teatral'noe obschchestvo, 1934).

amontillado, which corroborates Treadwell's appropriation of the story. Much like George H. Jones who craves expensive, imported commodities such as French underwear and Swiss watches, Fortunado in Poe's story is seduced by a rare bottle of sherry. And like Jones, he is condescending and has humiliated the narrator on various occasions. But the narrator bides his time; never letting on that something is amiss, until the appropriate moment when he offers Fortunado a rare bottle of amontillado. He then leads Fortunado to his catacomb of skeletal remains and precious wines, where he encases him behind a massive monolithic wall. Young Woman also selects a seemingly arbitrary, unprovoked moment after her affair is over to murder husband Jones with a pebble-filled bottle of her own. Fortunado's live burial behind an imponderable wall may have suggested to Treadwell a graphic depiction of Young Woman's feelings of claustrophobic containment in both her marriage and the skyscraper office. In her final autonomous act, Young Woman assumes control and has her husband "boxed" and buried.

The underground speakeasy extends to Roe's one-room basement apartment in Episode 6, encased by prisonlike bars, where Young Woman commences her extramarital affair. Although Roe calls her an angel and she feels purified by their encounter, the room's location "down there" establishes the illusory nature of her release and prefigures her demise. For the first time, however, her fragmented speech and confused ideation disappear and she imagines riding with him over the mountains. The nocturnal setting and appearance of a full moon identify her fantasies as both irrational and evil.

In accord with husband Jones, Roe admires her only for her aesthetic hands and her shapely body. Young Woman performs her femininity at the episode's denouement by posing before a mirror, assuming the posture of the volupté, with head thrown back and an arm lifted in a gesture of passivity and abandon. In mimicking the pose employed in "so many statues," Treadwell presents the power dynamic seen in five centuries of Western art.[47] In *Machinal*, women never possess the objectifying power of the gaze, the prerogative of men. Rather they are controlled and molded by it in public and private. Treadwell is perhaps the earliest feminist writer to define how visual imagery and the power of the gaze are determinants in the formation of gender identity and feminine subjectivity.[48]

82. "Prison" (New York production title: "A Machine") scene set for 1934 Russian production of *Machinal*. In M. A. Zelikson, comp., *Kamernyi teatr I ego Khudozhniki: 1914–1934*. (Moscow: Izd., Vserossiiskoe teatral'noe obschchestvo, 1934).

After Young Woman's desertion by Roe and her return to the domestic sphere in Episode 7, her neurasthenia, with its diverse symptomatology, returns with a vengeance. Jones concludes a financial transaction via telephone and approaches her with news of his success. Yet his announcement of the closed deal, coupled with his physical advances, emphasize her chattel status in the marriage. He brags, "the property's mine. It's not all that's mine! I got a first mortgage on her – I got a second mortgage on her – and she's mine!"[49] Young Woman recoils from his touch and becomes increasingly more disturbed, as he praises her purity and the abstract virtues of motherhood. Jones's oppressive monologue is echoed by his effort to contain her further by closing the windows, which exacerbates her agitation. She feels as if she is drowning and begins to experience difficulty breathing, bodily expressions of claustrophobia, which increase the tension of her chronic insomnia. A dissociative state ensues in which auditory hallucinations of Roe's voice and random voices recount his murder of Mexican banditos. References to small stones, millstones, and headstones announce that Jones's murder is imminent.

Clicking telegraph instruments and the robotic behavior of court personnel, which recall the clamor and actions of the skyscraper office, bring the play full circle in Episode 8. The arrangement of furniture and the planar, gridlike partitions in Ryndin's sets clearly function as variations of the metropolitan skyline (Figure 81). The accused murderer is identified for the first time as Helen Jones, her instrumental act providing her with an identity. When her lawyer asks where she lives, Mrs. Jones unwittingly replies, "in prison," which is how she viewed the skyscraper office and her marriage.[50] She denies killing her husband, insisting that they never so much as quarreled. Rather she blames the heinous deed on big dark men, at once a racial slur and a physical embodiment of her unconscious. But the prosecutor points to inconsistencies in her story and possesses a sworn affidavit from her lover, Richard Roe, turned Judas or *homme fatale* that they engaged in a year-long affair. Realizing that she is caught in a web of lies and fully surrounded by men and their masculine institutions, she admits murdering Jones to obtain her freedom. Her inability to seek a divorce because she did not want to hurt Jones accentuates that the moonlit murder was committed during Young Woman's mental decompensation, her pent-up hands releasing her repressed instincts. In Freud's aforementioned " 'Civilized' Sexual Morality and Modern Nervousness," he warned that if a woman did not love her husband, neurotic illness would inevitably ensue and "this neurosis will . . . [take] revenge upon the unloved husband."[51]

"A Machine" is the title of the final episode, in which male attorneys explain her motivations, male wardens regulate her body, and a priest tries to save her soul. Spatial and auditory representations of patriarchal ideology are realized in the steel grid of her prison cell, which faces the audience, and the whir of an airplane above, both meant to prompt vicarious identification with her plight (Figure 82). Prior to her execution by the ultimate machine, an electric chair, vulturelike reporters are invited to feast on the scoop. One queries, "Suppose the machine shouldn't work?" The other replies, "It'll work, it always works." Before a barber forcibly shaves her hair, a denial of her sexuality and a further recapitulation of her rape, she continues to resist submission. Yet her compulsive fixing of her hair and her plaintive call for "somebody, somebod . . . " signals that the all-pervasive forces of patriarchy and its material analogues have triumphed.[52]

Treadwell intended *Machinal* to awaken the audience to the plight of women in a patriarchal society.[53] Her interests in feminism and psychology may have led her to the writings of Karen Horney who extended the psychoanalytic enterprise to explain the particular functioning of the feminine psyche. Horney's "Flight from Womanhood: The Masculinity-Complex as Viewed by Men and Women," written two years before *Machinal*, could have provided Treadwell with further psychiatric and sociological ammunition to explain Young Woman's seemingly pathological deed.[54] Horney began her essay with the assertion that psychoanalytic research was predicated on the "minds of boys and men," hence the development of a masculine psychology, which was inadequate to explain the feminine psyche. Her lengthy paraphrase and quotation of Simmel may be applied to the psyche of Treadwell's Young Woman:

> Our whole civilization is a masculine civilization. The state, the laws, morality, religion and the sciences are the creation of men. Simmel by no means deduces from these facts . . . an inferiority in women, but he first of all gives considerable breadth and depth to this conception of masculine civilization: "The requirements of art, patriotism, morality . . . – all these categories which belong as it were . . . to humanity in general, but in their actual configuration are masculine throughout . . . in the history of our race the equation objective = masculine is a valid one."

Horney further redefined penis envy as a secondary function embodying all the disappointments and inferiorities in the development toward womanhood. Because of the "masculine character of our civilization," it was almost impossible for women to achieve sublimation or the healthy expression of the id.[55]

Treadwell employed current psychiatric discourse, simulations of material culture, and feminist theory to indict the skyscraper as the physical embodiment of the oppression of a symbolic every woman, infiltrating every facet of her existence. She invested the skyscraper with ideological power, an overarching signifier of patriarchal control, the enormity of which is pitted against Young Woman's individual desires and creative aspirations. However, Young Woman is able to seize the glass bottle or phallic signifier with instrumental hands for one elusive moment in a simultaneous act of freedom and autonomy, destroying it before she is ultimately crushed.

NOTES

1. James C. Young, "Titanic Forces Rear a New Skyline," *New York Times*, Nov. 15, 1925, sec. 4, p. 6.

2. Frederick Lewis Allen, *Only Yesterday* (New York: Harper & Row, 1931), 287. See also Orrick Jones, "Our Billion Dollar Building Year," *New York Times*, Sept. 14, 1924, sec. 1, p. 7; Gordon D. Macdonald, *Office Building Construction Manhattan 1901–1953* (New York: Real Estate Board of New York, 1953); "A Census of Skyscrapers," *American City* 41 (Sept. 1929):130.

3. For a comprehensive discussion of the debates concerning the viability of the American skyscraper, see my book *The Skyscraper in American Art, 1890–1931* (New York: DaCapo, 1990).

4. The most important contemporary writings on the play include Judith E. Barlow, "Introduction," in *Plays by American Women: The Early Years* (New York: Avon Books, 1981), ix–xxxii; Jennifer Parent, "Arthur Hopkins' Production of Sophie Treadwell's *Machinal*," *Drama Review* 26 (Spring 1982):87–100; Nancy Wynn, "Sophie Treadwell: The Career of a Twentieth Century American Feminist Playwright" (Ph.D. diss., City Univ. of New York, 1982); Louise Heck Rabi, "Sophie Treadwell: Agent for Change," in *Women in American Theatre*, eds. Helen Chinoy and Linda Walsh Jenkins, rev. ed. (New York: Theatre Group, 1987), 157–62; Barbara Bywaters, "Marriage, Madness and Murder in Sophie Treadwell's *Machinal*," in *Modern American Drama: The Female Canon*, ed. June Schlueter (Rutherford, NJ: Farleigh Dickinson Univ. Press, 1990), 97–110; Nancy Wynn, "Sophie Treadwell: Author of *Machinal*," *Journal of American Drama and Theatre* 3 (1991):29–47; Ginger Strand, "Treadwell's Neologism *Machinal*," *Theatre Journal* 44 (1992):163–75; Jennifer Jones, "In Defense of the Woman: Sophie Treadwell's *Machinal*," *Modern Drama* 37 (1994):485–96; Jerry Dickey, *Sophie Treadwell: A Research and Production Sourcebook* (Westport, CT: Greenwood Press, 1997); Jerry Dickey, "The 'Real Lives' of Sophie Treadwell: Expressionism and the Feminist Aesthetic in *Machinal* and 'For Saxophone'," in *Speaking the Other Self: American Women Writers*, ed. Jeanne Campbell Reesman (Athens, GA: Univ. of Georgia Press, 1997): 176–84; Jerry Dickey, "Sophie Visits Russia: Tairov's Production of *Machinal* and Treadwell's 'Awakening in the Promised Land'," *Women & Theatre*, Occasional Papers 4 (1997):1–17.

The Sophie Treadwell Papers are housed in the Univ. of Arizona Library Special Collections (UALSC) and consist of 52 boxes of material in two manuscript sets, MS 124 and MS 318. These include various versions of all her plays, clippings and correspondence, and reviews of her plays. In my analysis of *Machinal*, I have relied on the published versions: John Gassner ed. and Introduction, *Twenty Five Best Plays of the Modern American Theatre*, Early Series (New York: Crown, 1949) (hereafter referred to as *Machinal*/Gassner); Burns Mantle ed., *The Best Plays of 1928–9* (New York: Dodd, Mead, 1929) (hereafter referred to *Machinal*/Mantle), which includes summary notes and an abbreviated dialogue; and the original written version (1928), Sophie Treadwell Papers, UALSC, MS 124, Box 11, File 1 (hereafter referred to as *Machinal*/original). There are several other versions or parts of scenes in MS 124, Box 11. The original version contains eight episodes, the summary version contains ten, and the full published version contains nine.

There has been a recent interest in the relationship of space, the body, and mental life. See Anthony Vidler, "Bodies in Space/Subjects in the City: Psychopathologies of Modern Urbanism," *differences* 5 (1993):31–51 and *Warped Space: Art, Architecture and Anxiety in Modern Culture* (Boston: MIT Press, 2000); Esther Da Costa Meyer, "La Donna e Mobile: Agoraphobia, Women and Urban Space," in *The Sex of Architecture*, eds. Diana Agrest, Patricia Conway, and Leslie Kanes Weisman (New York: Harry N. Abrams, 1996):141–56. My reference to the imbrication of gender, mental health, and the metropolis is a paraphrase of Da Costa Meyer. See also Susan Bordo, "The Body and the Reproduction of Femininity: A Feminist Appropriation of Foucault," in *Gender/Body/Knowledge* (New Brunswick, NJ: Rutgers Univ. Press, 1989).

5. For discussions of the general effects of modernity, see Dana Brand, *The Spectator and the City in Nineteenth Century American Literature* (New York: Cambridge Univ. Press, 1995); Ben Singer, "Modernity, Hyperstimulus, and the Rise of Popular Sensationalism," in *Cinema and the Invention of Modern Life*, eds. Leo Charney and Vanessa Schwartz (Berkeley, CA: Univ. of California Press, 1995), 72–97; Ben Singer, *Melodrama and Modernity* (New York: Columbia Univ. Press, 2001).

6. For the effects of material culture, architecture, and space upon gender identity, see Louise Knapp

Howe, *Pink Collar Workers* (New York: G.P. Putnam's Sons, 1977); Margery Davies, *Woman's Place Is at the Typewriter: Office Work and Office Workers, 1870–1930* (Philadelphia: Temple Univ. Press, 1982); Griselda Pollock, "Modernity and the Spaces of Femininity," in *Vision and Difference: Femininity, Feminism and the Histories of Art* (London: Routledge, 1988):50–90; Daphne Spain, *Gendered Spaces* (Chapel Hill, NC: Univ. of North Carolina Press, 1990); Lisa M. Fine, *The Souls of the Skyscraper: Female Clerical Workers in Chicago, 1870–1930* (Philadelphia: Temple Univ. Press, 1990); Oliver Zunz, *Making America Corporate* (Chicago: Univ. of Chicago Press, 1990); Elizabeth Wilson, *The Sphinx in the City Urban Life, the Control of Disorder and Women* (Berkeley, CA: Univ. of California Press, 1991); Angel Kwolek-Folland, *Engendering Business: Men and Women in the Corporate Office, 1870–1930* (Baltimore: Johns Hopkins Univ. Press, 1990); Elizabeth Grosz, "Bodies–Cities," in *Sexuality and Space*, ed. Beatriz Colomina (Princeton, NJ: Princeton Architectural Press, 1992), 241–53; Sharon Hartman Strom, *Beyond the Typewriter: Gender, Class and the Origins of American Work, 1900–1936* (Urbana, IL: University of Illinois Press, 1992); Elizabeth Wilson, "Bodies in Public and Private," in *Public Bodies/Private States: New Views on Photography, Representation and Gender*, eds. Jane Brettle and Sally Rice (Manchester: Manchester Univ. Press, 1994), 6–23; Jane Rendell, Barbara Penner, Iain Borden, eds., *Gender Space Architecture* (London: Routledge, 2000).

7. Michel Foucault, *Discipline and Punish*, trans. Alan Sheridan (New York: Vintage, 1979). Since its inception as a building type, the skyscraper has been likened to a penis and a rapist. See my discussion in *The Skyscraper in American Art, 1890–1931*. For a discussion of the skyscraper as a perpetrator of rape, see Dolores Hayden, "Skyscraper Seduction Skyscraper Rape," *Heresies* 1 (May 1977):108–15. In addition, the phallic skyscraper architect Howard Roark commits rape in Ayn Rand's *The Fountainhead* (New York: Bobbs Merrill, 1943) and is justified by Rand in doing so. In this essay, I am analyzing the skyscraper not simply as the equivalent of the biological penis, but also in the Lacanian sense, as a signifier of power. See my "Ayn Rand and King Vidor's *The Fountainhead*: Architectural Modernism, the Gendered Body, and Political Ideology," *Journal of the Society of Architectural Historians* 61 (Sept. 2002):1–12.

8. I identified Young Woman as a sufferer of neurasthenia, with its diverse symptomatology in 1995. I presented these findings at the aforementioned Society of Architectural Historians annual conference in 1996. After further research, I discovered that Treadwell herself suffered from neurasthenia, hence came my thesis that *Machinal* is, in part, a case study of Treadwell's other self, pushed to the limit. I presented these findings at the aforementioned American Psychological Association, Division 39 conference in 1997. Jerry Dickey has recently provided an excellent chronicle of Treadwell's bouts with neurasthenia, which commenced in 1906 and continued intermittently throughout her life. He reports that she was hospitalized in 1910 at the St. Helena Sanitarium in California. See Dickey, *Sophie Treadwell: A Research and Production Sourcebook*, 1–3, 6–8. Treadwell may have used her experience for the sanitarium scene in her unpublished play, *Intimations for Saxophone* (1936). Women in wheelchairs and on stretchers serve as the backdrop for the maternity scene in *Machinal*.

As Dickey reported, Treadwell's mother was also a sufferer, leading Treadwell to ponder if the syndrome was, in part, hereditary. Her father thought of himself as somewhat of an expert on the subject. However, in evaluating an article by Judge Treadwell as given to Pauline Jacobson, "Neurasthenia, Not Fol-de-rol" (*San Francisco Bulletin*, Apr. 15, 1911, p. 13, clipping, Sophie Treadwell Papers, UALSC, MS 318, Box 16, File 11), it is clear that Treadwell Sr.'s ideas were antiquated and half-baked. He stated, "The strongest symptom in neurasthenia is where there is this terrible pulling at the base of the brain... When there is this pulling at the back of the neck, it's because the fibers of this big nerve at the base of the brain are affected – the – cer-boolum-cer(sic)."

Treadwell began saving clippings on the subject in 1911, perhaps as research. Her husband W. O. McGeehan reviewed the play *Le Bercail* or *The Redemption of Evelyn Vaudray*, which concerned female neurasthenia. See Henri Bernstein, *Le Bercail* (Paris: Modern Theatre, 1911). McGeehan stated "neurasthenia is an interesting complaint, but it is no excuse for a play" (unidentified clipping, Apr. 8, 1911, Sophie Treadwell Papers, UALSC, MS 124, Box 4, File 5). The main protagonist leaves her husband for a lover but ultimately returns for the sake of her child. McGeehan found the story implausible; however, some of its elements reappear in *Machinal*.

9. *Machinal*/original, 1. Most of the contemporary reviewers recognized the association between the trial and the play. As Nancy Wynn pointed out, Treadwell sat in on the trial on an informal basis. Both Snyder and Gray were convicted in May 1927 and executed in Jan. 1928. Treadwell completed most of the play by Jan. 1928 and finished it that Apr.; the New York production opened in Sept. 1928. See Nancy Wynn, "Sophie Treadwell: The Career of a Twentieth Century American Feminist Playwright," 108–9. Ginger Strand claims in "Treadwell's Neologism *Machinal*" that Treadwell borrowed much of *Machinal*'s language from the trial and the press

coverage. Although the content of the courtroom scene may have at times been similar, Treadwell also sought to simulate the mechanical speech of the office, its tempo and its clipped character, which mimicked both machines and advertising slogans. For the modernist appropriation of machine rhythms and jargon, see Cecelia Tichi, *Shifting Gears: Technology, Literature, Culture in Modernist America* (Chapel Hill, NC: Univ. of North Carolina Press, 1987).

10. Burns Mantle, "*Machinal*," *Daily News*, Sept. 8, 1928. Clipping, Sophie Treadwell Papers, UALSC, MS 318, Box 20, File 3.

11. As one reviewer reported in the *Theater*, "Whatever her faults Ruth Snyder had fire and vigor, and a great lust of life. This heroine is a whining neurotic girl full of self pity and repressions." Clipping, ca. Sept. 1928, Sophie Treadwell Papers, UALSC, MS 318, Box 20, File 3.

12. For a discussion of John Alden Carpenter's ballet *Skyscrapers* (1926) with sets by Robert Edmond Jones, see my *The Skyscraper in American Art, 1890–1931*. Illustrations of the stage designs and bibliography on the ballet are included. See also the more recent book by Howard Pollack, *Skyscraper Lullaby: The Life and Music of John Alden Carpenter* (Washington, DC: Smithsonian Institution Press, 1995). The ballet's macabre, skeletal set designs would also have served well in *Machinal*.

As W. David Sievers has pointed out in *Freud on Broadway: A History of Psychoanalysis and the American Drama* (New York: Hermitage House, 1955), 46, Arthur Hopkins was the first American to apply psychoanalytic concepts in the theater with his play *The Fatted Calf* (1912). As Hopkins stated, theater needs to bypass "the individual conscious reactions in order to reach the collective unconscious," quoted in Jennifer Parent, "Arthur Hopkins' Production of Sophie Treadwell's *Machinal*," 89. Echoing Hopkins, Robert Edmond Jones stated that "Eugene O'Neill's *Strange Interlude* and Sophie Treadwell's *Machinal* represent an effort to express directly to the audience the unspoken thoughts of the characters, to show us not only their conscious behavior but the actual pattern of their subconscious lives" (1929). Quoted in Delbert Unruh, ed., *Towards A New Theatre: The Lectures of Robert Edmond Jones* (New York: Limelight Editions, 1992), 89–90.

13. Sophie Treadwell, "Avtor o postanovke 'Mashinal'," *Vecherniaia Moskva*, May 22, 1934, quoted in Thomas Joseph Torda, "Alexander Tairov and the Scenic Artists of the Moscow Kamerny Theater, 1914–1935" (Ph.D. diss., Univ. of Denver, 1977), 595, as quoted in Dickey, "Sophie Visits Russia," 5.

14. *Machinal*/original.

15. *Machinal*/original. These lengthy descriptions of the sets were provided by Treadwell in the original version.

16. Richard Watts, Jr., "Moscow Sees 'Machinal' and Approves of It," *Times Herald*, June 18, 1933. Clipping, Sophie Treadwell Papers, UALSC, MS 318, Box 13, scrapbook. For a discussion of the Moscow production, see Jerry Dickey, "Sophie Visits Russia," 1–17. I thank Prof. Dickey for alerting me to the eleven original reproductions of the Moscow sets that initially appeared in M. A. Zelikson, comp., *Kamernyi teatr I ego Khudozhniki: 1914 – 1934* (Moscow: Izd., Vserossiiskoe teatral'noe obschchestvo, 1934). Dickey published four of the sets in "Sophie Visits Russia," including "The Family," "The Honeymoon," "Hearth," and "The Machine." However, as Dickey's concerns were different from my own, he did not analyze them in terms of the skyscraper as an overarching symbol of patriarchal ideology. The Soviets saw the skyscraper as the physical embodiment of capitalist exploitation.

17. George M. Beard, *American Nervousness: Its Causes and Consequences* (New York: Putnam, 1881). The literature on neurasthenia is exhaustive. The primary works by Beard and S. Weir Mitchell are useful for the nineteenth century views toward female sufferers, and the authoritarian administration of treatment. See George M. Beard, *Sexual Neurasthenia (Nervous Exhaustion): Its Hygiene, Causes, Symptoms and Treatment* (New York: Treat, 1884); S. Weir Mitchell, *Lectures on Diseases of the Nervous System, Especially in Women* (Philadelphia: Henry C. Lea's Son Co., 1881). For the secondary scholarship, consult Charles Rosenberg, "The Place of George M. Beard in Nineteenth Century Psychiatry," *Bulletin of the History of Medicine* 36 (1962):245–59; Barbara Ehrenreich and Deidre English, *Complaints and Disorders: The Sexual Politics of Sickness* (New York: Feminist Press, 1973); G. J. Barker-Benfield, *The Horrors of the Half Known Life* (New York: Harper & Row, 1976); Carroll Smith-Rosenberg, *Disorderly Conduct: Visions of Gender in Victorian America* (New York: Oxford Univ. Press, 1985); Elaine Showalter, *The Female Malady: Women, Madness, and English Culture, 1830–1980* (New York: Pantheon, 1985); George Frederick Drinka, M.D., *The Birth of Neurosis: Myth, Malady and the Victorians* (New York: Simon and Schuster, 1984). The literature on male nervousness continues to grow. See Michael Kimmel, "Consuming Manhood: The Feminization of American Culture and the Recreation of the Male Body, 1832–1920," in *The Male Body*, ed. Laurence Goldstein (Ann Arbor, MI: Univ. of Michigan Press, 1994), 12–41, and Kimmel, *Manhood in America: A Cultural History* (New York: Free Press, 1996); Joyce Henri

Robinson, " 'Hi Honey, I'm Home:' Weary (Neurasthenic) Businessman and the Formulation of a Serenely Modern Aesthetic," in *Not at Home: The Suppression of the Domestic in Modern Art and Architecture*, ed. Christopher Reed (London: Thames and Hudson, 1996), 98–112.

18. Herman Melville, "Bartleby the Scrivener. A Story of Wall Street," (1853) in *The Writings of Herman Melville, Vol. 9: The Piazza Tales and Other Prose Pieces* (Chicago: Northwestern Univ. Press, 1997), 13–45.

19. See S. Weir Mitchell, *Lectures on Diseases of the Nervous System, Especially in Women*.

20. Sigmund Freud, " 'Civilized' Sexual Morality and Modern Nervousness" (1908), in *Sigmund Freud Collected Papers*, vol. 2, trans. Joan Riviere (New York: Basic Books, 1959), 76–99. For the popularization of Freud in America, especially the adoption of his theories by artists and writers, see Nathan G. Hale, Jr., *Freud and the Americans, The Beginnings of Psychoanalysis in the United States, 1876–1917*, vol. 1 (New York: Oxford Univ. Press, 1971) and Hale's *Rise and Crisis of Psychoanalysis in the United States, Freud and the Americans, 1917–1985*, vol. 2 (New York: Oxford Univ. Press, 1995). The psychoanalyst Alfred Kuttner summarized Freud's ideas in the immensely popular *Civilization in the United States* (New York: Harcourt, Brace, 1922). His essay on "Nerves" coincided with the anthology's pessimistic assessment of the Machine Age. The influence of psychology on theatrical productions is examined in Sievers, *Freud on Broadway*.

21. Treadwell's unpublished play *Intimations for Saxophone* (1936) includes references to both Freud and Freudian modes of interpretation. Its main protagonist, who is in a boring marriage with a man lacking in sensuality, just as Young Woman was, develops a love–hate obsession with a Cossack dancer who throws knives to seduce women. Yet she meets a benevolent author-psychologist with whom she falls in love. Dr. Kartner tries to help her come to grips with her obsession by validating that in the "primitive primeval simplicities of life ... alone true happiness is found." She follows Kartner to Vienna, only to meet up again with her *homme fatale*. Unable to shake her obsession, she steps out on the dance floor just as he launches his knife, dying unable to integrate the "civilized" and bestial aspects of her character.

One of the characters in the play, Millie, is the voice of the Freudian mode of interpretation. She tries to analyze one of Lily's dreams, and when Lily will not come out of her room, she asserts, "this closed door is a symbol of your life, Lily. You are closed in. You are repressed. You are inhibited. Open the door." Sophie Treadwell Papers, UALSC, MS 124, Box 13, File 1.

The unpublished play *Ladies Leave* (1929) also features a bored wife who has an extramarital affair with her husband's more exciting subordinate. She finally leaves her husband for the Viennese psychologist Dr. Jeffers at the end of the drama. Sophie Treadwell Papers, UALSC, MS 124, Box 12, File 1.

In the short story "A Psychological Experiment," ca. 1920s, Treadwell features a narrator who assumes the role of the psychoanalyst, despite the fact that she holds a Ph.D. in science. Her old college roommate, now married to a conventional man, is suffering from a "severe mental complex from which the power of scientific psychology alone can save her." Recalling her study of Jung and Freud, she vows to help Babs by allowing her not to repress. Babs's "serious nervous condition" is caused in part by her confusion over an illicit affair she is carrying on with a poet. The ersatz psychoanalyst takes Babs to a serene natural setting to relieve her anxiety and appeals to her sense of duty and her rationality, both of which fail. Both hear about a pioneer woman who gave up everything to live with a younger lover who remained devoted to her for the remainder of her life. Although Babs's situation resolves itself when the poet breaks off the affair, the story of old Mrs. Norton prompts both women to ponder their respective life choices. Babs and the doctor may be seen as two sides of Treadwell's character, a divided self that is never resolved in her works. Sophie Treadwell Papers, UALSC, MS 124, Box 4, File 3. Treadwell's effort to forge a new psychological drama and her reliance on psychoanalytic theoreticians are the subjects of my forthcoming study.

22. George Simmel, "The Metropolis and Mental Life" (1903), in *On Individuality and Social Forms*, ed. Donald Levine (Chicago: Univ. of Chicago Press, 1971), 324–9.

23. *Machinal*/Mantle, 226.

24. For a discussion of William Henry Leffingwell and scientific office management, see Davies, *Woman's Place Is at the Typewriter*; Strom, *Beyond the Typewriter*; and Kwolek-Folland, *Engendering Business*.

25. Al Jolson as quoted by Gilbert Gabriel, "Last Night's First Night 'Machinal,' A Tragedy in Fine Stage Clothing, With Sudden Glory for Zita Johann," clipping, Sophie Treadwell Papers, UALSC, MS 318, Box 20, File 3.

26. *Machinal*/Gassner, 498–9.

27. *Machinal*/Gassner, 498–9.

28. *Machinal*/Gassner, 498–9.

29. Elizabeth Wilson, "Bodies in Public and Private," 12.

30. *Machinal*/Gassner, 499.

31. Karl Jaspers, *General Psychopathology*, trans. J. Hoenig and M. W. Hamilton (1923, 1946; repr.,

Manchester: Manchester Univ. Press, 1963). Treadwell also kept a file on Jaspers (Sophie Treadwell Papers, UALSC, MS 124, Box 4, File 5), although there is no mention of this particular text. Treadwell was also fluent in German, which suggests that she may have been familiar with Jaspers' work on abnormal psychology during her formulation of *Machinal.*

Articles in American journals began to reflect the concern for workers' mental statuses in ensuring efficient production. Elton Mayo of the Wharton School noted in "Reverie and Industrial Fatigue," *Personnel Journal* 3 (1924–25):273–83, in a section called "Psychological Interpretations" that the monotony of machine operation led to "pessimistic and bitter reflection."

32. Ruth Wanger, *What Girls Can Do* (New York: Henry Holt, 1926), 10–26. Consult Ellen Todd, *The New Woman: Painting and Gender Politics on Fourteenth Street* (Berkeley: Univ. of California Press, 1993) for further discussion of the advice literature aimed at female clerical workers.

33. See Davies, *Woman's Place Is at the Typewriter,* and Strom, *Beyond the Typewriter.*

34. Susan Bordo, "The Body and the Reproduction of Femininity."

35. *Machinal*/Gassner.

36. *Machinal*/Gassner, 501.

37. Sigmund Freud, *Totem and Taboo, Some Points of Agreement Between the Mental Life of Savages and Neurotics* (New York: Norton, 1952), 26–36. Treadwell's familiarity with the text is corroborated by her discussion of societal taboos in her play *Ladies Leave* of 1929 (Sophie Treadwell Papers, UALSC, MS 124, Box 12, File 1, pp. 8–9). Dr. Jeffers, one of the several psychologists who populate Treadwell's work, intimates that Zizi Powers, who is having an affair with her husband's more exciting subordinate, has "lost some taboos." After admitting to the doctor that she has just slapped a woman's face, she responds to his consternation by stating, "I've had a horrible reaction to it. That's the trouble with loosing your taboos. You don't know where to stop!" These lines could also have been uttered by Young Woman in *Machinal.*

38. Sigmund Freud, " 'Civilized' Sexual Morality and Modern Nervousness," 93.

39. Michel Foucault, "Of Other Spaces: Utopias and Heterotopias," *Lotus,* 48/49 (1985/86):9–17; repr. in *Rethinking Architecture, A Reader in Cultural Theory,* ed. Neil Leach (London: Routledge, 1997), 350–6.

40. *Machinal,* one of the unpublished versions, Sophie Treadwell Papers, UALSC, MS 124, Box 11, File 2. This description also appears in the Burns Mantle anthology, p. 234.

41. *Machinal*/Gassner, 508.

42. *Machinal*/Gassner, 507.

43. In the original version, Young Woman makes it clear that she does not want the baby because she reminds her of her husband. "I never wanted this one. HE gets on my nerves – every minute – on my nerves – every minute – She's HIM. I got enough of him – without her." Sophie Treadwell Papers, UALSC, MS 124, Box 11, File 1.

44. From 1920–21, Treadwell covered the effects of the Mexican Revolution. She was also the only Western journalist to interview Pancho Villa. It seems that Treadwell had a special fascination with, and an ambivalence toward, dark or swarthy men, often depicting them in her plays as the desirable, but repulsive exotic "other." In *Intimations for Saxophone* (1936), the main character's *homme fatale* is a Russian Cossack dancer. Although married, Treadwell herself had numerous affairs with artistic or bohemian types, including the painter Maynard Dixon and the Dadaist Arthur Cravan. The Dada enthusiast and art collector Louise Arensberg wrote to Treadwell in 1923, "What is Mac doing? I take for granted you are living *toute seule* with your Mex... but what about the proprieties? By this time he is doubtless growing a moustache again and will soon become dangerous." Feb. 7, 1923, Sophie Treadwell Papers, UALSC, MS 318, Box 4, File 6.

45. Funk and Wagnalls, *Standard Encyclopedic Dictionary* (Chicago: Ferguson, 1966), 577. The secondary definition of roe is "the milt of male fish." Milt means either fish sperm or the reproductive organs of the fish (p. 412). Roe also rhymes with Poe, who was also profligate and a heavy drinker.

46. Edgar Allen Poe, "The Cask of the Amontillado" (1846), in *Complete Stories & Poems of Edgar Allan Poe* (New York: Doubleday, 1966), 191–5. Treadwell was well versed in the writings of Poe. In 1920, she wrote a drama about him, with the title role for John Barrymore. Barrymore liked the script and he promised to play the leading role. Four years later and with the manuscript still not returned, Treadwell learned that he was to act in a drama about Poe written by his wife. Treadwell believed that Mrs. Barrymore's version was pirated from her own and she initiated a lawsuit. Later Treadwell wrote a play concerning Poe entitled *Plumes in the Dust.* For more information on Treadwell, Poe, and Barrymore, and a summary of "Plumes in the Dust" (1936), see Jerry Dickey, *Sophie Treadwell: A Research and a Production Sourcebook,* 82–6.

47. See Treadwell's production notes in *Machinal*/Mantle, 241–2.

48. David Nye in *American Technological Sublime* (Cambridge, MA: MIT Press, 1994), 96–7, discusses how

the businessman's gaze dominated images of the urban landscape. Skyscrapers were often depicted from panoramic perspectives, which Nye identifies as visualizations of the businessman's power. The infinitesimal specks of humanity seen from these vantage points suggest "subjugation as the obverse side of mastery." See also Roland Marchand, *Advertising the American Dream* (Berkeley, CA: Univ. of California Press, 1985).

49. *Machinal*/Gassner, 517.

50. *Machinal*/Gassner, 520.

51. Sigmund Freud, " 'Civilized' Sexual Morality and Modern Nervousness," 98.

52. *Machinal*/Gassner, 527–9.

53. For further information on Treadwell's feminism, see Ishbel Ross, *Ladies of the Press* (New York: Harper & Row, 1936) and Dickey, *Sophie Treadwell: A Research Guide and Production Sourcebook*.

54. Karen Horney, "The Flight from Womanhood: The Masculinity Complex as Viewed by Men and by Women" (1926), in *Feminine Psychology* (New York: Norton, 1967), 54–70.

55. Horney, "The Flight From Womanhood," 54–70; Georg Simmel, *Philosophische Kultur*, n.d., quoted in Horney, "The Flight From Womanhood," 55.

13

The Sublime and the Skyline

The New York Skyscraper

David E. Nye

When I used to try to explain America to Frenchmen of course before I had gone over this time, I used to tell them you see there is no sky over there there is only air, when you look up at the tall buildings at the time I left America the Flatiron was the tallest one and now it is not one at all it is just a house like any house but at that time it was the tallest one and I said you see you look up and you see the cornice way on top clear in the air but now in the new ones there is no cornice up there and that is right because why end anything.[1]

Gertrude Stein's stream-of-consciousness meditation on New York skyscrapers suggests how they were taken into consciousness, not as pure forms, but as experiences of air and sky that were immediately connected to American culture. There were no skyscrapers in France, and most Europeans found them vulgar and pretentious. Mark Girouard notes that in turn-of-the-century London, Paris, and Berlin "a sense of hierarchy led to high buildings being prohibited by law: it was for long unthinkable that cathedrals, palaces or public buildings should be overshadowed by commercial structures."[2] Henry James disliked skyscrapers, and much preferred the horizontality of the "great Palladian pile just erected by Messrs. Tiffany.... One is so thankful to it, I recognize, for not having twenty-five stories."[3] Architects trained to think in the Italian and French schools felt skyscrapers violated classical proportions and most genteel Americans agreed. The great World's Columbian Exhibition in Chicago was a self-conscious rejection of the tall building in favor of the Beaux-Arts style, which is to say in favor of the horizontal city. The fair's planners sought to show that they had absorbed classical European culture and were prepared to reproduce and sustain it.[4] They meant to show that they would maintain a European sense of sky, edged by the cornices of long horizontal buildings, reflected in great lagoons and framed like paintings. The skyscraper violated the sense of the sky, at first by thrusting up too high and later by eliminating the framing cornices, crowning domes, and other traditional ways of signifying the end of a building. Why, as Stein asked, end anything? Like her sentences, the skyscraper meant a landscape without a frame, a continuously unfolding sequence that ran into the future like the stream of consciousness itself, and which would later find expression in sheer glass towers and skyscrapers with mirrored surfaces.

Most architecture books adopt quite another style than Stein's as they seek to present skyscrapers as isolated things in themselves, not as part of an ensemble of buildings, and not as a rewriting of our relationship to air and sky. In such criticism each structure discussed represents a particular style or movement, and the illustrations are analogous to paintings hung in orderly sequence on a gallery wall. This representational strategy implies a stance in relationship to these buildings that is decontextualized, idealized, and shorn of human relation. In such an approach, skyscrapers are not seen as part of the flow of everyday life. Rather, even very good critics such as Paul Goldberger tended to see them as things apart, like art objects in the white space of a museum.[5] Photographs in such volumes seek to present the building by itself, with as little as possible of the surrounding architecture included in the frame. As this visualization suggests, the buildings are then discussed largely in terms of their formal qualities, as seen by architects, not in terms of their popular perception in an urban context. The building's appearance is discussed either from the perspective of someone standing on the ground or from an idealized position located twenty stories in the air. The view is from the outside, looking at the building.

The majority of the public are not architects, of course, and they take less interest in such views than in the panoramas available from the observation deck at the top of the building. For most people, the skyscraper achieves a good deal of its meaning as a vantage point, rather than as a view. In popular culture the skyscraper is not a thing in itself, but a platform from which other things can be seen and evaluated. This is not to say that people do not look at skyscrapers from the ground, but when they do it is seldom from immediately in front of the building. Even a colossus like the Empire State Building may be ignored by people walking right in front of it, not only because of the many distractions of the street, but also because the building is literally quite hard to see from nearby. Usually, skyscrapers are recognized at a distance and seen as part of a more general pattern. Except for a few famous buildings, most people cannot name skyscrapers, much less name their architects. Rather, the general public early on learned to appreciate a landscape of skyscrapers. A new word had entered the American language to describe what a city full of tall buildings looked like: people spoke of the "skyline." The following is a meditation on these two popular ways of understanding the skyscraper, first as part of an ensemble that made up a skyline and second as an Olympian vantage point.

Both of these popular responses to skyscrapers were part of the general revaluation of urban space, as it was transformed from the horizontal walking city of the mid-nineteenth century to the much larger vertical city of mass transportation.[6] A new aesthetics of the industrial sublime presented urban space as having the same awe-inspiring and uplifting qualities that in the eighteenth century had been attributed to natural phenomena such as mountains and spectacular sites such as Niagara Falls. The sense of awe before an overwhelming display of natural power and infinitude, which

83. "Inspiring Heights of World's Greatest Skyscraper – Empire State Building from Air, New York." Stereoview, ca. 1931. Keystone View Co. Collection of the editor.

Immanuel Kant and Edmund Burke had identified as the characteristic emotion of the sublime, was transferred by Americans to man-made artifacts, notably canals, railroads, great bridges, and skyscrapers.[7]

To ground these observations in a particular historical context, I will confine myself to the formative years when skyscrapers were being incorporated into the life of New York City, between roughly 1900 and 1930. Particularly during the 1920s a series of exhibitions, magazine articles, displays in department stores, and works of art manifested a public enthusiasm for the new buildings that Merrill Schleier calls "skyscraper mania." The image of the skyscraper as a sublime object "was adopted by optimists and pessimists alike. The numerous paintings and photographs of boundless towers rendered from disorienting perspectives were manifestations of the simultaneous amazement and inability to grasp the skyscraper's monumental proportions and symbolic implications" (Figure 83).[8] In personal terms, many came to grips with the skyscraper by seeing it from a distance as part of a new man-made equivalent of a cliff or by experiencing it from the top, as though from the summit of a mountain. These geological terms, like the language of the sublime, were used to describe the man-made phenomena.[9]

The Skyline

There is a moment in Sinclair Lewis's *Arrowsmith* (written in the early 1920s) when the medical researcher Martin Arrowsmith first responds to the New York skyline. While riding the elevated to the research center where he will begin a new job, he "beheld the Woolworth Tower" and "he was exalted. To him architecture had never existed; buildings were larger or smaller bulks containing more or less interesting objects. His most impassioned architectural comment had been, 'There's a cute bungalow; be a nice place to live.' Now, he pondered, 'Like to see that tower every day – clouds and storms behind it and everything – so sort of satisfying.'"[10] For Arrowsmith, the sublimity of the skyscraper objectifies his desire to excel and evokes an impassioned monologue on science.[11]

In 1926, the year after Lewis's novel appeared, Claude McKay published "Song of New York" in the *New Masses*.[12] McKay celebrated "the world's most splendid town,/ Grey stone and iron rushing to the sky." Comparing New York favorably to Paris ("a lovely whore,/ In jewelled dress attracting everyone") and Berlin ("a raw and bleeding sore") he has a double vision. On the one hand, he "realized New York" was "a demon holding in his hand a whip/ Driving me through the cold straight streets to work." Indeed, Arrowsmith also feels the pulse of the city and works harder in New York than he had anywhere before. Yet paradoxically, he scarcely looks up at the skyscrapers as he hurries to and from work each day. "The city of Magic was to become to Martin neither a city nor any sort of magic but merely a route: their flat, the subway, the Institute, a favorite inexpensive restaurant."[13]

Yet there was also another experience of the city of spires, if one stood outside it. McKay continues:

> Yet once you stand upon New Jersey's soil
> With a child's attitude and turn your face
> Toward the first citadel of modern toil,
> A great rock jutting grandly out in space,
> You'll never forget that marvel of these years,
> Around which wash the world's increasing tides,
> And, spurred by loves and hopes and stinging fears,
> Six millions scrambling up her steel-ribbed sides.[14]

By 1926, both Lewis and McKay could take for granted that their readers knew the skyline of New York. Here McKay does not seek to describe it, but rather focuses on what it represents: a "citadel," a "great rock" that six million people are trying to scale. He fuses several responses, admiring the view yet realizing that this marvel is surrounded by love, hope, and fear.

By the middle 1920s, McKay and Lewis had internalized the meanings of the skyscraper, as had their readers. To understand more fully what the panorama of New York meant, one has to go back to when it was new and its meanings were more openly discussed. In the 1890s people realized that the unintended outcome of skyscraper building would be a new view of Manhattan, seen from either the harbor or its two rivers (Figure 84). Before 1900 the term "skyline" had emerged as common coin, as a way of talking about this new vertical city. William R. Taylor found the first use of the term in the *New York Journal* in May 1896; Thomas A. P. van Leeuwen discovered scattered earlier examples.[15] Certainly by the end of the nineteenth century, the skyline emerged as a new visual category. In 1897, the architectural critic Montgomery Schuyler was among the first to admit that the silhouette of Manhattan visible from the surrounding shores had a new symbolic quality that was not a conscious intent of architects, but a concatenation of the whole: "It is in the aggregation that the immense impressiveness lies."[16] Schuyler's generation was responding to the creation of an artificial

84. New York City skyline from New Jersey, 1908. Courtesy of the Library of Congress, Prints and Photographs Div., Detroit Publishing Co. Collection [LC-D4-72997 DLC].

horizon, a completely man-made substitute for the geology of mountains, cliffs, and canyons.

In 1909 the Mayor of New York hosted the Hudson–Fulton celebration, which marked the tercentenary of Henry Hudson's discovery of the Hudson River and the centennial of Fulton's steamboat. The mayor freely admitted to a delegation of European dignitaries that "there are comparatively few buildings in New York City which, when taken by themselves, are not architecturally incorrect; there are only a few buildings that even by a stretch of the imagination can of themselves be called beautiful." Yet despite their individual inadequacies, the mayor argued, "Take the city altogether, the general effect of the city as a whole, the contrast of its blotches of vivid color, with the bright blue of the sky in the background, and of the waters of the harbor in the foreground, the huge masses of its office buildings, towering peak on peak and pinnacle above pinnacle to the sky, making of lower Manhattan, to the eye at least, a city that is set on a hill, and New York does have a beauty of her own, a beauty that is indescribable, that seizes one's sense of imagination, and holds one in its grip."[17] This statement was made when the Metropolitan Life and Singer buildings were the tallest in New York. The Woolworth Building would not be completed for three more years, and the heights reached by the Chrysler and Empire State buildings were scarcely imagined. Yet already the mayor had articulated what was to become standard praise for the skyline.

Note the reference to the Biblical "city on a hill" that was to be a model for all mankind. The mayor claimed for New York what the early Puritans had wished for their colonies. The "huge masses of office buildings" were thus metamorphosed from undistinguished commercial structures into representations of destiny. Montgomery Schuyler had already expressed a similar sentiment in 1903 when he wrote, "We can imagine quarters and avenues in New York in which a uniform row of skyscrapers might be not merely inoffensive but sublime."[18]

The British novelist Arnold Bennett voiced a characteristic response to this new landscape: "A great deal of the poetry of New York is due to the sky-scraper. At dusk the effect of the massed sky-scrapers from within, as seen from any high building up-town, is prodigiously beautiful, and it is unique in the cities of this world. The early night effect of the whole town, topped by the aforesaid Metropolitan Life Tower, seen from the New Jersey shore, is stupendous, and resembles some enchanted city of the next world rather than of this" (Figure 85).[19] This landscape told citizens that civil engineers and architects could perform wondrous feats, and that the owners of these buildings – insurance companies, newspapers, and captains of industry – were colossal. While banks and museums long clung to the low, horizontal building as being more refined, new businesses and new money quickly adopted the tall building, both as a way of focusing energies in a single concentrated location and as a way to proclaim their importance. While ground rents alone did not justify building particularly high, the publicity value of a great tower made additional stories well worth the investment.[20] The striving millions whom McKay saw swirling around the edges of these towers were pointedly reminded daily of the Singer sewing machine, the Woolworth stores, the newspapers they read, and the insurance they bought.

Yet the corporate skyscraper was not only a harbinger of change. In part because of their sheer bulk, skyscrapers soon became landmarks that provided spatial orientation, and architects adapted traditional elements of civic architecture to adorn them. Companies soon realized that it was good public relations to give people a reason to look at their buildings, and they installed giant illuminated clocks that could be seen from across town, day or night. These proud towers were thus more than giant billboards. If they manifested the economic might of corporations in terms of startling size and height, they also quoted from tradition, by selectively adopting elements of the past, as in the Woolworth Building's gothic elements or the Wrigley Building's imitation of the Giralda tower in Seville. If they literally asked Stein's question, "Why end anything?", they also sought a visual connection to the past.

The View from Above

Arrowsmith looked out at New York City from his new laboratory, located in a Manhattan skyscraper. He had left in succession private practice in North Dakota, public health work in Iowa, and a position in an expensive Chicago clinic, arriving at a new research position. Alone in his new lab for the first time,

> he looked out of the broad window above his [work] bench and saw that he did have the coveted Woolworth Tower, to keep and gloat on. Shut in to a joy of precisions, he would nevertheless not be walled out from the flowing life. He had, to the north, not the Woolworth Tower alone but the Singer Building, the arrogant magnificence of the City Investing Building. To the west, tall ships were riding, tugs were bustling, all the world went by. Below his cliff, the streets were feverish. Suddenly he loved humanity as he loved the decent, clean rows of test-tubes.[21]

Arrowsmith gloats over the Woolworth and other skyscrapers because they provide him with a new fantasy of domain. Lewis could quickly sketch his response because he knew that in the 1920s, readers had become familiar with precisely this view from the high office window. The city seen from a skyscraper had become a central part of popular iconography (Figure 86). Millions of postcards were

85. Night Scene, Southeast from 515 Madison Avenue, 1937. The Byron Collection, 93.1.1.2054. Reprinted with permission of the Museum of the City of New York.

sold of views from the most famous tall buildings. Likewise, artistic photographers such as Edward Steichen and Alfred Stieglitz explored the new upper world of glass and steel.[22] The penetration of the skyscraper view into the middle classes was further indicated by the fact that it had become a recurring motif in magazine advertising. Such images often silhouetted an executive against a window, as he looked out over the city, and the reader was expected to identify with this captain of commerce. Roland Marchand, the historian of advertising and public relations, has noted, "The panorama view through the window was always expansive and usually from a considerable height. It was never obstructed by another skyscraper across the street."[23] From this new vantage point, the businessman's magisterial gaze dominated the new man-made landscape.

Arrowsmith works for a research institute funded by a wealthy shipping mogul with extensive (and, one gathers, exploitative) investments in Latin America, and when he halts a plague on a Caribbean island this provides good public relations for the firm. Such ironies are lost on him, however, as he loves an abstract humanity, shorn of all its particularity and seen from an upper floor. One cannot, in practice, "love humanity as he loved the decent, clean rows of test-tubes." But such abstraction is a direct result of the skyscraper view, which promotes a magisterial vision in which abstract reasoning, whether applied to accounting, engineering, finance, or science, is naturalized as the normal

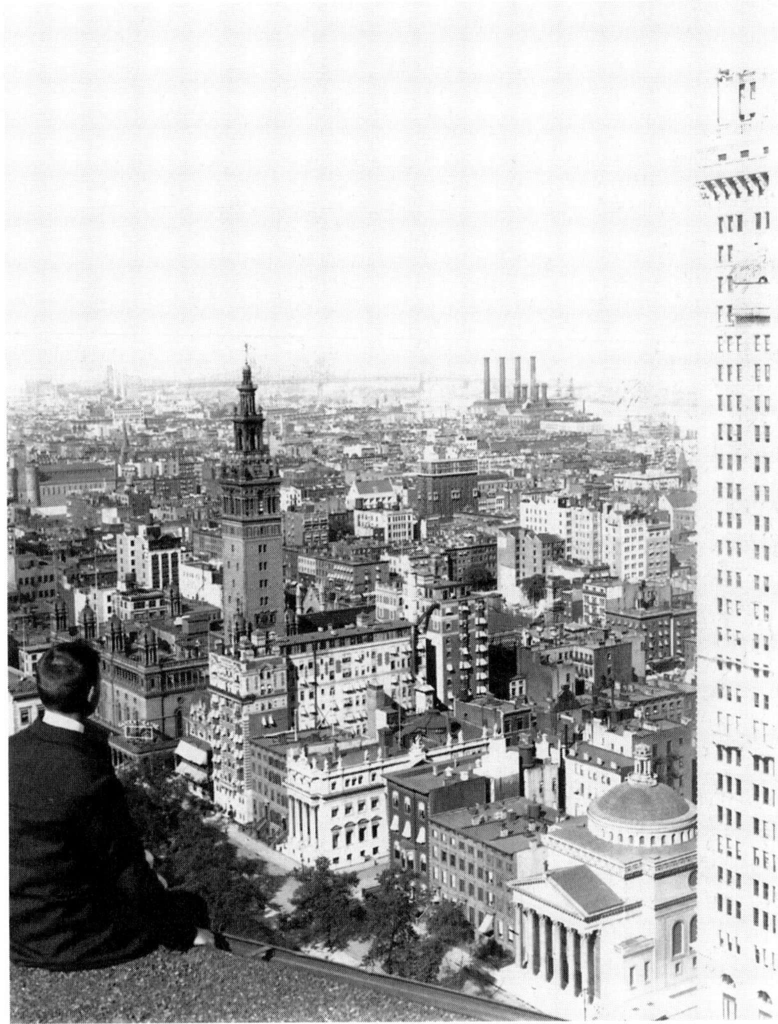

86. From the Flatiron Building looking northeast past Madison Square Garden to the Queensboro Bridge, New York. Reprinted with permission of the Keystone–Mast Collection, UCR/California Museum of Photography, University of California, Riverside.

way to think about the world. When Arrowsmith leaves his laboratory for the first time, he is in a buoyant mood, and on his walk back to the hotel immediately afterward he races along "seeing nothing yet in a blur seeing everything."[24] This blurred vision of the people around him is paralleled by his failure to think of his own needs. When he gets to the somewhat shabby hotel, his wife congratulates him on the new job but is dismayed to discover that he has no idea what salary he will be paid. The exaltation of the view has literally distracted him from asking.

The psychic economy of the skyscraper is far different from that of the horizontal city before 1875, whose characteristic office buildings had four or five stories. Before the elevator made building high attractive, the value of offices declined with each staircase the public had to climb. Above the shops at the street level, the most successful accountants, doctors, and lawyers were no more than one flight up.

87. "Up Broadway and Fifth Avenue from Flat Iron Building, New York." Stereoview, 1904. Collection of the editor.

Close to the street, they could observe the life around them from a slightly elevated position, but they were not cut off from scrutiny of the passers-by. They remained tied to the life of the street, its bustle, noise, and occasional traffic jams and confusion. During the warm months of the year, the windows were usually open, partially breaking down the distinction between inside and outside. The skyscraper changed this relationship completely. Built into its very architecture were exclusivity, remoteness, and climate control. The life of the street ceased to be a vibrant theater filled with identifiable people, and instead became a distant realm inhabited by figures so small as to become abstractions. From the higher floors it offered a fantasy of domain, in which individual personalities disappeared. By the time Lewis wrote *Arrowsmith* it seemed natural to speak of the flow of life as represented not by people but by the spectacle of other skyscrapers in the distance.

The world seen from such towers assumed a new aspect. As early as 1905 a journalist wrote of the view from the Flatiron Building that below "are things that you would take for beetles, others that seem to you ants. The beetles are cabs, the ants are [human] beings – primitive but human, hurrying grotesquely over the most expensive spot on earth" (Figure 87).[25] The brightness of the unobstructed sunlight at the top further heightened the sense of contrast between the observer and the people below. The perpetual twilight in that nether realm became a pleasing contrast to the powerful light at the top of the city, which was literally removed from the dirt, din, and darkness of the surface. People below seemed tiny figures without personal characteristics, mere insects whose humanity had disappeared. If the sublime made one appreciate human skill and ingenuity, at the same time it disconnected the observer from the masses below.

When the Empire State Building was opened in 1931, a characteristic newspaper item proclaimed:

> A new panorama of the metropolitan district – a vast panorama of shimmering water, tall towers, quiet suburban homes and busy Manhattan streets – was unfolded yesterday to visitors who ascended to the observatory above the eighty-fifth floor of the Empire State Building. From this highest vantage point steamers and tugs which appeared to be little more than rowboats could be seen far up the Hudson and the East River. Down the bay, beyond the Narrows and out to sea, a ship occasionally hove into view or faded in the distance. For miles in every direction the city was spread out before the gaze of the sightseers.... In Manhattan the tall buildings which from the streets below appeared as monsters of steel and stone, assumed a less awe-inspiring significance when viewed from above. Fifth Avenue and Broadway were little more than slender black ribbons which had cut their way sharply through masses of vari-colored brick. Among them Lilliputian vehicles jockeyed for position, halting or moving forward in groups, often like a processional.[26]

The new vantage point seemed to empower a visitor, inverting the sense of insignificance that skyscrapers could induce when seen from the ground. The observation platform offered a reconception of urban space, miniaturizing the city into a pattern. From the top floor of a skyscraper the congestion of the streets becomes a fascinating detail, and from "a height of more than 1,000 feet pedestrians were little more than ants and their movements hardly could be detected" (Figure 88).[27] The vision of humanity as a swarm of insects reappeared continually in such accounts and was early visualized in films, notably Fritz Lang's "Metropolis." Lifted up to the sky, one was invited to see the city as a vast three-dimensional map and to call into existence a new relationship between the self and this concrete abstraction. As one reporter from Boston wrote, "You may be awed by it, you can even be a little afraid of it; you cannot deny that it is Today in Steel and Stone."[28]

Roland Barthes' reflections on the Eiffel Tower are suggestive here.

> The Tower overlooks not nature, but the city; and yet, by its very position of a visited outlook, the Tower makes the city into a kind of nature; it constitutes the swarming of men into a landscape, it adds to the frequently grim urban myth a romantic dimension, a harmony, a mitigation; by it, starting from it, the city joins up with the great natural themes which are offered to the curiosity of men: the ocean, the storm, the mountains, the snow, the rivers. To visit the Tower then, is to enter into contact not with a historical Sacred, as is the case for the majority of monuments, but rather with a new nature, that of human space.[29]

In America the human relation to this new nature, the "beauty" and "romance" that Barthes suggests, is inflected by corporate power. The skyscraper provides a spectacular perch from which to contemplate the manufactured world as a totality created and controlled by capital.

Michel de Certeau makes a similar error in discussing the view from the World Trade Center. "To be lifted to the summit...is to be lifted out of the city's grasp. One's body is no longer clasped by the streets.... His elevation transfigures him into a voyeur. It puts him at a distance. It transforms the bewitching world by which one was 'possessed' into a text that lies before one's eyes. It allows one to read it, to be a solar Eye, looking down like a god."[30]

88. View of Broadway south from the Woolworth Building, ca. 1913. The Byron Collection, 93.1.1.18207. Reprinted with permission of the Museum of the City of New York.

The paradox that the tall building is at once within and outside the scene makes it a tourist attraction, but it is hardly an ideologically neutral space. To be sure, the panoramic vision permits anyone to view the city not as disconnected parts but rather as a unified structure, but not all citizens enjoy this fantasy of domain every day. The skyscraper seems to make the many parts of the city, in Barthes' words, comprehensible as "intelligible objects, yet without – and this is what is new – losing anything of their materiality; a new category appears, that of concrete abstraction."[31] This category is a visualization of capitalist "romance," however, the romance of rationalization, abstraction, and growth. If one is a voyeur when standing aloft, it is not because one looks at people far below who are unaware, but rather because one momentarily adopts the perspective of the captain of industry. One does not merely escape the clasp of the street; one enters the panopticon of corporate power.

This is not a static experience, but a new version of the sublime, an emotion of both awe and fear. There has always been an element of terror in looking at the city from a high place, in gazing down a sheer wall. This experience is further dramatized by the contrast between the confinement of being in a crowded elevator that whisks one up from the ground level and the openness one feels upon emerging suddenly on a windswept platform and staring out at a vast urban horizon. Many experience this sudden opening as a corresponding psychological expansion. Then they struggle to link the details of the scene below with their knowledge of the city seen from the ground. The mental activity of triangulation does not require that the scene appear infinite in extent. Rather it requires an apparently infinite series of mental transpositions of scale and orientation, forcing the viewer to perform Olympian calculations. The vast region visible from the top of a skyscraper appears intelligible, offering itself for decipherment like a huge hieroglyphic. Yet like all sublime landscapes (but unlike a text), its meaning remains unutterable, and for this very reason, the sense of power does not abate, but can be constantly renewed, as one looks out over the metropolis.

The view provides a sense of mastery for those who own and rent the skyscrapers. They prefer upper floors and the widest possible vistas, and rents ascend along with the elevator. The businessman hero of James Oppenheim's 1912 novel *The Olympian* reaches his apotheosis the first time he goes to the top of his own new skyscraper. Writing a decade before McKay and Lewis, during an earlier phase of the construction of the New York skyline, he articulated more directly what they took for granted.

> He was utterly alone in the skies. Below him rose the skyscrapers, giving slanting glimpses of deep streets busy with tiny black people and darting traffic, and from their tips curled white smoke in the boundless swim of sunlight. He saw the waters that circled the city like a hugging arm of the sea, and on the level stretches harbor-craft and ocean-liners. He saw the bridges suspended between Long Island and Manhattan, Brooklyn beyond; he saw the Jersey heights. . . . All the mighty metropolis stretched like a map below him, crowded to the circling horizon with millions of human beings.[32]

It would be difficult to find a better example of the magisterial gaze. But Oppenheim goes further by interpreting the scene. For his hero, the view was that of "Science tearing off the crust of the earth and releasing the powers and riches of Nature." Looking at the active scene below, he saw that "busily the race seized on these, a chaos of rough enterprise – mines, manufactories, laboratories, exchanges. And in the swift trade that followed three mighty gods began to roughly organize the chaos – Steam, Electricity, Steel." Putting them to work, men had made modern civilization. "The railroad came, the post, the mill and farm machinery, the typewriter, the telegraph, the telephone, the automobile. And all these were like nerves and blood vessels laid out through the chaos till it began to coalesce, the parts aware of each other, the Earth gradually shaping into one body."[33] The magisterial gaze from a skyscraper seemed to materialize a new historical relationship between human beings and their environment. A new "body" was created as materials are wrested from nature. Not merely a center of commerce, the skyscraper mediated the relationship between the ordinary citizen and great corporations. From the outside it was an overwhelming emblem of corporate power capable of awing the man in the street. Yet from the inside it was the site of the magisterial gaze. To experience either the immense vistas aloft or the insect life of the street below validated corporate power (Figure 89).

To describe the sublimity evoked in seeing the city from the top of a skyscraper, a new term may be useful. I have elsewhere suggested

89. Looking east from the Singer Tower. Courtesy of the Library of Congress, Prints and Photographs Div., Detroit Publishing Co. Collection [LC-D4-71388B DLC].

the utility of the "geometrical sublime," to supplement Kant's distinction between the mathematical and the dynamic sublime, both of which refer to nature. In contrast, the geometrical sublime refers to an experience of manmade infinitude, creating in the mind of the viewer not an awe of the divinity or of the natural world, but rather of human invention.[34] The skyscraper's fantasy of domain altered the phenomenology of the city, adding a new psychological dimension to everyday life. Where Jeremy Bentham's panopticon established a gaze of power that openly dominated prisoners who were always within view of an authority in a central tower, the skyscraper manifested both domination of those below and apparent visions of transcendence for anyone on the observation platform. The public could even be induced to pay for the experience of the magisterial gaze. The "concrete abstraction" glimpsed from the skyscraper awed them with half-articulated visions, which suggested the conquest of nature, the triumph of science, the rationalization of the modern city, the certainty of progress, and the apotheosis of corporate will.

The Inward Gaze

The elevator was one of the many technical innovations (including structural steel, the telephone, electric fans, incandescent lights, and new kinds of foundations) that made the skyscraper easier to both build and use. The visitor to a skyscraper typically had no reason to either notice or think about most of these technologies, but unlike a ceiling fan or recessed lighting, a personal encounter with an elevator usually was unavoidable. Yet one seldom reads anything of the elevator or its operators, who developed a unique perspective on the tall building, precisely because they seldom saw the view. Djuana Barnes, later known for her protofeminist novel *Nightwood*,[35] explored this unlikely vantage point early in her career while working as a reporter for the *Brooklyn Daily Eagle* in 1913. She interviewed an elevator operator who had lost a leg in the Civil War and had spent 40 years running up and down the insides of various New York buildings. Barnes adopted his Irish-American brogue and playful imagination to voice irreverent observations on the skyscraper city. Her critique was literally based on the marginal point of view within the elevator, which is not a precise location but a mobile platform. Unlike the observation deck that focuses the visitor's eye on the city panorama, the elevator forces attention back to a human scale and the individuality of its passengers.

Barnes's operator jokingly presents himself as ignorant of what the city now looks like, as though he had never once in the past 40 years experienced the magisterial gaze or viewed the skyline. Instead, he has cultivated the sympathetic gaze that literally comes from below, from the humble seat in the corner. His gift is "the reading of faces. Every new face – and there are many in a day – brings me a new problem."[36] In contrast, the individual face disappears into the vista for Arrowsmith, McKay, Bennett, or the business executive in a corporate office. By observing the passengers, Barnes shifts the focus from architectural form to its psychological effects. The operator notes, "There must have been a great increase in the height of the buildings, because while the ladies walk as though something was awing them, they always have their noses tilted as from watching bricks going up in the clouds. I should think there must be a monstrous fellow with a tail and horns who wields a stinging lash, for they hurry so in their little red boots and their black and tan pumps and their always-high heels."[37] Barnes transforms the awe and empowerment of the sublime into the ridiculous snobbery of women with upturned noses and high heels driven about the streets by the devil. Nor, from this humble perspective, are the businessmen impressive. By gendering the sublime, Barnes transforms it into pomposity: "I should say that the city was very magnificent and that men had builded it, because they are so pompous and proud, and they have such mighty gestures, and they talk so loud."[38] In the restricted space of the elevator, men are not Olympians exalted by contact with the sublime, nor are women scurrying insects at the bottom of the canyons of the city. Rather, within its narrow confines, for the brief period of the ride, people are momentarily forced to stand still with nothing to look at but themselves. Instead of the expansive scale of the city skyline, seen when "utterly alone in the skies," the passengers must endure a fleeting intimacy with strangers. The operator declares:

> I should sum it up by saying that it is some city, but that people are conceiving things which, when they cease to be dreams, become sometimes nightmares; for instead of bringing calm and the glory of having produced something, people hurry and hurry to get it, and the long shadow of the tallest skyscraper points a finger at them and says, 'Are you not thinking too much of your walls and too little of your gardens?'"[39]

Gardens are the characteristic site not of the sublime but of the beautiful. The marginal voice, arising from a mobile point of view neither on the ground nor in the air, challenges the magisterial gaze and the ideology of the technological sublime and questions the disturbing landscape of walls. If Lewis's Arrowsmith felt exaltation when viewing the Woolworth Building, Barnes's skyscraper points back accusingly at the observer.

NOTES

1. Gertrude Stein, *Everybody's Autobiography* (London: Virago, 1985), 174.

2. Mark Girouard, *Cities and People: A Social and Architectural History* (New Haven, CT: Yale Univ. Press, 1985), 329.

3. Henry James, *The American Scene* (London: Chapman and Hall, 1907), 185.

4. On the conflict between the horizontal, European style and the vertical, vernacular style, see William R. Taylor and Thomas Bender, "Culture and Architecture: Some Aesthetic Tensions in the Shaping of Modern New York City," in *Visions of the Modern City*, eds. William Sharpe and Leonard Wallock (Baltimore: Johns Hopkins Univ. Press, 1987), 189–219.

5. Paul Goldberger, *The Skyscraper* (New York: Knopf, 1981).

6. This terminology is discussed at greater length in David E. Nye, *American Technological Sublime* (Cambridge, MA: MIT Press, 1994), 56–7, 81–7, 96–108, 278.

7. Nye, *American Technological Sublime*, Chaps. 1–4.

8. Merrill Schleier, *The Skyscraper in American Art, 1890–1931* (New York: Da Capo, 1986), 10–15.

9. Another important dimension of the skyscraper, its appearance when illuminated at night, is treated in David E. Nye, *Electrifying America: Social Meanings of a New Technology* (Cambridge, MA: MIT Press, 1990), 66–7, 74, 78, 80, 84, as well as in Nye, *American Technological Sublime*, 180–1, 187–98.

10. Sinclair Lewis, *Arrowsmith* (New York: Harcourt, Brace and World, 1952), 287. I thank Ronald Martin of the Univ. of Delaware for drawing my attention to this passage.

11. Lewis, 292.

12. Claude McKay, "Song of New York," *New Masses* 1 (May 1926):15.

13. Lewis, 293.

14. McKay, "Song of New York," 15.

15. William R. Taylor, "New York and the Origin of the Skyline," *Prospects* 13 (1988):234. For earlier uses of the term in England and America, see Thomas A. P. van Leeuwen, *The Skyward Trend of Thought* (The Hague: AHA Books, 1986), 84–5.

16. Montgomery Schuyler, "The Sky-line of New York, 1881–1897," *Harper's Weekly* (March 20, 1897): 295.

17. Edgar H. Hall, *The Hudson Fulton Celebration, 1909*. vol. 1 (Albany: State of New York, 1910), 252. The mayor's comments echoed those of many critics in *Scribner's Magazine*. See Annette Larsen Benert, "Reading the Walls: The Politics of Architecture in *Scribner's Magazine*, 1887–1914," *Arizona Quarterly* 47, no. 1 (Spring 1991): 49–79.

18. Cited in Alan Trachtenberg, *Reading American Photographs* (New York: Hill and Wang, 1989), 213.

19. Arnold Bennett, *Those United States* (London: Martin Secker, 1912), 45–6.

20. Girouard, 320–1. See also Mona Domosh, "The Symbolism of the Skyscraper: Case Studies of New York's First Tall Buildings," *Journal of Urban History* 14 (May 1988):334.

21. Lewis, 291–2.

22. For examples of how a single building, the Flatiron, was photographed over the years, including the work of both Steichen and Stieglitz, see Philip William Kreitler, *Flatiron: A Photographic History of the World's First Steel Frame Skyscraper, 1901–1990* (Washington, DC: American Institute of Architects, 1990).

23. Roland Marchand, *Advertising the American Dream* (Berkeley, CA: Univ. of California Press, 1985), 240, 242.

24. Lewis, 292.

25. Edgar Saltus, "New York from the Flatiron," *Munsey's Magazine* 33 (July 1905):382–3. A widely distributed Underwood and Underwood stereograph made the same point (reproduced in Kreitler, 47).

26. "Panorama Viewed from 85th Story," *New York Times*, May 2, 1931:7.

27. "Panorama Viewed from 85th Story," 7.

28. "Sky Boys Who 'Rode the Ball' on Empire State," *Literary Digest* (May 23, 1931):33.

29. Roland Barthes, *The Eiffel Tower and Other Mythologies*, trans. Richard Howard (New York: Hill and Wang, 1979), 8.

30. Michel de Certeau, *The Practice of Everyday Life* (Berkeley, CA: Univ. of California Press, 1984), 92.

31. de Certeau, *The Practice of Everyday Life*, 9.

32. James Oppenheim, *The Olympian* (New York: Harper & Brothers, 1912), 416.

33. Oppenheim, *The Olympian*, 416–17.

34. See Nye, *American Technological Sublime*, Chap. 2 and passim.

35. Djuana Barnes, *Nightwood* (New York: Norton, 1988). When it first appeared in 1937, this novel was praised by T. S. Eliot.

36. Djuana Barnes, *New York*, ed. Alyce Barry (Los Angeles: Sun and Moon Press, 1989, [reprinted from the *Brooklyn Daily Eagle*'s series, Oct. 12 to Dec. 14, 1913]), 97.

37. Barnes, *New York*, 98.

38. Barnes, *New York*, 98.

39. Barnes, *New York*, 98.

Selected Bibliography

General

Bletter, Rosemarie. "The Invention of the Skyscraper: Notes on Its Diverse Histories." *Assemblage* (Feb. 1987):110–17.

Bluestone, Daniel. " 'A City Under One Roof': Skyscrapers, 1880–1895." Chap. 4 in *Constructing Chicago*. New Haven, CT: Yale University Press, 1991.

Bossom, Alfred Charles. *Building to the Skies: The Romance of the Skyscraper*. New York: Studio Publications, 1934.

Condit, Carl W. *The Rise of the Skyscraper*. Chicago: University of Chicago Press, 1952.

Domosh, Mona. "Constructing New York's Skyline." Chap. 3 in *Invented Cities: The Creation of Landscape in Nineteenth-Century New York and Boston*. New Haven, CT: Yale University Press, 1996.

Ferriss, Hugh. *The Metropolis of Tomorrow*. New York: Ives Washburn, 1929. Reprint, Princeton: Princeton Architectural Press, 1986.

Girouard, Mark. *Cities and People: A Social and Architectural History*. New Haven, CT: Yale University Press, 1985.

Goldberger, Paul. *The Skyscraper*. New York: Alfred A. Knopf, 1982.

Huxtable, Ada Louise. *The Tall Building Artistically Reconsidered: The Search for a Skyscraper Style*. New York: Pantheon Books, 1985.

Landau, Sarah Bradford, and Carl W. Condit. *Rise of the New York Skyscraper, 1865–1913*. New Haven, CT: Yale University Press, 1996.

Leeuwen, Thomas A. P. van. *The Skyward Trend of Thought: Five Essays on the Metaphysics of the American Skyscraper*. Cambridge, MA: MIT Press, 1988.

Lehman, Arnold L. "The New York Skyscraper: A History of Its Development, 1870–1939." Ph.D. dissertation, Yale University, 1974.

Mujica, Francisco. *History of the Skyscraper*. New York: Archaeology & Architecture Press, 1929. Reprint, New York: Da Capo Press, 1977.

Mumford, Lewis. *Sidewalk Critic: Lewis Mumford's Writings on New York*. Edited by Robert Wojtowiz. New York: Princeton Architectural Press, 1998.

Robinson, Cervin, and Rosemarie Haag Bletter. *Skyscraper Style: Art Deco, New York*. New York: Oxford University Press, 1975.

Saliga, Pauline, ed. *The Sky's the Limit: A Century of Chicago Skyscrapers.* New York: Rizzoli, 1990.

Schultz, Earle, and Walter Simmons. *Offices in the Sky.* New York: Bobbs-Merrill Co., 1959.

Sexton, R. W. *American Commercial Buildings of Today.* New York: Architectural Book Publishing Co., 1928.

Shepherd, Roger, ed. *Skyscraper: The Search for an American Style, 1891–1941.* New York: McGraw-Hill, 2002.

Tafuri, Manfredo. "The Disenchanted Mountain: The Skyscraper and the City." In Giorgio Ciucci et al., *The American City: From the Civil War to the New Deal,* 389–528. Cambridge, MA: MIT Press, 1979.

Taylor, William R., and Thomas Bender. "Culture and Architecture: Some Aesthetic Tensions in the Shaping of New York City." In *Visions of the Modern City: Essays in History, Art and Literature.* Edited by William Sharpe and Leonard Wallock, 185–215. Baltimore: Johns Hopkins University Press, 1987.

Willis, Carol. *Form Follows Finance: Skyscrapers and Skylines in New York and Chicago.* New York: Princeton Architectural Press, 1995.

Zukowsky, John, ed. *Chicago Architecture, 1872–1922: Birth of a Metropolis.* Munich: Prestel-Verlag, 1987.

Zukowsky, John, David Van Zanten, and Carol Herselle Krinsky. *Chicago and New York: Architectural Interactions.* Chicago: Art Institute of Chicago, 1984.

Makers and Users

Bruegmann, Robert. *The Architects and the City: Holabird and Roche of Chicago, 1880–1918.* Chicago: University of Chicago Press, 1997.

Clark, William Clifford. *The Skyscraper: A Study in the Economic Height of Modern Office Buildings.* New York: American Institute of Steel Construction, 1930.

Duffy, Francis. "Office Buildings and Organisational Change." Chap. 8 in *Buildings and Society: Essays on the Social Development of the Built Environment.* Edited by Anthony King, 255–80. London: Routledge and Kegan Paul, 1980.

Fenske, Gail. "The 'Skyscraper Problem' and the City Beautiful: The Woolworth Building." Ph.D. dissertation, MIT, 1988.

Fine, Lisa M. *The Souls of the Skyscraper: Female Clerical Workers in Chicago, 1870–1930.* Philadelphia: Temple University Press, 1990.

Forty, Adrian. "Design in the Office." Chap. 6 in *Objects of Desire: Design and Society from Wedgwood to IBM,* 120–55. New York: Pantheon, 1986.

Fuller, Henry B. *The Cliff Dwellers. A Novel.* New York: Harper and Bros., 1893.

Harris, Neil. *Building Lives: Constructing Rites and Passages.* New Haven, CT: Yale University Press, 1999.

Hoffmann, Donald. *Frank Lloyd Wright, Louis Sullivan and the Skyscraper.* Mineola, NY: Dover Publications, 1998.

Horowitz, Louis J., and Boyden Sparkes. *The Towers of New York: The Memoirs of a MasterBuilder.* New York: Simon and Schuster, 1937.

Schlereth, Thomas J. "The World and Workers of the Paper Empire." Chap. 5 in *Cultural History & Material Culture: Everyday Life, Landscapes, Museums,* 144–78. Charlottesville, VA: University Press of Virginia, 1990.

Starrett, Col. W. A. *Skyscrapers and the Men Who Build Them.* New York: Charles Scribner's Sons, 1928.

Starrett, Paul. *Changing the Skyline: An Autobiography.* New York: McGraw-Hill, 1938.

Ward, David, and Olivier Zunz, eds. *The Landscape of Modernity: Essays on New York City, 1900–1940.* New York: Russell Sage Foundation, 1992.

Willis, Carol, ed. *Building the Empire State.* New York: Norton, in association with the Skyscraper Museum, 1998.

In the Image of the Client

Abramson, Daniel M. *Skyscraper Rivals: The AIG Building and the Architecture of Wall Street.* New York: Princeton Architectural Press, 2001.

Fenske, Gail, and Deryck Holdsworth. "Corporate Identity and the New York Office Building: 1895–1915." Chap. 6 in *The Landscape of Modernity: Essays on New York City, 1900–1940.* Edited by David Ward and Olivier Zunz, 129–59. New York: Russell Sage Foundation, 1992.

Gad, Gunter, and Deryck Holdsworth. "Corporate Capitalism and the Emergence of the High-Rise Office Building." *Urban Geography* 8, no. 3 (May–June 1987):212–31.

Gibbs, Kenneth Turney. *Business Architectural Imagery*. Ann Arbor, MI: UMI Research Press, 1984.

Kwolek-Folland, Angel. *Engendering Business: Men and Women in the Corporate Office, 1870–1930*. Baltimore: Johns Hopkins University Press, 1994.

Marchand, Roland. "Confessions and Rebuttals: The Plight of the Soulless Corporation." Chap. 1 in *Creating the Corporate Soul: The Rise of Public Relations and Corporate Imagery in American Big Business*, 7–47. Berkeley, CA: The University of California Press, 1998.

Solomonson, Katherine. *The Chicago Tribune Tower Competition: Skyscraper Design and Cultural Change in the 1920s*. New York: Cambridge University Press, 2001.

Zunz, Olivier. "Inside the Skyscraper." Chap. 4 in *Making America Corporate, 1870–1920*, 103–24. Chicago: University of Chicago Press, 1990.

Urban Contexts

Balfour, Alan. *Rockefeller Center: Architecture as Theater*. New York: McGraw-Hill, 1978.

Bender, Thomas. *The Unfinished City: New York and the Metropolitan Idea*. New York: New Press, 2002.

Fenske, Gail. "Cass Gilbert's Skyscrapers in New York: The Twentieth-Century City and the Urban Picturesque." Chap. 5 in *Inventing the Skyline; The Architecture of Cass Gilbert*. Edited by Margaret Heilbrun, 229–88. New York: Columbia University Press, 2000.

Fogelson, Robert M. "The Sacred Skyline: The Battle over Height Limits." Chap. 3 in *Downtown: Its Rise and Fall, 1880–1950*, 112–82. New Haven, CT: Yale University Press, 2001.

Kantor, Harvey A. "Modern Urban Planning in New York City: Origins and Evolution, 1890–1933." Ph.D. dissertation, New York University, 1971.

Krinsky, Carol Herselle. *Rockefeller Center*. New York: Oxford University Press, 1978.

Page, Max. *The Creative Destruction of Manhattan, 1900–1940*. Chicago: University of Chicago Press, 1999.

Revell, Keith D. *Building Gotham: Civic Culture & Public Policy in New York City, 1898–1938*. Baltimore: Johns Hopkins University Press, 2003.

Revell, Keith D. "Regulating the Landscape: Real Estate Values, City Planning, and the 1916 Zoning Ordinance." Chap. 2 in *The Landscape of Modernity: Essays on New York City*. Edited by David Ward and Olivier Zunz, 19–45. New York: Russell Sage Foundation, 1992.

Popular Culture

Barthes, Roland. *The Eiffel Tower and Other Mythologies*. Translated by Richard Howard. New York: Hill and Wang, 1979.

Hales, Peter Bacon. *Silver Cities: The Photography of American Urbanism, 1839–1915*. Philadelphia: Temple University Press, 1984.

Hartmann, Sadakichi. *The Valiant Knights of Daguerre. Selected Critical Essays on Photography and Profiles of Photographic Pioneers by Sadakichi Hartmann*. Edited by Harry W. Lawton and George Knox. Berkeley, CA: University of California Press, 1978.

Kreitler, Philip William. *Flatiron: A Photographic History of the World's First Steel Frame Skyscraper, 1901–1990*. Washington, DC: American Institute of Architects, 1990.

Museum of the City of New York. *Painting the Town: Cityscapes of New York*. New Haven, CT: Museum of the City of New York in association with Yale University Press, 2000.

Neumann, Dietrich. *Film Architecture: Set Designs from Metropolis to Blade Runner*. Munich: Prestel, 1996.

Nye, David. *American Technological Sublime*. Cambridge, MA: MIT Press, 1994.

Schleier, Merrill. *The Skyscraper in American Art, 1890–1931*. New York: DaCapo Press, 1986.

Simmons, Peter. *Gotham Comes of Age: New York Through the Lens of the Byron Company, 1892–1942*. Exhibition catalog, Museum of the City of New York. San Francisco: Pomegranate, 1999.

Smith, Carl S. "Chicago Building." Chap. 6 in *Chicago and the American Literary Imagination, 1880–1920*, 121–51. Chicago: University of Chicago Press, 1984.

Taylor, William R. *In Pursuit of Gotham: Culture and Commerce in New York*. New York: Oxford University Press, 1992.

Trachtenberg, Alan. "Camera Work/Social Work." Chap. 4 in *Reading American Photographs: Images as History, Mathew Brady to Walker Evans*, 164–230. New York: Hill and Wang, 1989.

Trachtenberg, Alan. "Image and Ideology: New York in the Photographer's Eye." *Journal of Urban History* 10 (Aug. 1984):453–64.

Warner, Sam Bass, Jr. "Slums and Skyscrapers. Urban Images, Symbols, and Ideology." In *Cities of the Mind. Images and Themes of the City in the Social Sciences*. Edited by Lloyd Rodwin and Robert M. Hollister, 181–95. New York: Plenum, 1984.

Wigoder, Meir. "The 'Solar Eye' of Vision: Emergence of the Skyscraper-Viewer in the Discourse on Heights in New York City, 1890–1920." *Journal of the Society of Architectural Historians* 61, no. 2 (June 2002):152–69.

Index